Training for Certific

Taking An ASE Certifi

This study guide will help prepare you to take and pass the ASE test. It contains descriptions of the types of questions used on the test, the task list from which the test questions are derived, a review of the task list subject information, and a practice test containing ASE style questions.

ABOUT ASE

The National Institute for Automotive Service Excellence (ASE) is a non-profit organization founded in 1972 for the purpose of improving the quality of automotive service and repair through the voluntary testing and certification of automotive technicians. Currently, there are over 400,000 professional technicians certified by ASE in over 40 different specialist areas.

ASE certification recognizes your knowledge and experience, and since it is voluntary, taking and passing an ASE certification test also demonstrates to employers and customers your commitment to your profession. It can mean better compensation and increased employment opportunities as well.

ASE not only certifies technician competency, it also promotes the benefits of technician certification to the motoring public. Repair shops that employ at least one ASE technician can display the ASE sign. Establishments where 75 percent of technicians are certified, with at least one technician certified in each area of service offered by the business, are eligible for the ASE Blue Seal of Excellence program. ASE encourages consumers to patronize these shops through media campaigns and car care clinics.

To become ASE certified, you must pass at least one ASE exam and have at least two years of related work experience. Technicians that pass specified tests in a series earn Master Technician status. Your certification is valid for five years, after which time you must retest to retain certification, demonstrating that you have kept up with the changing technology in the field.

THE ASE TEST

An ASE test consists of forty to eighty multiple-choice questions. Test questions are written by a panel of technical experts from vehicle, parts and equipment manufacturers, as well as working technicians and technical education instructors. All questions have been pre-tested and quality checked on a national sample of technicians. The questions are derived from information presented in the task list, which details the knowledge that a technician must have to pass an ASE test and be recognized as competent in that category. The task list is periodically up-

© Advanstar Communications Inc. 2016.2
Customer Service 1-800-240-1968
FAX 218-740-6437
e-mail: PassTheASE@advanstar.com
URL: www.PassTheASE.com
A7 - HEATING AND AIR CONDITIONING

dated by ASE in response to changes in vehicle technology and repair techniques.

There are five types of questions on an ASE test:
- **Direct, or Completion**
- **MOST Likely**
- **Technician A and Technician B**
- **EXCEPT**
- **LEAST Likely**

Direct, or Completion

This type of question is the kind that is most familiar to anyone who has taken a multiple-choice test: you must answer a direct question or complete a statement with the correct answer. There are four choices given as potential answers, but only one is correct. Sometimes the correct answer to one of these questions is clear, however in other cases more than one answer may seem to be correct. In that case, read the question carefully and choose the answer that is most correct. Here is an example of this type of test question:

A compression test shows that one cylinder is too low. A leakage test on that cylinder shows that there is excessive leakage. During the test, air could be heard coming from the tailpipe. Which of the following could be the cause?
A. broken piston rings
B. bad head gasket
C. bad exhaust gasket
D. an exhaust valve not seating

Taking An ASE Certification Test

There is only one correct answer to this question, answer D. If an exhaust valve is not seated, air will leak from the combustion chamber by way of the valve out to the tailpipe and make an audible sound. Answer C is wrong because an exhaust gasket has nothing to do with combustion chamber sealing. Answers A and B are wrong because broken rings or a bad head gasket would have air leaking through the oil filler or coolant system.

MOST Likely

This type of question is similar to a direct question but it can be more challenging because all or some of the answers may be nearly correct. However, only one answer is the most correct. For example:

When a cylinder head with an overhead camshaft is discovered to be warped, which of the following is the most correct repair option?
A. replace the head
B. check for cracks, straighten the head, surface the head
C. surface the head, then straighten it
D. straighten the head, surface the head, check for cracks

The most correct answer is B. It makes no sense to perform repairs on a cylinder head that might not be usable. The head should first be checked for warpage and cracks. Therefore, answer B is more correct than answer D. The head could certainly be replaced, but the cost factor may be prohibitive and availability may be limited, so answer B is more correct than answer A. If the top of the head is warped enough to interfere with cam bore alignment and/or restrict free movement of the camshaft, the head must be straightened before it is resurfaced, so answer C is wrong.

Technician A and Technician B

These questions are the kind most commonly associated with the ASE test. With these questions you are asked to choose which technician statement is correct, or whether they both are correct or incorrect. This type of question can be difficult because very often you may find one technician's statement to be clearly correct or incorrect while the other may not be so obvious. Do you choose one technician or both? The key to answering these questions is to carefully examine each technician's statement independently and judge it on its own merit. Here is an example of this type of question:

A vehicle equipped with rack-and-pinion steering is having the front end inspected. Technician A says that the inner tie rod ends should be inspected while in their normal running position. Technician B says that if movement is felt between the tie rod stud and the socket while the tire is moved in and out, the inner tie rod should be replaced. Who is correct?
A. Technician A
B. Technician B
C. Both A and B
D. Neither A or B

The correct answer is C; both technicians' statements are correct. Technician B is clearly correct because any play felt between the tie-rod stud and the socket while the tire is moved in and out indicates that the assembly is worn and requires replacement. However, Technician A is also correct because inner tie- rods should be inspected while in their normal running position, to prevent binding that may occur when the suspension is allowed to hang free.

EXCEPT

This kind of question is sometimes called a negative question because you are asked to give the incorrect answer. All of the possible answers given are correct EXCEPT one. In effect, the correct answer to the question is the one that is wrong. The word EXCEPT is always capitalized in these questions. For example:
All of the following are true of torsion bars **EXCEPT**:
A. They can be mounted longitudinally or transversely.
B. They serve the same function as coil springs.
C. They are interchangeable from side-to-side
D. They can be used to adjust vehicle ride height.

The correct answer is C. Torsion bars are not normally interchangeable from side-to-side. This is because the direction of the twisting or torsion is not the same on the left and right sides. All of the other answers contain true statements regarding torsion bars.

LEAST Likely

This type of question is similar to EXCEPT in that once again you are asked to give the answer that is wrong. For example:

Blue-gray smoke comes from the exhaust of a vehicle during deceleration. Of the following, which cause is **LEAST** likely?
A. worn valve guides
B. broken valve seals
C. worn piston rings
D. clogged oil return passages

The correct answer is C. Worn piston rings will usually make an engine smoke worse under acceleration. All of the other causes can allow oil to be drawn through the valve guides under the high intake vacuum that occurs during deceleration.

PREPARING FOR THE ASE TEST

Begin preparing for the test by reading the task list. The task list describes the actual work performed by a technician in a particular specialty area. Each question on an ASE test is derived from a task or set of tasks in the list. Familiarizing yourself with the task list will help you to concentrate on the areas where you need to study.

The text section of this study guide contains information pertaining to each of the tasks in the task list. Reviewing this information will prepare you to take the practice test.

Take the practice test and compare your answers with the correct answer explanations. If you get an answer wrong and don't understand why, go back and read the information pertaining to that question in the text.

After reviewing the tasks and the subject information and taking the practice test, you should be prepared to take the ASE test or be aware of areas where further study is needed. When studying with this study guide or any other source of information, use the following guidelines to make sure the time spent is as productive as possible:

- Concentrate on the subject areas where you are weakest.
- Arrange your schedule to allow specific times for studying.
- Study in an area where you will not be distracted.
- Don't try to study after a full meal or when you are tired.
- Don't wait until the last minute and try to 'cram' for the test.

REGISTERING FOR ASE COMPUTER-BASED TESTING

Registration for the ASE CBT tests can be done online in myASE or over the phone. While not mandatory, it is recommended that you establish a myASE account on the ASE website (www.ase.com). This can be a big help in managing the ASE certification process, as your test scores and certification expiry dates are all listed there.

Test times are available during two-month windows with a one-month break in between. This means that there is a total of eight months over the period of the calendar year that ASE testing is available.

Testing can be scheduled during the daytime, night, and weekends for maximum flexibility. Also, results are available immediately after test completion. Printed certificates are mailed at the end of the two-month test window. If you fail a test, you will not be allowed to register for the same test until the next two-month test window.

TAKING THE ASE TEST – COMPUTER-BASED TESTING (CBT)

On test day, bring some form of photo identification with you and be sure to arrive at the test center 30 minutes early

to give sufficient time to check in. Once you have checked in, the test supervisor will issue you some scratch paper and pencils, as well as a composite vehicle test booklet if you are taking advanced tests. You will then be seated at a computer station and given a short online tutorial on how to complete the ASE CBT tests. You may skip the tutorial if you are already familiar with the CBT process.

The test question format is similar to those found in written ASE tests. Regular certification tests have a time limit of 1 to 2 hours, depending on the test. Re-certification tests are 30 to 45 minutes, and the L1 and L2 advanced level tests are capped at 2 hours. The time remaining for your test is displayed on the top left of the test window. You are given a warning when you have 5 minutes left to complete the test.

Read through each question carefully. If you don't know the answer to a question and need to think about it, click on the "Flag" button and move on to the next question. You may also go back to previous questions by pressing the "Previous Question" button. Don't spend too much time on any one question. After you have worked through to the end of the test, check your remaining time and go back and answer the questions you flagged. Very often, information found in questions later in the test can help answer some of the ones with which you had difficulty.

Some questions may have more content than what can fit on one screen. If this is the case, there will be a "More" button displayed where the "Next Question" button would ordinarily appear. A scrolling bar will also appear, showing what part of the question you are currently viewing. Once you have viewed all of the related content for the question, the "Next Question" button will reappear.

You can change answers on any of the questions before submitting the test for

scoring. At the end of the examination, you will be shown a table with all of the question numbers. This table will show which questions are answered, which are unanswered, and which have been flagged for review. You will be given the option to review all the questions, review the flagged questions, or review the unanswered questions from this page. This table can be reviewed at any time during the exam by clicking the "Review" button.

If you are running out of time and still have unanswered test questions, guess the answers if necessary to make sure every question is answered. Do not leave any answers blank. It is to your advantage to answer every question, because your test score is based on the number of correct answers. A guessed answer could be correct, but a blank answer can never be.

Once you are satisfied that all of the questions are complete and ready for scoring, click the "Submit for Scoring" button. If you are scheduled for more than one test, the next test will begin immediately. If you are done with testing, you will be asked to complete a short survey regarding the CBT test experience. As you are leaving the test center, your supervisor will give you a copy of your test results. Your scores will also be available on myASE within two business days.

To learn exactly where and when the ASE Certification Tests are available in your area, as well as the costs involved in becoming ASE certified, please contact ASE directly for registration information.

The National Institute for Automotive Service Excellence
101 Blue Seal Drive, S.E. Suite 101
Leesburg, VA 20175
1-800-390-6789
http://www.ase.com

Taking An ASE Certification Test

Table of Contents
A7 - Heating And Air Conditioning

Test Specifications And Task List 6

A/C System Service, Diagnosis And Repair 9

Refrigeration System Component Diagnosis And Repair 31

Heating And Engine Cooling Systems Diagnosis And Repair 48

Operating Systems And Related Controls Diagnosis And Repair . . 58

Sample Test Questions 73

Answers to Study-Guide Test Questions 85

Glossary 93

Advanstar endeavors to collect and include complete, correct and current information in this publication but does not warrant that any or all of such information is complete, correct or current. Publisher does not assume, and hereby disclaims, any liability to any person or entity for any loss or damage caused by errors or omissions of any kind, whether resulting from negligence, accident or any other cause. If you do notice any error, we would appreciate if you would bring such error to our attention.

4   A7 - Heating And Air Conditioning

The Building Blocks of Our Success

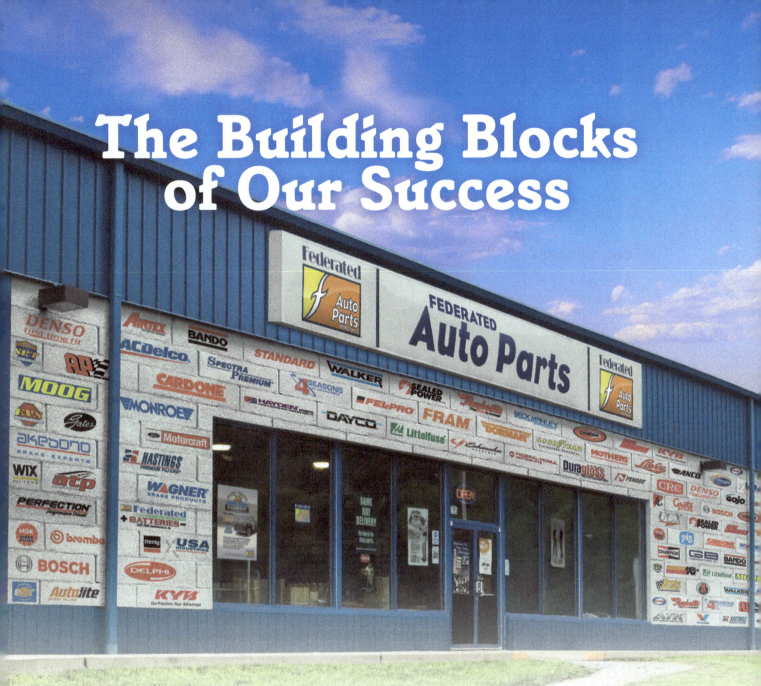

At Federated Auto Parts, you know you will always get great service and support from the most knowledgeable people in the business. You also know that you will get the best brand name, premium quality auto parts available. Parts that you can trust will help you get the job done right.

WWW.FEDERATEDAUTOPARTS.COM

Heating And Air Conditioning

TEST SPECIFICATIONS
FOR HEATING AND AIR CONDITIONING (TEST A7)

CONTENT AREA	NUMBER OF QUESTIONS IN ASE TEST	PERCENTAGE OF COVERAGE IN ASE TEST
A. Heating, Ventilation, A/C (HVAC) and Engine Cooling System Service, Diagnosis and Repair	21	42%
B. Refrigeration System Component Diagnosis And Repair	10	20%
D. Operating Systems And Related Controls Diagnosis And Repair	19	38%
Total	**50**	**100%**

The test could contain up to ten additional questions that are included for statistical research purposes only. Your answers to these questions will not affect your score, but since you do not know which ones they are, you should answer all questions in the test.

The 5-year Recertification Test will cover the same content areas as those listed above. However, the number of questions in each content area of the Recertification Test will be reduced by about one-half.

The following pages list the tasks covered in each content area. These task descriptions offer detailed information to technicians preparing for the test, and to persons who may be instructing Heating and Air Conditioning technicians. The task list may also serve as a guideline for question writers, reviewers and test assemblers.

It should be noted that the number of questions in each content area may not equal the number of tasks listed. Some of the tasks are complex and broad in scope, and may be covered by several questions. Other tasks are simple and narrow in scope; one question may cover several tasks. The main purpose for listing the tasks is to describe accurately what is done on the job, not to make each task correspond to a particular test question.

HEATING AND AIR CONDITIONING TEST TASK LIST

A. HEATING, VENTILATION, A/C (HVAC), AND ENGINE COOLING SYSTEM SERVICE, DIAGNOSIS, AND REPAIR
(21 questions)

Task 1 - Identify system type and conduct performance test on the A/C system; determine needed repairs.

Task 2 - Diagnose A/C system problems indicated by system pressures and/or temperature readings; determine needed repairs.

Task 3 - Diagnose A/C system problems indicated by sight, sound, smell, and touch procedures; determine needed repairs.

Task 4 - Leak test A/C system; determine needed repairs.

Task 5 - Identify A/C system refrigerant and existing charge amount; recover refrigerant.

Task 6 - Evacuate A/C system.

Task 7 - Inspect A/C system components for contamination; determine needed repairs.

Task 8 - Charge A/C system with refrigerant.

Task 9 - Identify A/C system lubricant type and capacity; replenish lubricant if necessary.

Task 10 - Inspect and replace passenger compartment (cabin air, pollen) filter.

Task 11 - Disarm and enable the airbag system for vehicle service following manufacturers' recommended procedures.

Task 12 - Read diagnostic trouble codes (DTCs) and interpret scan tool data stream.

Task 13 - Read & interpret technical literature (service publications, bulletins, recalls, and information including wiring schematics).

Test Specifications And Task List

Task 14 - Use a scan tool, digital multimeter (DMM), or digital storage oscilloscope (DSO) to test HVAC system sensors, actuators, circuits, and control modules; determine needed repairs.

Task 15 - Verify proper operation of certified equipment.

Task 16 - Recycle or properly dispose of refrigerant.

Task 17 - Label and store refrigerant.

Task 18 - Test refrigerant cylinders for non-condensable gases; identify refrigerant.

Task 19 - Identify the procedures and equipment necessary to service, diagnose, and repair A/C systems in hybrid/electric vehicles.

Task 20 - Diagnose the cause of temperature control problems in the heater/ventilation system; determine needed repairs.

Task 21 - Diagnose window fogging problems; determine needed repairs.

Task 22 - Perform engine cooling system tests (flow, pressure, electrolysis, concentration, and contamination); determine needed repairs.

Task 23 - Inspect and replace engine coolant hoses and pipes.

Task 24 - Inspect, test, and replace radiator, pressure cap, coolant recovery system, and water pump.

Task 25 - Inspect, test, and replace thermostat, thermostat by pass, and housing.

Task 26 - Identify, inspect, recover coolant; flush and refill system with proper coolant; bleed system as necessary.

Task 27 - Inspect, test, and replace fan (both electrical and mechanical), fan clutch, fan belts, fan shroud, and air dams.

Task 28 - Inspect, test, and replace heater coolant control valve (manual, vacuum, and electrical types), and auxiliary coolant pump.

Task 29 - Inspect, flush, and replace heater core.

B. REFRIGERATION SYSTEM COMPONENT DIAGNOSIS AND REPAIR
(10 questions)

Compressor and Clutch

Task 1 - Diagnose A/C system problems that cause the protection devices (pressure, thermal, and electronic controls) to interrupt system operation; determine needed repairs.

Task 2 - Inspect, test, and replace A/C system pressure, thermal, and electronic protection devices.

Task 3 - Inspect, adjust, and replace A/C compressor drive belts, pulleys, and tensioners.

Task 4 - Inspect, test, service, and replace A/C compressor clutch components or assembly.

Task 5 - Identify required lubricant type; inspect and correct level in A/C compressor.

Task 6 - Inspect, test, service, or replace A/C compressor, mounting, and fasteners.

Evaporator, Condenser and Related Components

Task 7 - Inspect, repair, or replace A/C system mufflers, hoses, lines, filters, fittings, and seals.

Task 8 - Inspect A/C condenser for proper air flow.

Task 9 - Inspect, test, and clean or replace A/C system condenser; check mountings and air seals.

Task 10 - Inspect and replace receiver/drier, accumulator/drier, or desiccant.

Task 11 - Inspect, test, and replace expansion valve(s).

Task 12 - Inspect and replace orifice tube(s).

Task 13 - Inspect A/C evaporator for proper air flow.

Task 14 - Inspect, test, clean, or replace evaporator(s).

Task 15 - Inspect, clean, and repair evaporator housing and water drain.

Task 16 - Inspect, test, and replace evaporator pressure/temperature control systems and devices.

Task 17 - Identify, inspect, and replace A/C system service valves and valve caps.

Task 18 - Inspect and replace A/C system high pressure relief device.

C. OPERATING SYSTEMS AND RELATED CONTROLS DIAGNOSIS AND REPAIR
(19 questions)

Electrical

Task 1 - Diagnose the cause of failures in the electrical control system of heating, ventilating, and A/C (HVAC) systems; determine needed repairs.

Task 2 - Inspect, test, repair, and replace HVAC blower motors, blower motor speed controls, resistors, switches, relays/modules, wiring, and protection devices.

Task 3 - Inspect, test, repair, and replace A/C compressor clutch coil, relay/ modules, wiring, sensors, switches, diodes, and protection devices.

Task 4 - Inspect, test, repair, and replace A/C related powertrain control systems and components.

Task 5 - Inspect, test, repair, and replace load sensitive A/C compressor cut off systems.

Task 6 - Inspect, test, repair, and replace engine cooling/condenser fan motors, relays/modules, switches, sensors, wiring, and protection devices.

Task 7 - Inspect, test, adjust, repair, and replace climate control system electric actuator motors, relays/ modules, switches, sensors, wiring, and protection devices (including dual/multi-zone systems).

Task 8 - Inspect, test, service, or replace HVAC panel assemblies.

Training for Certification

Vacuum/Mechanical

Task 9 - Diagnose the cause of failures of the heating, ventilating, and A/C (HVAC) vacuum and mechanical control systems; determine needed repairs.

Task 10 - Inspect, test, service, or replace HVAC Control panel assemblies.

Task 11 - Inspect, test, adjust, and replace HVAC control cables and linkages.

Task 12 - Inspect, test, and replace HVAC vacuum system actuators (diaphragms/motors), hoses, reservoir, check valve, and restrictors.

Task 13 - Inspect, test, adjust, repair, or replace HVAC ducts, doors, and outlets (including dual/multi-zone systems).

Automatic and Semi Automatic Heating, Ventilating, and A/C Systems

Task 14 - Diagnose temperature control system problems; determine

needed repairs (including dual/multi-zone systems).

Task 15 - Diagnose blower system problems; determine needed repairs (including dual/multi-zone systems).

Task 16 - Diagnose air distribution system problems; determine needed repairs (including dual/multi-zone systems).

Task 17 - Diagnose compressor clutch control system; determine needed repairs.

Task 18 - Inspect, test, or replace climate and blower control sensors.

Task 19 - Inspect, test, and replace door actuator(s).

Task 20 - Inspect, test, and replace heater coolant control valve and controls.

Task 21 - Inspect, test, and replace electric and vacuum motors, solenoids, and switches.

Task 22 - Inspect, test, or replace Automatic Temperature Control (ATC) control panel and/or climate control computer/module; program, code, or initialize as required.

Task 23 - Check and adjust calibration of Automatic Temperature Control (ATC) system.

Task 24 - Diagnose data communication issues, including diagnostic trouble codes (DTCs) that affect climate control system operation.

A/C System Service, Diagnosis And Repair

A/C SYSTEM OPERATION

In order to understand how an A/C system works, we must first understand a few basic principles. The first, and most important principle is that heat always moves toward a state of less heat. This is how an engine's cooling system works. Heat created by the combustion process in the engine's cylinders is transferred to the coolant in the water jackets next to the cylinders. The coolant is then pumped to the radiator where the heat is transferred to the cooler air traveling through it.

The second principle is that it requires a large amount of heat to change a liquid into a gas. Heat quantity is measured in British Thermal Units (BTUs) and a BTU is the amount of heat that is required to raise the temperature of one pound of water by 1°F. Consider that it takes only 180 BTUs of heat to raise the temperature of one pound of water from 32°F (0°C) to 212°F (100°C), but it requires another 970 BTUs to change that same pound of water into steam at the same temperature. The amount of heat needed for a liquid to change state to a vapor, without the temperature changing, is called the latent heat of evaporation.

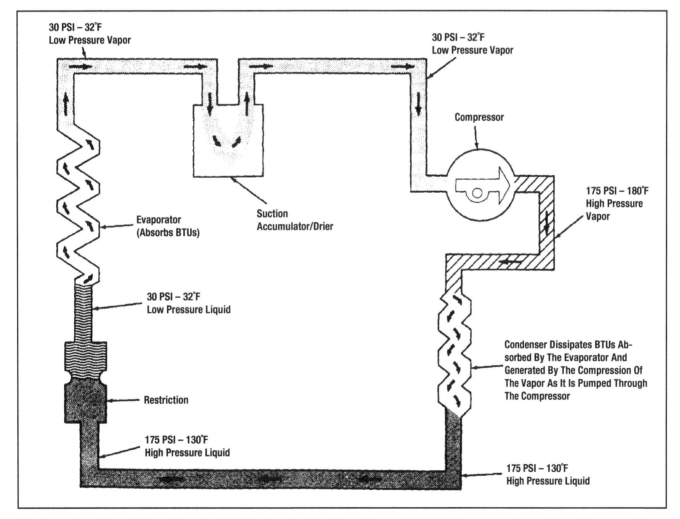

A schematic of the refrigerant cycle. Heat is absorbed as the refrigerant boils in the evaporator and heat is removed as it changes back to a liquid in the condenser.
(Courtesy: Ford Motor Co.)

A/C System Service, Diagnosis And Repair

Conversely, for a vapor to change back to a liquid it must release a large amount of heat. For steam to change back to liquid it must release 970 BTUs of heat. The amount of heat given off as a vapor changes state from a gas to a liquid, without the temperature changing, is called the latent heat of condensation.

The last principle is that when the pressure on a liquid increases, its boiling point also increases. This is why the cooling system on a modern vehicle is pressurized. To remove the heat from today's powerful, accessory laden engines, the coolant must be able to stay in liquid form and not boil over.

Armed with the knowledge of these principles, let's look at the A/C system. Since hot always moves to cold, to remove heat from inside a vehicle we must put something cold inside the vehicle that can carry the heat away: this is the refrigerant in the evaporator of the A/C system. Refrigerant has a boiling point below 32°F (0°C), which enables it to boil and absorb heat at low temperatures.

The A/C compressor pumps refrigerant through the system. Refrigerant is metered into the evaporator by a Thermostatic Expansion Valve (TXV) or an orifice tube, depending on the type of system. If the system is equipped with a TXV, liquid refrigerant will pass through a receiver/drier after it leaves the condenser and before it enters the TXV. If the system uses an orifice tube, the refrigerant flows through an accumulator before it enters the compressor.

Both the TXV and the orifice tube create a restriction in the system against which the compressor forces the refrigerant. Before the refrigerant passes through the TXV or orifice tube, it is under high pressure. Beyond that point the refrigerant is under low pressure. In fact, it is common to refer to the high side and low side of the A/C system when discussing function and problems. Everything between the compressor and the TXV (or orifice tube) is on the high side; everything from the TXV (or orifice tube) back to the compressor is on the low side.

Liquid refrigerant is metered into the evaporator, where warm air blown through the evaporator by the blower motor causes the liquid refrigerant to boil and change into a vapor, absorbing the latent heat of evaporation.

The refrigerant leaves the evaporator in the form of a gas and is drawn into the A/C compressor. The compressor raises the pressure of the refrigerant gas until its temperature is above ambient. The warmer refrigerant is pumped to the condenser, where relatively cooler ambient air removes the latent heat, changing the state of the refrigerant back to a liquid. The liquid refrigerant then leaves the condenser and returns to the refrigerant metering device, where it completes the refrigerant cycle.

The specifications for the high pressures and low pressures vary based on system design, and the type of refrigerant being used. These pressures must be kept in balance in order for the A/C system to function properly. Or, to put it more accurately, we must prevent the evaporator or condenser from becoming too cold or too warm. To insure proper service, always look up the system pressure specifications and testing

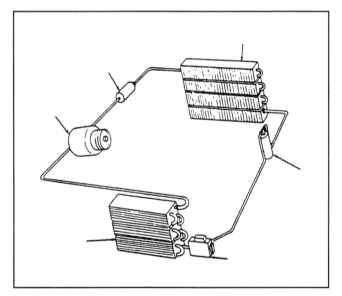

A typical expansion valve equipped air conditioning system.

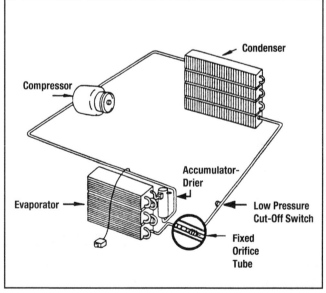

A typical orifice tube equipped air conditioning system.

A/C System Service, Diagnosis And Repair

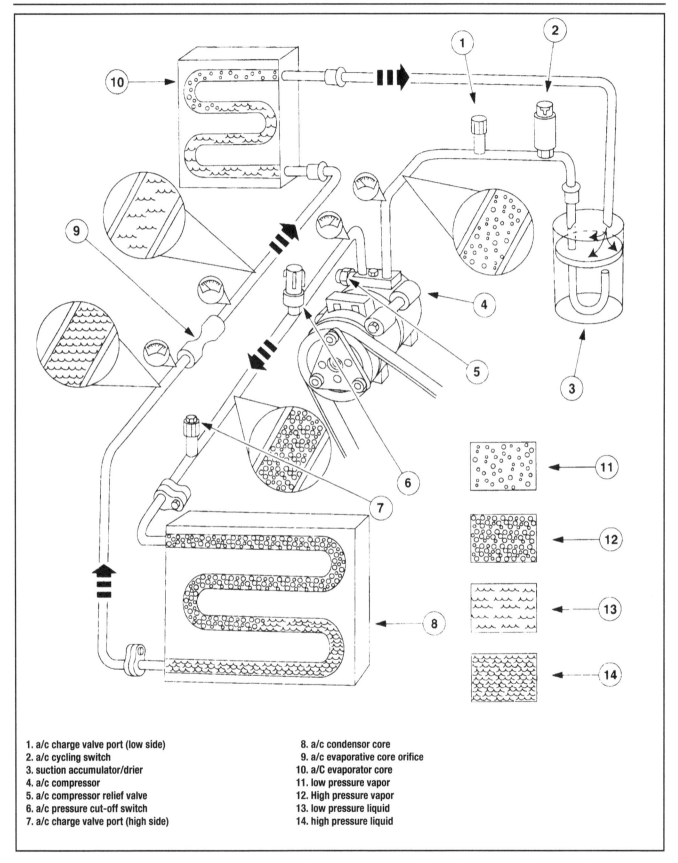

1. a/c charge valve port (low side)
2. a/c cycling switch
3. suction accumulator/drier
4. a/c compressor
5. a/c compressor relief valve
6. a/c pressure cut-off switch
7. a/c charge valve port (high side)
8. a/c condensor core
9. a/c evaporative core orifice
10. a/C evaporator core
11. low pressure vapor
12. High pressure vapor
13. low pressure liquid
14. high pressure liquid

A clutch cycling orifice tube type refrigerant system. Note the pressure cycling switch mounted just after the accumulator.

A/C System Service, Diagnosis And Repair

requirements in the appropriate service information source.

The TXV and orifice tube act as system control devices, but these components by themselves do not control the refrigerant flow accurately enough to maintain precise evaporator temperature. Over the years, various methods have been employed to achieve this, but today, there are two that are most common:
- Applying or removing electricity to the compressor electromagnetic clutch, having it engage and disengage
- By changing the actual operating displacement of the compressor.

Clutch Cycling Systems

Cycling the clutch is a simple way to control the A/C system. Cycling clutch control works with both the TXV and orifice tube systems, but because orifice tubes don't open and close like expansion valves, they will always be found working in conjunction with cycling clutch control.

The amount of heat that the evaporator must remove affects the system pressure. Refrigerant pressure and temperature are directly related (that is, if we increase system pressure we increase the refrigerant's temperature). So if we control the pressure within the evaporator, we also control its temperature. The compressor cycling rate automatically changes to control the temperature. The clutch is turned off and on by a switch to prevent the evaporator from icing. During operation, the clutch may be cycled several times each minute. As the change in heat load on the evaporator affects system pressures, the compressor cycling rate automatically changes to achieve the desired temperature.

Many orifice tube systems use some type of pressure cycling switch. It senses the low-side pressure (which is directly proportionate to temperature). Often, the pressure cycling switch is mounted on the accumulator. Since system pressure is quite low during cold weather, the pressure cycling switch keeps the compressor from running when it isn't needed. It also protects the compressor from damage should the refrigerant charge escape, since the compressor is lubricated by oil flowing with refrigerant.

A typical TXV system has a bulb and/or capillary tube or some other type of temperature sensing device embedded in the evaporator fins or attached to the evaporator outlet pipe. This device works in conjunction with a switch. When evaporator temperature increases, the switch closes and the compressor clutch engages. When evaporator temperature decreases, the switch opens and the clutch disengages.

For both orifice tube and expansion valve systems, the temperatures (and therefore pressures) at which the compressor clutch is cycled vary by system, vehicle and refrigerant.

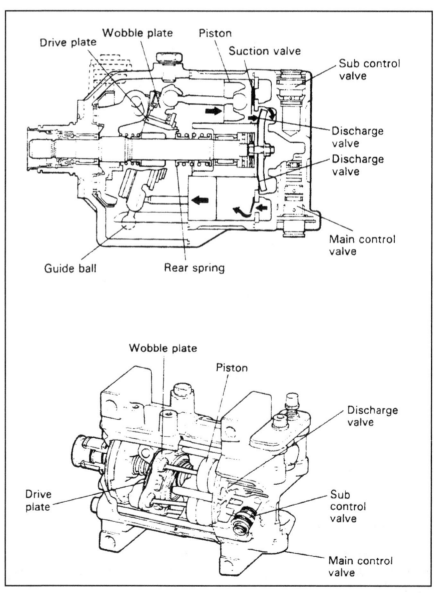

Cutaway view of a wobble plate variable displacement compressor.

Variable Displacement Compressors

A variable displacement compressor is usually an axial compressor, with the pistons arranged around and parallel to the driveshaft. One-way reed valves in the cylinder head control refrigerant flow into and out of each cylinder.

Depending on the design, the pistons are driven by a wobble plate or a swash plate. In a wobble plate compressor, the pistons are connected to the plate with short push rods. An angled yoke on the driveshaft causes the plate to wobble when the shaft rotates, driving the pistons back and forth in their bores.

In a swash plate compressor, the plate itself rotates with the driveshaft. A bearing in the bottom of each piston clamps around the edge and rides on either face of the swash plate. The plate is set at an angle to the shaft, so as it rotates, the pistons are forced back-and-forth in their bores.

The angle of the wobble plate or the swash plate determines the length of the piston stroke. In a variable displacement compressor, that angle can be changed, which changes the length of the pistons' stroke and, therefore, the amount of refrigerant displaced on each stroke. The angle is adjusted using springs and linkage that move lengthwise along the driveshaft, and it's controlled with refrigerant pressure in the compressor housing.

When housing pressure is increased, the pressure exerted on the back side of the pistons keeps them higher in their bores and closer to the cylinder head. This shortens the stroke, reducing displacement. When housing pressure is reduced, a spring pushes the adjusting linkage away from the cylinder head, increasing plate angle and lengthening the piston stroke to increase displacement.

Housing pressure is adjusted using a control valve with ports and passages that connect it to the suction (low side) and discharge (high side) chambers of the compressor head. Two different types of control valves are used. The traditional mechanical valve has a precision pressure-sensitive diaphragm that senses low-side pressure. When the temperature inside the vehicle is warm, evaporator temperature increases, which increases low-side pressure. This pushes on the diaphragm, opening a port that vents a little bit of housing pressure to the suction side. Reducing housing pressure increases piston stroke, which increases refrigerant flow volume through the system. As evaporator temperature decreases, so does low-side pressure. The diaphragm rebounds to close the low-side vent port and at the same time open a port that admits high-side pressure into the housing. This reduces piston stroke and, therefore, refrigerant flow volume.

Most new vehicles use a solenoid valve and temperature and pressure sensors in the refrigerant system instead of a diaphragm valve. This allows a computer to control the valve and adjust compressor displacement to control evaporator temperature, rather than using evaporator temperature to control displacement. Today almost all manufacturers offer electronically controlled variable displacement compressors, and some applications have no clutch, meaning the compressor runs whenever the engine is running. Most vehicles already operate the compressor any time the windshield defogger is turned on, even in winter. The electronic displacement control valve makes it easier to run the compressor continuously because displacement can be reduced closer to zero than with a mechanical valve. Continuous operation keeps seals lubricated, minimizes oil pooling and prevents other kinds of damage that result from long periods of inactivity.

An electronically controlled variable displacement compressor puts less load on the engine, improves fuel economy and improves idle quality by eliminating clutch cycling or the idle speed surge that sometimes accompanies it.

Additional A/C System Benefits

In addition to removing heat from the passenger compartment of the vehicle, the A/C system also removes moisture (humidity) from the air inside the vehicle as well as some airborne dust and pollen. Some vehicles are even equipped with dust and pollen filters.

The hot air inside the vehicle contains an elevated level of humidity. As it passes over the surface of the cooler evaporator, moisture is removed as it condenses and collects on the evaporator. This moisture collected on the surface of the evaporator then drips out of the evaporator case onto the ground. The airborne dust and pollen become trapped in the water droplets collected on the evaporator, and then drip out onto the ground with the moisture.

A/C SYSTEM PERFORMANCE TESTING

Refrigerants

The refrigerant used in automotive air conditioning systems from their inception until the early 1990s was a chemical compound called dichlorodiflouoro-methane, more commonly known as Freon˙ or R12. R12 is a member

A/C System Service, Diagnosis And Repair

of the chemical family known as chlorofluorocarbons (CFCs). Although R12 works extremely well as a heat transfer medium in an automotive air conditioning system, CFCs have been found to have a devastating effect on the earth's ozone layer, which protects all life on earth from harmful ultraviolet radiation from the sun. When a chlorine atom from a CFC like R12 is released, it can rise into the stratosphere and combine with one of the oxygen atoms of an ozone molecule to form chlorine monoxide and an oxygen molecule, destroying that ozone molecule. Since R12 was very inexpensive, it was a common practice to release it into the atmosphere during the servicing of an air conditioning system.

The Clean Air Act of 1990 required that the automotive industry stop releasing ozone-damaging refrigerant into the atmosphere. R12 was replaced with R134a and Section 609 of the Clean Air Act required that any person performing automotive air conditioning service "for compensation" be certified in the proper recovery and handling of refrigerants. These certifications can be obtained from a number of different sources, and failure to produce EPA certification when asked by any law enforcement representative can result in stiff Federal penalties. Repair facilities have additional requirements to meet to remain in compliance with the law as well. Contact the EPA for full information and details, or check with one of the several reference sources listed at the end of this study guide.

NOTE: *Successful completion of the A7 ASE certification exam DOES NOT substitute for the Section 609 certification.*

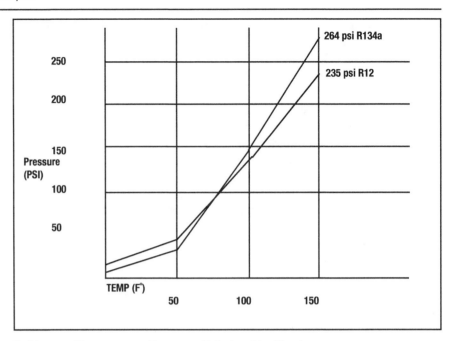

Refrigerant Temperature/Pressure Relationship Chart.

In 2006, the European Commission found that R134a was a contributor to global warming, with a GWP (Global Warming Potential) rating of 1300. It banned its use as an automotive refrigerant, and required that all vehicles offered for sale in the European Union starting with new model platforms in the 2011 model year be equipped with a refrigerant with a GWP under 150. The replacement choice is a product called HFO1234yf, also known as R1234yf. It is important to note that R134a is still approved for use in all vehicles that came originally equipped with it, and that, unlike the move from R12 so many years ago, there is no plan to "retrofit" any R134a vehicle to the new refrigerant. Additionally, the move to HFO1234yf is not a requirement in any other market. Here in the U.S., it is expected the transition will be voluntary as domestic manufacturers take advantage of the CAFE (Corporate Average Fuel Economy) credits that can be earned by switching over to more environmentally friendly materials, including refrigerants. GM was the first domestic manufacturer, offering at least two models equipped with HFO1234yf systems in the 2013 model year.

HFO1234yf is classified as a "mildly flammable" refrigerant, and as such will require special service procedures and equipment. In addition, evaporators for these systems will have to meet more stringent manufacturing standards and certification. In no case should an R1234yf evaporator be repaired or replaced with a salvaged unit. As of this writing, there are still pending EPA regulations that will likely require additional training and certification for technicians and shops. Regardless of the outcome of these pending rulings, all current Section 609 rules apply equally to HFO1234yf as they do to any other approved refrigerant. Those include the need for dedicated recovery and recycling equipment, and the ban on any form of venting refrigerant straight to the atmosphere..

Refrigerants are gasses at room temperature. Refrigerants have a

A/C System Service, Diagnosis And Repair

'roughly' one-to-one temperature to pressure relationship. The key word here is "roughly" though, because there are some differences. The one-to-one pressure and temperature relationship are close at low pressures, but as temperatures increase, the pressure-to-temperature relationships vary.

Refrigerants cannot be mixed. Even though they operate very similarly, they are distinctly different chemicals, and they require different approaches

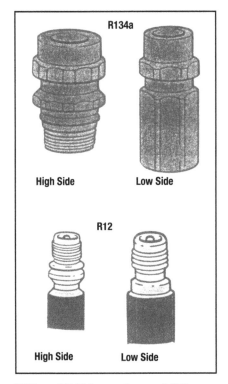

R12 and R134a service port fittings.

to certain system components, materials, and lubricating oils. If they are mixed, they form a compound with characteristics that are different from either refrigerant. A mixture of refrigerants can result in higher than normal pressures within a system, which can cause serious damage to system components. This can be such a serious matter that recovery/recycle/recharge equipment certified for use with HFO1234yf are required to first identify that the recovered refrigerant is pure HFO1234yf before the machine will begin. Refrigerant identifiers can be incorporated into the machine or tethered via USB cable.

NOTE: There a numerous refrigerants approved for use by the EPA, many of which contain blends of hydrocarbon compounds like propane and butane. NO OEM manufacturer approves of the use any of these substitutes and failure to use an identifier prior to recovering system's charge may result in the contamination of your shop's supply. It is considered a "best practice" to check every vehicle prior to service with a refrigerant identifer.

Refrigerant And System Identification

Before testing system performance, the type of refrigerant used and the design method used to regulate system pressures and temperatures must be identified. Each refrigerant has unique service fitting designs to help prevent accidental charging with another gas. Check the underhood label for system refrigerant identification, service precautions and specifications. It is also best practice to check for applicable TSBs (Technical Service Bulletins) issued by the manufacturer that may include modified/updated specifications.

However, labels and the type of service port fittings should not be regarded as proof of refrigerant type. There are a number of other refrigerants, as noted earlier, including refrigerant blends available that are marketed as replacements.

Be aware that the availablity of counterfiet refrigerants is an increasingly common problem, and these products may contain chemicals that are potentially dangerous to both you and your customer.

Mixing refrigerants in the same system contaminates the system and can result in damaged system components, reduced system performance, damaged recycling equipment and contaminated

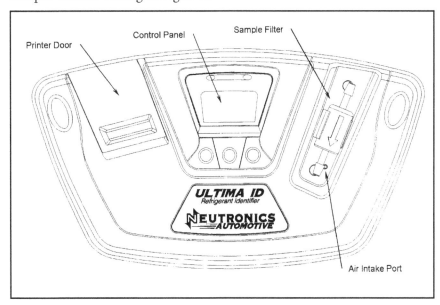

Some refrigerant identifiers have a built-in printer. A printout can be helpful when discussing needed repairs with a customer.
(Courtesy: Neutronics, Inc.)

Training for Certification

A/C System Service, Diagnosis And Repair

refrigerant supplies. In addition, some replacement refrigerants contain hydrocarbons such as propane or butane. These are highly flammable and could ignite during system servicing, possibly causing serious bodily injury and damaging equipment.

To prevent damaging A/C service equipment and contaminating refrigerant supplies, the refrigerant in the system should always be tested with a refrigerant identifier before connecting any equipment into the system. Some identifiers can detect R12, R134a, R22, air and hydrocarbons, displaying the percentages of each substance, while others may only give a pass/fail indication of purity. A pass is given if the purity is 98% or greater. Some identifiers are also equipped with an audible alarm if hydrocarbons are detected.

The refrigerant identifier is connected into the low side of the system. Before connecting the identifier, inspect the condition of the filter and hoses. Allow the tool to warm up and calibrate itself before operation. When the testing process is activated, the identifier will obtain and analyze a refrigerant vapor sample. If the refrigerant in the system is less than 98% pure, it should be considered contaminated and recovered using a dedicated recovery machine, so it can be reclaimed or destroyed.

As stated earlier, A/C systems can be identified by whether an expansion valve or orifice tube is used to control refrigerant flow into the evaporator and by whether the compressor cycles on and off or runs continuously. Systems using an expansion valve have a receiver/drier between the valve and condenser, while orifice tube systems have an accumulator between the evaporator and compressor.

A compressor that cycles on-and-off is usually used in conjunction with an orifice tube. Continuously running compressors can be either the conventional kind and used with an expansion valve to control evaporator temperature, or have variable displacement.

Variable displacement compressors use an internal valve to vary the angle of the compressor swash or wobble plate in response to changing evaporator pressures. When evaporator pressure is low, the angle of the plate is changed to reduce the pistons' stroke, in turn reducing the compressor's suction and output. When low-side pressure increases, the valve changes the plate angle to increase piston stroke and in turn raise compressor suction and output. Systems with variable displacement compressors usually employ an orifice tube but there are some that have an expansion valve.

Preliminary Inspection

Begin A/C system diagnosis by interviewing the customer to make sure you understand the complaint. Then check system operation and perform a visual inspection.

Functional Inspection

Start the engine and turn the A/C on-and-off several times, while listening for the sound of the compressor clutch. If the clutch cannot be heard engaging and disengaging, and there is no change in engine rpm when the A/C is turned on, there is a problem with the compressor's electrical control system or the refrigerant system may be low on refrigerant.

With the A/C turned on and set to full cold, check the air temperature at the dash panel duct outlets. If the air is cold or cool, then the compressor is operating and the system has some cooling capability. If the air is warmer than the temperature inside the vehicle, then there may be an air distribution problem. If the air is close to ambient temperature, then there is a problem with the refrigerant system.

Slowly move the temperature control from full cold to full hot and back again. The air temperature at the dash duct outlets should gradually become warmer as the control is moved toward hot and gradually become cooler when moved toward cold. Listen for the sound of the

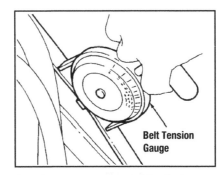

Checking compressor drive belt tension using a belt tension gauge. *(Courtesy: Ford Motor Co.)*

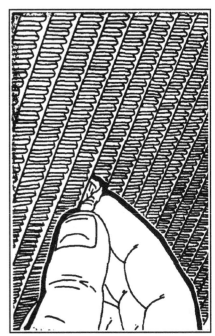

The position of the condenser in front of the radiator makes it particularly susceptible to collecting debris.

A/C System Service, Diagnosis And Repair

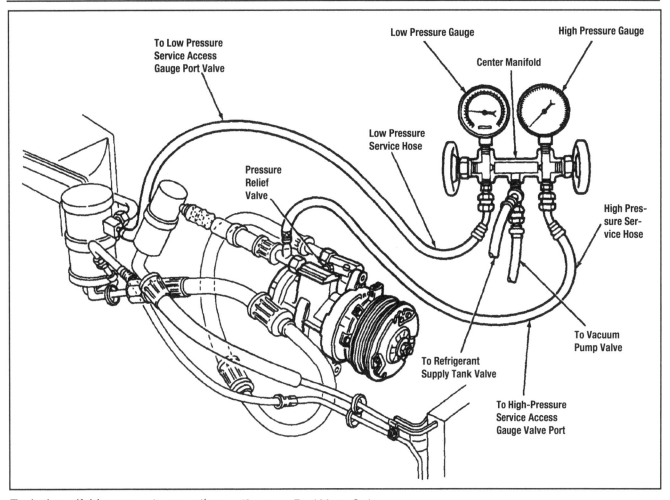

Typical manifold gauge set connections. *(Courtesy: Ford Motor Co.)*

temperature blend door closing in either direction. Move the function control from A/C to Heat and then to Defrost. The air flow should change from the dash outlets, to the floor and then to the windshield defrost outlets. If the temperature and/or function do not change properly, there may be a maladjusted or broken cable or a malfunctioning vacuum or electric door motor.

Move the blower motor control to each speed position. Listen and feel for a change in air volume according to control position. If the blower motor does not operate at all, there is a problem with the motor or the control circuit. If the motor operates but only on one speed, then the fault is in the control circuit.

Visual Inspection

Visually inspect the A/C system for obvious problems. Check the compressor drive belt for evidence of cracking, fraying, glazing or other damage and replace as necessary. If the belt is adjustable, check the belt tension by pressing against the belt with moderate pressure at a point midway along the longest span, and compare the deflection with specification, or check the tension using a belt tension gauge. Make sure the compressor is attached securely to its mounting brackets and the mounting bushings are in good condition.

Check the refrigerant lines and hoses for damage and signs of oil leakage, especially at any connections or unions. If oil has leaked out, most likely the refrigerant has as well. Pay particular attention to connections that are subject to engine vibrations, usually those on rubber lines. Check the front of the compressor. Oil here often indicates a bad front seal. Check all fittings and the pressure relief valve for signs of leaks.

Inspect the system electrical wiring to the compressor, blower motor and A/C switches for any damage. Make sure all connections are clean and tight. Check the vacuum hoses between the engine and firewall for evidence of cracks, splits, kinks or other damage that could cause a vacuum leak.

Inspect the condenser for debris that could obstruct air flow. If too many fins are bent, air flow will be

Training for Certification

A/C System Service, Diagnosis And Repair

reduced. Inspect the fan shroud for broken or missing parts, and make sure all air dams and condenser side and air seals are in place as they should be. Also, check the fresh air intakes in the cowl for leaves and other such debris.

If equipped with a mechanical fan, check the drive belt for wear and belt tension. A slipping belt will cause the fan to turn too slowly and not draw enough air through the condenser. Check the back of the fan clutch for an oily film, which would indicate that fluid is leaking and replacement is necessary. Turn the fan and clutch assembly by hand; there should be some viscous drag, but it should turn smoothly during a full rotation. Replace the fan clutch if it does not turn smoothly or if it does not turn at all. It should also be replaced if there is no viscous drag when hot or cold.

Have an assistant apply the parking brake and then start the engine and turn on the A/C. The clutch should engage and the compressor should turn. If equipped with an electric cooling fan, it should come on when the A/C is turned on. Some vehicles have two fans with one dedicated to the A/C system.

Manifold Gauges

A manifold gauge set is used to read the pressures on the low side and high side of the system. The gauge set has a low pressure gauge and a high pressure gauge. The gauges and hoses are often color coded blue for low, red for high. The low side is connected to the service fitting that is located somewhere between the evaporator outlet and the compressor. The high-side fitting is located somewhere between the compressor and the expansion valve or orifice tube.

A center hose or hoses, usually yellow in color, and often referred to as the service hose, connects to a vacuum pump or refrigerant source for evacuating or charging the system.

NOTE: Modern automotive air conditioning systems use much smaller system charges (refrigerant quantity), and proper charging is critical to system performance and component longevity. It is also critical that no venting of the refrigerant be allowed during service. For both of these reasons, it is recommended that only approved recovery/recycling/recharging equipment be used to service these systems. Leave the yellow service line alone.

All hoses must have a shutoff within 12 in. of their ends to prevent excess refrigerant from escaping during connection and disconnection. A Schrader valve or quick disconnect device at the hose end fitting is most common.

Ambient Air Temperature	Relative Humidity	Service Port Pressure		Maximum Left Center Discharge Air Temperature
		Low Side	High Side	
13–16°C (55–65°F)	0–100%	175–206 kPa (25–30 psi)	340–850 kPa (49–123 psi)	7°C (45°F)
19–24°C (66–75°F)	Below 40%	175–215 kPa (25–31 psi)	430–930 kPa (62–135 psi)	6°C (43°F)
	Above 40%	175–254 kPa (25–37 psi)	570–1070 kPa (83–155 psi)	9°C (48°F)
25–29°C (76–85°F)	Below 35%	175–249 kPa (25–36 psi)	760–1410 kPa (147–205 psi)	9°C (42°F)
	35–60%	175–261 kPa (26–38 psi)	830–1180 kPa (120–171 psi)	10°C (50°F)
	Above 60%	185–286 kPa (27–42 psi)	880–1250 kPa (128–181 psi)	11°C (52°F)
30–35°C (86–95°F)	Below 30%	193–293 kPa (28–43 psi)	1010–1410 kPa (146–205 psi)	12°C (54°F)
	30–50%	228–269 kPa (30–44 psi)	1050–1440 kPa (153–209 psi)	13°C (55°F)
	Above 50%	221–324 kPa (32–47 psi)	1100–1470 kPa (160–213 psi)	14°C (58°F)
36–41°C (96–105°F)	Below 20%	241–337 kPa (35–47 psi)	1310–1700 kPa (190–246 psi)	16°C (61°F)
	20–40%	247–345 kPa (36–50 psi)	1320–1700 kPa (190–230 psi)	16°C (61°F)
	Above 40%	259–353 kPa (37–52 psi)	1350–1690 kPa (196–246 psi)	16°C (61°F)
42–46°C (106–115°F)	Below 20%	292–378 kPa (42–55 psi)	1630–1950 kPa (238–283 psi)	17°C (62°F)
	Above 20%	297–383 kPa (43–55 psi)	1620–1930 kPa (235–280 psi)	19°C (66°F)
47–49°C (116–120°F)	Below 30%	338–405 kPa (50–59 psi)	187–2080 kPa (271–302 psi)	20°C (68°F)

A typical A/C performance specifications chart for an R134a vehicle. It shows how ambient temperature and relative humidity affect system operating pressures and outlet temperatures.
(Courtesy: GM Corp.)

A/C System Service, Diagnosis And Repair

WARNING: Always wear eye and skin protection when working with refrigerant, or personal injury may result.

To connect the gauge set, first locate the service fittings. Make sure the valves on the manifold and hoses are closed. Remove the cap from the low-side service fitting and connect the low-side hose to the fitting. Remove the high-side service fitting cap. Some older R12 high-side service ports require that an adapter be fitted to connect the high-side hose. If necessary, install the adapter and connect the hose to the adapter or fitting. On R134a and R1234yf systems there are no adapters required.

Open each hose valve but leave the manifold valves closed. The system pressure can now be read on the gauges.

Performance Testing

A performance test can determine whether the A/C system is functioning properly and if it is not can indicate what is wrong so the system can be repaired. Different vehicle manufacturers specify different methods to conduct system performance checks, but as a guideline, the following procedure may be used.

Connect a manifold gauge set as previously described. Hang the gauge set or place it where the gauges can be seen, making sure the hoses will not contact any hot or moving engine parts. With the engine off, the high and low-side pressures should be equal and the pressure should be correct for the ambient temperature. For example, at 70°F (21°C), the pressure in a system with R134a should be slightly higher at 71 psi. Check your service information system for these specifications and DO NOT rely on this as an indicator of proper system charge.

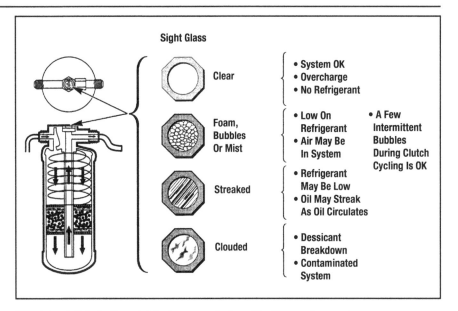

What is visible in the sight glass can help with diagnosing system malfunctions.

Place a thermometer at the center dash panel duct outlet to indicate the system temperature and place another thermometer at the center of the grille to register ambient temperature. Start the engine and turn on the A/C. Set the temperature control to the coldest setting. Turn on the blower motor and make sure it works on all speeds. Generally, if one of the blower speeds doesn't work, the problem is a faulty resistor. If the high speed doesn't work, the problem could be the high speed relay or fuse. If the blower is too slow at all speeds, perform a current draw test to see if the windings or brushes are bad.

At this point, if the A/C system is operating properly, there should be cool to cold air coming from the instrument panel air ducts. When the temperature control is moved from the coolest to the warmest setting, the air temperature should change to warm. When the function control lever is moved from A/C to heat, the air flow should move to the floor ducts.

Place the function control in the 'MAX A/C' or 'RECIRC' position and set the temperature control to the coldest position. Close all of the vehicle's doors and windows and make sure that all dash panel duct outlets are open.

Run the system on high for about five minutes, and then reduce the blower speed to low and allow the system to stabilize for about five more minutes. The thermometer at the center dash panel duct should read 35° - 55°F (2° - 13°C), depending on ambient temperature and humidity.

NOTE: Some vehicle manufacturers may recommend that you place a large fan in front of the grille to provide sufficient air flow over the condenser while performing test.

Check the vehicle manufacturer's specifications for proper system operating pressures, especially on R134a systems. Normal high-side gauge readings depend on the ambient temperature, so it is best to consult a temperature/pressure chart. Normal low-side readings vary depending on what is happening in the system, particularly in the evaporator, and what type of system it is.

A/C System Service, Diagnosis And Repair

The system controls (clutch cycling, expansion valve opening and closing, etc.) affect the readings and affect the evaporator temperature since there is roughly a one-to-one-relationship between temperature and pressure. Always look up the specifications for the system being worked on.

Here are some examples of gauge readings and what they may indicate:

Low side normal, high side normal (but poor cooling)
- air or moisture in the system
- blend door stuck open (admitting too much heat)
- defective or misadjusted thermostatic switch
- defective pressure cycling switch.
- Low side low, high side low
- low refrigerant charge (possible leak)
- expansion valve stuck closed
- restriction on the high side.

Low side high, high side high
- damaged compressor (bent or damaged valves)
- refrigerant overcharge
- condenser restriction or inoperative fan
- expansion valve stuck open.

Low side high, high side low
- damaged compressor (bent or damaged valves)
- loose drive belt or slipping clutch (if there's no compressor noise).

Low side low, high side normal to high
- expansion valve stuck closed
- clogged orifice tube.

Common causes of high pressure
- refrigerant overcharge
- restricted condenser (leaves, paper, bugs, etc.)
- clogged receiver/drier
- plugged orifice tube.

DIAGNOSIS BY SIGHT, SOUND, SMELL AND TOUCH

Sight
If the system has a sight glass, observe the refrigerant as it passes by. On older vehicles still equipped with R12, a clear flow indicates a proper charge. If there is foam, the charge is low, but if there are only a couple of bubbles, it is probably OK. A few bubbles when the compressor cycles on are normal. Oil streaks in the sight glass usually indicate a low charge and that the compressor is pumping oil from its sump. If the sight glass is cloudy, the desiccant bag has probably burst. Systems with orifice tubes and accumulators usually don't have sight glasses. While rare, if an R134a system has a sight glass, do not use it to try to perform diagnosis, as it is normal to observe bubbles in this type of system. If the refrigerant has color like yellow or green, someone has probably added refrigerant with a leak detection dye; this is no reason for concern.

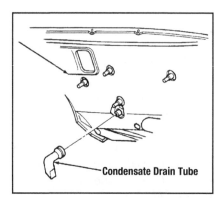

Typical evaporator case drain tube.
(Courtesy: DaimlerChrysler Corp.)

Look for frost buildup on the A/C lines and components. If there is a restriction in the system, frost will accumulate at the point of the restriction. A restricted receiver/drier will have frost buildup. A flooded evaporator, which can be caused by a restricted TXV, will have frost buildup at the evaporator outlet. Keep in mind that it is normal for light frost buildup at the outlet of the refrigerant metering device.

Sound
Squealing noise can be caused by loose or glazed belts. Sometimes belt noise sounds a lot like bearing noise. Spray some water on the belts and see if the noise goes away. If it does, the tension may need to be corrected or the belts may have to be replaced.

Bad compressor or clutch bearings may also make noise. Start the engine and engage the compressor clutch. Defective compressor bearings won't make noise until the compressor is operating, but bad clutch bearings will most often make noise without the clutch engaged. To verify defective pulley bearings, remove the belt(s) and turn the pulley by hand. If there is roughness, the bearings are bad. If there is no roughness, the compressor shaft bearing or thrust bearing may be the cause. Make sure you observe the proper clutch air gap specification if you need to replace a clutch or field coil assembly.

A clicking or buzzing noise coming from the compressor is a sign that the system is overcharged and liquid refrigerant is entering the compressor. Unless some refrigerant is removed, severe compressor damage may result. This noise could also result from air in the system.

Knocking or rattling sounds

A/C System Service, Diagnosis And Repair

usually indicate internal compressor damage, especially on piston type compressors. However, knocking or rattling noise can also be caused by loose compressor mounting brackets and/or bolts.

Noises from the blower motor could point to a bad bearing or debris, such as leaves, in the blower plenum.

A customer may voice concerns about noise that is normal for the A/C system, such as the random clicking of the compressor clutch when it engages, or a hissing noise when the A/C is turned off. The hissing noise is normal and caused by high-side pressure going through the refrigerant metering device as system pressures equalize.

Smell

Foul odors caused by bacterial growth can originate from the evaporator and evaporator case. As explained earlier, the evaporator removes moisture from the air as it condenses and collects on the cool evaporator surface. The moisture then drips from the evaporator and drains from a tube in the bottom of the evaporator case.

If the drain at the bottom of the evaporator case becomes clogged and water collects and stagnates, or if the surface of the evaporator remains too moist due to high humidity, bacteria can grow in the stagnant water or on the evaporator surface and cause an odor. This odor is then sent into the passenger compartment by the blower motor.

To prevent stagnant water from collecting, make sure the evaporator case drain is clear. In some instances, a clogged drain can cause the evaporator case to fill up and leak water into the passenger compartment. To prevent bacterial growth on the evaporator surface, the system should be run periodically on vent

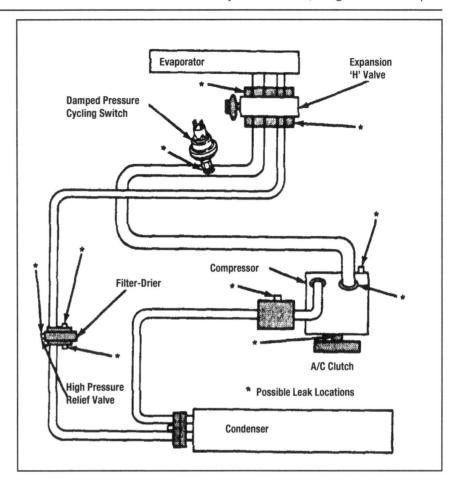

This schematic indicates areas where refrigerant leaks are most likely to occur. *(Courtesy: DaimlerChrysler Corp.)*

or heat with the A/C off, to dry the evaporator. If equipped, make sure the passenger compartment air filter is clean.

Chemical fungicides can be used to kill the bacteria, but they must be applied to the evaporator's surface. Depending on the vehicle, it may be possible to gain access to the evaporator through fresh air vents, by removing the blower motor resistor or by drilling holes in the evaporator case. In some cases the evaporator may have to be removed for cleaning.

Touch

Feel the temperature of the A/C lines and hoses during A/C operation. It is normal for the high-side components to be warm or hot and the low-side components to be cool or

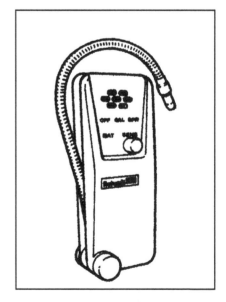

Typical electronic leak detector. *(Courtesy: Ford Motor Co.)*

cold. If you feel along the high-side components and suddenly the surface turns cold, you have

Training for Certification

A/C System Service, Diagnosis And Repair

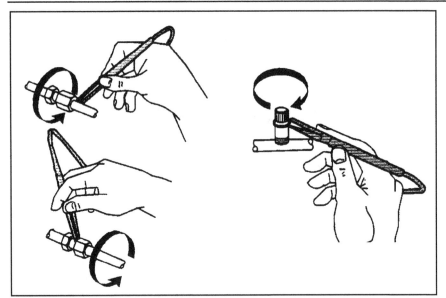

Move the leak detector probe all the away around fitting connections and service port fittings. Don't move the probe any faster than around one inch per second. *(Courtesy: GM Corp.)*

discovered a restriction in the system at the point of temperature change. On humid days, frost may even form at this point. If frost forms at the evaporator outlet, it could be caused by a defective thermostatic switch. If frost forms on the outside of the TXV, it may be stuck closed or clogged with ice.

A receiver/drier should be warm and an accumulator should be cool. The evaporator outlet should be cool; if it is not the system may be low on refrigerant or the proper amount of refrigerant may not be entering the evaporator. The line from the condenser to the TXV or orifice tube should be warm to hot. Feel the compressor itself. It may be warm, but if it is very hot, the valves may be broken or bent. This is particularly true of a piston-type compressor if the head is hot.

REFRIGERANT LEAK DETECTION

The presence of oil residue at a line connection is usually the sign of a refrigerant leak, because the refrigerant oil will escape along with the refrigerant. Visually inspect all line and hose connections, the area around the compressor seal, the service port fittings and the condenser and evaporator.

To find leaks, there must be at least 50 psi of pressure in the system. To be sure the system is under pressure connect the

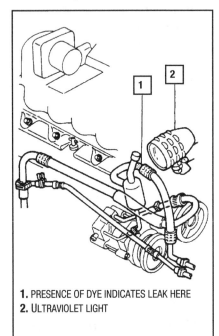

1. PRESENCE OF DYE INDICATES LEAK HERE
2. ULTRAVIOLET LIGHT

Using an ultraviolet light to detect dye and refrigerant leaks. *(Courtesy: Ford Motor Co.)*

manifold gauge set. If the pressure is below 50 lbs., add refrigerant to get enough pressure for testing.

A solution of soap and water is the simplest and cheapest leak detector. Simply apply the soapy water to the suspected area with a brush or spray bottle and look for the presence of bubbles or foam, which would be caused by a leak. The problem with this method is that it is only useful for a large leak.

Electronic leak detectors and fluorescent dye detectors are the preferred methods for finding refrigerant leaks.

Electronic Leak Detectors

Electronic leak detectors signal the presence of refrigerant by some type of audible indication, usually a beeping, clicking or buzzing tone. The more rapid the beeps, or the louder the tone, the larger the leak. Electronic leak detectors certfied to the latest SAE standards are lab-quality tools, and capable of detecting leaks as small as 4 grams per year. Treat them with care.

Perform the leak check in a location free of wind and drafts. If the area is contaminated with refrigerant or other gases, use a fan or compressed air to blow the excess refrigerant away. Make sure you pass the probe around the bottom of components and hoses as refrigerant is heavier than air and tends to settle. Don't move the probe too quickly and try to keep the probe tip no farther than 1/4" away, as this may cause you to miss small leaks. No faster than one inch per second is the general rule. Never allow the probe to contact any surface, to prevent contamination of the sensing tip.

Concentrate your efforts at connections and fittings, as these are the most likely leak sites. Also check the front of the compressor and the compressor crankcase, as these are common areas for seal leaks. Evaporator leaks can be hard to detect because of the lack of accessibility. It may be possible to insert the probe through the blower motor resistor-mounting hole or through the evaporator case drain tube. If using the latter, take care to prevent contaminating the sensing tip with moisture.

Leak detectors are different for different refrigerants. Be sure the tool you select is compatible with the system you are working on. When purchasing a new leak detector, be sure to check for the SAE certification label.

Leak Detection With Fluorescent Dye

Another way to find leaks is by injecting a special fluorescent dye into the system, operating it for a short time, and then passing an ultraviolet light over all of the components. This is a good method to find very small leaks, or leaks in inconvenient places. In fact, some vehicles come from the manufacturer with dye installed in the system.

There is a difference between the dyes to be used in different systems, so be sure to use the proper type for the system being worked on. Also be sure to follow proper procedures for adding dye. Too much can be as bad as overfilling the system with oil, and adding a PAG-based dye to an electric compressor can cause a high voltage leak that may require total system replacement to correct.

REFRIGERANT RECOVERY

Unless the refrigerant has completely drained from the A/C system due to a leak, before replacing any components that carry refrigerant through the system, the refrigerant must be removed. On a typical 80°F

(27°C) day, a fully charged system will have over 80 psi of pressure. Opening a fitting or union will allow the refrigerant to escape into the atmosphere. Such a procedure is not only unsafe, it is illegal and environmentally harmful. All refrigerant must be extracted and recycled using approved recovery/recycling equipment.

Most units operate similarly. Connect the service hoses to the vehicle's A/C system, and activate the equipment to draw out the refrigerant. The machine will weigh the amount of refrigerant that is removed from the system. Allow the system to empty until there is no pressure or a vacuum. Measure the amount of oil that is removed from the system so the proper amount of new oil can be added to the system during recharging.

Once the refrigerant is safely stored, repairs to the A/C system can be performed. Make sure the recovery/recycling equipment is operated in accordance with the manufacturer's instructions.

Recovery/recycling/recharge machines meeting SAE standard J2788 are more capable of removing all of the existing refrigerant charge than those made before this standard was enacted. These machines are also more accurate In measuring the amount of refrigerant recovered and the amount recharged to the system. Regardless of the machine used, it is considered best practice to allow the machine to sit for at least five minutes before completing the recovery process. Check the pressure in the system at the end of five minutes. If the pressure rises above "0", there is still refrigerant outgassing from the oil. Repeat recovery until stable system pressure remains in a vacuum (sealed system) or rises no higher than 0 psi (leaking system).

System Evacuation

After repairs have been performed on the A/C system, or any time the system has been opened, it must be evacuated. When repairs are made, air will enter the open system, and if not removed, the air can cause higher than normal operating pressures, leading to poor cooling performance.

Moisture from humidity in the air can form destructive chemicals inside the system when mixed with refrigerant and oils, and can cause a breakdown of the newer synthetic oils used in R134a systems. Also, water in the system can ice up in the expansion valve and block refrigerant flow. On systems with R12, water can combine with the chlorine in the R12 to form hydrochloric acid. These chemicals can corrode metals and attack rubber parts. During evacuation, as the pressure inside the system lowers, so does the boiling point of the water in the system. At 29 in/Hg, water can vaporize and be withdrawn by the vacuum pump.

While stand-alone vacuum pumps are commercially available, if you are using a charging station, the vacuum pump is most likely incorporated into the station. After properly connecting the service hoses, start the vacuum pump and open both sides of the system, exposing it to vacuum. Once the vacuum level reaches specification, continue pulling the vacuum for at least 30 to 60 minutes. The more humid the air, the longer the vacuum pump should be allowed to run. If the pump is turned off too soon, some of the moisture in the system will be left behind. Close all valves and turn the pump off. Wait for 5 minutes and note any vacuum loss. Loss of vacuum within 5 minutes indicates leakage.

A/C System Service, Diagnosis And Repair

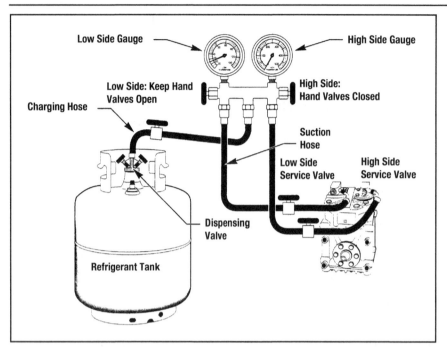

Although a charging station is more accurate, an A/C system can be charged from a refrigerant drum. The drum should be placed on a scale and the total weight noted before charging. During charging, the scale should be watched to determine the amount of refrigerant used.

NOTE: Recovery/recycling/recharging equipment meeting the latest SAE standard J2788 will perform an automatic leak check and may not allow the operator to recharge the system until the leaks have been repaired.

Before turning off the pump, close off the A/C system to the atmosphere to prevent air from being drawn back into it.

Although evacuating removes moisture, it won't remove debris. To help prevent any debris remaining in a repaired system from reaching the compressor, filters can be installed, usually in the liquid line. These filters are usually capable of trapping all debris normally encountered while allowing the refrigerant to pass freely. A system may also be flushed in accordance with the manufacturers recommendations, either with liquid refrigerant using specialized equipment or an approved solvent.

NOTE: Be sure to follow OEM recommendations on system flushing or component failure may result.

A common misconception is that any oil recovered during the recovery/evacuation process should be measured and added back into the system. The truth is that very little oil should be lost during this procedure. Typically, oil collected in the oil recovery bottle of the machine is a result of lack of machine maintenance and/or oil trapped in the internal lines after use of the onboard oil injection feature.

Refrigerant Charging

Although charging the system can be performed through either the high side or low side when the engine is not running, it must be done only through the low side when the engine is running. This safety measure prevents high-side pressure from entering the refrigerant container and possibly causing an explosion.

Obtain the refrigerant capacity specification for the system before charging. This is often printed on a sticker located somewhere under the hood, or in a service manual. The most accurate method to assure that the proper amount of refrigerant has been installed into the system is to use some type of charging station that can be programmed to deliver the exact amount. It is crucial that the exact amount of refrigerant called for is used. Overcharging can cause system damage, and undercharging will cause poor performance. With reduced system capacities, especially in R134a systems, charge amounts are more critical than ever.

When using a charging station or recovery/recycling equipment, follow the manufacturer's instructions for its use. Recharging equipment should also indicate

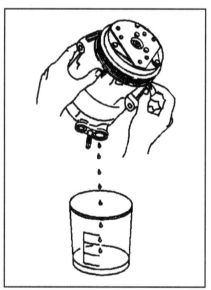

When replacing a compressor, drain the oil from the compressor being removed into a graduated container. Record the amount of refrigerant oil drained from the compressor and then properly dispose of the used oil. Drain any oil from the new compressor. Add the recorded amount of new refrigerant oil to the compressor prior to installation.

when the refrigerant oil should be injected. Allow the system to stabilize for a short period of time after charging. Then performance check the system, observing proper operating gauge pressures.

Refrigerant Oil

The main purpose of refrigerant oil is to provide compressor lubrication. The oil travels with the refrigerant throughout the entire system on some systems. On others, the system is designed to allow oil to stay in the sump of the compressor. The oil has a secondary purpose — to lubricate seals and O-rings and keep them pliable, and also to keep expansion valves moving freely.

Refrigerant oils are specific to the type of refrigerant used and to system design. Older R12 systems used a mineral oil, while modern R134a systems use various weights of PAG (polyalkyline glycol). HFO1234yf and systems using electric compressors use different oils still. It is imperative that the right oil be used in the right application, or serious system damage can result.

Be aware that some refrigerant oils are hygroscopic. That means they absorb water readily, even straight from the surrounding air. It is important these oils remain tightly sealed when not in use, and that contaminated oil be disposed of properly and NOT installed in the vehicle's air conditioning system.

Proper oil quantity is critical, just as it is in the engine. Too little oil will result in lack of lubrication to components and early failure of the compressor. Too much oil coats the inside of the heat exchangers (evaporator and condenser), reducing their efficiency. When replacing a component or servicing the system, always follow the OEM procedure for balancing the system charge. Typically, this is simply a matter of removing the oil from the replaced component, measuring the amount recovered, and adding a like amount back to the system.

NOTE: Replacement compressors may or may not come with oil already installed in them. In some cases, the installed oil is strictly lubrication for storage and is NOT the approved oil for the application. It is considered best practice to fully drain the oil from the replacement unit and adding the correct type and amount from an uncontaminated, sealed container.

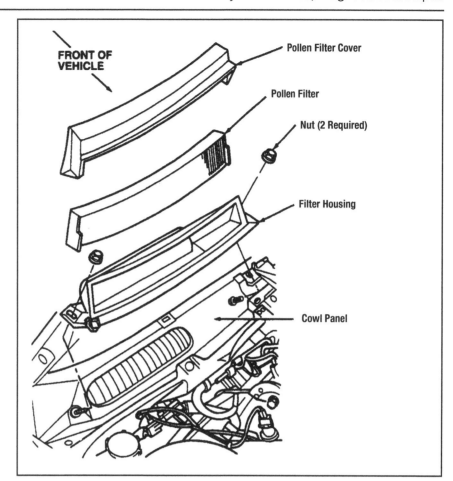

Typical passenger compartment air filter installation.
(Courtesy: Ford Motor Co.)

PASSENGER SIDE AIR FILTER

Many newer vehicles are equipped with passenger compartment air filters to trap dust, pollen and other pollutants. They are beneficial for vehicle occupants, and help protect the HVAC system downstream components. The filter should be replaced at the intervals specified in the manufacturer's scheduled maintenance information. Filters that are not changed regularly can cause an airflow restriction resulting in decreased heating and air conditioning performance.

On some vehicles the filter is located under the cowl screen and accessed from outside the vehicle, while on others it is installed in the evaporator case and is accessed

A/C System Service, Diagnosis And Repair

from under the dash. Refer to the vehicle service manual for specific procedures.

Air Bag System

Servicing the Heating, Ventilation and Air Conditioning (HVAC) system may require working around the SRS (Supplemental Restraint System) or air bag system. For example, procedures like heater core and evaporator core removal may require instrument panel and air bag module removal. To prevent accidental deployment and personal injury, the SRS must be properly disarmed.

In general, to disarm the air bag system, disconnect the negative battery cable from the battery terminal and tape the cable end to prevent it from accidentally contacting the battery terminal. Then, wait at least 10 minutes for the backup power supply to discharge. However, always consult the vehicle service manual for the exact disarming procedure.

When working on the air bag system, wear eye protection and follow all safety precautions. After an air bag module has been removed, carry the module with the cover pad facing away from the body. Store the module with the cover pad facing up, so that accidental deployment does not launch it into the air.

DIAGNOSING COMPUTER CONTROLLED HVAC SYSTEMS

Pre-OBD II

Vehicles built prior to the advent of OBD II (circa 1995-1996) typically used electronic control modules only to operate their automatic temperature control systems. On these models, the control module was typically contained in the HVAC control

head in the same unit housing the driver's system control switches. Warning indicators may or may not be included on the HVAC information display or instrument cluster. Access to any faults in these early electronic systems was generally performed by pressing control panel switches in a specified sequence, with a code numbers being displayed on the panel directly or by the flashing of an indicator light. Check the OEM service information for the specifics of the vehicle you are working on.

Once the trouble code number has been recovered, look up the definition of the code in your service information system. Most of these early systems set trouble codes for electrical problems in actuators or switches, and were diagnosed with simple voltage and resistance tests using a volt-ohmmeter. Often, the use of an automotive lab scope is an appropriate tool, allowing the technician to observe the function of an electrical component or circuit over time and helping him/her spot an intermittent loss like ones often found in components using a potentiometer as a variable voltage device.

NOTE: Understanding how any system functions is fundamental to effectively diagnosing them when they fail. Spend the time to review all the information you can before you pick up a tool or replace a component. Besides the service information, be sure to look for any Technical Service Bulletins (TSBs) that the manufacturer may have issued. There are also several after-market informational sources you should include while researching the potential cause of any vehicle performance issue.

Post-OBD II

Failures in the air conditioning system can impact vehicle emissions. For this reason, most late model vehicles rely on the engine management computer (more commonly referred to as the "ECM" or "PCM") to decide when the air conditioning compressor will turn on. Computer control of the compressor and other HVAC components is not limited to those models with automatic temperature control either. That makes it more important than ever for the technician to understand modern computer diagnostic strategies.

Diagnostic Trouble Codes

Diagnostic Trouble Codes (DTCs) are the computer reports of a failure within the system(s) it monitors. If it is a fault under the control of the ECM, it will turn on the Malfunction Indicator Lamp (MIL, also called a "Check Engine" light). However, if it is in a HVAC system module, there may be no visible warning that there is a problem.

DTCs are separated into four different types; "P" (powertrain), "B" (body), "C" (chassis), and "U" (communications). In addition, each type may have a generic SAE definition or a more unique manufacturer's definition. Regardless, never rely on the simple definition that may be displayed on your scan tool. Always look up the full definition, and the requirements needed for that fault to be recorded, in your service information system.

NOTE: Many electronic module code failures require that a module's software be recalibrated, a process called "reflashing". It is important that you check the OEM TSBs for this information before

26

A7 - Heating And Air Conditioning

wasting valuable diagnostic time.

"U" codes relate to the ability of individual modules to communicate with one another on the bus network. The operation of most modern HVAC systems relies on more than one module doing its job, and if it can't talk to the others on its network, DTCs will set and system function will suffer. Always diagnose and repair these "U" codes before moving on to any others stored in the system.

Diagnostic Procedure

The first step in any diagnostic procedure is to verify the customer's complaint. As well as following the basic system test procedures outlined earlier, make a habit of connecting an appropriate scan tool and checking all the vehicle modules for DTCs. Often, a fault in one may be the cause of a symptom in another. Record any DTCs found.

NOTE: Scan tools come in a variety of capabilities, from simple ECM code readers to full factory capable models. Most over-the-counter scan tools you see at local outlets or automotive parts houses are not capable of accessing body-related modules needed to properly diagnose and service modern HVAC systems.

Next, look up the individual definitions to see if any have shared requirements for failure detection. Understand fully how the specific system you are working on functions and what is needed by the module in question to log the failure. Be sure to check for any related TSBs as noted above for updated software and/or components.

Many scan tools offer what's called "bi-directional" control functions that allow the technician to command the operation of components like the compressor clutch, air blend doors, etc. Using these commands while monitoring the scan tool data stream can often assist you in locating a fault. Each Parameter Identifier (PID) on the scan tool screen has a meaning and use in troubleshooting.

Many manufacturers supply diagnostic flow charts, or "trouble trees", for their system codes. They can be a great aid in diagnosing HVAC DTCs but don't follow them blindly. Make sure you know why you are performing a specific test, perform them all, and in the order listed by the manufacturer, to get the most success from them.

There are also several sources of aftermarket information to assist you. With today's power of the internet, the answer may be only a few clicks away! Not all internet information is created equal, though, so be sure you verify the accuracy of what you find there. You can also access the factory information sites, albeit for a small fee, and have the same information as the dealer has. A link to these sites can be found at www.OEM1Stop.com, and is sponsored by the National Automotive Service Task Force (NASTF).

Once you have gathered the necessary information, its time to grab the appropriate tool and isolate the problem. In addition to a capable scan tool, you'll need a good volt-ohmmeter to perform any electrical tests outlined in the flow chart. Many technicians utilize digital storage oscilloscopes to perform performance tests of HVAC components like blend door actuators and potentiometers. Any circuit you would prefer to monitor over time and while its working is a good candidate for the use of this tool.

The last, and most important, step is to verify your repair after it's completed. Rescan the modules for DTCs and run a full-system performance test before you return the vehicle to your customer.

Refrigerant Recovery, Recycling and Handling

Section 609 of the Clean Air Act states that automotive air conditioning technicians are required to recover and recycle all refrigerant using a machine designed and approved to do the job. All A/C technicians must be certified to do so.

Equipment

According to the Clean Air Act, all equipment used for the recovery and recycling of refrigerant must meet SAE (Society of Automotive Engineers) standards, which provide equipment specifications for hardware related issues.

Recovery/recycling equipment both recovers the refrigerant from the motor vehicle and processes it through an oil separator, a filter, and a dryer. Equipment certified to SAE J2788 will automatically lock the user out of the machine when the filter requires changing. Replacement filters come with a code that must be entered to reset the machine.

Recover-only equipment removes the refrigerant from the A/C unit and transfers it into a holding tank. Technicians are then required by law either to recycle the used refrigerant on site or send it to an off-site reclamation facility to be purified.

Both styles of machine have on-board vacuum pumps used when evacuating the system. Proper maintenance of the pump, including periodic oil changes and inspection, are a key factor in insuring full performance from the equipment.

The two styles of recovery/recycling equipment: single-pass and multi-pass, draw the

A/C System Service, Diagnosis And Repair

refrigerant from the A/C system, filters and separates the oil, removes moisture and air, and stores the refrigerant until it's ready to be reused. The refrigerant goes through each stage before being stored and ready for reuse in single-pass systems. It may go through all or some of the stages before being stored in multi-pass systems.

Refrigerant Identification

Refrigerant contamination levels in excess of 5 percent can result in pressure control problems, air quality and flow problems, and valve blockage. In addition, resulting hose and seal degradation can contaminate the system further, causing more expensive repairs than anticipated.

Checking refrigerant pressures does not guarantee that you will recognize that refrigerant is contaminated or is a brand that is unfamiliar to you. However, refrigerant identification tools can help you. The identifier can confirm the chemical composition of refrigerant, and sometimes indicate flammable substances and air content.

Be aware that different refrigerant mixtures can result in a mixture that is not recognized by the identifier because the original intent was to identify R12 and R134a refrigerants. Because other refrigerants are now available, identification problems are now more complex. Service facilities should establish how these identifiers respond to different refrigerant mixtures and contamination.

Depending on the manufacturer, the identifier can be a hand-held tool, which will identify whether the refrigerant is pure R12 or R134a, or be part of a complete refrigerant recovery/ recycling station, which can aid in complete A/C diagnostics. Always follow the identifier manufacturer's instructions when using this type of equipment.

Should you identify contaminated refrigerant, recover that refrigerant using a dedicated machine and an approved recovery tank. When full, label appropriately and have the contaminated refrigerant recycled or disposed off by an approved agent.

Recovering Refrigerant

You must keep the discharge of refrigerant to a minimum when recovering refrigerant. All A/C service hoses must have shutoff valves within 12-in. (30cm) of the service ends: manual shutoff valves or Schrader valves, or quick disconnect fittings with automatic shutoff. The purpose of shutoff valves is to minimize the amount of refrigerant that escape into the atmosphere. Shutoff valves also minimize the amount of air that may enter the recycling equipment.

Always follow the equipment manufacturer's instructions. Recover the refrigerant from the vehicle and continue the process until the equipment gauges show a vacuum in the system. Turn off the recovery/recycling unit, but leave it connected to the vehicle for at least five minutes to see if the system has any residual pressure. If so, repeat the process to remove any remaining refrigerant until the A/C system holds a stable vacuum for at least five minutes.

Systems with accumulators usually require some extra time for recovery because accumulators can get very cold and refrigerant can become dissolved in the lubricant retained by the accumulator. Some refrigerant may remain in the accumulator and be released as it warms up. Running the engine to heat up the accumulator, or applying warm compresses to the accumulator itself can aid in full refrigerant recover. Make sure you remove all refrigerant before disconnecting any of the system's components.

Before disconnecting the equipment, close the valves in the service hoses. You may now make any necessary repairs to the A/C system.

Recycling

In general, properly recycled refrigerant can be removed from the vehicle's air conditioner, recycled on site, and then charged into the same or a different vehicle. Recycled refrigerant is identified as refrigerant that has been recovered from an A/C system and cleaned in accordance with SAE standards. The equipment is only designed to remove contaminants that are normally picked up during A/C operation. Recycling equipment meeting SAE standards for refrigerant must be labeled according to the specific refrigerant it is designed to recycle.

According to the EPA, once recovered, refrigerant should not be recycled on-site unless it is uncontaminated. Recovering contaminated refrigerant into recycling equipment may damage the equipment. In addition, the EPA regulations currently prohibit technicians from recycling blend substitute refrigerants (contaminated or not).

Storing and Disposal

It is illegal to use anything but "DOT CFR Title 49" containers for recycled refrigerant. Markings "4BA" or "4BW" on the side show that it meets DOT CFR Title 49 requirements. Never collect, salvage or store refrigerant in a disposable container.

Evacuate the container to at least 27-in. Hg vacuum (75mm

A/C System Service, Diagnosis And Repair

Hg absolute pressure) before transferring the refrigerant. To prevent overfilling during transfer of refrigerant, never fill a container to more than 60 percent of its gross weight rating. If the refrigerant is contaminated beyond the point where it can be cleaned, the contents should be recovered to be reclaimed by an EPA-certified refrigerant reclaimer.

Containers still have traces of refrigerant in them even though they may appear to be empty. Evacuate all remaining refrigerant using your recovery/recycling apparatus before disposing of the container. To remove any remaining refrigerant, connect your recovery/recycling unit to the container and recover the refrigerant. Once the container shows a vacuum, close its valve. Write the word 'EMPTY' on the container and dispose of it in accordance with all applicable laws.

Testing for Non-Condensable Gases

Before using recycled refrigerant, you must check it for excess non-condensable gases (air). After storing the container at 65°F (18°C) or above for 12 hours out of direct sunlight, connect a gauge, calibrated in 1-psi divisions, to the container and read the pressure.

Also check the air temperature within 4-in. of the container with an accurate thermometer. Compare your pressure reading to a standard temperature-pressure chart. Be sure the pressure is at, or below, the limits shown for a given temperature.

The refrigerant can be used as is, if the pressure of the recycled refrigerant is lower than the limit shown for a given temperature. If the pressure is higher than the limit shown for a given temperature, there is air in the tank. To purge the air, connect the tank to the recovery/recycling machine and slowly vent the air vapor from the top of the container. Continue venting until the pressure falls below the limit shown on your chart. If the pressure inside the container still exceeds the pressure limit shown, recycle the entire contents.

Refrigerant Handling Certification

Many organizations now provide the certification called for in the Clean Air Act, but such certification should not be confused with the regular ASE Heating and Air Conditioning Technician Certification Test A7.

Except in selected locales, the refrigerant recovery and recycling tests are open-book exams designed to acquaint the technician with the environmental issues, as well as proper techniques for handling CFCs. Once the test is passed, the technician will receive a certificate, which will entitle him or her to purchase CFCs, and also legally work on automotive refrigeration systems.

Organizations that provide certification include:

ASE Refrigerant Recovery and Recycling Review and Quiz
101 Blue Seal Drive
Suite 101
Leesburg, VA 20175
Phone 703-669-6600
http://www.asecert.org

Mobile Air Conditioning Society (MACS)
P.O. Box 88
Lansdale, PA 19446
Phone 215-631-7020
Fax 215-631-7017
http://www.macsw.org

In addition, you can check out the latest listing of certification sources at the EPA website. This list will be updated when other technician certification programs are approved.

Notes

Refrigeration System Component Diagnosis And Repair

COMPRESSOR AND CLUTCH

There are several different compressor designs, but all perform the same function: they move, or pump the refrigerant throughout the system, and they compress the low pressure vaporized refrigerant into a high pressure vapor.

Compressors may be of a piston, rotary vane or scroll design. Piston style compressors are the most popular, and are either in line, V-type, radial, axial or wobble plate. The most modern compressors are of a multi-piston design, ranging anywhere from 4 to 10 cylinders. Some compressors change displacement while operating, and have an effect on refrigerant flow in the system.

Most modern compressors have a clutch and drive pulley. The pulley is belt-driven by one or two V-belts directly from the engine's crankshaft or by a multi-ribbed V belt or serpentine belt. The pulley turns whenever the engine is running, although the compressor clutch is not engaged when the air conditioning is turned off.

NOTE: Electric compressors are increasingly used, and not only on hybrid cars. Some electric compressors are belt-driven as well. Read up on the specific system on any vehicle you're not familiar with before beginning service. These compressors are powered by extremely high voltage, and improper service techniques can result in personal injury. Special oils are used to keep the internal windings from shorting to the compressor case, and even small contamination with PAG left over in your service equipment is enough to cause total system failure. Only service equipment approved for hybrid/electric compressor service should be used.

Compressor Protection Devices

High-Pressure Cutout Switch

When certain malfunctions occur, high-side pressures could

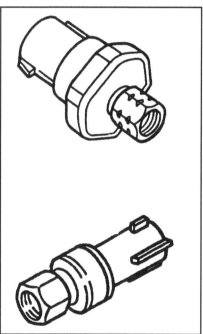

Two types of high-pressure cutout switches. The single function switch interrupts compressor function if system pressure becomes too high. The dual function switch first engages the high-speed cooling fan (on vehicles so equipped) in an attempt to lower pressure by increasing heat transfer at the condenser. However, if system pressure continues to rise after the fan has been engaged, then the switch will interrupt compressor operation.
(Courtesy: Ford Motor Co.)

exceed the safe operating limits of the compressor, hoses, or other components. To prevent this from happening, many systems are equipped with high-pressure cutout switches. These switches open the clutch circuit in the event that pressures become excessive. This function shuts down the compressor and stops the pressure from climbing higher. This serves two purposes: it protects the compressor from damage, and prevents venting of refrigerant through the pressure relief device (if equipped). Once repairs are made, the switch will allow normal clutch engagement.

High-pressure conditions can indicate failures such as a damaged compressor, refrigerant overcharge, condenser restriction, stuck open expansion valve, clogged orifice tube or receiver/drier.

Low-Pressure Cutout Switch

Some vehicles are equipped with low-pressure cutout switches. The purpose of this switch is also compressor protection. The compressor clutch circuit is opened if the pressure in the system drops too low. This would be an indication that the system has lost some or all of its refrigerant charge. Since the lubricating oil is carried by the refrigerant, a loss could cause damage to the compressor if it were allowed to operate without sufficient lubrication.

Low-pressure conditions can indicate failures such as a clogged orifice tube, low refrigerant charge, expansion valve stuck closed, or a restriction in the high side of the A/C system.

Refrigeration System Component Diagnosis And Repair

Ambient Temperature Switch

In non-automatic temperature control systems (ATC), the function of the ambient temperature switch is to inhibit compressor clutch operation in cold ambient temperatures. This sensor opens the electrical path to the compressor clutch when the temperature is below a specified range. This function mainly protects the compressor from poor or no lubrication, which could be the result of cold refrigerant oil.

Electronic Compressor Controls

Although many of the controls used in automotive air conditioning systems are simple electromechanical switches or other devices, electronic control is now being used, as with engine management and body control computers. Compressor clutch engagement can be determined by the computer when conditions like engine coolant temperature, ambient temperature, throttle position, engine load, etc. are optimum for proper system operation. Sensors report on these conditions to the electronic control module (ECM), and the ECM processes this information. If conditions are right, the ECM sends a command to engage the compressor clutch. Conversely, when a problem is detected where conditions are not optimum, the compressor is disengaged by the ECM. Some of the most common sensors that computers use to help them make clutch operation decisions are:

Engine Coolant and Ambient Temperature Sensors

These sensors are thermistors, which are resistors whose values change with temperature. Under cold or hot engine, or cold ambient temperature conditions,

compressor clutch engagement may not be desirable.

Wide Open Throttle Switch

Some vehicles with smaller engines are equipped with a Wide Open Throttle (WOT) switch. When the accelerator pedal is pressed all the way to the floor, this switch opens the electrical circuit to the compressor clutch to temporarily disable the compressor. This eliminates the load it places on the engine, as it is most often assumed that the pedal on the floor means it is more important to go fast at that moment than to remain cool inside the car. When the accelerator is released from the floor, the compressor clutch will re-enable the compressor.

Throttle Position Sensor

The throttle position sensor reports to the engine management computer on engine demand conditions. It works in a capacity like that of the wide open throttle switch.

Manifold Absolute Pressure (MAP) And Mass Airflow (MAF) Sensors

These are engine load sensors. The computer may decide to prevent clutch operation under conditions of high engine load.

Power Steering Pressure Switch

This switch is installed in the power steering system and reports on high pressure conditions. High pressure means that there is a load being placed on the engine by the power steering pump. The computer may decide to temporarily shut down the compressor to prevent engine stalling or low idle speed. It could also raise idle speed through control of an idle speed control device.

Drive Belts, Pulleys And Tensioners

Squealing noises from the engine compartment that increase in frequency as the engine rpm is raised, or when the A/C compressor is engaged, can usually be attributed to loose belt(s). In addition, pulley misalignment can cause the belt to enter the compressor pulley on an angle, also causing noise.

Check the compressor belt(s) for wear and proper adjustment as described under Preliminary Inspection in the A/C System Performance Testing section of this study guide. If replacement is necessary, loosen the belt tensioner or compressor pivot, move the tensioner or compressor to eliminate belt tension, and remove the belt. Never pry the belt from its pulley. It may be necessary to remove other accessory drive belts to gain access to the compressor belt.

Before removing a serpentine V-ribbed belt, make sure there is a belt routing diagram handy or draw one prior to belt removal, to prevent installation problems. Use a socket or wrench to tilt the automatic tensioner away from the belt, and then remove the belt from the pulleys.

After the belt is removed, spin the pulley to determine if it wobbles or has any noticeable bearing wear. Inspect the pulleys for chips, nicks, cracks, tool marks, bent sidewalls, severe corrosion or other damage. Check for hard objects such as small stones or sand that may become imbedded in the bottom of the pulley grooves.

When replacing belt(s), inspect the A/C compressor and its corresponding pulley(s) for improper alignment. Aligned pulleys reduce both pulley and belt wear, and vibration of engine components. If the belt pulleys are severely

32   A7 - Heating And Air Conditioning

Refrigeration System Component Diagnosis And Repair

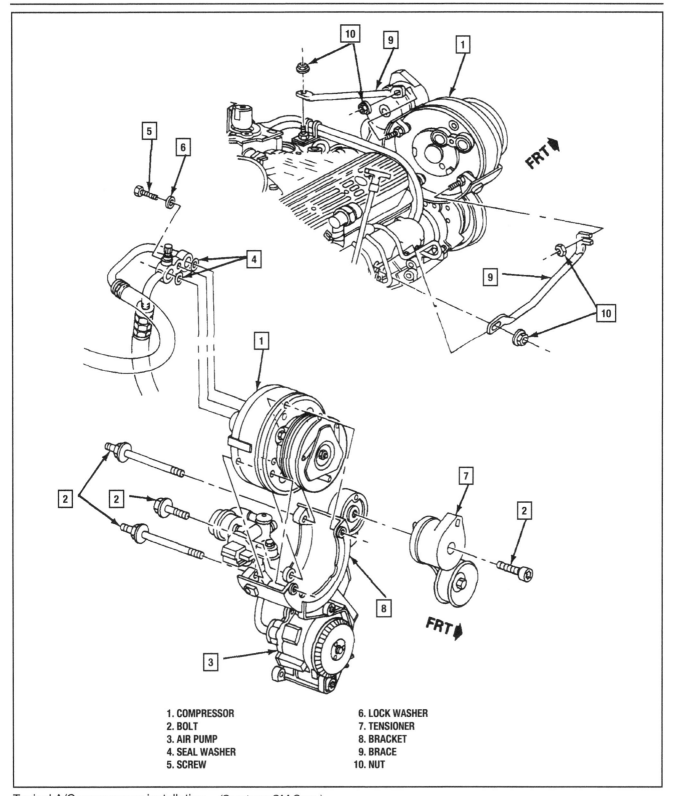

1. COMPRESSOR
2. BOLT
3. AIR PUMP
4. SEAL WASHER
5. SCREW
6. LOCK WASHER
7. TENSIONER
8. BRACKET
9. BRACE
10. NUT

Typical A/C compressor installation. *(Courtesy: GM Corp.)*

misaligned, look for improper positioning of the A/C compressor or its corresponding pulley, improper fit of the pulley or shaft, or incorrect components installed.

Install a new belt by correctly positioning it in its pulley grooves. Using the proper tools, move the compressor to tighten the belt, or in the case of automatically tensioned drives, move the tensioner to a position where the belt can be installed onto the pulleys. Always use manufacturer's tension recommendations.

Training for Certification 33

Refrigeration System Component Diagnosis And Repair

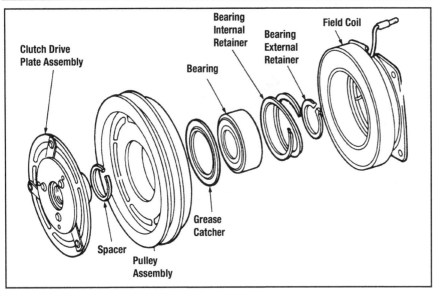

The stationary field coil creates a magnetic field when it receives an electrical signal. The field pulls the clutch drive plate into the pulley assembly so the engine-driven belt can rotate the input shaft of the A/C compressor.

Compressor Assembly

Knocking noises from the compressor usually indicate internal damage, especially on piston-type compressors. Although technically the compressor can be rebuilt, it is usually replaced. Always check the compressor mounting and brackets before condemning the compressor for noise. A loose mounting can cause knocking noises from the compressor area that may be mistaken for internal compressor noise. In addition, loose compressor mounting can cause misalignment of the pulleys.

To remove the compressor, first recover the refrigerant from the system using the proper equipment. Disconnect the electrical connectors from the compressor and remove the compressor drive belt. Disconnect the pressure hoses from the compressor and plug the hoses to prevent system contamination. Remove the compressor mounting bolts and lift the compressor from the engine compartment.

Drain the replacement compressor of any oil it contained during shipment. Follow the vehicle or compressor manufacturer's procedure for adding oil to the new or replacement unit. As discussed in the section on lubricants, correct oil levels is critical to system performance and component life.

Install the compressor in the engine compartment and secure the mounting bolts. Be sure to torque the mountings as outlined in the service information to avoid binding the compressor's internal mechanism. Remove the plugs from the refrigerant hoses and install them onto the compressor assembly, using new seals or O-rings. Rotate the compressor through by hand at least 20 complete revolutions to thoroughly lubricate the compressor before initial start-up.

Install the compressor drive belt and adjust if necessary. Reconnect the electrical connectors. Evacuate and recharge the A/C system and check for leaks. Finally, check system performance.

Compressor Clutch

An electromagnetic clutch provides the mechanical link between the pulley and the compressor input shaft whenever air conditioning is demanded. The compressor drive hub is usually found at the front of the pulley and is attached directly to the compressor driveshaft. A stationary electromagnetic coil is attached to the face of the compressor, behind the pulley.

When current flows through the coil windings, a magnetic field pulls the drive hub snug against the pulley. Now functioning as a unit, they drive the compressor as long as the coil is energized.

Compressor Clutch Inspection

Inspect the front of the compressor for oil, which could indicate a leaking front compressor seal. This would not only cause a refrigerant leak, but the oil could cause the compressor clutch to slip.

Connect manifold gauges and make sure there is adequate refrigerant in the system. Start the engine and turn on the A/C. If the compressor clutch does not engage, turn off the engine. Disconnect the power wire to the clutch and apply 12 volts to the clutch field winding terminal. If the clutch engages, then check the power supply to the clutch, including the system

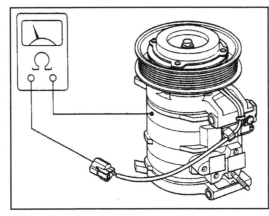

Measuring compressor clutch field coil resistance. *(Courtesy: Honda Motor Co., Ltd.)*

Refrigeration System Component Diagnosis And Repair

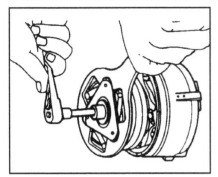

Hold the clutch hub with a suitable tool while the bolt or nut is removed.
(Courtesy: GM Corp.)

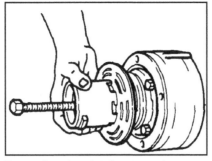

Removing the clutch rotor using a puller.
(Courtesy: GM Corp.)

protection devices and electronic compressor controls.

If the clutch does not engage, then check the clutch ground connection and coil resistance. If resistance is not within specification, then replace the coil or clutch assembly. If the compressor clutch engages noisily, suspect a defective compressor clutch plate, hub, or rotor.

Compressor Clutch Replacement

Although most compressor clutch and drive pulley components can be serviced in the engine compartment, it is advisable to recover the refrigerant and remove the compressor from the vehicle. After the compressor is removed, clamp it in a suitable holding device with the clutch facing upward. If the clutch plate and hub are fastened to the shaft using a retainer such as a C-clip, remove the clip using the appropriate removal tool. If the clutch plate and hub are fastened to the shaft using a bolt or nut, hold the clutch plate using an appropriate clutch hub holding tool and remove the bolt or nut.

After the retainer has been removed, attach a clutch plate and hub puller into the hub assembly. Turn the center screw of the puller into the puller body until the clutch plate and hub have been separated from the shaft. Remove the Woodruff key from the hub and place it aside for future use.

To remove the clutch rotor assembly, remove the rotor and bearing retaining ring and install the appropriate puller. Hold the puller in place and tighten the puller screw against the guide to remove the pulley rotor and bearing assembly.

After the rotor has been removed, inspect it to see if the bearing can be replaced. On some compressors, the bearing and rotor must be replaced as an assembly. However, if the bearing is replaceable, drive the bearing out of the rotor hub with a rotor bearing removal tool.

Next, remove the clutch coil by installing the appropriate puller on the front head of the compressor. Tighten the forcing screw against the puller pilot to remove the coil assembly.

When installing the coil, place the assembly on the front head of the compressor with the terminals in the proper position. Place a suitable installation tool over the opening of the clutch coil housing and align the installer with the compressor front head. Turn the installation tool forcing screw to force the clutch coil onto the front head until it is properly seated. Make sure the installation tool is properly aligned during installation.

Install the bearing into the clutch rotor (if applicable) by placing the rotor on a support. Align the bearing squarely with the hub bore, and using the installation tool, drive the bearing fully into the hub.

Now, install the compressor clutch rotor and bearing assembly on the front head. Position a rotor and bearing installation tool directly over the rotor and tighten the center screw to force the assembly onto the compressor front head. Make sure the installation tool is properly aligned during installation. Once the assembly is properly seated, install the retainer ring.

When installing the replacement clutch and hub, place the Woodruff

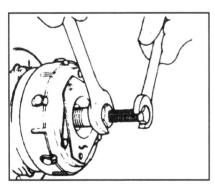

Removing the clutch plate and hub using a puller.
(Courtesy: GM Corp.)

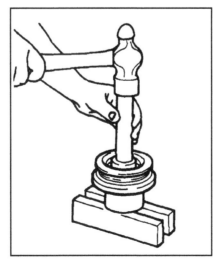

Removing the bearing from the clutch rotor.
(Courtesy: GM Corp.)

Refrigeration System Component Diagnosis And Repair

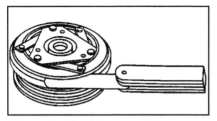

Measuring the clearance between the compressor clutch friction surfaces.
(Courtesy: GM Corp.)

key into the hub groove. Make sure that the frictional surfaces of the clutch plate and clutch rotor are free of dirt, oil and debris before installation. Align the shaft keyway with the Woodruff key and place the clutch plate and hub assembly onto the compressor shaft.

CAUTION: Do not drive or pound on the clutch hub or shaft. Internal damage to the compressor can result.

Using a clutch plate and hub installation tool, press the hub onto the shaft. Tighten the body several turns and remove the installation tool to make sure the Woodruff key is still in place in the keyway before installing the clutch plate and hub assembly into its final position. After the clutch plate and hub have been seated, compare the air gap between the frictional surfaces with manufacturer's specifications.

If the air gap is sufficient, remove the installation tool, and double-check for proper Woodruff key positioning. If the retainer is a C-clip, install the clip. If the retainer is a bolt or a nut, hold the clutch and hub with the appropriate tool, and install the bolt or nut. Torque to manufacturer's specifications.

If the compressor clutch components have been replaced with the compressor off the vehicle, reinstall the compressor and connect the pressure lines and electrical connectors. Evacuate and recharge the A/C system using the proper equipment, and check for leaks. Finally, check system performance.

Servicing Hybrid Electric Compressors

Most hybrid vehicles make use of air conditioning compressors that are either fully electric or partially electric. The reason for this is to allow the compressor to function when the ICE (Internal Combustion Engine) is in "Idle Stop" mode and not running. The electrical portion of these compressors uses high voltage (HV), just like other hybrid components, and the safety precautions needed to work on any HV system should be followed when removing or replacing one of these compressors. To verify that the hybrid you're working on uses an HV compressor, check the specifications pages in the service information system of your choice and look carefully for the blue or orange wire harness connecting to the compressor assembly.

Diagnosing compressor issues on electric compressors is not all that different from diagnosing belt-driven units. The job of the compressor is the same – to compress the refrigerant charge. Servicing these systems, though, does have its unique precautions you must follow to avoid damage to the compressor or the need to replace expensive system components.

HV air condition systems have a unique warning label under the hood that can help you identify these systems.

Be sure to follow the OEM procedures for disabling the HV system before you attempt to disconnect any HV wiring from the compressor. This involves the use of specialized equipment, like protective gloves and digital voltmeters capable of handling the requirements of an HV system. If you are not hybrid trained, be sure to get at least basic training before you attempt to service any HV component. After you've properly isolated the HV battery from the vehicle, most manufacturers recommend waiting for a period of time to allow the HV capacitors to bleed off before you disconnect any wiring from an HV component. A voltmeter rated for HV use should be used to verify that the voltage at the connector has reached a safe level before proceeding. Again, follow the published OEM service procedure to insure your safety.

Routine compressor and system services are very similar to the non-hybrid systems. Follow the same steps you would in any other to properly recover and recharge a hybrid system, or to balance the oil charge when replacing a component in a hybrid system.

There is one notable exception to these normal procedures. That is the use of a POE (Polyolester) oil instead of the PAG oil used in non-electric designs. PAG oil is conductive, and the addition of even a minute amount can contaminate the entire system in a hybrid HV A/C system. The small amount of PAG oil is typically introduced by using a service machine on both system designs, where the minute traces of oil recovered from a previous job are pumped back into the hybrid system during its recharge. The result is a HV insulation failure and a DTC (Diagnostic Trouble Code), often accompanied by a vehicle "no start" complaint that

Refrigeration System Component Diagnosis And Repair

To disconnect spring lock fittings, a special tool is required.
(Courtesy: Ford Motor Co.)

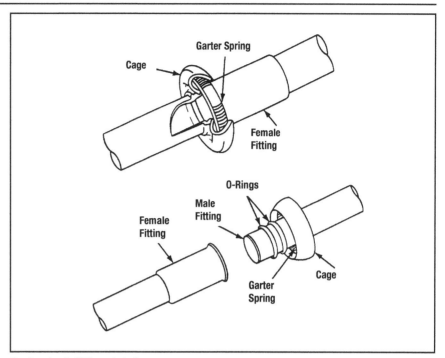

Spring lock fitting details.

will not be solved until every component in the system (if the a/c has been run for even a short time after the PAG oil is introduced) has been replaced. And no, a system flush will NOT correct the problem.

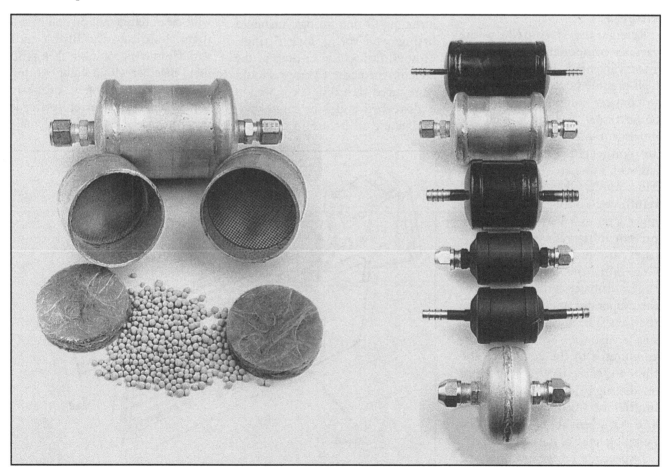

In-line filters come in many different designs. Many manufacturers recommend that filters be installed after a compressor failure to protect the new compressor from metal particles that may remain in the system.

Training for Certification

Refrigeration System Component Diagnosis And Repair

WARNING: *Even a few drops of PAG oil introduced into a hybrid electric system can be enough to contaminate the entire system and cause HV insulation faults.*

To avoid these issues, use only the correct oil specified by the OEM. In addition, use a dedicated service machine or one that is hybrid certified and has a published procedure for clearing the lines of any oil remaining between vehicles. In addition, these machines are often set up so that the oil charge function many offer is disabled.

EVAPORATOR, CONDENSER AND RELATED COMPONENTS

A/C Hoses, Lines And Fittings

Refrigerant is routed to the various components in the A/C system by rigid lines and flexible high-pressure hoses. Hoses are used to connect components with the compressor, to allow for engine movement. Most other components are connected with rigid lines, although hoses are sometimes used. Most modern hoses are made of reinforced rubber with a nylon inner layer as a barrier material to prevent refrigerant leakage. Most lines are made of aluminum. Generally, the line or hose of largest diameter is the one between the evaporator and compressor on the low side of the system. The smaller diameter lines connect the compressor to the condenser and the condenser to the evaporator on the high side. Often there is a muffler between the compressor and condenser to quiet the pumping noise of the compressor.

Inspect the refrigerant lines and hoses for leaks, kinks, dents and any other damage. Damaged lines and hoses are usually replaced, but in some cases they can be repaired. The fittings and crimping tool equipment used by some shops to custom make hoses can also be used to repair an existing hose. Rigid lines can be repaired by cutting out the damaged section of tubing. A new section is then installed and connected to the existing line using special collars that are crimped on.

When installing a new hose or line, make sure it is routed properly and that all guides and retainers are in place, if equipped. Do not replace a line or hose with one that is longer or shorter than the original, as damage from vibration or interference with other components may result.

Hoses and lines are connected to components and one another using several types of fittings, including O-ring fittings, manifold fittings and spring lock fittings. Most all fittings use O-rings at the attachment ends. O-rings should be replaced each time a connection is disturbed and lubricated with refrigerant oil before installation. Replacement O-rings must also be selected with refrigerant compatibility in mind.

Spring Lock Fittings

Spring lock fittings require a special tool to disconnect them. To disconnect a spring lock fitting, first properly recover the refrigerant from the system, then fit the tool over the fitting. Push the tool into the cage opening to release the female fitting from the garter spring, then pull the male and female fittings apart. Remove the tool from the fitting.

Remove and discard the O-rings, being careful not to scratch the tubing. Inspect the garter spring and remove it if broken or damaged. Clean the ends of the fittings.

Install a new garter spring, if removed. Lubricate new O-rings with clean refrigerant oil and install them. Lubricate the fitting ends with clean refrigerant oil, then push them together with a slight twisting motion. The fitting is properly connected if the garter spring is over the flared end of the female

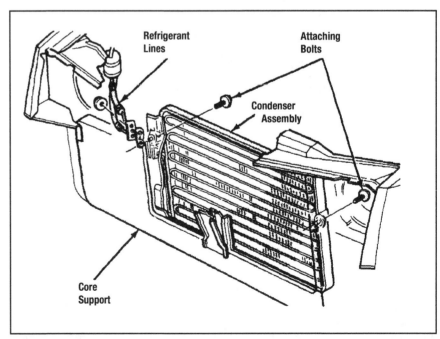

Typical condenser mounting. *(Courtesy: DaimlerChrysler Corp.)*

fitting. Evacuate and recharge the system, then check for leaks.

Service Port Fittings

As described earlier, service valve fittings are unique to the type of refrigerant originally fitted to the system. The high and low-side fittings are different to prevent connecting service hoses to the wrong fittings. The reason for the different fitting designs is to prevent cross contamination of systems, refrigerant supplies, and service equipment. The fittings are covered with caps also containing O-rings. Always re-install the caps after service, and replace any damaged O-rings in the caps.

A worn Schrader valve core in a service port fitting is often the cause of a refrigerant leak. After recovering the refrigerant, the valve core can be removed using a valve core removal tool. Lubricate the new core with refrigerant oil and install it finger tight. Evacuate and recharge the system, then check for leaks

Filters

Although not usually installed as original equipment, many vehicle manufacturers recommend installation of in-line filters in a system that has suffered a compressor failure. The main reason is for protection of the new compressor from metal chips or other debris that could be in the system from the original compressor failure. The other reason is that the debris could also clog orifice tube or expansion valve filters, or wedge in an expansion valve and keep it from operating properly. There are filters that fit into both the high and low sides of the system.

Condenser

The condenser is a heat exchanger much like a radiator. In fact, it is usually located just

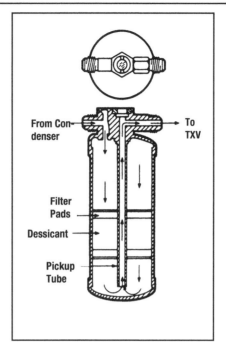

The receiver/drier is usually located on the output line of the condenser. The refrigerant enters the unit, flows through a desiccant, which helps keep moisture out of circulation, and then is routed to the expansion valve. The receiver/ drier should be replaced if the system is left open or if major service is being performed, especially if the compressor is being replaced.

in front of the radiator on most vehicles. Air flow across the condenser is provided by an engine driven or electric motor operated fan, and at higher road speeds, by ram air.

The hot, vaporized refrigerant is pumped from the compressor into the condenser. As the refrigerant winds its way through the condenser coils, it loses much of its heat to the surrounding air through its tubes and fins. As it cools, the high pressure vapor condenses into a warm, high pressure liquid.

There are three basic types of condensers: tube and fin, serpentine, and parallel flow. The tube and fin style has pipes that pass through fins, with U-shaped fittings on the ends of the pipes connecting one to the next. The serpentine condenser has a flat, continuous piece of tubing that snakes through the fins. This type is more efficient than the tube and fin design, and it's more compact. The parallel flow condenser is most similar to a radiator in its construction and is the most efficient of the designs in terms of heat transfer.

Condenser replacement is required if the unit leaks or if it is damaged or clogged. Suspect a defective condenser if high-side pressures are excessive or if there has been a compressor failure and debris is suspected to be clogging the condenser. A restriction in the condenser is indicated by frost forming near the condenser outlet. Frost can also form on the condenser itself at the point of restriction in the condenser.

To replace a condenser, first recover the refrigerant from the system. Disconnect the negative battery cable and remove any components necessary to gain access to the condenser. Disconnect the refrigerant lines from the condenser and cap the lines to prevent system contamination. Remove the fasteners that secure the condenser and remove the condenser from the vehicle.

Measure the amount of oil found in the condenser that was removed, and then add the same amount of fresh refrigerant oil into the replacement condenser. If oil has leaked out of the system, use the manufacturer's recommended amount. Position the condenser in the vehicle and install the mounting fasteners. Tighten all fasteners to specifications. Using new, lubricated O-rings, connect the refrigerant lines. Install any components that were removed for condenser access. Reconnect the negative

Refrigeration System Component Diagnosis And Repair

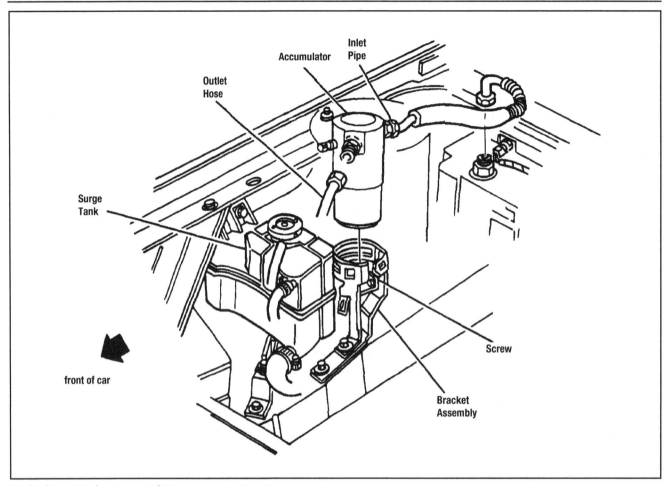

Typical accumulator mounting. *(Courtesy: GM Corp.)*

battery cable. Next, evacuate and recharge the A/C system and check for leaks. Finally, check system performance.

Receiver/Drier

As its name implies, the receiver/drier stores and dries the refrigerant. More accurately, a desiccant inside of it absorbs moisture from refrigerant. Receiver/driers are only used on systems that use expansion valves. They are located between the condenser and evaporator in the high pressure side of the system, ahead of the expansion valve.

Inside the receiver/drier housing is a filter, a bag of desiccant (drying agent) and a pickup tube. If the air conditioning system has a sight glass, it is often located on the top of the receiver/drier.

In its 'receiver' function, the unit stores liquid refrigerant until the evaporator needs it. How long and how much refrigerant is stored depends on cooling demand. On hot, humid days, demand is high and refrigerant isn't stored long.

In its 'drier' function, the receiver/drier protects the rest of the system from the damaging effects of moisture. Water in the system can combine with refrigerant and lubricant, form corrosive substances, and even change the chemical composition of refrigerant and lubricant. The desiccant, which usually looks like very large granules of salt, is contained within a porous bag. This bag sometimes breaks, which allows the desiccant to leave the receiver/drier and flow throughout

the system. This obviously renders it ineffective as a moisture absorbent.

The desiccant can only absorb and hold so much moisture. If too much water gets in the system, the desiccant must be replaced. In most cases, you have to replace the whole receiver/drier unit to achieve this. Desiccants are not universal. Different types must often be used with different refrigerants and lubricating oils.

The receiver/drier should be replaced if it leaks, if it is clogged, if the system has been left open for a period of time or if major system service has been performed, such as compressor replacement. Suspect a defective receiver/drier if desiccant is found in other parts of the system, if there is moisture or

Refrigeration System Component Diagnosis And Repair

debris in the system, or if there is a significant temperature difference in the liquid line before and after the receiver/drier or there is frost on the receiver/drier, which would indicate a restriction.

To replace a receiver/drier, first recover the refrigerant from the system. Disconnect the negative battery cable and disconnect any electrical connectors from the receiver/drier. Remove any components necessary to gain access to the unit. Disconnect the refrigerant lines from the receiver/drier and cap the lines to prevent system contamination. Remove the fasteners that secure the receiver/drier and remove it from the vehicle. If equipped, remove any switches or sensors that are mounted on the receiver/drier.

If necessary, install any switches or sensors that were removed onto the replacement receiver/drier. Measure the amount of oil found in the receiver/drier that was removed, and then add the same amount of fresh refrigerant oil into the replacement receiver/drier. If oil has leaked out of the system, use the manufacturer's recommended amount. Position the receiver/drier in the vehicle and install the mounting fasteners. Tighten all fasteners to specifications. Using new, lubricated O-rings, connect the refrigerant lines. Install any components that were removed for receiver/drier access. Reconnect the electrical connectors to the receiver/drier, if necessary, and reconnect the negative battery cable. Next, evacuate and recharge the A/C system and check for leaks. Finally, check system performance.

Accumulator

On a system with an orifice tube rather than an expansion valve, the receiver/drier is substituted for by a component called an accumulator. The accumulator is usually located near the outlet of the evaporator. Refrigerant flowing out of the evaporator enters the accumulator to be stored, especially if it all has not vaporized in the evaporator. Because a liquid cannot be compressed, the accumulator ensures that only vaporized refrigerant reaches the compressor. The accumulator also contains a desiccant to keep the system free of moisture. Accumulators are similar in appearance to receiver/driers but usually bigger. Also, they never contain a sight glass. Their function is similar to that of receiver/driers in most every way, but they are located in the low pressure side of the system.

The accumulator should be replaced if it is leaking, if the system has been left open for a period of time, or whenever any other major A/C system components are replaced. The accumulator cannot be serviced and can only be replaced as a unit.

To replace an accumulator, first recover the refrigerant from the system. Disconnect the negative battery cable and disconnect any electrical connectors from the accumulator. Disconnect the refrigerant lines from the accumulator and cap the lines to prevent system contamination. Remove the fasteners that secure the accumulator and remove it from the vehicle. If equipped, remove any switches or sensors that are mounted on the accumulator.

If necessary, install any switches or sensors that were removed onto the replacement accumulator. Measure the amount of oil found in the accumulator that was removed, and then add the same amount of fresh refrigerant oil into the replacement accumulator. If oil has leaked out of the system, use the manufacturer's recommended amount. Position the accumulator in the vehicle and install the mounting fasteners. Tighten all fasteners to specifications. Using new, lubricated O-rings, connect the refrigerant lines. Reconnect the electrical connectors to the accumulator, if necessary, and reconnect the negative battery cable. Next, evacuate and recharge

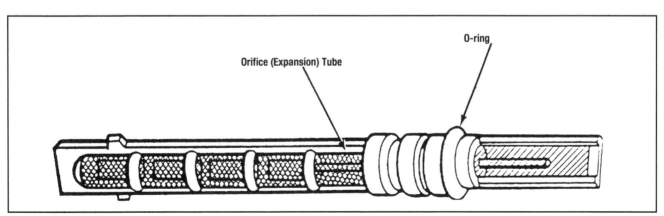

This is a typical orifice tube assembly. The actual tube is contained within a plastic housing made up mostly of a filter screen.

Refrigeration System Component Diagnosis And Repair

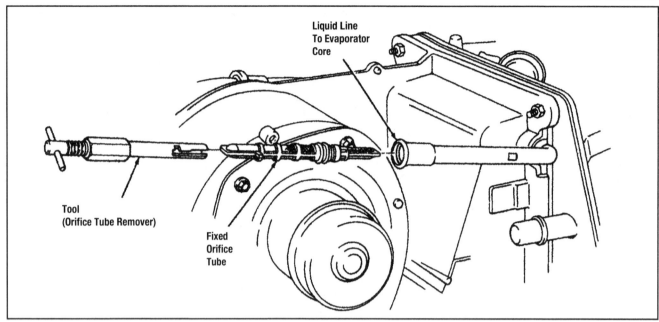

Fixed orifice tube removal. *(Courtesy: Ford Motor Co.)*

the A/C system and check for leaks. Finally, check system performance.

Orifice Tube

Refrigerant entering the evaporator must be metered, or sprayed in as a low pressure liquid at a controlled rate. If too much refrigerant enters the evaporator at too fast a rate, it can cause evaporator icing. If too little refrigerant enters the evaporator at too slow a rate, it can cause poor cooling performance. Also, the refrigerant's pressure must be kept low enough so that it will vaporize (boil) around the temperature of the vehicle's interior. The orifice tube acts as a restriction in the system, which creates the pressure drop. On its outlet side, pressure is lower than its inlet side. The orifice tube is usually located at the evaporator inlet.

As the low pressure liquid refrigerant exits the orifice tube, it sprays into the evaporator. As the refrigerant's pressure drops, so does its temperature. The refrigerant is now colder than the air inside the vehicle so it readily boils, or vaporizes. It absorbs heat from the passenger compartment, which it carries away as it is drawn out to the compressor. However, the orifice tube has a fixed inside diameter and cannot change in response to evaporator temperature. When the cooling load is low, an orifice tube flows too much refrigerant and floods the evaporator with liquid refrigerant. Because of this, an orifice tube system always has an accumulator to catch and store the liquid refrigerant.

Air conditioning systems with orifice tubes usually cycle the compressor on and off to control refrigerant flow. When the temperature/pressure in the evaporator drops, the compressor is stopped until the temperature/pressure rises to a certain level, when compressor operation

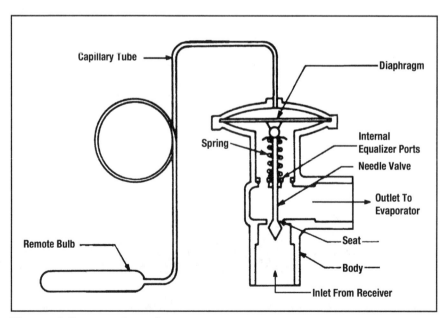

Thermostatic expansion valve.

Refrigeration System Component Diagnosis And Repair

resumes. Because evaporator pressure and temperature are closely linked, the cut-out and cut-in signals can be provided by a temperature sensing thermistor located near the evaporator or a pressure switch mounted on the accumulator or low pressure hose.

Most orifice tubes look very similar to each other externally. Internally, the difference is the actual diameter of the opening inside the tube that the refrigerant passes through. This tube, often made of brass, has a very small inside diameter. (It could be as small as 0.050-in.). The external 'housing' of an orifice tube is usually plastic with a filter screen to trap debris so it doesn't plug the tiny inside diameter of the tube. There is also usually an O-ring seal on the external housing. This wedges the orifice tube in tightly against the inside walls of the portion of the A/C system plumbing it is contained in, which prevents refrigerant bypass.

The most common reason for replacing an orifice tube is if it is plugged. If there is a complaint that the A/C is not cold enough or not cold at all, and if the low-side pressure is very low and there is frost on the line between the orifice tube and the evaporator, suspect a plugged orifice tube.

NOTE: On some vehicles the orifice tube cannot be removed from the line. If orifice tube replacement is required, a new line must be installed or a kit that provides a new line segment including the orifice tube can be installed.

A special tool is usually required to remove an orifice tube. To replace an orifice tube, first recover the refrigerant from the system. Disconnect the negative battery cable. Disconnect the liquid line from the evaporator inlet line and plug the liquid line to prevent contamination.

Pour a small amount of clean refrigerant oil into the evaporator inlet line to lubricate the line and orifice O-rings during removal. Engage the tangs on the orifice tube with the special tool. Hold the tool stationary and run the sleeve on the tool down against the evaporator inlet line until the orifice tube is pulled from the line. Do not twist or rotate the orifice tube in the line as it can break. Special tools are available to extract broken orifice tubes.

Lubricate the O-rings on the replacement orifice tube with clean refrigerant oil, then install it into the evaporator inlet line until it is seated. Using a new O-ring, connect the liquid line to the evaporator inlet line. Connect the negative battery cable. Evacuate and recharge the A/C system and check for leaks, then check system performance.

Expansion Valve

Many A/C systems use a Thermostatic Expansion Valve (TXV) to restrict the amount of refrigerant entering the evaporator. Systems with expansion valves operate differently from those with orifice tubes. Instead of cycling the clutch on and off to control refrigerant flow, the expansion valve opens and closes as necessary to maintain proper evaporator pressure and temperature.

The TXV reduces the high pressure liquid refrigerant to low pressure liquid, which it meters to the evaporator at a controlled rate. There is a metered orifice at the expansion valve's outlet, but there is also a 'plunger' that opens and closes to control the amount of refrigerant that goes through the orifice to the evaporator.

The amount of TXV opening is determined by a signal it receives from the outlet side of the evaporator. A capillary tube bulb mounted to the outlet pipe of the evaporator is insulated against ambient heat. If outlet temperature is too high, the capillary bulb signals the TXV to allow more refrigerant to flow; if temperature is too low, the bulb signals the TXV to restrict the flow.

Although all expansion valves operate on a similar principle, they are not all identical. Usually they are spring loaded devices with a diaphragm that is linked to the plunger. Some diaphragms are internally equalized while others are connected to the low pressure side of the A/C system via an equalizer tube. Some expansion valves have a screen on the inlet side.

Expansion valves need devices to report to them what the conditions are at the evaporator. This is the job of the capillary tube. This tube is filled with gas that expands and contracts to move the diaphragm against its internal or external equalizing pressure. On the end of the capillary tube there is usually a sensing bulb that is in contact with the evaporator or the evaporator's outlet pipe. It is insulated by a special tape to prevent ambient air temperature from affecting its operation. Regular electrician's tape cannot be substituted for this special insulated tape.

As the temperature at the evaporator outlet increases, the pressure in the capillary tube increases. This pressure acts on the diaphragm, which in turn opens the expansion valve and allows more refrigerant to enter the evaporator. Conversely, when the evaporator temperature decreases, pressure in the capillary tube decreases. Less pressure acts on the diaphragm, which in turn allows the expansion valve to close, and less refrigerant enters the evaporator. This dithering constantly controls the amount of

Training for Certification

43

Refrigeration System Component Diagnosis And Repair

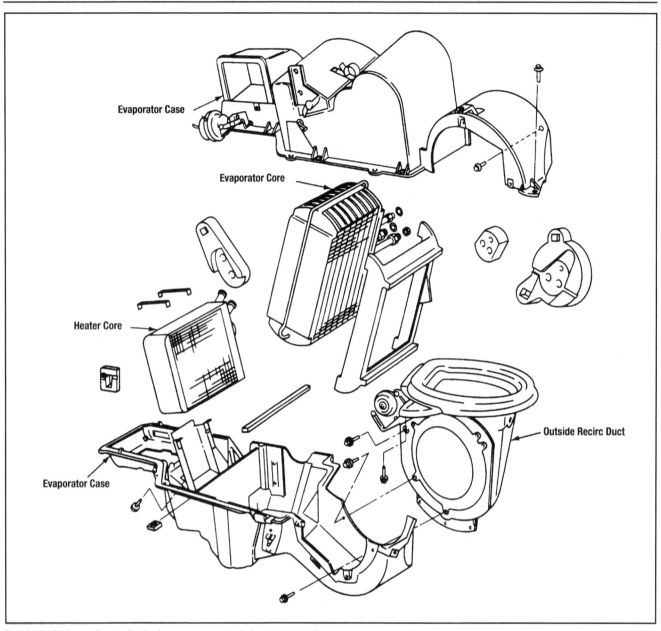

Exploded view of a typical plenum case and duct assembly.

refrigerant entering the evaporator, thereby controlling evaporator pressure and temperature.

On evaporators with large pressure drops between the inlet and outlet, an equalizing tube may be used between the evaporator outlet and the TXV. In essence, this equalizer eliminates the effect of the large pressure drop on TXV operation. These equalizers can be internal or external.

Expansion valves are usually non serviceable. If one malfunctions, you must replace it. However, some are equipped with filter screens, and if this is the case, it should be cleaned whenever the system is opened for service of other components.

A TXV should be replaced if it becomes clogged or stuck in position due to debris, contamination or corrosion, or if the capillary tube is damaged. If the TXV is stuck closed, restricting the refrigerant flow, the air flow inside the vehicle will not be cold, the low and high-side pressures will be low and there may be frost on the valve. If the TXV is stuck open, flooding the evaporator with excess refrigerant, the air flow inside the vehicle will not be cold and the system low-side pressure will be high.

To replace a TXV, first recover the refrigerant from the system. Disconnect the negative battery cable. Remove the insulation covering the capillary tube and bulb and remove the capillary tube

44　　A7 - Heating And Air Conditioning

Refrigeration System Component Diagnosis And Repair

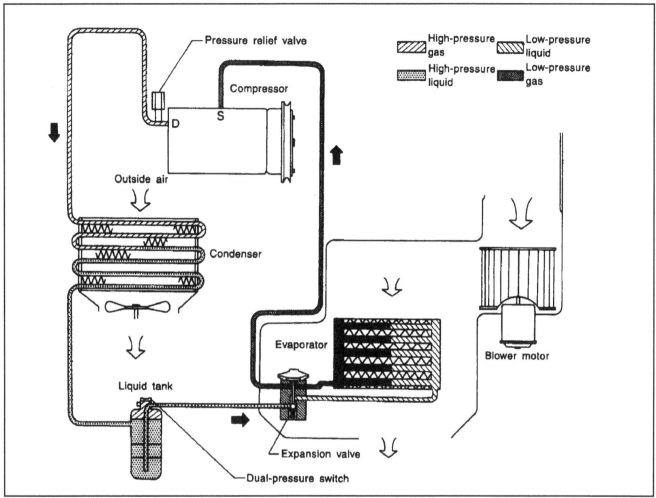

On this system, the high-pressure relief valve is located in the line just past the compressor discharge port.

from its mounting. Disconnect the refrigerant lines from the TXV and cap the lines to prevent contamination. Remove the TXV from the vehicle.

Install the replacement TXV and connect the refrigerant lines using new O-rings lubricated with clean refrigerant oil. Properly position the capillary tube and bulb along with the insulation. Connect the negative battery cable. Evacuate and recharge the A/C system and check for leaks, then check system performance.

Evaporator

The evaporator is a heat exchanger not much different in appearance or design from a heater core, but with one main operational difference. Cool air passing over a heater core picks up heat from it and becomes warmer. Heat from the air passing over an evaporator is absorbed by it and the air becomes colder. The evaporator is aptly named because it reflects the fact that inside of it the refrigerant turns from a liquid to a gas (boils). Liquids boil sooner under low pressure than high pressure and refrigerant inside the evaporator has a pressure of about 30 psi.

Evaporator temperature should hover at 32° - 40°F (0° - 4°C). At temperatures above this range, it does a poor job of cooling the inside of the vehicle. At lower temperatures, ice will form from condensation on the evaporator's fins, blocking air flow and rendering it ineffective as a heat exchanger. The key is to keep the evaporator temperature within the narrow 32° - 40°F (0° - 4°C) range.

The evaporator is housed in a case, often the same one housing the heater core and blower. This case is usually called the plenum. The plenum also contains air routing and/or temperature blend doors, and is essentially a ductwork system. At the bottom of the evaporator case is a drain hole with a hose that directs the condensed water outside the vehicle. Make sure the drain is kept clear or stagnant water can collect and allow bacteria to grow, causing odors. A clogged drain can also cause the case to fill up with water and leak into the passenger compartment.

Training for Certification

Refrigeration System Component Diagnosis And Repair

Replace the evaporator if it is leaking, clogged or corroded from moisture. Depending on the vehicle, it may be possible to remove the evaporator from the plenum with the plenum installed in the vehicle, or the entire plenum may have to be removed to access the evaporator. Begin by recovering the refrigerant from the system. Disconnect the negative battery cable. Disconnect the refrigerant lines from the evaporator and plug the lines to prevent contamination.

NOTE: Evaporators used in HFO1234yf systems must meet more stringent construction standards than those used in R134a systems. It is imperative that you DO NOT attempt to repair these evaporators, nor replace one with one taken from a salvaged vehicle.

If the plenum is being removed and it also houses the heater core, drain the cooling system and disconnect the heater hoses. Label and disconnect the necessary electrical connectors and vacuum hoses. Remove all other components necessary for evaporator or plenum removal, then remove the evaporator or plenum. If the plenum was removed, disassemble it as necessary to remove the evaporator.

Measure the amount of oil found in the evaporator that was removed, and then add the same amount of fresh refrigerant oil into the replacement evaporator. If oil has leaked out of the system, use the manufacturer's recommended amount. If necessary, install the evaporator into the plenum. Install the evaporator or plenum into the vehicle. Install all components that were removed for access and connect the necessary electrical connectors and vacuum hoses.

If the heater core was removed with the plenum, connect the heater hoses and add coolant to the proper level. Connect the refrigerant lines using new O-rings lubricated with clean refrigerant oil. Connect the negative battery cable. Evacuate and recharge the A/C system and check for leaks. Check system performance.

Other Evaporator Pressure/Temperature Controls

Before the advent of orifice tubes and cycling compressors, some older vehicles used evaporator pressure controls like the Suction Throttling Valve (SVT) and the Pilot Operated Absolute (POA) valve. These devices maintain pressure in the evaporator by regulating the flow of refrigerant out of the evaporator, thereby controlling evaporator temperature. They are located in the suction line between the evaporator and compressor and are used in systems where the compressor operates continuously when the A/C is on.

The valve should be replaced if it sticks due to debris, contamination or corrosion. Symptoms of a valve that is stuck closed include high low-side pressure, poor cooling and high evaporator pressure combined with low suction pressure. A valve that is stuck open is indicated by low evaporator pressure or a frozen evaporator.

To replace a valve, first recover the refrigerant from the system. Disconnect the negative battery cable. Disconnect the refrigerant lines from the valve and cap the lines to prevent contamination. Remove the valve from the vehicle.

Install the replacement valve and connect the refrigerant lines using new O-rings lubricated with clean refrigerant oil. Connect the negative battery cable. Evacuate and recharge the A/C system and check for leaks, then check system performance.

High Pressure Relief Device

A high pressure relief valve is used to release pressure in the system before excessive high pressure can damage system components. When a predetermined pressure is reached, the valve opens, allowing refrigerant to escape until the pressure drops below the discharge point, when the valve closes. The high pressure relief valve is located in the high side of the system.

Notes

Heating And Engine Cooling Systems Diagnosis And Repair

HEATING AND ENGINE COOLING SYSTEM OPERATION

The function of the cooling system is to cause a rapid and even warm up of the engine and to keep it operating within a narrow temperature range. This keeps the engine at the temperature for the most efficient and safe operation. A cooling system is probably more accurately described as an engine temperature control system.

All engine cooling systems contain four major components, the water pump, thermostat, radiator, and heater core (these last two items are devices known as heat exchangers). As a convenient starting point, lets think of the water pump as the heart of the cooling system. In a conventional cooling system, the water pump moves the coolant through the engine block's water jackets, to the cylinder head(s), possibly through a passage in the intake manifold, and then to the thermostat. As the coolant flows through the engine, it absorbs the heat that is generated in the engine's cylinders by the combustion process.

The thermostat, which is simply a valve that opens and closes depending on temperature, will open to allow coolant past it when the temperature of the coolant reaches a certain point. Cooling systems require a thermostat to control temperature and to assure quick warm up. If left to full flow, the cooling system would over-cool the engine. When cold, the thermostat restricts coolant flow from the engine to the radiator. A bypass system is used to permit coolant circulation through the engine to provide an even engine warm up. As the engine warms, the thermostat opens to permit coolant flow from the engine to the radiator. Most thermostats are designed to start opening around 190°F (88°C), and to be fully open around 210°F (99°C).

From the thermostat, the coolant flows through the upper hose to the radiator, and then through the internal tubes of the radiator, which have external fins attached to them. The heat from the coolant moves from the tubes to the fins, which provide a large surface area for heat dissipation to the cooler outside air. The cooled coolant then exits the radiator and returns to the water pump and engine to repeat the cycle.

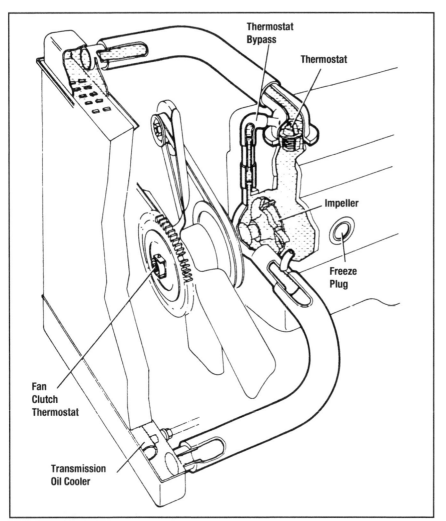

The cooling system will over-cool the engine if coolant flows unimpeded. When the engine is cold, the thermostat restricts coolant flow from the engine to the radiator, so that the engine can quickly come to normal operating temperature.

Heating And Engine Cooling Systems Diagnosis And Repair

The interior heater works in the same manner. Hot coolant is pumped through the heater core by the water pump, and heat from the coolant moves from the heater core to the passenger compartment as the blower fan forces air through the heater core.

TEMPERATURE CONTROL DIAGNOSIS

The engine cooling system must be in good working order to ensure proper heating system operation. It is also critical to engine emissions control, and problems in the cooling system can result in a powertrain-related DTC. If coolant flow is restricted, it may not route through the heater core. If this is the case, outlet air temperature may be lower than anticipated, and interior heating will be insufficient.

If there is a complaint of not enough heat, first check to see if the cooling system needs servicing. Check for coolant leakage, both from the heater core and the engine compartment, and hose problems such as collapsing and blockage. Telltale signs of heater core leakage are if the floor of the passenger compartment is damp, or the windows are fogged. Fog that smears when wiped is a sign of coolant on the glass. You may also detect the odor of antifreeze in the passenger compartment.

Make sure the coolant level is OK and the thermostat is opening and closing properly. This allows the engine to heat the coolant to the proper temperature. Remember, a thermostat that is stuck open will cause lower-than-normal engine temperatures, causing the coolant to enter the heater core colder than it should be.

Start the engine and allow it to reach normal operating temperature. Check the temperature of the heater hoses going to, and from, the heater core. If the heater is working correctly, the return hose leading to the engine water pump will be nearly as hot as the feed hose. If the return hose is cooler, the heater core is generally either plugged or air-locked. An air pocket in the heater can usually be burped by loosening the outlet hose until coolant runs out while the engine is running.

If equipped, check the heater control valve for proper operation. Make sure the cable (if equipped) is connected and adjusted properly, and that it is not kinked or misrouted. If equipped with a vacuum-controlled valve, check the hose for vacuum and make sure the valve works when vacuum is applied. This valve is the critical temperature control component that allows the maximum amount of hot coolant to flow through the heater core.

Make sure that all heater ductwork is intact and routed to the proper flanges. Operate the blower through its entire speed range, leaving it on high. Operate the heater controls, making sure that when a particular mode

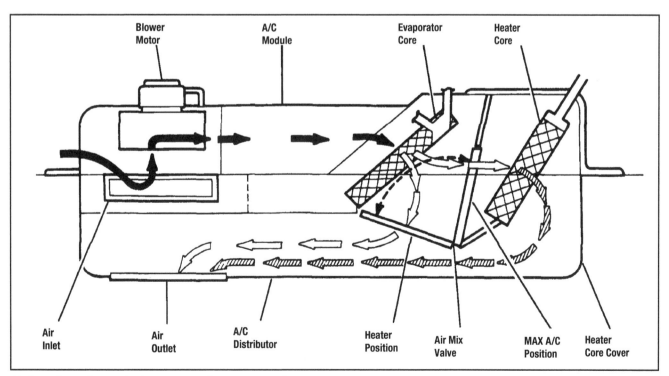

Air flow through a typical evaporator/heater core plenum.
(Courtesy: GM Corp.)

Heating And Engine Cooling Systems Diagnosis And Repair

is selected (such as defrost, floor vents, etc.) the outlet air is routed to that particular function. If not, check for proper operation of the air doors in the heater plenum. If the air doors are cable operated, make sure the cables are connected and adjusted properly, and that they are not kinked or misrouted. If the doors are vacuum or electronically operated, make sure there is vacuum or current to the actuator, and that the actuator functions properly. Note that if a door is shared by two functions (such as floor heat and defrost) it may bind halfway, routing heat in two different directions. This will give the impression that the heater is not performing properly.

COOLING SYSTEM INSPECTION

Begin cooling system inspection by checking the coolant appearance, level and freeze protection. The coolant should appear clean and translucent; a cloudy or muddy appearance is evidence of contamination. Check the coolant level in the expansion or overflow tank. The coolant should be at the level indicated for the temperature of the coolant.

Check coolant concentration using approved test strips or a refractometer. A refractometer takes a small fluid sample and measures the amount of light refracted, relating that to the specific gravity of the coolant mixture. The specific gravity of coolant changes according to the antifreeze concentration; the specific gravity increases as the concentration of the antifreeze increases.

It is best to obtain a coolant sample directly from the radiator, as the overflow tank may have recently been topped off with water or pure antifreeze. Always use caution when removing the radiator cap from a pressurized system; only remove the cap when the system is cold. Draw the coolant into the hydrometer and read the specific gravity on the float. The protection level should be at least –34ºF (–37ºC), which represents a 50/50 mixture of antifreeze and water.

Visually inspect the cooling system for problems. Check for signs of coolant leaks at all hose connections, core plugs (freeze plugs), head gasket(s), thermostat housing, water pump and radiator. Inspect all hoses for cracks, ballooning or brittleness and replace if necessary. If the hoses feel soft or mushy when they are squeezed, replace them.

Check the radiator cap rating to make sure it is the right one for the vehicle. Check the cap's relief valve spring action, and inspect the seal for brittleness. Check the filler neck on the radiator or surge tank mating surface.

Check the water pump drive belt for wear, glazing and belt tension. A slipping belt will not turn the pump impeller at the proper speed to circulate coolant. If the engine is equipped with a mechanical fan, a slipping belt will cause the fan to turn too slowly, not draw enough air through the radiator, and possibly cause the engine to overheat. Replace or adjust the belt as necessary.

Inspect the fan for missing, cracked or bent blades. If equipped with a fan clutch, check the back of the clutch for an oily film, which would indicate that fluid is leaking and replacement is necessary. Turn the fan and clutch assembly by hand; there should be some viscous drag, but it should turn smoothly during a full rotation. Gently rock the fan fore and aft; there should be no or very little movement. Replace the fan clutch if it does not turn smoothly or if it does not turn at all. It should also be replaced if there is no viscous drag when hot or cold. If the fan is electric, make sure it runs when the engine warms up and also when the A/C is switched on.

Inspect the fan shroud and any air dams and deflectors. Make

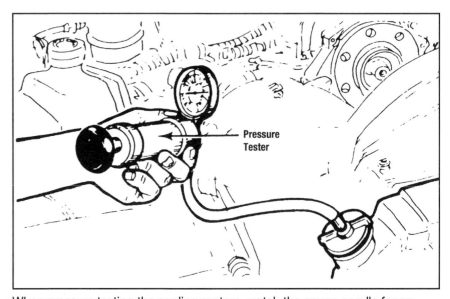

When pressure testing the cooling system, watch the gauge needle for an indication of a leak. Make sure all hose clamps are tight and that the heater core is not leaking. Remember that coolant can also leak into the engine and transmission lubricant systems.

Heating And Engine Cooling Systems Diagnosis And Repair

sure all are in place and properly mounted, including any seals.

Start the engine and listen for unusual noises. A hammering sound may indicate a restriction in the water jacket or air in the

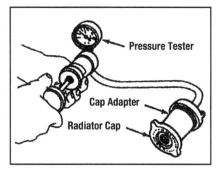

When pressure testing the radiator cap, the proper cap adapter must be used. The cap should be capable of holding the pressure recommended for the vehicle. Pressure test the cooling system at approximately the release pressure of the radiator cap.

system. Squealing noises indicate a bad belt or water pump bearing damage. Gurgling from the radiator may point to air in the system.

Cooling System Pressure Testing

Use a hand-held pump with a pressure gauge that is designed for cooling system testing. While the engine is cold, remove the pressure cap from the radiator or expansion tank. Make sure the system is filled to capacity, then attach the tester. Pump it up to the rated system pressure and watch the gauge needle; it should not drop rapidly. If pressure drops, check for leaks at the radiator and heater hoses, water pump, radiator, intake manifold, sensor fittings, water control valves and heater core. Repair leaks as required and retest.

If you can't spot the leak, it may be internal such as a head gasket, cracked cylinder head or cracked block. Inspect the engine oil for signs of coolant; if it is thick and milky, that's a dead giveaway. Start the engine and watch the tester gauge. If the pressure immediately increases, there could be a head gasket leak, but not into the crankcase. The coolant may be going out the tailpipe, however, which would be indicated by white smoke from the exhaust pipe and a somewhat sweet antifreeze odor in the exhaust. Remember that catalytic converters can mask small coolant leak symptoms because the converter super-heats the coolant into such a fine vapor that it is not noticeable.

Use the system tester's cap adapter to check the pressure cap. Pump it up to the cap's rating. It should hold for about 10 seconds and then decrease just a bit. If it drops too much, replace the cap. Pump the cap to exceed its pressure rating. The cap should release pressure; if not it should be replaced.

THERMOSTAT

The thermostat's function is to allow the engine to come to operating temperature quickly and then maintain a minimum operating temperature. If the thermostat is good, the radiator hose bringing coolant from the

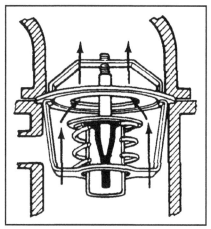

The thermostat is designed to open when the engine coolant reaches a specified temperature.

engine to the radiator should be hot to the touch after the engine has been idling and warm. If the hose is not hot, the thermostat is most likely stuck open, especially if there has also been a complaint of poor heater performance. If the thermostat was stuck closed, the engine would quickly overheat.

To test the thermostat operation, remove the radiator cap while the engine is cold. Put a thermometer in the radiator fill neck and

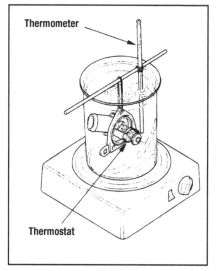

Thermostat testing.
(Courtesy: Honda Motor Co., Ltd.)

start the engine. Keep an eye on the coolant in the radiator and occasionally feel the upper radiator hose. When the hose gets warm, the coolant should be moving in the radiator. Check the thermometer. If it doesn't go above 150°F, the thermostat is either stuck open or missing.

On systems where access to the radiator fluid level is not possible, connect a capable scan tool and access the date for the Engine Coolant Temperature (ECT) sensor. It is best to access this in the scan tool's "generic" mode to get a true reading and not a substitute value. Use a temperature probe or infrared temperature gun to monitor the engine line to the

Heating And Engine Cooling Systems Diagnosis And Repair

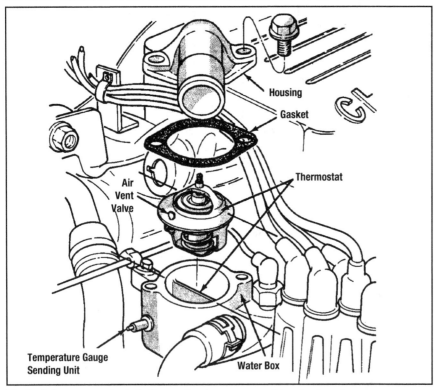

Typical thermostat installation. *(Courtesy: DaimlerChrysler Corp.)*

radiator. You should see a change in temperature at roughly the same time the ECT PID reaches the specifiec value for thermostat opening.

The thermostat can be checked more precisely by removing it from the vehicle and submerging it in a container of water with a thermometer. Suspend the thermostat so it does not contact the container or thermometer. Heat the water and observe the temperature when the thermostat opens. The opening temperature should match the thermostat's temperature rating +/- 3°F. It should be fully open approximately 25°F above the temperature rating. Remove the thermostat from the water. The valve should close slowly when exposed to cooler ambient temperature. Replace the thermostat if it does not function as specified.

To replace the thermostat, drain the cooling system and disconnect the hose from the thermostat housing. Remove the thermostat housing and remove the thermostat. Clean all gasket material from the sealing surfaces and check the surfaces for nicks or burrs.

Properly seat the thermostat in its flange on the engine. Make sure the heat sensing portion of the thermostat is installed so as to expose it to the hot coolant side. Using a new gasket, install the thermostat housing and torque the bolts to specification. Refill the cooling system, start the engine and check for leaks and proper operation.

RADIATOR

Coolant from the engine flows through a series of tubes in the radiator. These tubes are surrounded by a network of fins designed to direct air flow to the tubes. The cooled liquid is then circulated back through the engine in order to maintain proper operating temperature.

Clean the radiator fins of debris, bugs or leaves that may have been drawn in while driving. Sometimes, debris may collect between the radiator and condenser. Make sure all fins are intact, and not bent so as to misdirect air flow. Distorted fins can be straightened using a suitable tool, however, be careful when straightening because the fins are very delicate.

Inspect the radiator for damage and any signs of leakage from the core tubes, radiator tanks and hose collars. Look inside the radiator for large amounts of mineral deposits at the ends of the core tubes, as mineral buildup can cause an internal restriction. If blockage inside the radiator is suspected, an infrared surface thermometer can be used to scan the surface of the radiator when the engine is hot and idling. The radiator should be warmest near the inlet and gradually cool toward the outlet. If there are areas that are considerably cooler than the inlet, then there may be restrictions at those areas.

If visual inspection and/or testing indicate that radiator replacement is required, drain the cooling system and disconnect the hoses and transmission cooler lines, if equipped. Separate the radiator from the fan shroud and electric cooling fan, if equipped, and remove the radiator mounting fasteners. Remove the radiator from the vehicle.

Transfer fittings and/or temperature sending units to the replacement radiator, as required. Position the radiator in the vehicle and tighten the mounting fasteners to specification. Install the shroud and electric cooling fan, if equipped. Connect the radiator hoses and transmission cooler lines, if equipped. Refill the cooling system, start the engine and check for leaks.

Heating And Engine Cooling Systems Diagnosis And Repair

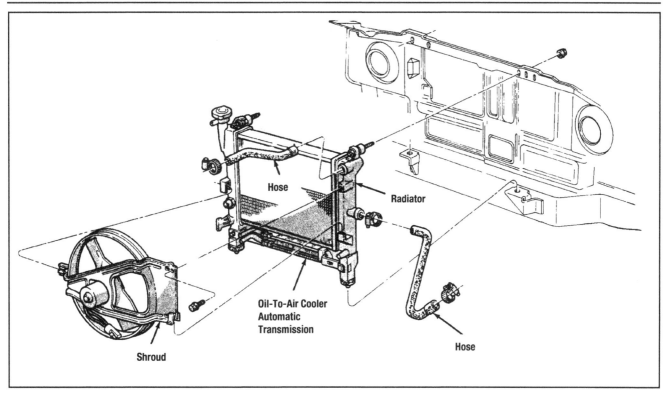

Typical radiator installation. *(Courtesy: DaimlerChrysler Corp.)*

WATER PUMP

The water pump is mounted on the engine and driven by a belt. The pump employs an impeller fan designed to pump coolant throughout the engine via specially placed water jackets. While some water pumps are mounted directly behind the radiator fan and its pulley, others are mounted independently on the front of the engine.

Check for a coolant leak from the vent hole at the bottom of the pump shaft housing. Check the water pump bearings by grasping the fan or pulley and attempt to move the impeller shaft back and forth. If there is any movement, the water pump bearings are defective. Remove the drive belt and turn the pulley by hand. The pulley should turn smoothly. If there is noise and/or binding, the bearings are defective. Replace the pump if it leaks or the bearings are defective.

To replace a water pump, drain the cooling system and disconnect the hoses from the pump. Remove the water pump drive belt and pulley. Remove any brackets or other components necessary for water pump removal. Remove the water pump mounting bolts and remove the water pump. Clean all gasket material from the sealing surfaces and check the surfaces for nicks or burrs.

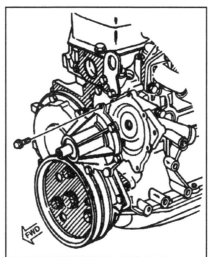

Typical water pump installation. *(Courtesy: GM Corp.)*

Install the water pump using new gaskets and torque the mounting bolts to specification. Install any brackets or other components that were removed. Install the water pump pulley and the drive belt. Properly tension the belt, as required. Connect the coolant hoses to the water pump. Refill the cooling system, start the engine and check for leaks.

FLUSHING, FILLING AND BLEEDING THE COOLING SYSTEM

Engine overheating can be caused by a clogged cooling system. If you suspect that the system is clogged, drain it and then flush the system using one of the commercially available flushing kits. Flush the system according to the directions supplied with the kit.

All used coolants pick up heavy metals such as lead from the solder used in the assembly of heat exchangers, so drained coolant

Heating And Engine Cooling Systems Diagnosis And Repair

must either be disposed of properly or recycled.

After flushing, or whenever the cooling system has been drained for service, the system should be refilled with the vehicle manufacturer's specified coolant mixture. Ethylene glycol is the most widely used substance mixed with water to form engine coolant. Ethylene glycol lowers the freezing point of water and raises the boiling point. Not all ethylene glycol antifreeze is the same, however. Most antifreeze consists of about 90% ethylene glycol, with the remaining percentage being additives. The additives prevent corrosion and lubricate pump seals, and it is with the additive packages that antifreeze differs.

NOTE: Be sure to use water that meets OEM requirements. Many areas have "hard" water, or water with high mineral content. These minerals can lead to corrosion and damage to the cooling system passages and/or components. Many coolant manufacturers offer "pre-mixed" coolant to help technicians avoid this issue.

The traditional "green" anti-freeze that has been around for years uses Inorganic Additive Technology (IAT), meaning that the additives used to protect against corrosion are inorganic. The inorganic phosphates and silicates work quickly to apply a corrosion fighting coating in the cooling system, however these additives also deplete quickly, which is why it is necessary to frequently change this type of coolant.

Organic Additive Technology (OAT) antifreeze uses additive packages consisting of organic acids. These coolants don't lay down a coating but rather help preserve the self-protective layers that naturally develop over time on both iron and aluminum. This process uses up additives much more slowly than traditional coolant. The most well known type of OAT antifreeze is GM's Dex-Cool.

HOAT stands for Hybrid Organic Additive Technology. As its name suggests, HOAT antifreeze uses both silicate and organic acid corrosion inhibitors for extended service life.

Do not try to rely on color to identify the type of coolant in the system. Raw coolant is colorless and manufacturers can dye it any color they want. Most experts say that mixing coolant will not cause any damaging chemical reactions and the coolant will still carry away heat and protect against freezing. However, mixing some types will affect the service life. OAT and HOAT are considered long life coolants. If IAT coolant is mixed with either, the change interval will degrade to that of a shorter life coolant. For optimum system protection, use the type of coolant specified by the vehicle manufacturer.

A mix of 50 percent water/50 percent antifreeze is usually the most effective mixture, but some vehicle manufacturers may specify otherwise. Drain and replace the coolant at the vehicle manufacturer's recommended interval.

When filling the cooling system, be aware that some vehicles have bleeder valves to release air trapped in the system and require that a specific bleeding procedure be followed. If there are no bleeders, to prevent air from becoming trapped in the system you can remove a hose from the highest point (usually at the heater core) and fill the system until coolant begins to come out at this point. Start the engine, and as soon as the level in the radiator drops, top it off and install the cap. Fill the reservoir to the indicated level.

NOTE: Trapped air in modern cooling systems can cause symptoms of "lack of cabin heat" and even cooling system component damage. On some models, the use of special equipment is needed to insure that all air is purged from the system.

Most all cooling systems in use today are equipped with a coolant reservoir. The radiator cap in the

ETHYLENE GLYCOL-BASED ENGINE COOLANT PROTECTION

Capacity Cooling System (Quarts)	PROTECTION CHART — Quarts of Engine Coolant Required for Protection to Temperatures (°F) Shown										
	2	3	4	5	6	7	8	9	10	11	12
6	0	-34									
7	6	-18	-54								
8	10	-8	-34								
9	14	0	-21	-50							
10	16	4	-12	-34	-62						
11	18	8	-6	-23	-47						
12	19	10	0	-15	-34	-57					
13	21	13	3	-9	-25	-45					
14	22	15	6	-5	-18	-34	-54				
15	23	16	8	0	-12	-26	-43				
16	23	17	10	2	-8	-19	-34	-52			
17	24	18	12	5	-4	-14	-27	-42			
18	24	19	14	7	0	-10	-21	-34	-50		
19	25	20	15	9	2	-7	-16	-28	-42		
20	25	21	16	10	4	-3	-12	-22	-34	-48	
21		22	17	12	6	0	-9	-17	-28	-41	
22		22	18	13	8	2	-6	-14	-23	-34	-47

A 50/50 mixture (coolant/distilled water) is recommended as it provides freeze protection down to -34°F (-36.7°C) and boiling protection up to 265°F (129°C). DO NOT ALLOW the concentration of coolant to fall below 40% or exceed 60% as engine parts could become damaged or not work properly. Shaded blocks show 50% concentration to the next higher full quart.

ETHYLENE GLYCOL HYDROMETER SCALE - For cooling systems larger than shown, use double the quantity required for a system one-half as large. For systems smaller than shown, use half the quantity required for a system twice as large.

Heating And Engine Cooling Systems Diagnosis And Repair

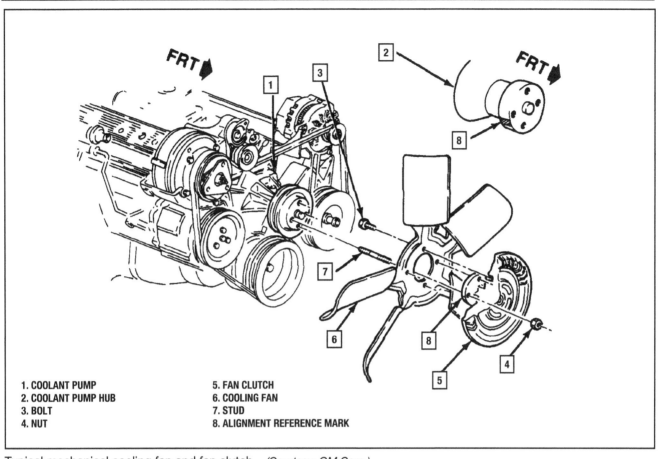

1. COOLANT PUMP
2. COOLANT PUMP HUB
3. BOLT
4. NUT
5. FAN CLUTCH
6. COOLING FAN
7. STUD
8. ALIGNMENT REFERENCE MARK

Typical mechanical cooling fan and fan clutch. *(Courtesy: GM Corp.)*

system functions as a two-way check valve: It has a limit that, once exceeded, allows the coolant to escape from the radiator and into the reservoir. This happens normally as the coolant heats up and expands. As the system cools, it creates a partial vacuum and sucks coolant from the reservoir back into the radiator. It is a closed system where, ideally, no coolant escapes and no air gets into the cooling system. Air in the system contributes to corrosion.

When adding coolant to this type of system, add it to the reservoir. The tank is usually marked with the proper hot and cold fill levels. The overflow tank serves as a receptacle for coolant forced out of the radiator overflow pipe and provides for its return to the system. As the engine cools, the balancing of pressures causes the coolant to siphon back into the radiator.

NOTE: Hybrids often have two or more cooling systems under the hood. One is for the ICE, or gasoline engine, and the other is for the high voltage components. Some even have "thermos bottles" designed to keep coolant hot for long periods to provide instant cabin heat when the car is in electric-only mode. Be sure to follow all OE service procedures and precautions before attempting hybrid cooling system service and repair.

COOLING FANS

Mechanical Cooling Fan

Most rear-wheel drive cars and trucks have belt-driven, mechanical fans equipped with a fan clutch. The fan clutch is designed to slip when cold and rotate the fan at certain maximum speeds when hot. Fan clutches improve gas mileage and reduce noise levels.

Inspect the fan clutch as described under Cooling System Inspection in this study guide. To test the fan clutch, attach a thermometer or electronic temperature probe to the radiator near the inlet and connect a timing light to the engine. Start the engine and strobe the fan to 'freeze' the blades; note the engine speed. When the engine warms up (check the thermometer), the fan speed should increase and the blades will appear to be moving in the strobe light. As the temperature drops, the fan should slow down. A quick check of fan clutches is to shut down a hot engine, then observe how long it takes for the fan to stop spinning. A properly operating clutch should stop the fan from spinning within two seconds.

Replace the fan clutch if it fails inspection or testing.

Heating And Engine Cooling Systems Diagnosis And Repair

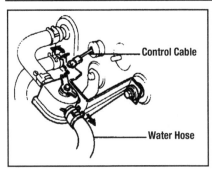

Typical cable-operated heater control valve.
(Courtesy: Toyota Motor Corp.)

Electric Cooling Fan

Many vehicles, especially those with transverse engines, use electric cooling fans. Besides not needing a belt to drive them, electric fans conserve energy since they run only when needed.

When the engine slightly exceeds proper operating temperature, the electric fan should come on. It may cycle on and off as the coolant warms and cools. On most vehicles, the fan also should run whenever the A/C is switched on. (Some vehicles have two fans with one dedicated to the A/C system. That one may not run for engine cooling alone.)

If the fan doesn't run, check for power at its connector using a test light. If there is power, the fan motor is faulty. If there is no power, the problem may be a blown fuse, a bad relay, the fan's temperature switch, the engine coolant temperature sensor, the computer controls or wiring. In most cases, the fan motor can be replaced by removing the entire assembly, and then removing the fan from its motor. Use caution not to damage the radiator fins or core tubes when removing the fan.

HEATER CONTROL VALVE

Although they are becoming less common, many vehicles still have water valves in the engine compartment to stop the flow of coolant to the heater core when it is not needed. Start the engine and run it until it reaches normal operating temperature. Switch the heater to its hottest setting and feel the hose between the heater control valve and the heater core. It should feel about the same temperature (hot) as the inlet hose to the heater control valve. If both hoses are not equally as hot, chances are the heater control valve is inoperative. Make sure the cable (if equipped) is connected to the valve and adjusted properly, and that it is not kinked or misrouted. If equipped with a vacuum-controlled valve, check the hose for vacuum and make sure the valve works when the vacuum is applied.

If the valve is leaking or inoperative, it must be replaced. Drain the cooling system, then disconnect the vacuum hose or cable from the valve. Disconnect the heater hoses and remove the valve. Inspect the condition of the heater hoses and clamps and replace as necessary.

Connect the valve to the heater hoses, observing the proper coolant flow direction, and secure with the clamps. Reconnect the vacuum line or cable. Refill the cooling system. Start the engine and allow it to warm up to operating temperature. Turn the heater to its highest temperature and check for proper operation.

HEATER CORE

As mentioned earlier, moisture on the passenger floor or a slimy film on the windows is a sign of heater core leakage. You can test the heater core using the cooling system pressure tester and an adapter to connect to the heater core inlet pipe. After capping the outlet, pressurize the core and replace it if it doesn't hold pressure. If, during the cooling system inspection it was found that

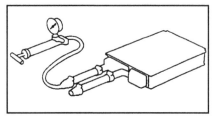

Pressure testing a heater core.
(Courtesy: Ford Motor Co.)

the return hose leading to the water pump was much cooler, the heater core is most likely plugged or air bound. An air bound heater can be burped by loosening the outlet hose until coolant runs out while the engine is running. However, a plugged core must be corrected by reverse flushing or replacement.

Replace the heater core if it is leaking or plugged. Depending on the vehicle, it may be possible to remove the heater core from the plenum with the plenum installed in the vehicle, or the entire plenum may have to be removed to access the heater core. Disconnect the negative battery cable and drain the cooling system. Disconnect the heater hoses from the heater core.

If the plenum is being removed, label and disconnect the necessary electrical connectors and vacuum hoses. Remove all other components necessary for heater core or plenum removal, then remove the heater core or plenum. If the plenum was removed, disassemble it as necessary to remove the heater core.

If necessary, install the heater core into the plenum. Install the heater core or plenum into the vehicle. Install all components that were removed for access and connect the necessary electrical connectors and vacuum hoses. Connect the heater hoses to the heater core. Connect the negative battery cable. Refill the cooling system. Start the engine and allow it to warm up to operating temperature. Turn the heater to its highest temperature and check for leaks and proper operation.

Notes

Operating Systems And Related Controls Diagnosis And Repair

MANUAL HEATING, VENTILATING AND A/C SYSTEMS

System Operation

Vacuum and mechanical controls are combined with electrical controls to operate the Heating, Ventilation and Air Conditioning (HVAC) system. The items being controlled are activated by vacuum, cables, electricity or any combination of these. The instrument panel controls may operate vacuum switches to select the routings to the various vacuum motors that control A/C, defrost and heat modes. They may also be connected to cables that control a door or valve's position, or they can be electrical switches or potentiometers that can control electric motors or vacuum solenoids.

Controlling the temperature of the air entering the passenger compartment is usually achieved by means of a door in the plenum assembly, often referred to as the blend door. The blend door controls the amount of air flowing through the heater core. The door's position is controlled by a cable or small electric motor. On some vehicles the temperature of the air flowing through the heater core can also be controlled by a heater control valve (water valve) mounted in the hose to the heater core. The heater control valve controls the flow of hot coolant through the heater core. Its position can also be controlled by a vacuum motor or cable.

Air routing is controlled very much the same way as temperature. Cable, vacuum, or electric motor operated doors inside the plenum assembly either open or block passages or ducts to dash vents, floor outlet, windshield defroster, etc. depending on which panel control position the driver has selected. Air can enter the HVAC system from either the interior of the vehicle ('RECIRC'), or from the outside ('FRESH'). Inside a vacuum motor housing is a spring loaded vacuum diaphragm, one side of which is connected to the vacuum source. The other side is attached to an arm that moves the air door.

System Diagnosis

Complaints of insufficient cooling or heating, or improper air routing, can often be traced to problems with vacuum or mechanical controls. Many failures or partial malfunctions of air conditioning systems can be caused by controls that are out of adjustment. Also, vacuum leaks or disconnected hoses will cause air doors to stay in the wrong position. To diagnose the positions of the doors in relation to the positions of the control head levers, a good air conditioning diagram is necessary.

If the problem seems to lie with an electrical device, check the necessary fuses, relay, diodes and wiring connections. Verify that the blower works at all speeds. Common sense will tell you a lot about the condition of electrical parts. For example, if the blower works on one speed only, you know that the blower motor is OK. The trouble then, would have to be in the switch or resistor. For slower speeds, current is routed through one or more resistors in a resistor block. It is often found in the plenum where air flow can keep the resistor coils cool. Failure to work on one or more resistor speeds means that a portion of the resistor assembly is probably burned out or the high-speed relay is defective.

On some vehicles, the mode doors are moved by DC motors that push or pull levers as necessary. Total failure may indicate a blown fuse, but if individual components malfunction, check for power to the motor and check the motor itself. Occasionally, the selector switch may be at fault, but this is less common.

If problems arise concerning air routing or temperature control, keep in mind that vacuum leaks are usually caused by bad hoses. It is more unusual to find a bad vacuum motor or switch. Vacuum is often maintained in the system by a vacuum reservoir. The reservoir may have a check valve in its supply hose, or the check valve may be part of the reservoir. If, during hard acceleration, air routing changes by itself, it's probably due to a leak in the system or a faulty check valve. A complaint that the mode shifts from the floor to defrost at wide open throttle is evidence that the system isn't holding vacuum. Hissing sounds also point to vacuum leaks. Some vacuum operated doors also have an adjustment in the length of the arm that attaches the door to the diaphragm.

Control cables usually have an adjustment at the end opposite the control panel. Air doors that are operated by cables should be adjusted so that the doors shut

58   A7 - Heating And Air Conditioning

Operating Systems And Related Controls Diagnosis And Repair

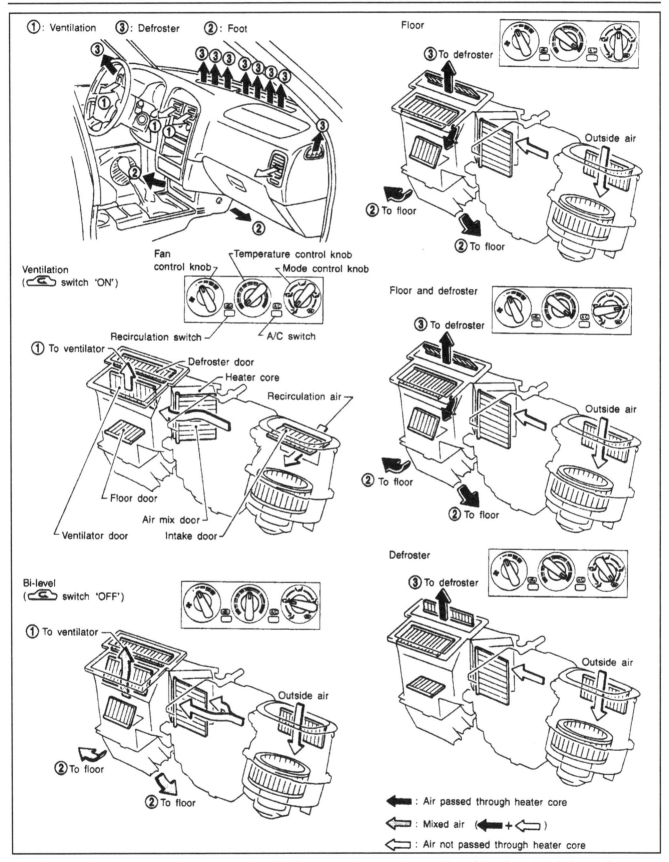

This diagram illustrates the air flow through the HVAC system. It shows the position of the doors in relation to the various control head positions. *(Courtesy: Nissan Motor Co., Ltd.)*

Operating Systems And Related Controls Diagnosis And Repair

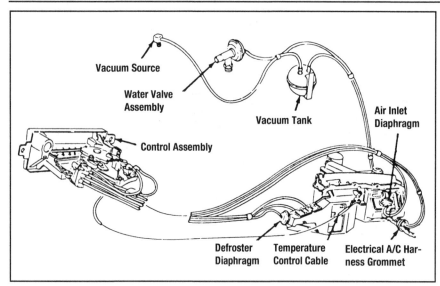

A/C systems acquire the control vacuum from a vacuum reservoir equipped with a check valve. The vacuum supply of this manual A/C system is routed from the reservoir to the dashboard control panel, where the mode selection lever distributes the vacuum signal to the appropriate plenum door vacuum servos and the heater hot water valve. The blower motor speeds are selected by a switch and a relay, and the temperature blend door is operated by a cable.

tightly enough to stop air flow. This adjustment is made in most cases by shifting the cable housing in its clamp bracket near the door. Many cables today are self adjusting and if there is a problem with operation, the cable may have become disconnected from the lever to which it was attached.

If control cables must be replaced, it is usually easier to drop the control panel out of the dash than to try to fit a new cable with the panel in place. Also, replacing a vacuum control switch on the control panel usually means the entire panel must be replaced as a unit.

If the complaint is generally insufficient air flow, the cause may not be the blower motor. Leaves and other debris can make their way into the fresh air intake, especially if the screen is missing, and obstruct air flow. A shop vac can be used to clean the air intake. Many new vehicles are equipped with passenger compartment air filters. These filters can become clogged and restrict air flow if not replaced regularly.

Some interior air 'problems' may be caused by operator error. For instance, if the windows fog in cool weather, the motorist may be selecting RECIRC believing it best to keep the warm air inside. In fact, he or she is recirculating moisture laden air, and the windows will clear if fresh air is chosen.

Electrical Components

Blower Motor

If the blower motor doesn't work, check the fuse or circuit breaker, and check for voltage at the connector at the resistor block. Generally, if one or two of the blower speeds don't work, the problem is a faulty resistor. If the high speed doesn't work, the problem could be the high-speed relay or a fuse. Don't overlook the switch on the dashboard or the ground for the blower motor. If the blower is too slow at all speeds, perform a current draw test to see if the windings or brushes are bad. Noises from the blower could point to a bad bearing or debris in the fan.

Blown fuses or breakers most often indicate a short circuit in the wiring. However, a short can sometimes occur in the blower motor itself. It is obvious that for the motor to work, two things are necessary, power (voltage) to the motor, and continuity to ground. So, the first thing to check for is voltage available at the motor. While a test light will indicate whether voltage is present, a Digital Multimeter (DMM) will indicate how much voltage is present.

To test for proper voltage, place the panel selector levers in the manufacturer's recommended positions and insert the probes of a DMM into the back of the connector at the blower motor. Compare the measured voltage with

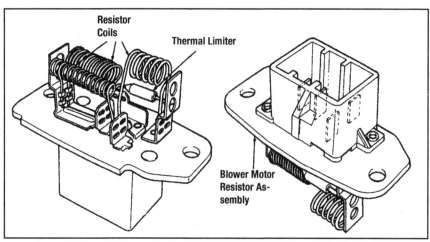

Typical blower motor resistor. *(Courtesy: Ford Motor Co.)*

Operating Systems And Related Controls Diagnosis And Repair

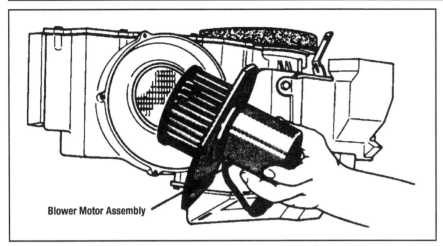

Typical blower motor installation.
(Courtesy: DaimlerChrysler Corp.)

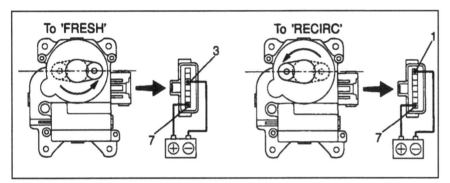

This servomotor is tested by applying 12 volts to terminal 7 and grounding terminal 3. The motor arm should then rotate to the 'FRESH' position. When terminal 1 is grounded the arm should rotate to the 'RECIRC' position.
(Courtesy: Toyota Motor Corp.)

Condition	Fan operation (Fan speed)
Engine coolant temperature 88 °C (190 °F) or below	Rotate (Low speed)
Engine coolant temperature 98 °C (208 °F) or above	Rotate (High speed)
Refrigerant pressure is less than 1,520 kPa (15.5 kgf/cm^2, 220 psi)	Rotate (Low speed)
Refrigerant pressure is 1,520 kPa (15.5 kgf/cm^2, 220 psi) or above	Rotate (High speed)

An example of condenser fan operating specifications.
(Courtesy: Toyota Motor Corp.)

Place the panel selector levers in the manufacturer's recommended positions and start the engine. Operate the blower at all speeds, recording the current draw for each speed. Compare with manufacturer's specifications.

NOTE: Many DMMs are not capable of measuring the high current draw of some blower motors. Instead, use a low amp clamp that you can close around one of the blower motor leads. Low amp clamps are available as standalone tools or as an accessory for your DMM or DSO (digital storage oscilloscope).

NOTE: Many newer vehicles have done away with blower motor resistors and have replaced them with blower motor electronic modules. These can be electrically diagnosed using similar methods, but may require the use of a scan tool.

Actuators And Servomotors

As explained earlier, electric actuators and servomotors are used in many systems to move air doors within the plenum, opening or blocking plenum passages. An actuator may directly operate a door or, when activated, may operate a vacuum motor, which in turn operates the door.

There are two-position actuators, which open or close, and continuous position actuators that can stop anywhere within a range. The latter are usually used for temperature blend door operation.

If there is a function or temperature problem caused by a malfunctioning air door, first make sure there is power to the actuator. If there is no power, check the circuit back to the control head. If there is power to the actuator, the actuator should be tested. Refer to the manufacturer's service info for specific testing procedures.

manufacturer's specifications.

To test for blower motor current draw, disconnect the blower motor wire connector and connect a DMM (in the amps position) between the positive terminal on the motor and the corresponding terminal of the wire connector. Connect a jumper wire between the ground terminal on the motor and the corresponding terminal of the wire harness connector.

Operating Systems And Related Controls Diagnosis And Repair

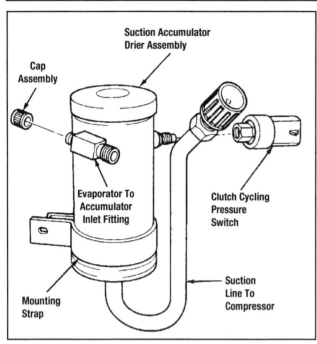

Typical pressure cycling switch mounting location.
(Courtesy: Ford Motor Co.)

Condenser Fan

Some vehicles have a separate cooling fan for the condenser. The fan may have low and high speed operating modes. Some vehicles have two fans, with one being the low speed and fan and the other the high speed fan.

Inspect the fan for missing, cracked or bent blades. Make sure the fan shroud is in place and not broken.

If the condenser fan doesn't run when the A/C is on, check for power at its connector using a test light. If there is power, the fan motor is faulty. If there is no power, the problem may be a blown fuse, a bad relay, the A/C pressure switch, the engine coolant temperature sensor, the computer controls or wiring.

Even if the condenser fan runs, refer to the factory service information to determine what constitutes proper fan operation. For example, the specifications may state that a two speed fan should run at low speed if the engine coolant is below a certain temperature and the refrigerant is below a certain pressure, and run at high speed when that coolant temperature or refrigerant pressure is exceeded.

In most cases, the fan motor can be replaced by removing the entire assembly, and then removing the fan from its motor. Use caution not to damage the condenser fins or core tubes when removing the fan.

Potentiometer

Some vehicles have a potentiometer located in the HVAC control panel that relays the position of the temperature control lever to the ECM. The information is processed by the ECM and air conditioning output is regulated accordingly.

To test the potentiometer, locate the air conditioning control module. Connect a DMM switched to the ohms position across the potentiometer wires at the end of the module connector. Check the resistance of the potentiometer while moving the temperature control lever. Compare the readings with manufacturer's specifications.

If the readings are not within specifications, replace the potentiometer. Disconnect the negative battery cable and remove the HVAC control head from the instrument panel. Disconnect the potentiometer wiring and remove it from the HVAC control head.

Compressor Clutch Controls

As previously discussed, cycling the compressor clutch is a method of controlling evaporator pressure and hence, its temperature. Whenever pressure approaches the high limit, the controls simply switch off the clutch until pressure drops. The clutch is turned off and on automatically to prevent the evaporator from icing up. During operation, the clutch may cycle on and off several times each minute. As the change in heat load on the evaporator affects system pressures, the compressor cycling rate automatically changes to achieve the desired temperature. However, if the clutch cycles rapidly, it may be a sign of low refrigerant charge.

It is important to visually inspect the wiring and connectors to the various cycling and protection devices to make sure they are intact. Check for loose or broken wire connections, and damaged terminals. Ensure that all grounds are clean and making good contact.

The A/C electrical circuit must be opened or closed on demand from the system, or by the driver. Current will flow only in a closed circuit. In the case of the A/C compressor, the system must be performing at its optimum in order for the circuit to close, and the compressor clutch to engage. Proper operation of all compressor clutch control switches is crucial to maintaining system performance levels.

A/C Clutch Relay

The relay is composed of a coil and a set of contacts. When current is passed through the coil, a magnetic field is formed, and this field causes the contacts to move together, completing the circuit. Most relays are normally open, preventing current from passing through.

The operation of the A/C clutch relay on pre-OBD II vehicles is directly affected by the A/C switch input circuit. When the switch is turned on, high pressure, low

Operating Systems And Related Controls Diagnosis And Repair

pressure, and temperature switches sense the correct conditions, and the relay closes to complete the circuit to the compressor clutch. However, any changes in pressure or temperature sensed by the control switches that would indicate an out-of-range condition will shut off current to the relay, and disengage the compressor clutch.

On OBD II vehicles, the ECM controls the function of the relay. Many of the parameters are the same, but instead of a hard wire in series with the relay, the inputs are fed as data PIDs to the ECM, which then makes a "go-no go" decision based on those inputs.

NOTE: Relays are often used in a variety of circuits controlled by an electronic control module. This protects the sensitive module electronics from high current applications. To prevent unwanted voltage surges when the relay is shut off, diodes are often built into the relay itself. Failure to replace a failed relay with one of the same design can lead to circuit board damage and eventual failure of the controlling module. This includes swapping the relay with a "known good" for testing!

Thermostatic and Pressure Switches

To cycle the compressor, some systems use a thermostatic switch. It has a capillary tube attached to the evaporator outlet or inserted between the evaporator core fins to sense the temperature. This capillary is attached to a switch that opens and closes as necessary to cycle the compressor. Most thermostatic switches are factory-set and not adjustable. If the switch is defective, the compressor clutch will cycle on and off quickly.

The more modern controls use a thermistor, which reacts faster than a mechanical thermostat to sense temperature changes. This keeps the temperature constant, as opposed to the temperature swings that are typical of mechanical thermostats. Additionally, thermistors do not need the constant air flow necessary to operate mechanical thermostats.

Although some orifice tube systems use a thermostatic switch to control compressor clutch cycling, others use a pressure cycling switch. It senses the low-side pressure (which is directly proportionate to temperature) near the evaporator outlet. Usually the pressure cycling switch is found on the accumulator, and is often mounted in a Schrader fitting so it can be replaced without the loss of refrigerant. When system pressure is low, the switch opens; when it is high, the switch closes. The more heat the refrigerant picks up in the evaporator core, the higher the pressure becomes.

On expansion valve systems, the compressor is switched on around 25 psi and off about 10 psi. Orifice tube systems usually switch on around 45 psi and turn off at 25 psi. Since system pressure is quite low during cold weather, the pressure cycling switch keeps the compressor from running when it isn't needed. It also protects the compressor from damage should the refrigerant charge escape.

Low-Pressure Cutout Switch

The low-pressure cutout switch may be found in either the high or low side of the system, but its function is the same: it disengages the compressor clutch if the pressure drops below a preset level, keeping the compressor from being destroyed due to lack of lubrication, which normally flows with the refrigerant. Whenever there is a leak of refrigerant, oil leaks out as well.

To check the low-pressure cutout switch, disconnect the electrical connector and connect a jumper wire across the terminals. Start

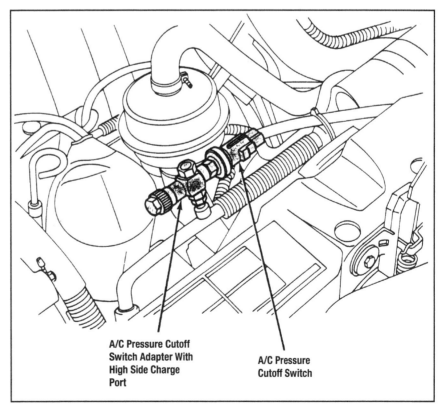

A compressor high-pressure cutout switch along with a service port.

Operating Systems And Related Controls Diagnosis And Repair

the engine and engage the A/C system. If the compressor engages after a brief period, suspect a defective low-pressure cutout switch. If the compressor does not engage, the wiring, fuse, or ambient temperature switch may be defective. If the clutch engages, connect a manifold gauge set, read the compressor discharge pressure and compare with manufacturer's specifications. At a specified pressure and ambient temperature, the switch should engage the compressor.

Recover the refrigerant using the proper equipment before servicing the switch. Disconnect the negative battery cable and the electrical connector from the switch. Remove the switch and its O-ring from its mounting. Install the replacement switch with a new O-ring. Connect the electrical connector and the negative battery cable. Next, evacuate and recharge the A/C system and check for leaks. Finally, check system performance.

High-Pressure Cutout Switch

Like the low-pressure cutout switch, the high-pressure cutout switch protects the compressor from damage. It breaks the circuit to the compressor clutch if it detects pressures above a preset level. This switch is usually located in the high-pressure side of the refrigeration system.

A quick way to check the high-pressure cutout switch operation is to connect the manifold gauge assembly, start the engine and engage the A/C system. To create a high pressure situation, restrict air flow through the condenser. The compressor should disengage once the pressure reaches the threshold of the switch calibration.

To replace the switch, disconnect the negative battery cable and the electrical connector to the switch. Remove the switch from the valve

and discard the O-ring. Install the replacement switch with a new O-ring; connect the electrical connector and the negative battery cable. Finally, check system performance.

Thermal Limiter

Older General Motors systems used a remote-mounted, thermal limiter in conjunction with a superheat switch on the back of the compressor, to disengage the compressor clutch in the event of low refrigerant charge. When the superheat switch engages, electric current to a heater in the thermal limiter heats up a fuse, which then melts and breaks the circuit to the compressor clutch coil.

Early thermal limiters were sensitive to sudden pressure changes, but were redesigned to blow slower. Thermal limiters cannot be reused. However, they should only be replaced after the underlying cause of failure has been repaired.

Electronic Controls

HVAC control is increasingly being handled by computers. Sensors installed in the system report to the ECM, which then sends the command to cycle the clutch. Thermistors-resistors whose values change rapidly with temperature-are the most common type of sensors.

Some electronic engine controls have a direct relationship to A/C system operation. The goal is to optimize engine operation while minimizing the impact on A/C performance. Therefore, some engine sensors are also used in a dual capacity. While they inform the ECM of critical engine operating parameters, others combine to control operation of the A/C system in certain instances.

For instance, if an A/C belt becomes loose, a compressor rpm

sensor can relay slower-than-normal pulley revolution to the ECM. The ECM then compares this rotation with the engine rpm, and disengages the compressor clutch if the variance is too high. The compressor rpm sensor can be located on or inside the compressor. These sensors are of the magnetic type, similar to a crankshaft position sensor.

On some vehicles, the vehicle speed sensor will inform the ECM that it has reached an acceptable speed to turn off the electronically controlled cooling fan. Since enough ram air is supplied at higher vehicle speeds, it is not necessary to run the cooling fan. As the vehicle slows down and ram air decreases, the speed sensor will tell the ECM to activate the cooling fan.

The coolant temperature sensor performs a similar function, only it senses when the coolant temperature has reached a level where the engine cooling fan should be turned on. The sensor changes value with temperature, and in some cases, tells the ECM to disengage the compressor clutch when an overheat condition is present. When coolant temperature has stabilized, the coolant temperature sensor informs the ECM, and the ECM re-engages the compressor clutch.

The wide open throttle switch or throttle position sensor tells the ECM to open the circuit to the compressor clutch when critical engine speed is in demand. The switches temporarily disable the compressor, eliminating the load it places on the engine. After acceleration, the switches inform the ECM that throttle demand has been reduced, and the ECM then engages the compressor clutch.

When a sensor malfunctions, a fault code is generated. The fault code is stored in the ECM memory. Active fault codes indicate a current

Operating Systems And Related Controls Diagnosis And Repair

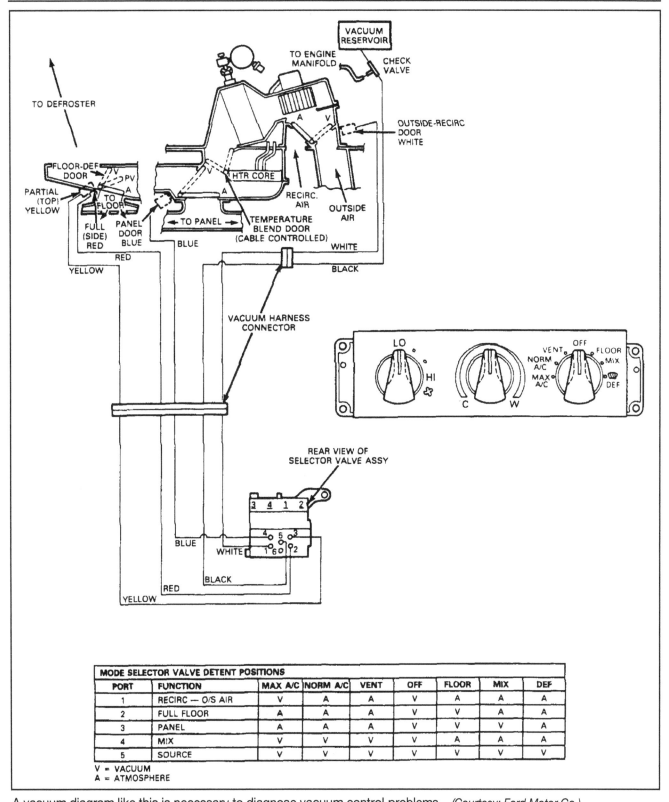

A vacuum diagram like this is necessary to diagnose vacuum control problems. *(Courtesy: Ford Motor Co.)*

problem of some kind. Inactive fault codes suggest a problem that may be temporary, or a problem that has been repaired or corrected since being stored in memory. Inactive fault codes may be helpful in finding intermittent problems. On some vehicles, information codes are generated when a specific function is active (air conditioner on, for instance).

Fault codes usually only indicate

Operating Systems And Related Controls Diagnosis And Repair

which circuit the problem is in; they don't necessarily indicate which component in the circuit has failed. The problem could be caused by a loose connection, improper modification, or a broken wire, so perform a thorough inspection when diagnosing a malfunction. Ensure that all grounds are clean and making good contact. If basic mechanical and electrical checks fail to locate the problem, follow manufacturer's electronic system test procedures.

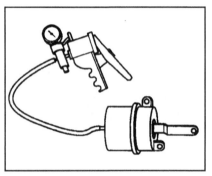

Testing a vacuum operated actuator.
(Courtesy: Ford Motor Co.)

Vacuum Actuators

As stated earlier, the vacuum actuator contains a spring-loaded diaphragm, one side of which is connected to the vacuum source. The other side is attached to an arm that moves the air door. Leaks or disconnected hoses will cause the doors to stay in the wrong position. To diagnose the positions of the doors in relation to the positions of the control head levers, a good system vacuum diagram is necessary.

First, check for proper operation. Under all driving conditions, air should come from the appropriate vents when the corresponding mode is selected. If a problem is detected, use the system vacuum diagram to check vacuum flow.

Check the vacuum reservoir check valve to see if it holds vacuum in one direction. Inspect all interior vacuum lines, especially the multi-connection behind the instrument panel. Check the control head for leaky ports or damage, and check all actuators for the ability to hold vacuum. Finally, disconnect the vacuum line from the actuator and attach a hand-held vacuum pump. Apply vacuum to the actuator. The actuator lever should move to its engaged position and remain there while vacuum is applied. When vacuum is released, the actuator lever should move back to its normal position. Make sure the lever operates smoothly without binding.

To replace the actuator, remove the vacuum line(s) and linkage. Remove the actuator fasteners and the actuator from the vehicle. Reinstall the replacement actuator and fasteners, and reconnect the vacuum lines and linkage. Check for proper operation.

Ducts, Doors And Outlets

Air entering the plenum is directed to whatever vent is selected by a series of ducts underneath the dash. When the desired selection is made at the HVAC control panel, actuators either close or open doors to route the air in the desired direction.

It is important to inspect the plenum doors to make sure they are opening and closing properly. Check door hinges and actuator connections to make sure they are not binding. Check the adjustment (if equipped) of the actuator arm to make sure all doors are opening fully and closing tightly. Remember, improperly routed air can result in ineffective heating, cooling and defrosting. In addition, unwanted outside air can enter the passenger compartment when inside air is desired, or vice-versa if the ducts and doors don't operate properly.

NOTE: *The use of electronic actuators is no longer limited to systems offering automatic temperature control. Many of these actuators can be permanently damaged if operated when not installed on the vehicle. Others require a recalibra-*

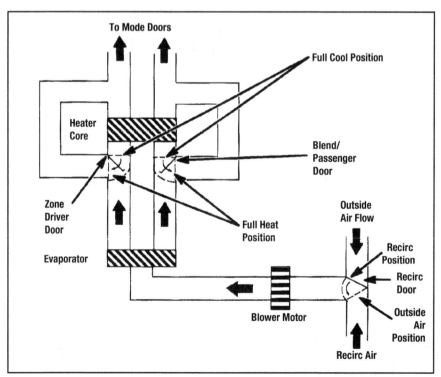

Dual zone climate control air distribution functional diagram.
(Courtesy: DaimlerChrysler Corp.)

Operating Systems And Related Controls Diagnosis And Repair

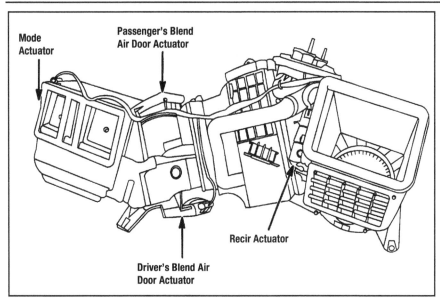

A plenum from a vehicle with dual zone climate control.
(Courtesy: DaimlerChrysler Corp.)

tion procedure when replaced, or when a loss of battery power to its command module has been lost. Be sure to read and follow the published service information and precautions before beginning any troubleshooting or repair of these systems. See "Diagnosing Computer Controlled HVAC Systems" in section A.

AUTOMATIC AND SEMI-AUTOMATIC HEATING, VENTILATING AND A/C SYSTEMS

The main difference between manual HVAC and Automatic Temperature Control (ATC) systems is the more precise control of air temperature and routing provided by the ATC system. With automatic controls, the motorist can choose a given temperature, and have this temperature setting maintained by the A/C and heater control system. Sensors determine the present temperature and the system uses actuators to move the air doors to the positions necessary to achieve the desired temperature.

Some newer ATC systems incorporate a feature known as Dual Zone, in which the driver and

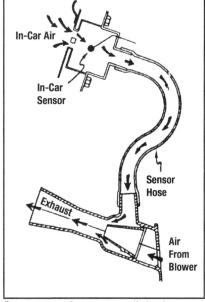

Some manufacturers call the in-car temperature sensor an aspirator. Through the use of a venturi cone in the blower pressure-side air flow, the interior air is drawn through the sensor body.

front passenger can select different temperatures for individual comfort. These work exactly the same way as conventional systems, the only difference being an additional temperature control and blend door for the passenger.

There are two kinds of ATC systems, Semi-Automatic Temperature Control (SATC) and Electronic Automatic Temperature Control (EATC). Semi-automatic systems usually control only the outlet air temperature. In this type of system, the driver still must select the mode of operation and blower speed. As in manual A/C, a switch in the control panel is usually activated to turn on the compressor when the system is placed into the A/C mode, and the water control valve is opened in any mode in which heat may be desired.

EATC systems usually control most of the specific functions of mode of operation, temperature control, blower speeds and, if equipped, water valve action. The system will automatically maintain the desired air temperature and quantity for each mode, and will route the air according to driver selection. In addition, EATC systems have self-diagnostic capabilities.

SATC Systems

SATC system components include the control panel, the programmer and various sensors and actuators. All SATC systems do not have all of the components described here.

The instrument panel mounted control panel is the interface between the driver and the system. The driver selects the desired temperature, the operating mode and the fan speed. The programmer receives the input from the control panel and the system sensors, and in turn controls the blower speed, the air door actuators, the compressor clutch and the heater water valve.

The input sensors include the in-vehicle temperature sensor, the ambient sensor, the sunload sensor and the evaporator temperature sensor. The in-vehicle temperature sensor is an NTC (Negative Temperature Coefficient) thermistor that measures the

Operating Systems And Related Controls Diagnosis And Repair

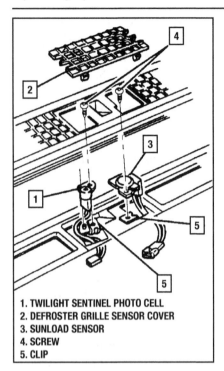

1. TWILIGHT SENTINEL PHOTO CELL
2. DEFROSTER GRILLE SENSOR COVER
3. SUNLOAD SENSOR
4. SCREW
5. CLIP

temperature inside the vehicle. It is located in the aspirator, which is located in the dashboard. The aspirator tube is connected to a heater-A/C duct. The air flowing in the duct past the tube creates a vacuum, drawing in-vehicle air past the sensor. The change in voltage drop across the sensor, as the sensor resistance changes in response to the in-vehicle air temperature, is sent to the programmer.

The ambient temperature sensor is used to measure the temperature of the air outside the vehicle. It is also an NTC thermistor and functions similarly to the in-vehicle temperature sensor. The ambient temperature sensor is usually located in the front of the vehicle, behind the grill.

The sunload sensor is a photovoltaic diode that is usually mounted on the top of the dashboard, sometimes in a speaker grill. Varying amounts of sunlight striking it modify its electrical return signal to the programmer. Bright sunlight will cause the programmer to adjust system output toward cooler; less sunlight will cause the programmer to adjust system output toward warmer. Some dual zone climate control systems have driver and passenger side sunload sensors.

The evaporator temperature sensor is mounted in the plenum and may have a pickup directly attached to the evaporator fins. The evaporator temperature sensor is usually an NTC thermistor.

The outputs from the programmer include the air door actuators, compressor clutch control and the heater water valve. The air door actuators can be electric or vacuum motors. The blend door actuator controls the position of the blend door so that the temperature in the vehicle selected by the driver can be maintained. For example, if a cooler temperature is desired, the programmer will move the blend door to partially or completely block air flow through the heater core. If a warmer temperature is desired, the programmer will move the blend door to allow partial or

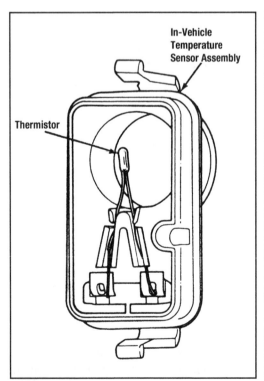

View of the inside of an in-car temperature sensor, showing the thermistor.
(Courtesy: Ford Motor Co.)

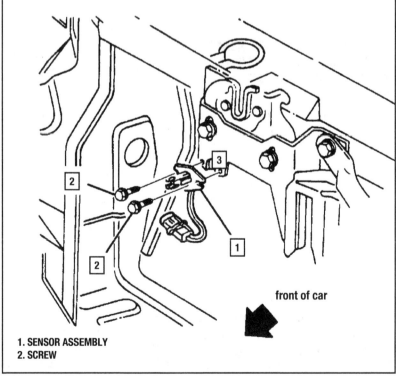

1. SENSOR ASSEMBLY
2. SCREW

Typical ambient temperature sensor mounting location.
(Courtesy: GM Corp.)

A7 - Heating And Air Conditioning

Operating Systems And Related Controls Diagnosis And Repair

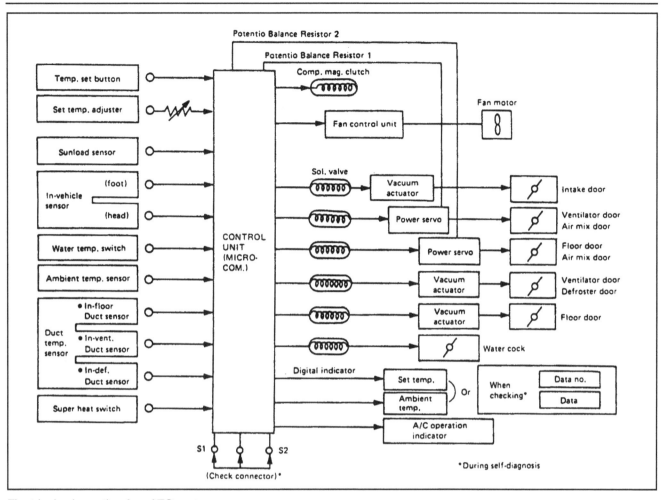

Electrical schematic of an ATC system.

full air flow through the heater core.

The mode door actuator controls the position of the mode door. The programmer, in response to the driver's input, moves the mode door to the position necessary to supply air flow to the desired outlets: the floor ducts, panel ducts or defrost ducts. Some systems have a mix mode, where air flow can be supplied to two ducts, such as when heat and defrost is desired. Some systems will also automatically set air flow to the panel ducts when A/C is selected.

The air inlet door actuator controls the air inlet door so that outside air can be blocked off from inside the vehicle, if desired. When "MAX A/C" or "RECIRC" is selected, the programmer will move the air inlet door to block air from outside the vehicle, in order to provide faster cooling.

When "MAX A/C" is desired, the programmer in some systems will also move the actuator that controls the heater water valve to close, blocking the flow of hot coolant into the heater core.

EATC Systems

The programmer in EATC systems is computer controlled. Control is either through a BCM (Body Control Module) or a computer dedicated to the climate control system. In addition to the computer, a control panel, programmer and the sensors described in the SATC system, EATC systems may also use inputs from the engine coolant temperature sensor, vehicle speed sensor, and throttle position sensor.

The door actuators in EATC systems also have potentiometers attached to them. These provide feedback to the computer so the computer knows the exact door position. The resistance in the potentiometer changes according to door position, and the computer reads the voltage drop across the potentiometer.

The BCM, or climate control computer, monitors driver and sensor input and uses the information to calculate air door position, blower speed and compressor control. The computer then commands the programmer to operate the actuators.

The BCM, or climate control computer, also monitors the input and feedback signals and

Operating Systems And Related Controls Diagnosis And Repair

compares them to pre-programmed information. If any signals are found to be outside of expected parameters, the computer will store the information in the form of a DTC (Diagnostic Trouble Code) in its memory, and will turn on a light on the instrument panel to alert the driver that service is needed.

System Diagnosis

Troubleshooting automatic temperature control systems is a lot like troubleshooting manual systems. In each case most failures are vacuum or mechanical in nature. Always start by checking the less complicated items first, just as if the vehicle had a manual A/C system. Inspect the air or vacuum supply in addition to the lines and hoses. It is possible that the problem could be caused by leaks in lines, fittings and unions.

Start with a system performance check as on a manual system, but as there are differences in how many of these systems operate, obtain the manufacturer's service information. Use a heat gun to warm the in-vehicle and ambient temperature sensors and see if the system responds with cooler air out of the dash outlets and increased blower speeds. Next, chill the air flow to the sensors to produce the opposite effect; heat from the lower floor vent, and high blower speeds. (Aerosol chilling agents are available at many electronic supply stores.) Place a light source over the sunload sensor to see if the system responds with cooler air output.

If the system reacts with a change to one or two inputs but not to the third, the problem is most likely confined to the single sensor or its circuit. But if no reaction is observed on any of the units, or only a partial reaction is seen, the problem is usually with the programmer or its output units.

Have a helper repeat the tests while you observe components such as vacuum or electric motors throughout the system for movement. If the programmer is good, some movement should occur in response to at least one of the three sensor inputs or the instrument panel controls, since it is unlikely that all of the circuits will simultaneously go bad.

By carefully analyzing the results of sensor and instrument panel control tests, you should be able to pinpoint a problem area.

Many EATC systems require scan tools for in-depth diagnosis, but many provide a method to output fault information on their instrument panel displays, often represented by numerical codes.

The proper function of the EATC system depends upon the electrical inputs of the sensors. The programming that enables the computer to provide control of the system naturally tells the computer how to interpret these signals. To help the technician find trouble, the computer is instructed to know the difference between a reasonable sensor input and one that indicates the sensor is not functioning properly.

Should the system begin to operate erratically, the computer will record that fact and store a DTC that will tell the technician what has happened. The goal of this system is not only to lead the technician in the right direction, but also to retain information about

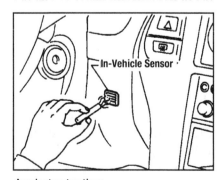

Aspirator testing.
(Courtesy: Nissan Motor Co., Ltd.)

a fault that might be intermittent and may not be evident when the vehicle is brought in for service.

If the control panel has a digital display, the temperature indication on the display would be replaced by the failure code number when in the diagnostic mode. Start the engine and let it warm up to operating temperature. Following the manufacturer's instructions, activate the digital display to read the diagnostic codes. Record all codes displayed during the test. If error codes appear during the test, follow the diagnostic procedures outlined by the manufacturer.

If the control panel does not have a digital display, connect a suitable scan tool to the diagnostic data link and read active or stored DTCs. Compare these codes with the manufacturer's trouble code list to pinpoint the problem.

Most temperature sensors can

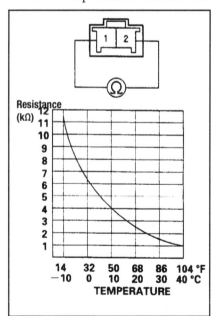

An example of resistance specifications for an in-vehicle temperature sensor.
(Courtesy: Honda Motor Co., Ltd.)

be tested for resistance and voltage drop. Refer to the vehicle service information for specifications and testing procedures. In general,

Operating Systems And Related Controls Diagnosis And Repair

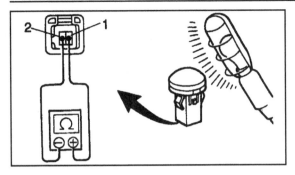

Sunload sensor testing.
(Courtesy: Toyota Motor Corp.)

the sensor should be replaced if its resistance is not within specification. If resistance is infinite, check for an open circuit in the wiring upstream of the sensor. Since a temperature sensor's resistance varies with temperature, check the sensor voltage against temperature and compare with manufacturer's specifications.

Aspirator Testing

If air is not drawn past the in-vehicle temperature sensor, the sensor will not be able to accurately measure the temperature inside the vehicle. To check aspirator function, place the blower on high and the function mode on heat. Place a small piece of paper over the aspirator inlet in front of the aspirator inlet. The paper should be held against the aspirator inlet due to suction. You can also use the smoke function of your EVAP tester. The smoke from the machine should be sucked into the aspirator.

If the aspirator does not function as indicated, check for an obstruction in the duct or aspirator tube or for a loose connection.

In-Vehicle And Ambient Temperature Sensor Testing

Disconnect the sensor harness connector. Connect the leads of a DMM in the ohms position to the sensor terminals. Heat or cool the sensor as necessary and compare the resistance with manufacturer's specifications. Replace the sensor if it is not within specifications.

Sunload Sensor Testing

Remove the sensor from the vehicle. Connect the leads of a DMM in the ohms position to the sensor terminals. Cover the sensor with a cloth and check that no continuity exists between the terminals. If continuity exists, replace the sensor.

Remove the cloth and place a light over the sensor. Continuity should now exist between the

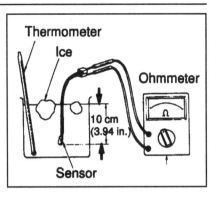

Evaporator temperature sensor testing.
(Courtesy: Toyota Motor Co.)

terminals. If no continuity exists, replace the sensor.

Evaporator Temperature Sensor Testing

Remove the evaporator temperature sensor from the vehicle. Place the sensor and a thermometer in a container of cold water. Connect the leads of a DMM in the ohms position to the sensor terminals. Gradually heat the water, noting the change in temperature and resistance.

Compare the resistance/temperature readings with manufacturer's specifications and replace the sensor as necessary.

MADE FOR DURABILITY.

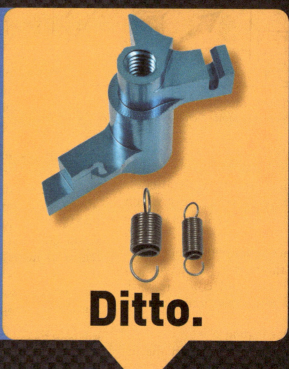

Ditto.

When OE plastic shift interlock levers break, their cars get stuck in "park." TechSmart's Shift Interlock Lever is machined out of billet aluminum and anodized for long-lasting strength and durability. So when the going gets tough, you can count on our parts to keep going.

TechSmart® Shift Interlock Levers

- Machined out of billet aluminum and anodized for long-lasting strength, durability and smooth shifting operation
- No need to replace the entire shifter assembly when only the original lever fails

The Evolution of Parts

Armadillos are mammals with a leathery armor shell. The word armadillo means "little armored one" in Spanish.

  TechSmartParts.com

Prepare yourself for ASE testing with these questions on HEATING AND AIR CONDITIONING

NOTE: The following questions are written in the ASE style. They are similar to the kinds of questions that you will see on the ASE test, however, none of these questions will actually appear on the test.

1. Technician A says that evacuating an A/C system will remove air and moisture from the system. Technician B says that evacuating an A/C system will remove dirt particles from the system. Who is right?
   A. Technician A only
   B. Technician B only
   C. Both A and B
   D. Neither A or B

2. There is a growling or rumbling noise at the A/C compressor when the system is off and the engine is running. The noise stops when the system is turned on. Technician A says that a bad compressor bearing could be the cause. Technician B says that a bad compressor clutch bearing could be the cause. Who is right?
   A. Technician A only
   B. Technician B only
   C. Both A and B
   D. Neither A or B

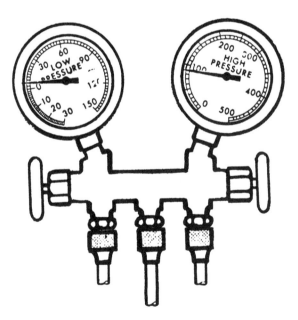

3. The readings shown above are taken with the A/C system operating at an ambient (outside) temperature of 85°F (29°C). What do the readings indicate?
   A. normal operation
   B. low refrigerant level
   C. a restriction in the high side
   D. damaged compressor

4. Recovery/recycling equipment must have shutoff valves located within 12-in. (30 cm) of the hoses' service ends so that:
   A. oil can be added to the refrigerant
   B. the unit can be isolated from the refrigerant source
   C. the filter can be changed without disconnecting the hoses
   D. refrigerant discharge can be kept to a minimum

5. When recovering refrigerant from an A/C system, how long should the technician wait after the recovery/recycling unit has been turned off to see if there is any residual pressure in the system?
   A. 1 minute
   B. 5 minutes
   C. 10 minutes
   D. 15 minutes

6. A system with a low pressure on the low side and a heavy frost accumulation on the inlet side of the Thermostatic Expansion Valve (TXV) indicates a:
   A. TXV stuck open
   B. clogged condenser
   C. defective compressor
   D. clogged screen or TXV stuck closed

7. A blower motor only works on high speed. Which of the following causes is the MOST LIKELY?
   A. defective blower relay
   B. defective blower resistor
   C. defective blower switch
   D. blown fuse or tripped circuit breaker

8. A customer complains that when accelerating his car with the A/C on, the cold air flow from the dash outlets shifts to the floor. Technician A says that this is caused by a faulty check valve in the vacuum reservoir. Technician B says that this condition is due to a vacuum leak. Who is right?
   A. Technician A only
   B. Technician B only
   C. Both A and B
   D. Neither A or B

Training for Certification

Prepare yourself for ASE testing with these questions on
HEATING AND AIR CONDITIONING

9. When pressure testing the cooling system on a late model gasoline engine vehicle, the pressure on the tester drops but no leaks can be found in the engine compartment. Technician A starts the engine and, seeing the pressure on the tester gauge increase, says that there is an internal leak, a blown head gasket. Technician B says that there cannot be an internal leak because the engine oil looks normal, not milky like it would be if coolant were present, and there is no white smoke coming from the exhaust pipe. Who is right?
   A. Technician A only
   B. Technician B only
   C. Both A and B
   D. Neither A or B

10. When identifying an A/C system, Technician A says that an accumulator located between the evaporator and compressor is an indication that the system has an orifice tube. Technician B says that when the high-side service port fitting is smaller than the one on the low side, the system uses R134a refrigerant. Who is right?
   A. Technician A only
   B. Technician B only
   C. Both A and B
   D. Neither A or B

11. When troubleshooting an ATC system, the system responds when the ambient and in-vehicle temperature sensors are heated and cooled. However, there is no response when the sunload sensor is exposed to a light source. Technician A says that the problem is with the system's programmer. Technician B says that the problem is with the sunload sensor. Who is right?
   A. Technician A only
   B. Technician B only
   C. Both A and B
   D. Neither A or B

12. The following are all methods of orifice tube replacement EXCEPT:
   A. Replace the line that incorporates the orifice tube.
   B. Disconnect the liquid line from the evaporator inlet line and pull the orifice tube straight out with an extractor tool.
   C. Disconnect the liquid line from the evaporator inlet line and, using a twisting motion to break free of the line, pull out the orifice tube with an extractor tool.
   D. Cut out the section of line containing the orifice tube and, using a kit, install a new orifice tube line segment.

13. Technician A say when there is a "U" DTC, it should be repaired before any further diagnostics can be performed. Technician B says "U" DTCs indicate there is nothing wrong with the AC system. Who is correct?
   A. Technician A only
   B. Technician B only
   C. Both Technician A and B
   D. Neither Technician A or B

14. A vehicle with R134a refrigerant in the A/C system has a refrigerant leak. Technician A says that a propane gas leak detector should be used to find the location of the leak. Technician B says that an electronic leak detector should be used to check for leaks. Who is right?
   A. Technician A only
   B. Technician B only
   C. Both A and B
   D. Neither A or B

15. Which of the following is a true statement regarding R134a refrigerant?
   A. It is harmful to the ozone layer.
   B. It mixes with mineral oil.
   C. It requires a different desiccant than R12.
   D. It operates at lower pressures than R12.

16. The compressor in an A/C system does not run. When a jumper wire is used to connect the battery positive terminal to the power connector, the compressor clutch engages. Technician A says that the clutch coil is defective. Technician B says that the pressure cycling switch could be defective. Who is right?
   A. Technician A only
   B. Technician B only
   C. Both A and B
   D. Neither A or B

17. The floor inside a vehicle is wet and there is a slimy film on the windows. Technician A says that the heater core is leaking. Technician B says that the evaporator case drain plug is clogged. Who is right?
   A. Technician A only
   B. Technician B only
   C. Both A and B
   D. Neither A or B

74   A7 - Heating And Air Conditioning

Prepare yourself for ASE testing with these questions on
HEATING AND AIR CONDITIONING

18. During A/C system operation, a knocking sound can be heard coming from the compressor. Technician A says that there could be internal compressor damage. Technician B says that the compressor mounting brackets and bushings should be checked. Who is right?
    A. Technician A only
    B. Technician B only
    C. Both A and B
    D. Neither A or B

19. All of the following could cause poor heater performance EXCEPT:
    A. defective temperature blend door actuator
    B. radiator coolant temperature below 150°F (66°C)
    C. heater core return hose much cooler than inlet hose
    D. stuck open heater control valve

20. During an A/C system performance test, the air temperature at the center outlet duct is warm to slightly cool and the low and high-side pressures on the manifold gauge set are both low. All of the following could be the cause of these symptoms EXCEPT:
    A. clogged orifice tube
    B. expansion valve stuck closed
    C. restricted receiver/drier
    D. plugged condenser

21. What is the minimum system pressure necessary to leak test with an electronic leak detector?
    A. 25 psi
    B. 50 psi
    C. 75 psi
    D. 100 psi

22. Observing the data stream while operating a HVAC system on a late model vehicle the counts for the blend door change when the vehicle is moved outside in the mid day sun. Technician A says there is an intermittent problem with the blend door actuator that will eventually set a DTC. Technician B says that under no circumstances should the counts change on the blend door motor. Who is correct?
    A. Technician A only
    B. Technician B only
    C. Both A and B
    D. Neither A or B

23. When diagnosing an ATC system, most of the system temperature sensors can be tested for:
    A. resistance and current flow
    B. resistance and voltage drop
    C. voltage drop and current flow
    D. current flow and continuity

24. During an A/C system performance test, high-side pressure was found to be excessive and the A/C compressor continued to run. Technician A says that the high-pressure cutout switch could be defective. Technician B says that there could be an air flow obstruction at the condenser. Who is right?
    A. Technician A only
    B. Technician B only
    C. Both A and B
    D. Neither A or B

25. The A/C compressor cycles rapidly, and air coming from the vents is only slightly cool. Technician A says the problem could be a low refrigerant charge. Technician B says the problem could be a defective thermostatic switch. Who is right?
    A. Technician A only
    B. Technician B only
    C. Both A and B
    D. Neither A or B

26. To properly evacuate an A/C system, the vacuum pump should be operated a minimum of:
    A. 5 minutes
    B. 10 minutes
    C. 20 minutes
    D. 30 minutes

27. Technician A says that a special tool is required to disconnect and connect spring lock fittings. Technician B says that new when assembling spring lock fittings, new O-rings lubricated with clean refrigerant oil should be used. Who is right?
    A. Technician A only
    B. Technician B only
    C. Both A and B
    D. Neither A or B

Training for Certification

Prepare yourself for ASE testing with these questions on
HEATING AND AIR CONDITIONING

28. All of the following are true statements concerning in-line filters EXCEPT:
    A. They are usually installed in a system that has suffered a compressor failure.
    B. They are installed to protect the new compressor from metal chips or other debris that could be in the system from the original compressor failure.
    C. They are installed to collect debris that could clog the orifice tube or expansion valve filters.
    D. Filters are only installed in the high side of the system.

29. Two technicians are discussing sight glass observations. Technician A says that if foam is seen in the sight glass, the refrigerant charge is low. Technician B says that if oil streaks are seen in the sight glass, the refrigerant charge is low. Who is right?
    A. Technician A only
    B. Technician B only
    C. Both A and B
    D. Neither A or B

30. Technician A says that moisture in an A/C system can freeze in the expansion valve and stop the system from cooling. Technician B says that moisture in the A/C system will react with R12 to form an acid that can cause corrosion. Who is right?
    A. Technician A only
    B. Technician B only
    C. Both A and B
    D. Neither A or B

31. Low heater output can be caused by all of the following EXCEPT:
    A. an engine low on coolant
    B. a stuck open cooling system thermostat
    C. a restricted heater control valve
    D. a disengaged clutch type radiator fan

32. The high-side pressure in an A/C system is above specifications. All of the following could cause this problem EXCEPT:
    A. an overcharge of refrigerant
    B. restricted air flow across the condenser
    C. a slipping fan belt
    D. a broken compressor reed valve

33. When filling a container with recycled refrigerant, to what percentage of the container's gross weight rating should it be filled?
    A. 50 percent
    B. 60 percent
    C. 70 percent
    D. 80 percent

34. A vacuum door actuator is being tested. When vacuum is applied with a hand held vacuum pump, the door does not move and the reading on the vacuum gauge is zero. Technician A says that the door does not move because it is binding or obstructed. Technician B says that the door does not move because the actuator is defective. Who is right?
    A. Technician A only
    B. Technician B only
    C. Both A and B
    D. Neither A or B

35. A customer complains of a foul odor coming from the dash outlets whenever the A/C and blower are on. Technician A says that this is caused by a clogged evaporator drain. Technician B says that this is caused by bacterial growth on the evaporator. Who is right?
    A. Technician A only
    B. Technician B only
    C. Both A and B
    D. Neither A or B

36. When an A/C system is operating, a clicking or buzzing noise is heard coming from the compressor. Technician A says that this noise means that the system is overcharged. Technician B says that the noise could be due to air in the system. Who is right?
    A. Technician A only
    B. Technician B only
    C. Both A and B
    D. Neither A or B

37. A customer complains that when parallel parking, his car repeatedly stalls, but only when the air conditioning is on. Technician A says that the power steering pressure switch is defective. Technician B says that there is a problem with the power steering pump. Who is right?
    A. Technician A only
    B. Technician B only
    C. Both A and B
    D. Neither A or B

Prepare yourself for ASE testing with these questions on
HEATING AND AIR CONDITIONING

38. All of the following are true statements about receiver/driers EXCEPT:
   A. They may have a sight glass located on the top.
   B. They store liquid refrigerant.
   C. They keep liquid refrigerant from entering the compressor.
   D. They contain a desiccant to absorb moisture from the system.

39. Technician A says that the pressure cycling switch is usually located on the accumulator. Technician B says that the refrigerant must be recovered from the system before the switch can be removed. Who is right?
   A. Technician A only
   B. Technician B only
   C. Both A and B
   D. Neither A or B

40. Technician A says that the A/C system can be charged through the high or low side only when the engine is not running. Technician B says that the A/C system can be charged though the low side when the engine is running. Who is right?
   A. Technician A only
   B. Technician B only
   C. Both A and B
   D. Neither A or B

41. An air conditioning check has uncovered a discharge in the system and compressor damage. Technician A says that after the repairs are made, to check the low-pressure cutoff switch. Technician B says lubricating oil is carried by the refrigerant through the system. Who is right?
   A. Technician A only
   B. Technician B only
   C. Both A and B
   D. Neither A or B

42. When checking recycled refrigerant for excess non-condensable gases (air), Technician A says that the container must be stored at 65°F (18°C) or above for 8 hours out of direct sunlight, before checking the pressure. Technician B says if the pressure is higher than the limit shown for a given temperature, there is air in the tank. Who is right?
   A. Technician A only
   B. Technician B only
   C. Both A and B
   D. Neither A or B

43. The operation of the thermostatic switch depends on the temperature of the:
   A. condenser
   B. compressor
   C. evaporator
   D. outside air

44. All of the following are causes for fan clutch replacement EXCEPT:
   A. oil film on the back of the clutch
   B. no viscous drag
   C. fan speed does not increase as engine warms up
   D. when engine is hot, fan stops spinning in only two seconds after shut down

45. Technician A says that an ambient temperature switch protects the compressor from damage. Technician B says that an ambient temperature sensor provides input for the Automatic Temperature Control (ATC) system. Who is right?
   A. Technician A only
   B. Technician B only
   C. Both A and B
   D. Neither A or B

46. If a capillary tube were to break at some point between its sensing bulb and the expansion valve, what affect would it have on the valve?
   A. The expansion valve would stick open.
   B. The expansion valve would stick closed.
   C. The expansion valve would stick in whatever position it was in at the time of the break.
   D. There would be no affect on the expansion valve.

Training for Certification

Prepare yourself for ASE testing with these questions on
HEATING AND AIR CONDITIONING

47. A customer has a complaint of poor heat output. After checking the hoses running from the heater core and finding them both to be hot, Technician A says the problem could be a clogged heater core. Technician B says a misadjusted temperature control cable could be the problem. Who is right?
   A. Technician A only
   B. Technician B only
   C. Both A and B
   D. Neither A or B

Refer to the statement below to answer the next question.

The sunload sensor is a 2 – wire photo diode. The vehicle uses two sunload sensors, left and right. They are built into the sunload sensor assembly along with the ambient light sensor. Low reference (ground) and signal circuits run to each sensor. As the brightness of the sun increases, the sensor signal level decreases. The sensor operates in a range between completely dark and very bright. The sensor signal between 0-5 volts goes into the HVAC module and is converted to between 0 and 255 counts. The sunload sensor tells the HVAC control module the amount of light shining on the vehicle. Bright or high intensity light causes the vehicles interior temperature to increase. The HVAC system compensates for the increased temperature by diverting additional cool air into the vehicle.

48. Technician A says to measure the Sunload Sensor Signal you must use a DVOM and measure its signal voltage changes. Technician B says to use a scan tool and observe the data stream to see the counts change when the light is varied to the sensor. Who is correct?

   A. Technician A only
   B. Technician B only
   C. Both Technician A and B
   D. Neither Technician A or B

49. During the diagnosis of an ATC system, a trouble code is obtained that references the blend door feedback sensor. Technician A says that the sensor should be replaced. Technician B says that the sensor circuit should be tested. Who is right?
   A. Technician A only
   B. Technician B only
   C. Both A and B
   D. Neither A or B

50. A major cause for the depletion of the ozone layer has been attributed to:
   A. carbon monoxide (CO) fumes from automotive exhaust
   B. unburned hydrocarbon (HC) emissions from automobile exhaust
   C. the release of chlorofluorocarbons (CFCs) into the atmosphere
   D. all of the above

51. Which of the following sensors is NOT an NTC thermistor?
   A. in-vehicle sensor
   B. ambient sensor
   C. sunload sensor
   D. engine coolant temperature sensor

52. A customer with an SATC equipped vehicle complains that the car does not get cool enough on hot days. Technician A says that the blend door actuator is probably malfunctioning. Technician B says that the programmer is the problem. Who is right?
   A. Technician A only
   B. Technician B only
   C. Both A and B
   D. Neither A or B

53. A compressor clutch will not engage. All of the following could be the cause EXCEPT:
   A. a closed high-pressure cutout switch
   B. low refrigerant level
   C. an open ambient temperature switch
   D. faulty compressor clutch coil

54. The inside of an EATC equipped vehicle never feels as cool as the temperature setting. The A/C system checks out OK, including the sensors. Technician A says there could be an obstruction in the aspirator tube. Technician B says the aspirator tube could be disconnected from the duct. Who is right?
   A. Technician A only
   B. Technician B only
   C. Both A and B
   D. Neither A or B

Prepare yourself for ASE testing with these questions on HEATING AND AIR CONDITIONING

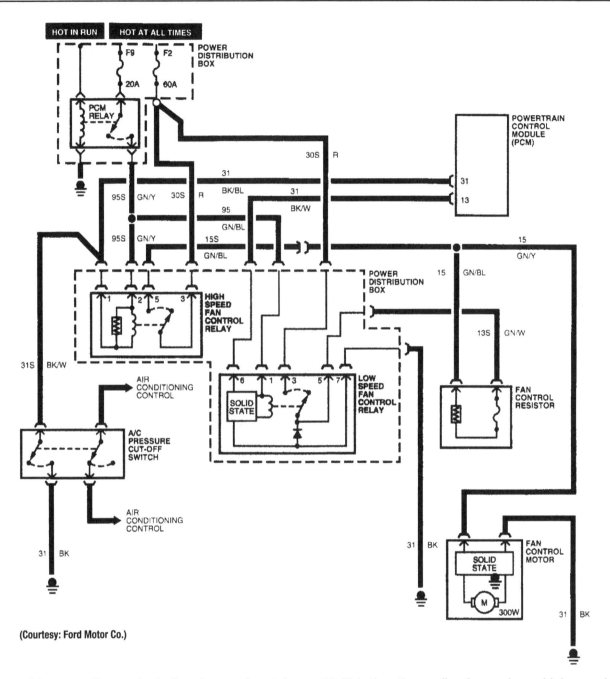

(Courtesy: Ford Motor Co.)

The next two questions refer to the above schematic.

55. The cooling fan works on low speed but not on high speed. Which of the following could be the cause?
    A. a faulty fan control resistor
    B. an open in circuit 95S between the 95/95S splice and the high speed relay
    C. a short to ground in circuit 95S between the 95/95S splice and the high speed relay
    D. a blown 60 amp fuse

56. This time the cooling fan works on high speed but not on low speed. All of the following are possible causes **EXCEPT**:
    A. a poor connection at the junction of circuit 13S and the power distribution box
    B. an open in circuit 30S
    C. a faulty fan control resistor
    D. an open in circuit 15 between the 15/15S splice and the fan motor.

Training for Certification

Prepare yourself for ASE testing with these questions on
HEATING AND AIR CONDITIONING

57. The ambient temperature sensor in an EATC system is being tested. Technician A says that the resistance of the sensor should increase as it is heated. Technician B says that, as the sensor resistance changes, the computer reads the change in voltage drop across the sensor. Who is right?
   A. Technician A only
   B. Technician B only
   C. Both A and B
   D. Neither A or B

58. At what percentage is refrigerant considered to be pure and safe for recovery?
   A. 90%
   B. 95%
   C. 98%
   D. 100%

59. All of the following could cause lower than normal high-side pressure **EXCEPT**:
   A. missing air dam
   B. low refrigerant charge
   C. worn compressor
   D. restricted orifice tube

60. Two Technicians are discussing an A/C system retrofit. Technician A says that a high-pressure cutout switch must be added to the system. Technician B says that the receiver/drier should be replaced. Who is right?
   A. Technician A only
   B. Technician B only
   C. Both A and B
   D. Neither A or B

61. A customer complains about a hissing noise coming from under the hood after turning off the car. A Technician says the noise is coming from the A/C system and is:
   A. a normal condition
   B. system pressures equalizing
   C. a refrigerant leak
   D. both A and B

62. A customer complains of low air flow through the instrument panel duct outlets. Which of the following could be the cause?
   A. faulty blower motor
   B. clogged passenger compartment air filter
   C. stuck mode door
   D. all of the above

63. All of the following are classifications of antifreeze **EXCEPT**:
   A. Inorganic Additive Technology (IAT)
   B. Organic Additive Technology (OAT)
   C. Hybrid Inorganic Additive Technology (HIAT)
   D. Hybrid Organic Additive Technology (HOAT)

64. Vehicles with Dual Zone climate control have a separate _____ for the passenger side of the vehicle.
   A. mode door
   B. blend door
   C. heater core
   D. evaporator core

65. When using an electronic refrigerant leak detector, all of the following should be observed **EXCEPT**:
   A. Leak detectors are very sensitive to many types of gases. If the area is contaminated with refrigerant or other gases, use a fan or compressed air to blow the excess refrigerant away.
   B. Pass the probe around the top of components and hoses as refrigerant is lighter than air and tends to rise.
   C. Don't move the probe faster than one inch per second.
   D. Never allow the probe to contact any surface, to prevent contamination of the sensing tip.

66. Technician A says that mineral deposits can restrict air flow through the radiator. Technician B says that internal restrictions in the radiator can be detected from the outside. Who is right?
   A. Technician A only
   B. Technician B only
   C. Both A and B
   D. Neither A or B

67. A typical refrigerant identifier can detect all of the following **EXCEPT**:
   A. R134a
   B. Hydrocarbons
   C. Air
   D. R744

Prepare yourself for ASE testing with these questions on
HEATING AND AIR CONDITIONING

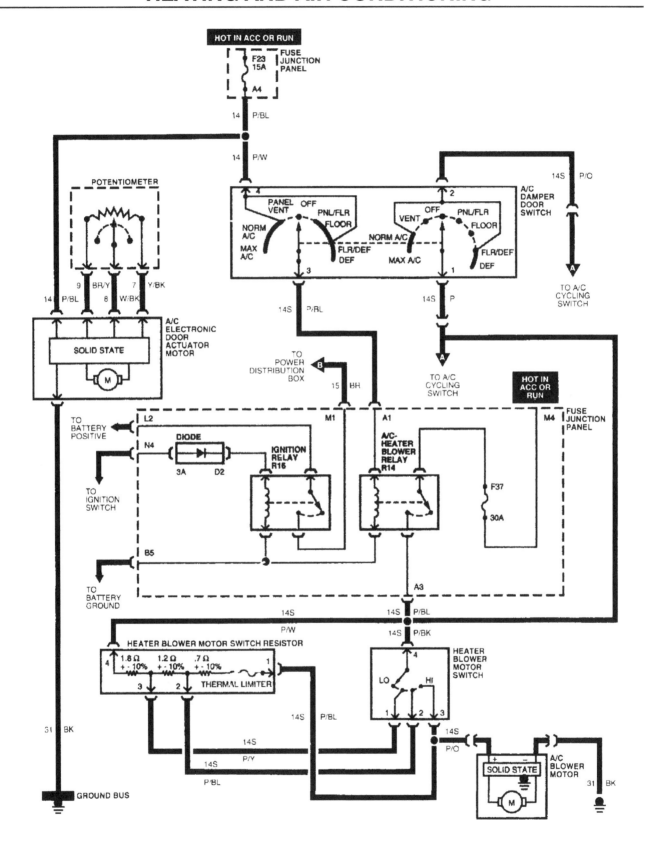

(Courtesy: Ford Motor Co.)

Prepare yourself for ASE testing with these questions on
HEATING AND AIR CONDITIONING

The following three questions refer to the schematic on the left:

68. The blower motor works on all speeds except low. Technician A says that this could be caused by an open in the 1.8-ohm resistor. Technician B says that this could be caused by an open in circuit 14S between the P/BL and P/O splice and the motor. Who is right?
    A. Technician A only
    B. Technician B only
    C. Both A and B
    D. Neither A or B

69. The blower motor only works on high. Which of the following could be the cause?
    A. an open thermal limiter
    B. a blown 30 amp fuse
    C. an open in circuit 31
    D. an open in the P/BK wire between the P/BL and P/BK splice and the blower switch

70. When the A/C damper door switch is placed in the MAX A/C position, the compressor clutch does not engage. However, a test light illuminates when placed at pin 1 of the A/C damper door switch. Which of the following could be the cause?
    A. an open in the P/BL wire of circuit 14S
    B. a faulty A/C damper door switch
    C. a blown 30 amp fuse
    D. a faulty A/C heater blower relay

71. A vehicle comes into the shop with a complaint of "no cold air". Technician A says to first turn the key off, set the DVOM to DC volts and measure the voltage present at the electromagnet clutch. If there is no voltage present, replace the compressor. Technician B says set the DVOM to DC volts and measure the continuity of the compressor clutch. Who is correct?
    A. Technician A only
    B. Technician B only
    C. Both Technician A and B
    D. Neither Technician A or B

72. When replacing a blend door actuator, Technician A says that after installing the actuator, the control module will automatically know what the step the actuator is on and there is no need for calibration. Technician B says that after replacing the actuator, one procedure for recalibrating the control module would be to remove the fuse for the module for at least 60 seconds, then replace the fuse and perform an operational test of the system. Who is correct?

A. Technician A only
B. Technician B only
C. Both Technician A and B
D. Neither Technician A or B.

73. Technician A says that any compressor that uses a belt is a belt-driven compressor and not a HV component. Technician B says that some hybrids use a combination belt/electric compressor. Who is correct?

A. Technician A
B. Technician B
C. Neither Technician A or B
D. Both Technician A and B

74. Technician A is finishing his repair on a hybrid HV electric compressor and is preparing to recharge the system using a service machine that is used to service all of the shop's customers cars. In the process, he introduces a small amount of PAG oil into the system. Knowing this, which of the following statements is NOT true about what Technician A should do next.

A. If the air conditioning compressor has not been engaged, he can replace the compressor and recharge using a service machine dedicated to hybrid service.
B. If the air conditioning compressor has been engaged, he will need to follow OEM procedure to remove the contaminated oil charge from the system.
C. There is no issue. PAG oil is approved for use in a HV air conditioning system.
D. The introduction of the PAG oil remaining in the service machine's internal lines and service hoses is enough to cause a HV insulation fault in the hybrid vehicle.

75. Technician A says that he can safely remove a HV A/C compressor without following any of the published OEM HV safety guidelines. Technician B says that in order to safely remove and replace a HV compressor a technician will need basic hybrid safety training, proper safety equipment and tooling (including protective gloves and voltmeter rated for use on hybrid systems) and will need to adhere to published OEM service procedures. Who is correct?

A. Technician A
B. Technician B
C. Neither Technician A or B
D. Both Technician A and B

82   A7 - Heating And Air Conditioning

Notes

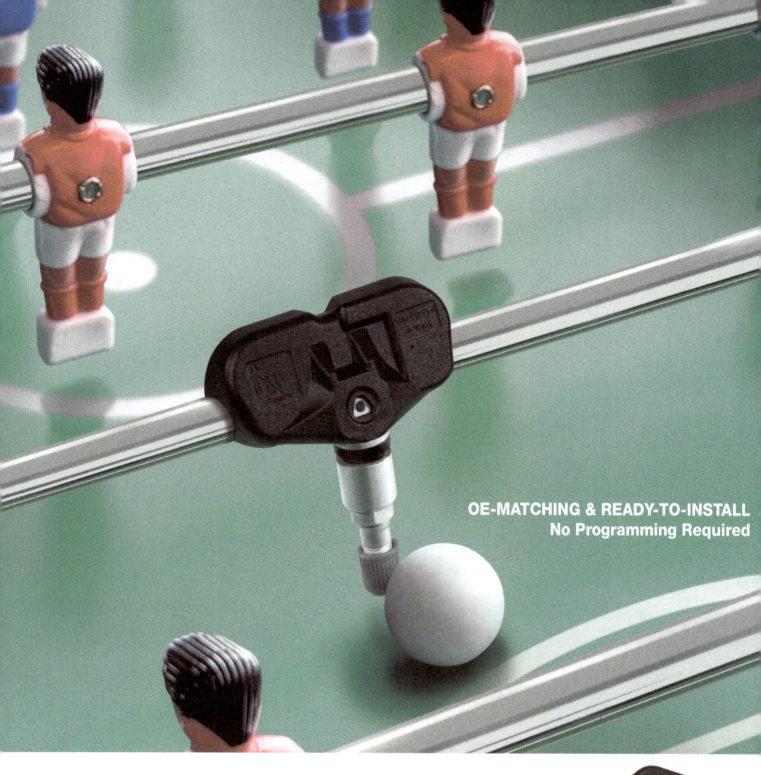

OE SENSOR REPLACEMENT – PERFECT
(FOOSBALL PLAYER REPLACEMENT – BAD CALL)

When your OE TPMS sensors fail, there's only one replacement brand you need to know: Standard®. With over 98% coverage and OE-matching, direct-fit TPMS sensors that can be OE-relearned or ID-cloned, Standard® is the perfect TPMS solution for you and your customers.

standardbrand.com

OE-MATCHING & READY-TO-INSTALL
No Programming Required

Answers to Study-Guide Test Questions

1. The correct answer is A. Evacuating an A/C system removes air and moisture from the system. The receiver/drier may contain a filter or strainer to catch and trap foreign particles and dirt, but this remains in the receiver/drier and is not removed during the evacuation procedure.

2. The correct answer is B. The compressor clutch bearing allows the rotor/pulley assembly to spin independently of the compressor shaft when the A/C system is off. When the engine is running and the A/C system is off, the compressor clutch bearing is spinning. When the A/C system is turned on, the rotor/pulley assembly and the armature are locked together by the magnetic action of the compressor clutch coil.

3. The correct answer is B. Low pressure on both the low side and the high side indicates a low refrigerant charge.

4. The correct answer is D. According to the Clean Air Act, recovery/recycling equipment must have shutoff valves located within 12-in. (30 cm) of the hoses' service ends so that refrigerant discharge to the atmosphere can be kept to a minimum.

5. The correct answer is B. The technician should wait five minutes and watch the gauges to see if there is any residual pressure. If there is, repeat the process to remove any remaining refrigerant until the A/C system holds a stable vacuum for at least five minutes.

6. The correct answer is D. A low pressure reading on the low side and a heavy frost accumulation on the inlet side of the TXV indicates a clogged screen at the expansion valve inlet or a TXV stuck closed.

7. The correct answer is B. Answer D is incorrect because if the blower fuse was blown or circuit breaker tripped, the blower would not work at all. Answer A is incorrect because a blower relay is generally only used for the high blower speed and this is working. Answer C, the blower switch is a possible cause but the most likely cause for operation on only high speed is that a portion of the resistor assembly is burned out.

8. The correct answer is C. If, during hard acceleration, air routing changes by itself, it's probably due to a leak in the system or a faulty check valve in the vacuum reservoir. A complaint that the mode shifts from the dash to the floor at wide-open throttle is evidence that the system isn't holding vacuum.

9. The correct answer is A. If the engine is started while pressure testing a cooling system and the pressure immediately increases, there could be a head gasket leak, but not into the crankcase. The coolant may be going out the tailpipe, but since this is a late model gasoline engine vehicle and equipped with a catalytic converter, there is no white smoke from the exhaust because the converter super-heats the coolant into such a fine vapor that it is not noticeable.

10. The correct answer is A. Systems using an expansion valve have a receiver/drier between the valve and condenser, while orifice tube systems have an accumulator between the evaporator and compressor. Technician B is wrong because on R134a systems, the low-side service port is the smaller one.

11. The correct answer is B. If the system reacts with a change to one or two inputs but not to the third, the problem is most likely confined to the single sensor or its circuit. But if no reaction is observed on any of the units, or only a partial reaction is seen, the problem is usually with the programmer.

12. The correct answer is C. When removing the orifice tube with an extractor tool, do not twist or rotate the orifice tube in the line as it can break. If an orifice tube breaks during removal, special tools are available to extract broken orifice tubes. All of the other answers are methods of orifice tube replacement.

13. The correct answer is A. A "U" DTC indicates there is a problem with the present modules not being able to communicate with each other. It is likely that the module responsible for generating a DTC for the AC problem can't report the problem until it is able to communicate on the network. Repair the "U" DTC first then rescan for any present DTCs.

Answers to Study-Guide Test Questions

14. The correct answer is B. Technician A is wrong because propane gas leak detectors cannot detect R134a. Technician B is right, but he must make sure the electronic leak detector is designed for R134a, as many older units are not.

15. The correct answer is C. Desiccants are not universal and different types must be used with different refrigerants and lubricating oils. When a system is retrofitted, the replacement receiver/drier or accumulator has XH-7 or XH-9 desiccant.

16. The correct answer is B. Technician A is wrong because if the clutch coil was defective, the compressor clutch would not engage. Technician B is correct because, since the compressor clutch engages when 12 volts is directly applied, the problem is in the compressor control circuit, which includes the pressure cycling switch.

17. The correct answer is A. Fogged windows that smear when wiped and moisture on the passenger floor are telltale signs of a leaking heater core. Technician B is incorrect because, while a clogged evaporator case drain could cause the case to fill up with moisture and spill out onto the floor, it would not cause a slimy film on the windows.

18. The correct answer is C. Knocking noises from the compressor usually indicate internal damage, especially on piston-type compressors. However, always check the compressor mounting and brackets before condemning the compressor for noise. A loose mounting can cause knocking noises from the compressor area that may be mistaken for internal compressor noise.

19. The correct answer is D. A stuck open heater control valve could cause problems when heat is not wanted, but because coolant flow to the heater core is not interrupted, the heater valve would not cause poor heater performance. A defective temperature blend door actuator could cause poor heat if the blend door was stuck in the wrong position. Radiator coolant temperature below 150°F (66°C) would indicate a missing or stuck open thermostat, which could also cause poor heater performance. A heater core return hose that is much cooler than the inlet hose means that the heater core is plugged or air bound, also causing poor heat.

20. The correct answer is D. Although the air temperature at the center outlet would be about the same, if the condenser is plugged, the manifold gauge readings would be high. All of the other answers are possible causes for the symptoms in the question.

21. The correct answer is B. There must be at least 50 psi of refrigerant pressure in the system in order for a leak detector to be able to sense a leak. Refrigerant may have to be added to the system to achieve this.

22. The correct answer is D. The blend door motor counts change as the position of the door is changed. This is it's normal operation. The easiest was to determine the blend door is functions is to read the data stream from the scan tool while observing the system's operation.

23. The correct answer is B. Most temperature sensors can be tested for resistance and voltage drop. In general, the sensor should be replaced if its resistance is not within specification. Since a temperature sensor's resistance varies with temperature, check the sensor voltage against temperature and compare to manufacturer's specifications.

24. The correct answer is C. Technician A is correct because the high-pressure cutout switch should break the circuit to the compressor clutch if it detects pressures above a preset level. If the compressor continues to run when pressure passes the threshold of the switch calibration, the switch is defective. Technician B is also right because an obstruction to air flow through the condenser can cause excessive high-side pressure.

25. The correct answer is C. During operation, the clutch may cycle on and off several times each minute. Insufficient refrigerant causes rapid change in heat load on the evaporator, which affects system pressures. If the clutch cycles rapidly, it may be a sign of low refrigerant charge. A defective thermostatic switch may not be engaging the compressor clutch long enough. The thermostatic switch has a capillary tube attached to the evaporator outlet or inserted between the evaporator core fins to sense the temperature. This capillary is attached to a switch that opens and closes, as necessary, to cycle the compressor.

Answers to Study-Guide Test Questions

26. The correct answer is D. To properly evacuate an A/C system, the vacuum pump should be operated for a minimum of 30 minutes.

27. The correct answer is B. Technician A is wrong because a special tool is only required to disconnect spring lock fittings.

28. The correct answer is D. There are filters that fit into both the high and low sides of the system. All of the other statements ate true concerning in-line filters.

29. The correct answer is C. If there is foam, the charge is low, but if there are only a couple of bubbles, it is probably OK. A few bubbles when the compressor cycles on is normal. Oil streaks in the sight glass usually indicate a low charge and that the compressor is pumping oil from its sump.

30. The correct answer is C. Moisture in the A/C system can ice up in the expansion valve and block refrigerant flow. On systems with R12, moisture can combine with the chlorine in the R12 to form hydrochloric acid. These chemicals can corrode metals and attack rubber parts.

31. The correct answer is D. A disengaged clutch type radiator fan would not cause low heater output. All of the other answers are possible causes of low heater output.

32. The correct answer is D. A broken compressor reed valve could not cause the high-side pressure to be above specifications.

33. The correct answer is B. To prevent overfilling during transfer of refrigerant, never fill a container to more than 60 percent of its gross weight rating.

34. The correct answer is B. Regardless of what condition the door is in, the key here is that the gauge reading is zero, meaning there is a vacuum leak in the actuator.

35. The correct answer is C. If the drain at the bottom of the evaporator case becomes clogged and water collects and stagnates, or if the surface of the evaporator remains too moist due to high humidity, bacteria can grow in the stagnant water or on the evaporator surface and cause an odor. This odor is then sent into the passenger compartment by the blower motor.

36. The correct answer is C. A clicking or buzzing noise coming from the compressor is a sign that the system is overcharged and liquid refrigerant is entering the compressor. Unless some refrigerant is removed, severe compressor damage may result. This noise could also result from air in the system.

37. The correct answer is A. The power steering pressure switch is installed in the power steering system and reports on high pressure conditions caused by a load being placed on the engine by the power steering pump. The computer may decide to temporarily shut down the compressor to prevent engine stalling or low idle speed, or it could also raise idle speed through control of an idle speed control device. During parallel parking maneuvers, the steering wheel is most likely being moved to full lock at some point, increasing pressure. Technician A is right because, if this increased pressure is not being communicated to the computer by the switch, the A/C compressor will continue to run with its load on the engine or the idle speed will not be raised enough to keep the engine from stalling. Technician B is wrong because if the problem was with the power steering pump, the stalling would occur regardless of whether the A/C was on.

38. The correct answer is C. The receiver/drier is located in the high side of the system, between the condenser and evaporator, ahead of the expansion valve. It stores liquid refrigerant until needed by the evaporator. The accumulator is the component that keeps liquid refrigerant from entering the compressor, but accumulators are used in systems with orifice tubes, not expansion valves.

39. The correct answer is A. The pressure cycling switch senses the low-side pressure near the evaporator outlet and is usually found on the accumulator. Technician B is wrong because the switch is often mounted in a Schrader fitting so it can be replaced without the loss of refrigerant.

Training for Certification

87

Answers to Study-Guide Test Questions

40. The correct answer is C. Charging the system can be performed through either the high side or low side when the engine is not running, but must be done only through the low side when the engine is running. This safety measure prevents high-side pressure from entering the refrigerant container and possibly causing an explosion.

41. The correct answer is C. The purpose of the low-pressure cutoff switch is compressor protection. The compressor clutch circuit is opened if the pressure in the system drops too low. This would be an indication that the system has lost some or all of its refrigerant charge. Since the lubricating oil is carried by the refrigerant, a loss could cause damage to the compressor if it were allowed to operate without sufficient lubrication.

42. The correct answer is B. To purge the air, connect the tank to the recovery/recycling machine and slowly vent the air vapor from the top of the container. Continue venting until the pressure falls below the limit shown on your chart. If the pressure inside the container still exceeds the pressure limit shown, recycle the entire contents. Technician A is wrong because the container must be stored for 12 hours, not eight.

43. The correct answer is C. The thermostatic switch, which is used to cycle the A/C compressor on and off, depends on the temperature of the evaporator in order to operate.

44. The correct answer is D. A properly operating clutch should stop the fan from spinning within two seconds after a hot engine shut down. All of the other answers are indications of a defective fan clutch.

45. The correct answer is C. In non-ATC systems, the function of the ambient temperature switch is to inhibit compressor clutch operation in cold ambient temperatures. This function mainly protects the compressor from poor or no lubrication, which could be the result of cold refrigerant oil. In ATC systems, the ambient temperature sensor senses ambient outside temperature. As ambient or interior temperatures stray, the sensors pick up the change and the system adjusts the outlet duct temperature accordingly to compensate for the temperature changes.

46. The correct answer is B. Expansion valves are usually spring loaded devices with a diaphragm that is linked to a plunger. Without any pressure against the diaphragm from the gas in the capillary tube, the spring inside the expansion valve would cause the valve to stick closed.

47. The correct answer is B. If both hoses leading to the heater core are hot, coolant is circulating through the heater core. One hose that is significantly cooler than the other would indicate a clogged heater core. However, if the temperature control cable is incorrectly adjusted, the temperature blend door may not allow enough warm air to enter the passenger compartment for sufficient heating.

48. The correct answer is C. The signal can be measured from the Sunload sensor itself be taping into the signal wire coming from the sensor, but it is very hard to do that. The easier way is the use the scan tool and read the input changes in counts as you vary the light being applied to the sensor. However if you are repairing a code, you would go through this procedure to ensure the sensor and circuit is working.

49. The correct answer is B. Fault codes usually only indicate which circuit the problem is in; they don't necessarily indicate which component in the circuit has failed. The problem could be caused by a loose connection, improper modification, or a broken wire, so perform a thorough inspection when diagnosing a malfunction. Ensure that all grounds are clean and making good contact. If basic mechanical and electrical checks fail to locate the problem, follow manufacturer's electronic system test procedures.

50. The correct answer is C. The release of CFCs into the atmosphere has been found to be a major cause of ozone layer depletion.

51. The correct answer is C. The sunload sensor is a photovoltaic diode. All of the other sensors listed are NTC thermistors.

Answers to Study-Guide Test Questions

52. The correct answer is D, neither technician is right. Both technicians are jumping to conclusions. To a find the problem, a logical diagnostic procedure must be followed or parts may be replaced unnecessarily. This includes performing a preliminary inspection of the A/C system and checking refrigerant pressures before condemning any part of the ATC system.

53. The correct answer is A. The high-pressure cutout switch is normally closed. It opens the compressor clutch circuit when high-side pressures are excessive in order to protect the compressor. All of the other answers would cause the compressor clutch not to engage.

54. The correct answer is C, both technicians are right. The in-vehicle temperature sensor is located in the aspirator, which is located in the dashboard. The aspirator tube is connected to a heater-A/C duct. The air flowing in the duct past the tube creates a vacuum, drawing in-vehicle air past the sensor. If there is an obstruction in the aspirator tube or the tube is disconnected from the duct, air will not be drawn past the in-vehicle temperature sensor and the sensor will not be able to accurately measure the temperature inside the vehicle. This could account for the discrepancy between the temperature setting and the actual temperature inside the vehicle.

55. The correct answer is B. Answer A is wrong because the fan control resistor does not affect high-speed fan operation. Answer C is wrong because a short to ground here will blow the 20-amp fuse and neither fan will work. Answer D is wrong because if the 60-amp fuse is blown, neither fan will work..

56. The correct answer is D. If there is an open in circuit 15 between the 15/15S splice and the fan motor, the motor will not run at all. All of the other answers are possible causes for no low speed blower motor operation.

57. The correct answer is B. The ambient temperature sensor is an NTC (Negative Temperature Coefficient) thermistor. When an NTC thermistor is heated, the resistance should drop, and when it is cooled, resistance should increase.

58. The correct answer is C. Refrigerant is considered pure and safe for recovery if it is at least 98% by weight of a single type of refrigerant. If the refrigerant in the system is less than 98% pure, it should be considered contaminated and reclaimed or destroyed.

59. The correct answer is A. A lower than normal refrigerant charge and excessive internal wear would both cause the compressor to develop less discharge pressure. A restricted orifice tube would cause refrigerant flow through the system to be slowed. When the refrigerant spends more time in the evaporator, its temperature and pressure are slightly reduced. A missing air dam would cause an air flow problem through the condenser and the radiator. The reduced air flow and possible engine overheating would both cause higher than normal high side pressure.

60. The correct answer is C. If it does not have one, a high-pressure cutout switch must be added to the system to stop compressor operation before high-side pressure reaches the point of opening the high-pressure relief valve and releasing refrigerant into the atmosphere. The receiver/drier should be replaced because all refrigerants do not use the same type of desiccant. R134a systems use XH-7 or XH-9 desiccant.

61. The correct answer is D. The hissing noise is normal and caused by high-side pressure going through the refrigerant metering device as system pressures equalize.

62. The correct answer is D. A blower motor that does not run on high speed or higher speeds due to a defective relay or resistor would cause reduced air flow. A clogged passenger compartment air filter would create an obstruction and also reduce air flow. Finally, a mode door stuck between two positions would create the impression of reduced air flow because the available air would be routed to two places (i.e., the floor and the dash) instead of one.

63. The correct answer is C. Inorganic Additive Technology (IAT) antifreeze uses inorganic phosphates and silicates to provide corrosion protection. Organic Additive Technology (OAT) antifreeze uses organic acids to protect then iron and aluminum in the cooling system. Hybrid Organic Additive Technology (HOAT) antifreeze uses both silicate and organic acid corrosion inhibitors for extended service life.

Training for Certification

Answers to Study-Guide Test Questions

64. The correct answer is B. Vehicles with Dual Zone climate control have a separate blend door for the passenger side. The passenger can adjust a separate temperature control, which in turn controls the blend door and the amount of air flowing through the heater core for the passenger side of the vehicle.

65. The correct answer is B. Make sure that you pass the probe around the bottom of components and hoses as refrigerant is heavier than air and tends to settle.

66. The correct answer is B. Technician A is wrong because mineral deposits can restrict coolant flow inside the radiator, not air flow through the radiator. Look inside the radiator for large amounts of mineral deposits at the ends of the core tubes. Technician B is right because an infrared surface thermometer can be used to scan the surface of the radiator. With the engine hot and idling, the radiator should be warmest near the inlet and gradually cool toward the outlet. If there are areas that are considerably cooler than the inlet, then there may be restrictions at those areas.

67. The correct answer is D. Systems that use R744 refrigerant, which is pure CO_2, are still under development. Typical refrigerant identifiers that are currently available can detect R12, R134a, R22, air and hydrocarbons.

68. The correct answer is A. Technician B is wrong because if there is an open between the P/BL and P/O splice and the motor, the motor will not run at all.

69. The correct answer is A. An open thermal limiter would prevent the blower motor from working on any speed but high. The other answers are incorrect because any of these causes would prevent the blower motor from working at all.

70. The correct answer is B. A faulty A/C damper door switch or a problem in the circuit between the switch and the A/C clutch cycling switch could be the problem. Since the test light showed that there is power going to the A/C damper door switch, all of the other components listed are OK.

71. The correct answer is D. In the case of Technician A, in order to measure voltage present at the compressor clutch, the key must be turned on, AC set to a cold AC position and the engine should be running. If there is no voltage present, it would mean there is a problem with the circuit leading to the compressor clutch coil. In the case of Technician B, in order to measure the compressor clutch continuity, the DVOM would need to be set to the Ohm position not the DC volt position.

72. The correct answer is B. On some Automatic AC systems the Body Control Module/HVAC module will automatically control the actuator and position it within limits for normal operation when the module is reset by removing its power for more than 60 seconds.

73. Answer B is correct. Many Honda models use a compressor that is both belt driven and electrically driven. The HV portion of the compressor is used to maintain occupant comfort when the engine goes into "Idle Stop" mode.

74. Answer C is correct (not true). Even a minute amount of PAG oil introduced into a HV system can be enough to cause a HV insulation fault. If the compressor has run, and allowed to pump that contaminated oil through the entire system, it may be necessary to replace all the system components in order to correct the problem.

75. Technician B is correct. Failure to follow hybrid safety procedures could result in personal injury or damage to expensive HV components. At a minimum, a technician will need to isolate the HV battery source while wearing protective rubber gloves rated "OO" (1000 volts) which in turn are protected by leather linesmen's gloves. A CAT III rated voltmeter may also be needed to safely check that any HV voltage remaining at the compressor connector has dissipated to a safe level.

Notes

Notes

Glossary of Terms

--a--

accumulator - a component used to store or hold liquid refrigerant in an air conditioning system that also contains a desiccant.

actuator - a control device that delivers mechanical action in response to a vacuum or electrical signal.

air conditioning (A/C) - a system that cools and dehumidifies the air entering the passenger compartment of a vehicle.

air ducts - tubes, channels or other tubular structures used to carry air to a specific location.

air gap - the space or gap between the compressor drive hub and pulley assembly.

ambient temperature - the temperature of the air surrounding an object.

ambient temperature switch - a switch that prevents air conditioner operation below a certain ambient temperature.

amplifier - a circuit or device used to increase the voltage or current of a signal.

antifreeze - a material such as ethylene glycol which is added to water to lower its freezing point; used in an automobile's cooling system.

atmospheric pressure - the weight of the air at sea level (14.7 lbs. per sq. in.) or at higher altitudes.

automatic temperature control (ATC) system - a climate control system that uses the heating and air conditioning systems to maintain the interior temperature selected by the vehicle's passengers.

axial - having the same direction or being parallel to the axis or rotation.

--b--

blend door - a door in the heating and air conditioning system that controls the temperature of the air going into the passenger compartment.

blower motor - the electric motor, which drives the fan that circulates air inside the vehicle passenger compartment.

boiling point - the temperature at which a liquid turns to vapor.

British Thermal Unit (BTU) - a unit of measurement; the amount of heat that is required to raise the temperature of one pound of water by one degree F.

--c--

capillary tube - a thin, gas-filled tube that senses the temperature of the evaporator and relays this information to the thermostat and/or expansion valve.

Celsius - the basis of the metric system of temperature measurement in which water's boiling point is 100°C and its freezing point is 0°C.

charge - to fill, or bring up to the specific level, an A/C system with refrigerant; the required amount of refrigerant for an A/C system.

chlorofluorocarbon (CFC) - any organic chemical compounds made up of carbon, chlorine and fluorine atoms, usually used in refrigeration. R12 is a CFC.

clutch cycling switch - a device that opens and closes the circuit that engages the air conditioning compressor clutch based on pressure or temperature.

compressor - an engine driven device that compresses refrigerant gas and pumps it through the air conditioning system.

condensation - the process of a vapor becoming a liquid; the opposite of evaporation

condense - to cool a vapor to below its boiling point, where it then condenses into a liquid

condenser - a device, similar to a radiator, in which the refrigerant loses heat and changes state from a high-pressure gas to a high-pressure liquid as it dissipates heat to the surrounding air.

coolant - a mixture of water and ethylene glycol based antifreeze that circulates through the engine to help maintain proper temperatures

cooling fan - a mechanically or electrically driven propeller that draws air through the radiator.

Training for Certification

Glossary of Terms

cooling system - the system used to remove excess heat from an engine and transfer it to the atmosphere. Includes the radiator, cooling fan, hoses, water pump, thermostat and engine coolant passages.

core - in automotive terminology, the main part of a heat exchanger, such as a radiator, evaporator or heater. Usually made of tubes, surrounded by cooling fins, used to transfer heat from the coolant to the air.

corrosion - the eating into or wearing away of a substance gradually by rusting or chemical action.

crossflow radiator - a radiator in which coolant enters on one side, travels through tubes, and collects on the opposite side (see downflow radiator).

cycling clutch system - an A/C system that controls temperature by switching the compressor clutch on-and-off.

--d--

deflection - a turning aside, bending or deviation; bending or movement away from the normal position due to loading.

degree - used to designate temperature readings or 1 degree as a 1/360 part of a circle.

dehumidify - to remove moisture (humidity) from the air.

desiccant - any hygroscopic material that removes and traps moisture, usually found in a bag in the accumulator or receiver/drier in air conditioning systems.

diagnostic trouble code (DTC) - a code that represents and can be used to identify a malfunction in a computer control system.

diaphragm - a flexible, impermeable membrane on which pressure acts to produce mechanical movement.

diode - a simple semiconductor device that permits flow of electricity in one direction but not the other.

discharge - to remove the refrigerant from an air conditioning system.

displacement - the volume the cylinder holds between the top dead center and bottom dead center positions of the piston.

downflow radiator - a radiator in which coolant enters the top of the radiator and is drawn downward by gravity (see crossflow radiator).

--e--

electromagnet - a magnet formed by electrical flow through a conductor.

electromagnetic induction - moving a wire through a magnetic field to create current flow in the wire.

electromechanical - refers to a device that incorporates both electrical and mechanical principles together in its operation.

electronic - pertaining to the control of systems or devices by the use of small electrical signals and various semiconductor devices and circuits.

electronic control module (ECM) - the computer in an electronic control system, also known as an electronic control unit (ECU).

engine coolant temperature (ECT) sensor - a sensor, which works by a negative coefficient thermistor, that loses resistance as its temperature goes up (just like the intake air temperature sensor). When the computer applies its 5-volt reference signal to the sensor, this voltage is reduced through a ground circuit by an amount corresponding to the temperature of the engine coolant.

evacuate - the process of applying vacuum to a closed refrigeration system to remove air and moisture.

evaporation - the process through which a liquid is turned into vapor.

evaporator - a heat exchanger, in which low-pressure refrigerant flows and changes state, absorbing heat from the surrounding air.

--f--

Fahrenheit - a scale of temperature measurement with the boiling point of water at 212°F. In the metric system, water's boiling point is 100°Celsius.

Glossary of Terms

fan - a mechanically or electrically driven propeller that draws or pushes air through the radiator, condenser, heater core or evaporator core.

fan clutch - a device attached to a mechanically driven cooling fan that allows the fan to freewheel when the engine is cold or the vehicle is driven at speed.

fan shroud - an enclosure that routes air through the radiator cooling fins.

Freon - Dupont registered trade name for R12 refrigerant (dichlorodifluoromethane).

--*g*--

gauge set - the set of gauges that attaches to the high and low side of the A/C system and used for diagnosis. Also called a manifold gauge set.

ground - the negatively charged side of a circuit. A ground can be a wire, the negative side of the battery or the vehicle chassis.

--*h*--

head pressure - the pressure of the refrigerant at the compressor outlet.

heater core - a radiator-like device used to heat the inside of a vehicle. Hot coolant is pumped through it by the water pump, and heat from the coolant moves from the heater core to the passenger compartment as the blower fan forces air through it.

high side - the high-pressure half of an A/C system, usually refers to all components between the compressor outlet and the expansion valve or orifice tube.

--*l*--

latent heat of condensation - the amount of heat given off as a vapor changes state from a gas to a liquid without the temperature changing.

latent heat of evaporation - the amount of heat needed for a liquid to change state to a vapor without the temperature changing.

leak detector - a tool used to locate refrigerant leaks.

liquid line - the tube and/or hose leading from the outlet of the condenser to the expansion valve or orifice tube.

low side - the suction side of an A/C system between the evaporator core inlet (after the expansion valve or orifice tube) and the compressor.

lubrication - reducing friction between moving parts.

--*m*--

magnet - any body with the property of attracting iron or steel.

magnetic field - the areas surrounding the poles of a magnet, which are affected by its forces of attraction or repulsion.

microprocessor - the portion of a microcomputer that receives sensor input and handles all calculations.

multimeter - a tool that combines the functions of a voltmeter, ohmmeter and ammeter together in one diagnostic instrument.

--*n*--

negative temperature coefficient thermistor - a thermistor that loses electrical resistance as it gets warmer. The temperature sensors for the computer control system are negative temperature coefficient thermistors. The effect is to systematically lower the 5-volt reference voltage sent them by the computer, yielding a signal that corresponds to the temperature of the measured source. Typically the ECT and IAT sensors use this principle.

--*o*--

ohm - a unit of measured electrical resistance.

open circuit - electrical circuit that has an intentional (switch) or unintentional (bad connection) break in the wire.

orifice - a precisely sized hole that controls the flow of fluid.

Training for Certification

Glossary of Terms

orifice tube - used in some air conditioning systems, a component with a fixed opening through which refrigerant passes as it is metered into the evaporator core.

--*p*--

polyalkyline glycol (PAG) oil - lubricant used with A/C systems containing R-134a refrigerant.

pressure - the exertion of force upon a body. Pressure is developed within the cooling or A/C system and is measured in pounds per square inch on a gauge.

psi - measurement of pressure in pounds per square inch.

--*r*--

R12 - the generic term for CFC refrigerant used in older A/C systems. Also called Freon.

R134a - generic term for a modern refrigerant that does not contain CFCs and does not harm the ozone layer.

radiator - the part of the cooling system that acts as a heat exchanger, transferring heat to atmosphere. It consists of a core and holding tanks connected to the cooling system by hoses.

radiator cap - a device that seals the radiator and maintains a set pressure in the cooling system.

receiver/drier - an A/C system component into which high-pressure liquid refrigerant flows and is temporarily stored and dehydrated, usually located between the condenser outlet and expansion valve.

reclaim - to send refrigerant to an off-site facility where it is restored to its original purity so that it may be reused.

reciprocating - an up-and-down or back-and-forth motion.

recover - to remove refrigerant from a system and store it temporarily.

recycle - to remove contaminants such as moisture, particulates, etc. from refrigerant and re-introduce it into the A/C system.

refrigerant - a chemical compound used in an A/C system to remove heat from the evaporator and transfer it to the condenser.

refrigerant cycle - the complete loop or circuit that refrigerant passes through as it changes state from a vapor, to a liquid, then back to a vapor.

refrigerant oil - either a mineral or synthetic oil designed specifically for A/C systems.

relay - an electromagnetic switch that uses low amperage current to control a circuit with high amperage.

residual pressure - remaining or leftover pressure.

residue - surplus; what remains after a separation.

resistance - the opposition offered by a substance or body to the passage of electric current through it.

retrofit - to convert an older A/C system that used R12 to use R134a refrigerant, usually by replacing various components.

rotary - refers to a circular motion.

--*s*--

Schrader valve - a spring operated valve used to open and close the service outlets in an A/C system. They are the service valves used to attach manifold gauges and to charge or evacuate the system.

serpentine belt - multiple ribbed belts that wrap around and drive various engine mounted components.

service port - any of the various designs of fittings that allow service tools such as manifold gauges to be attached to an A/C system. See also Schrader valve.

servo - a device, such as an electric motor or hydraulic piston that is controlled by an amplified signal from a low power command device.

sight glass - a window in the high-pressure side of the A/C system, usually in the receiver/drier, to observe the refrigerant for signs of bubbles and/or moisture.

slip - condition caused when a driving part rotates faster than a driven part.

Glossary of Terms

suction - suction exists in a vessel when the pressure is lower than the atmospheric pressure.

suction line - the low-side tube and/or hose leading from the evaporator core outlet to the compressor inlet.

superheat - the addition of more heat to a gas after it has already vaporized; the heat added to vaporized refrigerant after it has changed state from a liquid to a gas.

superheat switch - a switch, usually mounted on the compressor on certain A/C systems, which completes the circuit to the thermal limiter switch.

--t--

technical service bulletin (TSB) - information published by vehicle manufacturers that describe updated service procedures that should be used to handle vehicle defects.

tension - effort that elongates or stretches material.

thermal limiter - a component, similar to a fuse, which blows to open the compressor clutch circuit when the superheat switch detects low A/C system pressure.

thermistor - a temperature sensitive variable resistor in which the resistance decreases as its temperature increases.

thermostat - a device installed in the cooling system that allows the engine to come to operating temperature quickly and then maintains a minimum operating temperature.

thermostatic expansion valve (TXV) - used on some air conditioning systems, a temperature sensitive device that meters the flow of refrigerant into the evaporator core. Also called an expansion valve.

--v--

vapor - a substance in a gaseous state. Liquid becomes vapor when brought above the boiling point.

volt - a unit of measurement of electromotive force. One volt of electromotive force applied steadily to a conductor of one-ohm resistance produces a current of one ampere.

voltage drop - voltage lost by the passage of electrical current through resistance.

voltmeter - a tool used to measure the voltage available at any point in an electrical system.

--w--

water pump - device used to circulate coolant through the engine.

water valve - a device used to control the flow of hot coolant to the heater core, operated by cable, vacuum or electrically.

Training for Certification

Notes

The Parent Partnership Toolkit for Early Years

Pat Brunton
and
Linda Thornton

© Pat Brunton and Linda Thornton 2010

ISBN: 978-1-905538-69-0

A catalogue record for this book is available from the British Library.

All rights reserved. No part of this publication may be reproduced, stored in a retrieval system, copied or transmitted without written permission from the publisher except that the materials may be photocopied for use within the purchasing institution only.

Edited by Giles Flitney

Designed by Lorraine Gourlay and Tom Kington

Printed in China by 1010 Printing

Published by Optimus Education, a division of Optimus Professional Publishing Limited.
Registered office: 33-41 Dallington Street, London EC1V 0BB.
Registered number: 05791519
Tel: 0845 450 6406
Fax:0845 450 6410

www.optimus-education.com

Contents

Introduction	1

Section 1

Introduction	3
Research evidence	3
Government policy	4
Training for practitioners to support parental engagement	8

Section 2

Introduction	13
Parental responsibility	13
Maintaining parents' confidentiality	14
How to engage families	15
Structure of Section 2	15
2.1 Establishing the vision and values	19
2.2 Creating a welcoming environment	37
2.3 Listening to parents	49
2.4 Communicating with parents	77
2.5 Key person working	95
2.6 Supporting parent-child relationships	113
2.7 Auditing your provision	129

Section 3

Introduction	135
Structure of Section 3	135
3.1 Creating links with home	139
3.2 Using collections of everyday things	153
3.3 Out and about	167
3.4 Family workshops – exploring together	181
3.5 Family members as visitors to your setting	209
3.6 The value of play	217

THE PARENT PARTNERSHIP TOOLKIT FOR EARLY YEARS

Introduction

The Parent Partnership Toolkit for Early Years is a resource to help early years practitioners to develop strong, positive relationships with the families who use their setting. The resource has been put together to:

- recognise the contribution that effective parent partnership can make to high-quality early years services and good outcomes for children and families

- support the belief that 'all parents are interested in the development and progress of their own children' and that the role of practitioners is to find ways of overcoming the barriers that may prevent parents from expressing this interest effectively (Whalley et al, 2007)

- underpin a model of parent partnership in which practitioners make consistent efforts to engage and involve parents in all aspects of their children's development, aware of the need to refine and adapt services to the needs and aspirations of the individual families with whom they are working (Robins and Callan, 2009).

The resource is organised into three sections:

Section 1 takes a strategic view of parent partnership. It looks at the context in which the emphasis on partnership with parents is developing. It reviews the research evidence, summarises government policy in this area and looks at initiatives to develop the skills of early years practitioners in working with parents.

Section 2 looks at how to create a 'parent-friendly ethos'. It provides a framework for planning the improvement of parent partnership in an early years setting. It demonstrates how attitudes to working in partnership with parents affect all aspects of an early years setting and provides a range of tools and resources to support quality improvement in this area.

Section 3 consists of a wide range of practical resources to support parental engagement. These range from ways to incorporate partnership with parents into the everyday planning and organisation of the setting, 'one-off' activities to engage with groups of parents and information leaflets for parents about different aspects of children's play and learning.

References

- Robins, A and Callan, S (eds) (2009) *Managing Early Years Settings*, SAGE, London
- Whalley, M and the Pen Green Centre Team (2007) *Involving Parents in Their Children's Learning*, SAGE, London

THE PARENT PARTNERSHIP TOOLKIT FOR EARLY YEARS

Section 1

Introduction

The benefit to young children and their families of positive, mutually respectful relationships between parents and early years practitioners has been evidenced through research studies carried out over a number of years (Desforges and Abouchaar, 2003) and it has become increasingly embedded in government policy. The development and growth of the Pre-school Learning Alliance has demonstrated the impact that empowerment of parents can have on children's learning and on the lives of parents themselves (*see Section 2.1: Establishing the vision and values*), and it is now more than 30 years since the Warnock Committee, reviewing provision for children with special educational needs, identified the importance of 'supporting parents as their child's primary educators' (Warnock, 1978). The remainder of this section looks in more detail at recent research and government policy developments that emphasise the importance of early years practitioners making partnerships with parents a core feature of their early years provision.

Research evidence

Research studies carried out over the last 10 years have demonstrated the benefits of supporting parents to be fully involved in their young children's welfare, learning and development. The findings of the extensive literature review carried out by Charles Desforges in 2003 showed that the influence of the home learning environment was 'enduring, pervasive and direct' (Desforges and Abouchaar, 2003). The influence of what parents do with their children at home has a significant positive effect on children's wellbeing and achievement after all other variables have been eliminated. Large-scale research projects, such as the EPPE (Effective Provision of Pre-School Education), REPEY (Researching Effective Pedagogy in the Early Years) and the ELPP (Early Learning Partnership Project), which focused specifically on children under five and their families, have consolidated these findings.

EPPE and REPEY studies

The Effective Provision of Pre-School Education (EPPE) research, a comprehensive longitudinal study to measure the impact on children's learning and development of different forms of preschool provision, produced several important findings (Sylva et al, 2004). These have subsequently been used as the evidence base for much of the policy development in this area. The EPPE research showed that:

- the home learning environment and what parents and carers do makes a real difference to young children's development
- irrespective of children's backgrounds, the home learning environment has a greater influence on their intellectual and social development than the occupation, income or level of education of the parents
- there is a range of activities that parents undertake with pre-school children that have a positive effect on their development. These include reading with their child, teaching songs and nursery rhymes, painting and drawing, playing with letters and numbers, visiting the

library, teaching the alphabet and numbers, taking children on visits and creating regular opportunities for them to play with their friends at home.

Overall, when comparing different forms of preschool provision, the EPPE research found that there were more intellectual gains for children in settings that encouraged parent engagement in their children's learning. The most effective settings shared child-related information between parents and practitioners, often involving parents in decisions about their child's learning. The best outcomes were achieved when settings shared their educational aims with parents, enabling them to support children at home with activities or materials that complemented their experiences in the setting.

The Researching Effective Pedagogy in the Early Years (REPEY) study was based on an in-depth study of settings identified as high quality in the EPPE project (Siraj-Blatchford et al, 2002). The REPEY research demonstrated that involvement in learning activities at home was closely associated with better cognitive attainment in the early years. The settings that encouraged continuity of learning between the setting and the home achieved consistently better cognitive outcomes.

ELPP

The Early Learning Partnership Project focused on working with voluntary sector organisations to develop practices that could help parents of children aged one to three, who were at risk of learning delay, to engage in their children's learning. The findings of the study with these vulnerable and 'hard-to-reach' families are significant. They demonstrated that parents participating in structured programmes designed to support their involvement in early learning became more aware of their children's needs and more confident in providing their children with appropriate learning opportunities. The evaluation report of this project is a very useful and comprehensive source of information on the challenges to be addressed when working with disadvantaged and vulnerable families (Evangelou et al, 2008).

Government policy

The importance of developing effective partnerships with parents to support their children's welfare, learning and development has been a theme of government policy and action over the last decade (Baldock et al, 2009). There has been a shift in emphasis from parental involvement being considered an optional extra to an expectation that early years providers will establish strong, positive relationships with parents, acknowledging them as their children's first and most enduring educators. Government policy has taken a strategic, cross-departmental approach to moving forward the parent participation agenda through initiatives such as Sure Start children's centres (DfES, 2006), the implementation of the Every Child Matters framework (DfES, 2004a, 2004b) and the introduction of initiatives arising from the Children's Plan (DCSF, 2007a, 2007b). Partnership with parents is integral to the Early Years Foundation Stage framework (DfES, 2007) and an essential element of the Ofsted self-evaluation form (SEF) and inspection framework (Ofsted, 2009).

Sure Start children's centres

The Sure Start programme, launched in 1999, has evolved into a comprehensive programme of more than 3,000 children's centres, providing services for young children and their families. Through the deployment of multi-agency teams, centres provide access to high-quality early years provision, information and support for parents, health and family-support services. Outreach work and the development of approaches to reach disadvantaged and 'hard-to-reach' families are a particular feature of Sure Start provision (DfES, 2006, DCSF, 2008).

Since January 2010, Sure Start children's centres have been established as a legally recognised part of universal services for children, mothers, fathers and grandparents. Ofsted is responsible for inspecting the quality of services delivered through children's centres, assessing the whole range of care, education, family support and outreach services that these centres provide (DCSF, 2009).

Every Child Matters

In 2003, the government published a green paper based on the recommendations of the Laming report into the death of Victoria Climbié, which prompted a widespread consultation with providers of children's services and with children, young people and families on the key issues affecting children's wellbeing (Laming, 2003). Every Child Matters: Next Steps (DfES, 2004a) was published in 2004 and the Children Act 2004 was passed to provide the legislative framework to improve the delivery of services to make them more focused around the needs of children and families. Later in 2004, Every Child Matters: Change for Children (DfES, 2004b) set out the aim that every child, whatever his or her background or circumstances, should be supported to:

- be healthy
- stay safe
- enjoy and achieve
- make a positive contribution
- achieve economic wellbeing.

These five Every Child Matters outcomes create the framework within which the quality of all provision for young children and families is judged and they link closely to the themes and commitments of the Early Years Foundation Stage (EYFS) framework.

Children's Plan

The Children's Plan: Building Brighter Futures (DCSF, 2007a) developed the principles of Every Child Matters and set out a 10-year strategy for developing services for children, young people and families. The stated aim of the plan is:

'to improve educational outcomes for children, improve children's health, reduce offending rates among young people and eradicate child poverty by 2020, thereby contributing to the achievement of the five Every Child Matters outcomes.'

The involvement of parents in their children's welfare and education is a core theme of the Children's Plan, epitomised by the recurring use of the statement, 'Government does not bring up children – families do.' Building Brighter Futures - the Children's Plan for Families (DCSF, 2007b) was produced specifically for parents and set out the aim to put children and families at the centre of everything government does. The value of engaging with and involving parents is highlighted in the statement:

'Because parents and carers are the most important people in children's lives, we have produced this separate, shorter version specially designed for parents and others who care for children. It describes what we are planning to do, how it will affect you and your family and how we will involve families and children in what we do in the future.'

The plan places a particular emphasis on improving the way services engage with fathers, highlighting the importance of providing training for practitioners and acknowledging the preference expressed by many fathers for accessing information and support via the internet.

A number of initiatives affecting the relationship between families and providers of early years services have been developed to implement the Children's Plan.

- **Every Parent Matters**

  Published in 2007, Every Parent Matters focused on developing a strategy for service development that recognised that 'parents and the home environment they create are the single most important factor in shaping their children's wellbeing, achievements and prospects.' (DfES, 2007a). The strategy is based on the premise that:

  - the overwhelming majority of parents want to do the very best for their children
  - the majority say they expect to need advice or help at some time
  - mainstream services are not as good as they should be at recognising and responding to parents' needs
  - parents can be effective in very different ways but there is a growing understanding, evidenced from research, about the characteristics of effective parenting
  - it is vital to support the development of a wide range of services for parents to access as and when they need to
  - parents should be helped to feel empowered to influence and shape public services such as schools, health and children's services.

  The policy document sets out what is being done to promote the development of services for parents, as well as their involvement in shaping services for themselves and their children. It also seeks to initiate a national debate with parents, children and young people, as well as service planners and providers, as to how best to support and engage parents.

- **Healthy Lives, Brighter Futures: the Strategy for Children and Young People's Health**

  Healthy Lives, Brighter Futures is a child-health strategy, produced jointly by the Department of Health and the Department for Children, Schools and Families (DCSF, 2009a). The strategy:

- recognises that parents are the key to achieving the best physical and mental health outcomes for their children

- sets out the principles of the relationship between parents and services and what parents and their children can expect from those services

- emphasises the role of Sure Start children's centres in delivering the Healthy Child Programme as well as helping to provide all parents with a source of easily accessible advice about how they can effectively support their child's early learning, development and mental health

- discusses the need for each centre to tailor the services it provides to the needs of the communities it serves as well as individual parents.

- **Early Home Learning Matters** (*www.earlyhomelearning.org.uk*)

  Developed by the Family and Parenting Institute (*www.familyandparenting.org*), Early Home Learning Matters is a website dedicated to providing information and advice to support parents and practitioners in developing effective partnerships to support the learning and development of children under five. It cites the evidence for the importance of supporting parents to create a good home learning environment and hosts a range of practical resources for parents and practitioners. The DCSF has also funded the production of a publication, *Early Home Learning Matters, A Good Practice Guide* (Roberts, 2009). This brings together much of the evidence from the ELPP (DCSF, 2008a) and Parents as Partners in Early Learning (PPEL) project (DCSF, 2008b) on good practice in working with parents.

- **Investors in Families** (*www.investorsinfamilies.org.uk*)

  Investors in Families, an accreditation that schools and early years settings can apply for, has been established to recognise and promote the importance of developing parent partnerships and family-friendly approaches. It aims to value and support the role that families play in the life of the child, support families in developing their children's achievement and self-esteem and promote social inclusion and a sense of wellbeing through positive participation in family life. Piloted in Buckinghamshire since 2007, this model is currently being rolled out by local authorities across the country.

Early Years Foundation Stage framework

The value of establishing effective partnerships with parents underpins the structure of the EYFS framework and is clearly set out in the 'positive relationships' theme in the commitment 2.4: 'Parents as partners':

'Parents are children's first and most enduring educators. When parents and practitioners work together in early years settings, the results have a positive impact on children's development and learning.'

The EYFS highlights the importance of respecting diversity in family make-up and background, of creating a welcoming atmosphere, communicating well and respecting the wealth of knowledge that parents have about their children. The emphasis is on creating an equal partnership between the family and the setting, with parents and practitioners each having knowledge and experience that they can share with one another. Support for practitioners in delivering this aspect of the EYFS is available through an e-learning course, 'Working with parents and carers' (DCSF National Strategies *http://nationalstrategies.standards.dcsf.gov.uk/node/170946*).

Ofsted self-evaluation framework (SEF)

The Ofsted inspection framework for early years provision places an emphasis on practitioners engaging with parents, seeking their views on the setting and taking action in response to consultation with parents and children (Ofsted, 2009, 2009a, 2009b).

It looks at how well parents and carers are provided with good-quality information about the early years provision and informed about their children's achievements and progress. It asks providers to demonstrate the extent to which parents and carers are encouraged to share what they know about their child, particularly when the child first starts to attend, and for evidence of how parents and carers have been encouraged to be involved in supporting their children's learning and development.

Partnership with parents is considered a key element of the leadership and management of any early years setting. The update of the SEF in October 2009 (Ofsted 2009c) included a new requirement that asks practitioners to evaluate and make a judgement about the effectiveness of their engagement with parents and carers. This effectively raises the profile of partnership with parents and places it at the core of high-quality early years provision.

Training for practitioners to support parental engagement

Although early years practitioners are trained in working with children, very few have received any in-depth training in working with parents. However, the following personal qualities that underpin successful relationships and partnerships with parents have been identified (Braun et al, 2006, cited in Roberts, 2009):

- **respect:** valuing parents as individuals, believing in their fundamental ability to cope and make a difference in their family lives, and working within an ethos of partnership
- **empathy:** showing an understanding of the challenges a parent is facing in their lives and being able to see the situation from their point of view
- **genuineness:** being sensitive, honest, undefensive and trustworthy
- **humility:** working in the context of an equal relationship and using parents' strengths, views and knowledge alongside your own at every stage of the process
- **quiet enthusiasm:** bringing a friendly, positive energy to the relationship and a consistently calm, steady and warm approach
- **personal integrity:** in addition to empathising with the parent, being able to hold alternative views and offer these when appropriate
- **expertise:** the knowledge and experience that the helper (practitioner) brings to the work to complement the parents' existing knowledge and skills, both in building the relationship and in providing information and support.

The Key Elements of Effective Practice (KEEP) document highlights the importance of initial and ongoing training and development to help practitioners to develop, demonstrate and continuously improve their work with parents, carers and the wider community (DfES, 2005). This is substantiated by the work of the research team at the Pen Green Centre (Whalley et al, 2007) and the evaluation of the ELPP, which highlighted the importance of equipping early years practitioners with the skills they need to engage effectively with parents, particularly in more vulnerable families (Evangelou et al, 2008).

To address the need for training, initiatives such as the Parents, Early Years and Learning (PEAL) project have developed training programmes 'to support and inspire practitioners' to increase their parent-partnership work (*www.peal.org.uk*). The PEAL project has also identified many of the barriers to parent participation and collated examples of good practice in overcoming these barriers (Wheeler and Connor, 2009). Training for practitioners is also a feature of the programmes designed to address specific aspects of parenting described in more detail in *Section 2.6: Supporting parent-child relationships*

Currently the Children's Workforce Development Council (CWDC) is developing a new training Qualifications Credit Framework (QCF) for early years practitioners. The early years pathway for the Level 3 Children and Young People's Diploma includes partnership with parents as a key element of the first mandatory unit covering the context and principles of early years provision (CWDC, 2009a). In addition, a career framework to support practitioners working with parents is being developed by CWDC (2009b), building on the work done by the National Academy for Parenting Practitioners.

Early years leadership

The importance of leadership in early years settings in determining the quality of provision for children and families is increasingly being recognised. The National Professional Qualification for Integrated Centre Leadership (NPQICL) supports the development of leadership skills and qualities for managers of multi-agency teams working in children's centres, while Early Years Professional Status (EYPS) is designed largely for individuals leading practice in the private, voluntary and independent sectors. In both instances, working with families and developing effective partnerships with parents are identified as key skills for early years leaders (Ward, 2009).

National standards for leaders of Sure Start children's centres (DCSF, 2007c) highlight the importance of establishing effective partnerships with parents in Standard 6: 'Stronger families, stronger communities'. This charges the head of a children's centre with the responsibility to:

- raise expectations and aspirations so that families and the local community are encouraged to enjoy new opportunities for learning and better health
- ensure effective and sustained outreach into the community so that the most disadvantaged families are identified and encouraged to engage with the centre
- create imaginative opportunities to include the wider community in the activities of the centre and ensure that parents' views and feedback shape services.

To achieve EYPS (CWDC, 2008) practitioners have to demonstrate how they meet the following standards and can lead and support others to:

- recognise and respect the influential and enduring contribution that families can make to children's development, wellbeing and learning

- establish fair, respectful, trusting and constructive relationships with families and communicate sensitively and effectively with them

- work in partnership with families, at home and in the setting, to nurture children, to help them to develop and improve outcomes for them

- provide formal and informal opportunities through which information about children's wellbeing, development and learning can be shared between the setting and families.

References

Baldock, P, Fitzgerald, D and Kay, J (2009) *Understanding Early Years Policy*, SAGE, London

Braun, D, Davis, H and Mansfield P (2006) *How Helping Works: Towards a Shared Model of Process*, Parentline Plus/Centre for Parent and Child Support/One Plus One, see: *www.parentlineplus.org.uk*

Children Act 2004, see: *www.opsi.gov.uk/acts/acts2004/ukpga_20040031_en_1*

CWDC (2008) Guidance to the Standards for the Award of Early Years Professional status, see: *www.cwdcouncil.org.uk/ assets/0000/2398/EYP_Guidance_to_standards.pdf*

CWDC (2009a) Qualifications Credit Framework, see: *www.cwdcouncil.org.uk/qualifications-credit-framework*

CWDC (2009b) *Children and Young People's Workforce Practitioners Specialised in Supporting Mothers, Fathers and Carers*, see: *www.cwdcouncil.org.uk/working-with-families*

DCSF (2007a) *The Children's Plan: Building Brighter Futures*, see: *www.dcsf.gov.uk/childrensplan/*

DCSF (2007b) *Building Brighter Futures: The Children's Plan for Families*, see: *http://publications.dcsf.gov.uk/eOrderingDownload/ Childrens_Plan_Parents_Families.pdf*

DCSF (2007c) *National Standards for Leaders of Sure Start Children's Centres*, see: *www.nationalcollege.org.uk/index/ leadershiplibrary/leading-early years/early years-national-standards.htm*

DCSF (2008) *The Sure Start Journey: A Summary of Evidence*, see: *http://publications.everychildmatters.gov.uk/ eOrderingDownload/Sure_start_journey.pdf*

DCSF (2008a) *Supporting Parents to Engage in Their Child's Early Learning*, see: *www.familyandparenting.org/item/1555*

DCSF (2008b) *Parents as Partners in Early Learning (PPEL)*, see: *http://nationalstrategies.standards.dcsf.gov.uk/primary/features/ foundation_stage/parents_partners/*

DCSF (2009) The Children's Plan: 2 Years On, see: *www.dcsf.gov.uk/childrensplan*

DCSF (2009a) *Healthy lives, Brighter Futures: The strategy for children and young people's health*, see: *www.dh.gov.uk/en/ Publicationsandstatistics/Publications/PublicationsPolicyAndGuidance/DH_094400*

Desforges, C and Abouchaar, A (2003) *The Impact of Family Involvement, Parental Support and Family Education on Pupil Achievements and Adjustment: a Literature Review*, DfES RR433, see: *www.bgfl.org/bgfl/custom/files_uploaded/uploaded_ resources/18617/Desforges.pdf*

DfES (2004a) *Every Child Matters: Next Steps*, DfES/0240/2004

DfES (2004b) *Every Child Matters: Change for Children*, see: *www.dcsf.gov.uk/everychildmatters/about/background/background*

DfES (2005) *Key Elements of Effective Practice (KEEP)*, see: *http://nationalstrategies.standards.dcsf.gov.uk/node/88576*

DfES (2006) *Sure Start Children's Centres: Practice Guidance*, see: *www.dcsf.gov.uk/everychildmatters/research/publications/ surestartpublications/1854*

DfES (2007) *The Early Years Foundation Stage: Setting the Standards for Learning, Development and Care for Children from Birth to Five*, see: *http://nationalstrategies.standards.dcsf.gov.uk/earlyyears*

DfES (2007a) *Every Parent Matters*, see: *www.teachernet.gov.uk/wholeschool/familyandcommunity/workingwithparents/ everyparentmatters*

Evangelou, M, Sylva, K, Edwards, A and Smith, T (2008) *Supporting Parents in Promoting Early Learning: the Evaluation of the Early Learning Partnership Project*, DCSF RB039, see: *www.dcsf.gov.uk/research/data/uploadfiles/DCSF-RB039A.pdf*

Laming, H (2003) *The Victoria Climbié Inquiry. Report of an Inquiry by Lord Laming*. HMSO, London

Ofsted (2009) *Early Years Online Self-Evaluation Form (SEF) and Guidance – for Settings Delivering the Early Years Foundation Stage*, see *https://online.ofsted.gov.uk/onlineofsted/public/launchportal.aspx*

Ofsted (2009a) *Are You Ready for Your Inspection? A Guide to Inspections of Provision on Ofsted's Childcare and Early Years Registers*, see: *www.ofsted.gov.uk/Ofsted-home/Forms-and-guidance/Browse-all-by/Other/General/Are-you-ready-for-your-inspection-A-guide-to-inspections-of-provision-on-Ofsted-s-Childcare-and-Early-Years-Registers*

Ofsted (2009b) *Early Years Self Evaluation Form Guidance*, see: *www.ofsted.gov.uk/publications/080104*

Ofsted (2009c) *Online Self-Evaluation Form Amendments*, see: *www.ofsted.gov.uk/Ofsted-home/Forms-and-guidance/Browse-all-by/ Other/General/Online-early-years-self-evaluation-form-amendments*

Roberts, K (2009) *Early Home Learning Matters, A Good Practice Guide*, Family and Parenting Institute, London, see: *www. earlyhomelearning.org.uk*

Siraj-Blatchford, I, Sylva, K, Muttock, S, Gilden, R and Bell, D (2002) *Researching Effective Pedagogy in the Early Years (REPEY)*, DfES RR356, see: *www.dcsf.gov.uk/research/data/uploadfiles/RR356.pdf*

Sylva, K, Melhuish, E, Sammons, S, Siraj-Blatchford, I and Taggart, B (2004) *The Effective Provision of Pre-School Education Project: Final Report*, see: *www.dcsf.gov.uk/research/data/uploadfiles/SSU_FR_2004_01.pdf*

Ward, U (2009) *Working with Parents in Early Years Settings: Achieving Early Years Professional Status*, Learning Matters, Exeter

Warnock, M (1978) *Special Educational Needs* (report by the Committee of Enquiry into the Education of Handicapped Children and Young People), London: HMSO

Whalley, M and the Pen Green Centre Team (2007) *Involving Parents in their Children's Learning*, SAGE, London

Wheeler, H and Connor, J (2009) *Parents, Early Years and Learning. Parents as Partners in the Early Years Foundation Stage*, National Children's Bureau, London

Working with Parents and Carers e-Learning course: *http://nationalstrategies.standards.dcsf.gov.uk/node/170946*

Section 2

Introduction

Section 2 looks in more detail at the many different aspects that practitioners need to consider when creating an ethos and way of working which values and supports the role that parents play in the care and education of their young children.

Section 2 is arranged into seven parts which look in turn at:

2.1 establishing the vision and values

2.2 creating a welcoming environment

2.3 listening to parents

2.4 communicating with parents

2.5 key person working

2.6 supporting parent-child relationships

2.7 auditing your provision.

Section 2.7 provides an overview that draws together all the information discussed in Sections 2.1 to 2.6 and relates this to the EYFS framework and the Ofsted SEF. This provides a useful summary, but can also be used as a starting point for deciding which aspects of your existing provision it would be most useful to focus on first.

Parental responsibility

Throughout the text the term 'parent' is used to include not only the child's birth parents but also members of their immediate family, including grandparents and family members, as well as guardians and foster carers. This definition is broader and encompasses more of the adults who might have an important influence on a child's wellbeing, learning and development. However, it is important that practitioners are also aware of the strict legal definition of parental responsibility. As stated on the government website, Directgov:

> 'In England and Wales, if the parents of a child are married to each other at the time of the birth, or if they have jointly adopted a child, then they both have parental responsibility. Parents do not lose parental responsibility if they divorce, and this applies to both the resident and the non-resident parent.
>
> This is not automatically the case for unmarried parents. According to current law, a mother always has parental responsibility for her child. A father, however, has this responsibility only if he is married to the mother when the child is born or has acquired legal responsibility for his child through one of these three routes:
>
> - (from 1 December 2003) by jointly registering the birth of the child with the mother
> - by a parental responsibility agreement with the mother
> - by a parental responsibility order, made by a court.

Living with the mother, even for a long time, does not give a father parental responsibility and if the parents are not married, parental responsibility does not always pass to the natural father if the mother dies.

All parents (including adoptive parents) have a legal duty to financially support their child, whether they have parental responsibility or not.'

www.direct.gov.uk/en/Parents/ParentsRights/DG_4002954

The responsibilities of a parent are not defined in detail by law but are generally taken to include the following:

- providing a home for the child
- having contact with and living with the child
- protecting and maintaining the child
- disciplining the child
- choosing and providing for the child's education
- determining the religion of the child
- agreeing to the child's medical treatment
- naming the child and agreeing to any change of the child's name
- accompanying the child outside the UK and agreeing to the child's emigration, should the issue arise
- being responsible for the child's property
- appointing a guardian for the child, if necessary
- allowing confidential information about the child to be disclosed.

Reading through this list, practitioners will immediately be aware of some key responsibilities which lie only with a child's legal parent. For example, signing a consent form on behalf of the child or giving permission for the child to be collected from the setting by another adult. Care must be taken to adhere to the requirements of the law in this regard while at the same time seeking to establish effective relationships with all the significant adults in a child's life.

Maintaining parents' confidentiality

Building a relationship of trust and respect is important for all families using the setting, but particularly for those who may have more complex family arrangements resulting in particular needs for help and support. The rights of a parent who does not live with a child to receive appropriate information from the early years setting must be acknowledged and respected.

Managers and setting leaders must consider carefully how much information about family circumstances is shared with a child's key person. Clearly the key person (*see Section 2.5: Key person working*) is entitled to have sufficient information to enable him or her to fulfil the role effectively, but maintaining parents' confidentiality is also vitally important. Ensuring information is only made available on a 'need to know' basis will help to maintain this important balance.

How to engage families

There is no simple answer to the question, 'How do we engage with families?' There will be a variety of different answers to this question depending on the age of the children, the size and nature of the early years setting and the social and ethnic mix of the families using it. Perhaps the most useful question to ask first is, '*Why* do we want to engage with families?' Thinking about the answer to this question will often be the first step on the road to finding the route to answering the 'How' question.

Why do we want to engage with families?

- to establish a shared vision of childhood on which to base the policies and working practices of the setting (see *Section 2.1: Establishing the vision and values*)

- to understand more about the children we work with so we can better support their learning and development (see *Section 2.3: Listening to parents, Section 2.5: Key person working and Section 3*)

- to help parents understand more about how their child learns so they can support this process at home (see *Section 2.2: Creating a welcoming environment, Section 2.4: Communicating with parents and Section 3*)

- to help parents acquire the information and skills they need to enjoy their parenting role (see *Section 2.6: Supporting parent-child relationships*)

- to add value to the experiences the children encounter in the setting (see *Section 3*)

- to enhance the role of the early years setting in the local community (see *Section 2.1: Establishing the vision and values and Section 3*)

- to help parents acquire the skills they need to be independent and economically active (see *Section 2.6: Supporting parent-child relationships*).

Structure of Section 2

2.1 Establishing the vision and values

This section looks at the fundamental importance of establishing the overall vision and values of an early years setting and at how these can be used to define policy and practice. It looks at different models of practitioner-parent relationships, addresses the question, 'Why involve parents?' and provides examples of early years approaches that particularly value the role of parents. There is information on how to create a parent partnership policy, including checklists and audit sheets, and an example of how to present information for parents in an easily accessible format. Finally, the content of the section is summarised in a series of key points and reflective questions that can be used for staff training and professional development.

2.2 Creating a welcoming environment

In this section we take a closer look at the different elements of the physical and emotional environment that will influence how comfortable parents will feel in a setting. It reviews the important role that the architecture of the building – the layout and organisation of space –

play in supporting or impeding the implementation of the setting's vision and values. The importance of creating a good first impression through paying attention to the physical space and to the welcome that parents experience is also considered. A series of audit sheets are provided to support a review of the physical layout and organisational structures of the setting to ensure they support effective parent partnership. The content of the section is summarised in a series of key points and there is a series of reflective questions to initiate further discussion and staff training.

2.3 Listening to parents

This section reviews what is involved in creating a listening culture that demonstrates to parents that their views, of their own child and about the work of the setting, are welcomed and valued. It looks at good practice in listening to specific parental groups – families from ethnic minorities, fathers, teenage parents and parents of children with additional needs. The question, 'Why consult with parents?' is reviewed and there is information on how to manage consultation groups and how to design an effective consultation questionnaire. Examples of questionnaires that would be appropriate for different early years settings are provided along with sample letters to parents setting out the framework and purpose of the consultation process. The content of the section is then summarised in several key points and reflective questions are provided for use in staff training and professional development.

2.4 Communicating with parents

This section looks at the range of information that practitioners may want to provide for parents and considers the different ways in which this information could be presented. It highlights the importance of really trying to get to know children and valuing the parents' perspectives on and knowledge of their child. The importance of creating a shared view of childhood is highlighted, identifying some of the key messages to share with parents. Ways of sharing information about children's learning and development are considered and there is guidance on how to make letters and documents readable and visually attractive. Techniques for organising meetings where parents feel welcome and comfortable are reviewed as is the key area of supporting staff to develop their verbal and non-verbal communication skills. There are checklists for assessing how well you currently communicate and guidelines for producing easily readable written information. The key points covering the content of the section are summarised and there are reflective questions to prompt personal study and to use for staff training.

2.5 Key person working

In this section we look at the important role played by the key person in consolidating the link between the early years setting and the family. The role of the key person and what it entails is discussed, highlighting the differences between a key worker and a key person. A brief introduction to attachment theory provides the basis on which to build key person working. The practical considerations of organisation and management of key person working are considered, including resources for auditing and reviewing current systems. The importance of home visits and of managing transitions is discussed and there are checklists and proformas to support these processes. For staff training and professional development purposes there is a summary of key points at the end of the section and a series of reflective questions for group discussion or personal reflection.

2.6 Supporting parent-child relationships

This section looks in more detail at some key information that practitioners can share with parents to support them in their role as parents. It identifies the aspects of child development that many parent would appreciate advice and guidance on and focuses in more detail on helping parents to understand and manage young children's behaviour. The benefits of involving parents in creating the setting's behaviour management policy are discussed, highlighting this as an opportunity to come to a common understanding of what is important for young children. Discussing the setting's approach to safeguarding children can help parents to appreciate the roles and responsibilities that parents and the early years setting share in ensuring children are kept safe from harm. The wide range of programmes to help parents to develop their parenting skills is reviewed, accompanied by an information grid identifying the wide range of resources and programmes available. A series of key points summarises the section and there are reflective questions to assist with personal study and staff training initiatives.

2.7 Auditing your provision

This section reviews the place of developing parent partnerships in the Early Years Foundation Stage (EYFS) framework and looks at the requirements of the Ofsted self-evaluation form (SEF). It then brings together all the aspects of developing partnerships with parents that are considered in Sections 2.1 to 2.6 to create an audit tool for measuring all aspects of your provision to see how effectively it supports partnership with parents. This provides essential information for completing the Ofsted SEF and for planning for improvement.

THE PARENT PARTNERSHIP TOOLKIT FOR EARLY YEARS SECTION 2

Establishing the vision and values

This section looks at the fundamental importance of establishing the overall vision and values of an early years setting and at how these can be used to define policy and practice. It looks at different models of practitioner-parent relationships, addresses the question, 'Why involve parents?' and provides examples of early years approaches that particularly value the role of parents. There is information on how to create a parent partnership policy, including checklists and audit sheets and an example of how to present information for parents in an easily accessible format. Finally, the content of the section is summarised in a series of key points and reflective questions that can be used for staff training and professional development.

Working in partnership with parents will be an integral part of the vision and values of any early years setting. Before looking specifically at how partnerships with parents can be promoted within the ethos of a setting, it is important to look at the wider context of establishing or reviewing the overall vision and values that define how the setting operates.

Establishing the overall vision and values

Having an overall vision for the setting based on an agreed set of shared values creates a firm foundation on which to build all aspects of quality early years practice. The process of establishing the vision and values of the setting provides an opportunity for the staff team to:

- see the big picture and understand the overall aims and purpose of the job they are doing
- share ideas and opinions and get to know one another better
- appreciate the key part they play in the provision of services for children and their families
- take responsibility for playing their part in the quality of care and education provided by the setting
- develop a sense of pride in their work.

Making use of the vision and values

The process of establishing the setting's vision and values is a very useful and productive staff development exercise, clarifying the aims of the setting and building a shared understanding of its aim and purpose. However, the vision and values are not simply to be written down, put on the shelf and forgotten about. Instead, they should underpin everything that happens within the setting. The vision and values should be used:

- to help parents to understand what it is that the setting believes is important
- to evaluate progress and to provide direction when making plans for future development
- when drawing up policies and procedures
- to promote the setting to potential new staff members
- to remind staff of the culture and ethos of the setting
- as a starting point for creating partnerships with other organisations
- to support the setting's promotion and marketing campaign.

Agreeing shared values

The process of agreeing a set of values that are shared by everyone involved in the setting is not likely to be a simple and straightforward process. Each one of us has our own set of values that determines how we live our lives, based on the:

- values of our parents and other adults who have had a significant influence on our own early childhood experiences

- societal, cultural, ethical, political and religious influences and beliefs that affect our daily thoughts and actions.

The principles that underpin the Early Years Foundation Stage (EYFS) guidance (DCSF, 2008a) provide a good framework for starting a discussion about the values of the setting. The four themes of the EYFS are:

- a unique child

- positive relationships

- enabling environments

- learning and development.

Looking at each of these themes in turn, it is useful to pose a series of questions that will help to reveal different people's attitudes and opinions (see figure 2.1a on p27). Use this checklist as the starting point for a team discussion about what the values of the staff team are and how these values will underpin practice within the setting.

Be prepared for the discussion to be wide ranging and, at times, controversial, as people will be expressing views and opinions that they hold very dear. It is vital that everyone is given the opportunity to express their opinion in some way – some people may feel more comfortable writing things down rather than speaking out in a large group.

The key issues that are likely to come up during a discussion on the setting's values can probably be grouped together under five broad headings, which cover:

- children's learning and development

- children's welfare and safety

- relationships with parents, children and colleagues

- organisation and management

- physical environment.

Out of this, it should be possible to agree five or six core values that everyone agrees are fundamental to the effective running of the setting. The core values define the quality of the setting and will underpin all the setting's policies and day-to-day practices.

Agreeing the values underpinning partnership with parents

Different models exist to describe the relationship that can exist between parents and practitioners in an early years setting. Robins and Callan (2009) have categorised these as:

- **The 'expert' model** – where the practitioner has a negative view of a child's experiences

SECTION 2.1   THE PARENT PARTNERSHIP TOOLKIT FOR EARLY YEARS

outside the setting, with the focus on what the child cannot do, or what the parents do not provide. The practitioner takes control of decision making and does not encourage active involvement from parents and carers.

- **The 'transplant' model** – where the practitioner cedes some responsibility to the parent or carer but does not actively encourage them to become involved in the decision-making process. This tends to create a distant relationship between the practitioner and the parent, with the practitioner being perceived as an authority figure. Evidence suggests that this could be regarded as the default model that will prevail in early years settings unless active steps are taken to develop practice.

- **The 'consumer' model** – based on an understanding of the interests and rights of all parents to be involved in their young children's wellbeing, learning and development. It is based on the principles underpinning the provision of high-quality early years services set out in the Start Right report (Ball, 1994). Practitioners make consistent efforts to engage and involve parents in all aspects of their children's development, aware of the need to refine and adapt services to the needs and aspirations of the individual families with whom they are working.

The ideas, resources and suggestions contained in this publication are all designed to help you develop the 'consumer' model in your setting. Using the different models described above as the basis for discussion with the staff team provides a good starting point for coming to a shared agreement about the setting's values that underpin partnership with parents.

As part of this process it is useful to ask the question, 'Why involve parents?' The answer to this question will be different for every setting and will be influenced by the nature of the setting, the services it provides and the perceived needs of the local community. However, there are likely to be some very important and broad-ranging areas of agreement. The research evidence on which many of the national priorities around involving parents are based is reviewed in Section 1. These studies have shown that establishing strong partnerships with parents:

- recognises the prime role parents play as their child's first and most enduring educators
- empowers parents to be fully involved in their child's education, building positive attitudes for the future
- enables children to experience the benefits of positive relationships between the home and the setting
- increases parents' understanding of early learning and development, leading to better home-learning environments
- promotes the wellbeing and welfare of young children, helping to keep them safe from harm
- helps parents to ask for the support and assistance they might need at different times
- adds value to the work of the setting, keeping it in touch with the views, opinions and aspirations of the families it serves
- builds community cohesion.

National Strategies has produced several resources that highlight the importance of building partnerships with parents and provide examples of good practice in involving parents in their children's learning (DfES 2004, DfES 2005, DCSF 2007, DCSF 2008b). See also Section 1 and Section 2.6: Supporting parent-child relationships.

Establishing the vision of the setting

Once established, the values will help to define the vision for the setting. Every setting's agreed values will be unique, but probably largely similar, and the vision of the setting will also be influenced by:

- national priorities and objectives
- local aims and objectives that take into account the economic, cultural and social identity of the community it serves
- the aims and aspirations of the key individuals involved in running the setting
- the objectives of sponsoring organisations and key strategic partners.

Creating a vision statement helps to capture the essence of what the setting is aiming to achieve. This will be a forward-looking statement that focuses on the aspirations of the setting and where it would like to be in the future. Putting together a vision statement can be a time-consuming process, and it may need several redrafts before it is finalised. However, the time spent on this process, ideally by the key group of people responsible for leading practice in the setting, is time well spent. The final vision statement should be meaningful, thoughtful and inspirational, defining a future that is more appealing than the present. Ideally, it should draw people in and make them feel they want to be a part of it. For example:

'Our vision is to create an environment in which children, families and staff enjoy strong positive relationships and exciting learning experiences that give them the opportunity to fulfil their inbuilt potential.'

Willow Tree Children's Centre

The value of parent participation and the contribution it makes to high-quality outcomes for children is well demonstrated by the underpinning ethos of the Pre-school Learning Alliance in the United Kingdom and the values and principles of the Reggio Approach to early childhood in Northern Italy (*see the box on page 23*).

Creating a parent partnership policy

The purpose of a parent partnership policy is to define what needs to be done to turn the setting's vision and values regarding parent partnership into reality. Developing a parent partnership policy will help to:

- define the approach of the setting and make this understandable to everyone
- meet any legal requirements governing the setting's operation
- provide a framework for decision making and help to ensure that actions are carried out in a consistent way.

The policy should consist of a description of principles, expectations and procedures clearly written so that anyone reading it will know what has been agreed. It should also make it clear what actions an individual is expected to take in any particular circumstances.

Valuing parent participation

Pre-school Learning Alliance

The Pre-school Learning Alliance (PLA), established in 1962 as the Pre-school Playgroups Association, was set up by parents in response to the lack of nursery school places for their children. The original aims of the organisation were the mutual support for those running groups and the lobbying of government for the expansion of early years provision. However, it quickly became apparent that the involvement and empowerment of the children's parents had a powerful effect, not only on children's learning, but also on the parents themselves. Over the last 40 years the Pre-school Learning Alliance has grown to become a leading educational charity supporting 15,000 early years settings and over 800,000 young children and their families. Parental involvement remains at the heart of the alliance's approach, through its committee-based structure and encouragement of parent volunteers. Many parents access PLA training courses, which set them on the road to further training and employment, and national programmes, such as Jump Start and Looking at Learning Together, act as awareness-raising initiatives to promote family learning and adult literacy.
www.pre-school.org.uk

Reggio Approach

The world-renowned preschools and infant-toddler centres of Reggio Emilia in Northern Italy began in the period immediately following the Second World War. Ravaged by the devastation of the war, the women and few surviving men of the village of Villa Cella just outside Reggio Emilia worked together to build a preschool out of the rubble that surrounded them. Their stated aim was to provide a different form of education for their young children, so they would never again bring up a generation of children who did not question what was happening to them. The preschools were organised, funded and managed by parents and remained so until 1963 when the Municipality of Reggio Emilia took over responsibility for their running.

The reciprocal relationships that exist between parents, children and teachers are at the heart of the Reggio Approach. Parents remain a very powerful and proactive force involved in defining the direction and evolving philosophy of the Reggio preschools. The preschools and infant-toddler centres see themselves as an essential part of the local community, providing a focal point for parents to meet, debate and participate in the life of their child's setting. The 'Rights of Parents' is a parents' charter, which sets out what the parent can expect of the setting and what the setting can expect of parents.

During their time in an infant-toddler centre, children remain with the same two teachers, allowing time for strong relationships to be developed between teachers, parents and children. The whole process of documenting children's learning creates a detailed illustrated record of a child's preschool experience, which is shared and discussed regularly with parents.

(Thornton and Brunton, 2009).

Examples of model parent partnership policy documents, such as the one shown in *figure 2.1c on p29*, will provide a useful guide as to how to construct a policy. However, as every setting has its own identity and ethos and is situated in its own cultural context, it is very important to create a policy with input from all the key people that it affects to ensure that it is owned and supported by everyone associated with the setting.

Writing the parent partnership policy

Regardless of who is charged with the responsibility for writing the policy – manager, director, headteacher, senior leadership team, management committee or policy working group – it is vital to consult widely to gather a diverse range of views. This not only helps to ensure that the policy is appropriate and comprehensive, but also helps people feel that they have 'ownership' of the issues covered by the policy and that they share a responsibility for making sure it works in practice.

Like all other policies the setting has, the parent partnership policy and its associated procedures is there to give consistency to the way the setting operates. It should make clear to everyone what they can expect to happen and what is expected of them. The parent partnership policy must therefore be known to, and understood by, everybody. It is important to think carefully about:

- the complexity of the language used

- how the policy is presented to encourage people to read it

- whether it needs to be translated into different languages.

1. Preparation

Before writing the policy it is important to carry out some research to look at the background information on the key areas the policy should cover. Useful questions to ask at this stage of the process are:

- What are the statutory requirements?

- What are we currently doing in the setting to support partnership with parents? Use the audit sheet (*figure 2.1b on p28 'Involving parents – How are we doing?'*) to help with this process.

- Who are the key groups who should be consulted? This is likely to include parents, other family members, staff, and other agencies.

- What is the best way to consult with them? (*See Section 2.3: Listening to parents*)

- Where else could we find out about good practice in consulting with parents?

2. Writing

The background research should enable you to identify the key features to be included in the policy and how best to put them into practice. Much of this information will come from consulting with parents and then analysing and using the results of this consultation (*see Section 2.3: Listening to parents*).

Using the same standard format for all the setting's policy documents helps to ensure that they are clear and consistent and simplifies the review process. Key points to include in the written policy include the legal framework within which the policy sits, who will be responsible for ensuring the policy is implemented, who will monitor the policy's effectiveness and the date when the policy will be reviewed. This will help to ensure that the policy is effective in practice and is responsive to the changing needs of the parent population.

Questions to ask at this stage include:

- Who will be responsible for writing the policy?
- What have we learned from the consultation process?
- Are there any staff training needs that should be addressed?
- Is the document easy to understand?
- Who needs to know about the policy?
- How will it be publicised and made widely available?

The policy is likely to include information on how the setting:

- values the key role that parents, family members and carers play in the life of the young children who attend the setting
- will consult with parents and take their opinions into account
- operates on a daily basis, including where to find out more about its policies and procedures
- provides information on the experiences that children are involved in, to support their learning and development
- will address any concerns the parent or setting may have about a child's progress
- provides information for parents to enhance children's welfare and wellbeing
- signposts parents to help and advice available from external organisations
- provides opportunities for parents to become involved in the life of the setting.

When writing the parent partnership policy, try to keep it as short and clear as possible. Include the procedures to be followed to put the policy into practice and set these out in a simple step-by-step way.

Figure 2.1c on p29 gives an example of what a model policy document might look like, while *Figure 2.1d on p31* demonstrates how the same document could be presented in a more user-friendly format for wider distribution by making use of the guidelines for providing information for parents outlined in *Section 2.4: Communicating with parents.*

The parent partnership policy may have an effect on several of the other policies of the setting. List these at the end of the policy document to simplify the review process.

3. Review

The parent partnership policy will need to be reviewed periodically to see how well it fits the current needs of the setting. An ongoing process of consultation with parents will help you to identify how well the policy is working in practice and highlight any changes that need to be made. Policies are often reviewed on a three-year rolling programme to establish whether:

- the policy has been fully implemented
- the procedures are being followed
- the policy is achieving its aims of increasing parental involvement

- it needs to be modified to improve its effectiveness.

Use the audit sheet in *figure 2.1e on p33* as a checklist to monitor how effectively the parent partnership policy has been put into practice.

References

Ball, C (1994) *Start Right: The Importance of Early Learning*, Royal Society for the Encouragement of Arts, Manufactures and Commerce, see: *www.eric.ed.gov/ERICWebPortal/search/detailmini.jsp?_nfpb=true&_&ERICExtSearch_SearchValue_0=ED37283 3&ERICExtSearch_SearchType_0=no&accno=ED372833*

DfES (2004) *Parents: Partners in learning*, DfES 0413-2004G, see: *http://nationalstrategies.standards.dcsf.gov.uk/node/154658*

DfES (2005) *Foundation Stage Parents: Partners in Learning*, DfES 1210-2005G, see: *http://nationalstrategies.standards.dcsf.gov. uk/node/154690*

DCSF (2007) *Playing and learning together DVD*, DCSF 00671-2007DVD-EN, see: *https://nationalstrategies.standards.dcsf.gov. uk/node/113036*

DCSF (2008a) *The Early Years Foundation Stage: Setting the Standards for Learning, Development and Care for Children from Birth to Five*, DCSF 00261-2008PCK-EN, see *http://nationalstrategies.standards.dcsf.gov.uk/node/157774*

DCSF (2008b) *Parents as Partners in Early Learning* (case studies) DCSF ref. 00196-2008-PCK-EN, see *http://nationalstrategies.standards.dcsf.gov.uk/node/151972*

Pre-school Learning Alliance, see *www.pre-school.org.uk*

Robins, A and Callan, S (eds) (2009) *Managing Early Years Settings: Supporting and Leading Teams*, SAGE, London

Thornton, L and Brunton, P (2009) *Understanding the Reggio Approach: Early Years Education in Practice*, Routledge, Abingdon

SECTION 2.1 THE PARENT PARTNERSHIP TOOLKIT FOR EARLY YEARS

Figure 2.1a

Exploring and agreeing our values

EYFS theme	Questions to ask
A unique child Every child is a competent learner from birth who can be resilient, capable, confident and self-assured.	• How do we view children? • How do we value differences? • Are we overprotective of children? • Do we value healthy lifestyles and act as good role models?
Positive relationships Children learn to be strong and independent from a base of loving and secure relationships with parents and/or a key person.	• As a staff team, do we demonstrate respect for one another? • What view do we have of the role of parents? • Are we knowledgeable enough to support young children's learning effectively? • How well do we carry out the key person role?
Enabling environments The environment plays a key role in supporting and extending children's learning and development.	• For whose benefit are the settings' routines organised? • Do we respect parents' views of their children to help us to really get to know them? • How well are children's ideas and interests used as a basis for planning? • Do we show real respect for our environment and resources? • Have we created genuine partnerships with external agencies?
Learning and development Children develop and learn in different ways and at different rates and all areas of learning and development are equally important and inter-connected.	• What is our understanding of play? • Do we create opportunities for risk and challenge? • Are we creative practitioners? • What is our role as early years professionals? • Do we place enough value on professional development?

27

Figure 2.1b

Involving parents – how are we doing?

	Never	Sometimes	Usually	Always
Parents are greeted when they enter the building.				
The entrance area is tidy and inviting.				
All parents have a copy of the prospectus.				
Important information is available in different languages as appropriate.				
Contact information is kept up to date.				
Parents know where to look to find information about the setting.				
Parents are consulted on key aspects affecting the life of the setting.				
The results of consultations are fed back to parents and acted on.				
Information leaflets are available and there is space to look at them.				
Activities and courses for parents are widely advertised and promoted.				
Family support groups are organised so they are responsive to parents' needs.				
All staff photographs are up to date.				
All staff wear name badges.				
Parents know who their key person is and what the role entails.				
Staff are trained in how to talk to parents and share information with them.				
There is time at the beginning and end of the day to talk to parents.				
Parents know who to talk to if they are concerned about any aspect of their child's development.				
The setting has books and resources that reflect the diversity of the local community.				
Regular events are organised to help parents understand more about early learning and development.				
Parents are encouraged to borrow resources to help them support their child's learning at home.				
Parents are encouraged to share their skills with the children in the setting.				
Social events are organised to develop the relationship between the setting and the community it serves.				

SECTION 2.1   THE PARENT PARTNERSHIP TOOLKIT FOR EARLY YEARS

Figure 2.1c

Model parent partnership policy

Parent partnership policy

Date: **Review date:**

Person responsible for implementing this policy:

Legal framework:

- Children Act 1989, 2004
- Childcare Act 2006
- Data Protection Act 1998
- Every Child Matters – Change for Children 2004
- Freedom of Information Act 2000
- UN Convention on the Rights of the Child
- Human Rights Act 2000
- EYFS Welfare Requirements: Safeguarding and Promoting Children's Welfare, Organisation, Documentation
- EYFS Learning and Development Requirements

Policy

As a setting we are fully committed to supporting parents, family members and carers in their role as the first and most enduring educators of their young children. We see this as underpinning everything that we do to secure children's welfare and wellbeing and nurture their learning and development. To build strong positive relationships between the staff of the setting and children's families, we share information, consult with parents and family members, listen to what they have to say and respond to their views. The family forum also provides a focus for consultation and for exchanging views and ideas.

Throughout the year we organise a wide range of activities and initiatives to help parents feel fully involved with the life of the setting. These include family learning events, information sessions, opportunities to learn new skills and chances to meet representatives of partner organisations and agencies. Social events and outings are held throughout the year to build a real sense of community within our early years setting.

Information about the management, operating practices and daily routines of the setting is set out in the prospectus and in more detail in the policies and procedures file. All families are given a copy of the prospectus when they join the setting and a copy of the policies and procedures file can be found in the reception area. The setting leader is happy to explain what these policies mean and how they are translated into practice. The parents' noticeboard in the reception area has key information, dates and the setting's monthly newsletter, containing news and information about important events and staff changes. It is distributed by email and/or as a paper copy.

Staff members all wear name badges and their photographs are displayed in the rooms they work in. Every family has a designated key person who acts as the first point of contact between the family and the setting and will ensure parents are kept fully informed about their child's welfare and wellbeing. Information about the learning and development experiences that children of different ages are involved in will be provided by the key person, room or section leaders. Parents receive regular updates and there are also photographs and written information displayed around the setting. Individual children's experiences are shared at the end of each day. Parents are encouraged to look at their child's developmental record at regular intervals and to meet with staff for a progress review twice a year.

THE PARENT PARTNERSHIP TOOLKIT FOR EARLY YEARS SECTION 2.1

Figure 2.1c *cont*

Staff will listen to and address any concerns that a parent may have about their child's progress and will keep parents fully informed by discussing any issues relating to progress that they feel are significant. The setting will provide parents with information about other services or organisations they feel parents may find helpful to further their child's learning and development, or to support them in their parenting role.

Parents and other family members make an enormous contribution to the life of our setting. We greatly value the many different ways in which families support us, through spending time helping in the setting, assisting with specific projects, sharing their skills and expertise and acting as advocates for the setting in the local community.

Links to other policies: Key person, Equal opportunities, Learning and development, Inclusion and special needs, Behaviour

Person responsible for monitoring this policy:

Procedures:
List here the procedures to put in place to translate the parent partnership policy into practice. These procedures are likely to involve many different aspects of the running of the setting including:

1. Providing information for parents:
- the type of information to be provided
- the format it will be in
- where and when it will be made available.

2. Consulting on key issues:
- what aspects of the setting's organisation are consulted on
- how consultation takes place
- when consultation happens
- how feedback is given to show that consultation has been acted on.

3. Providing information for staff:
- what staff need to know about the parent partnership policy
- how this information will be provided
- how training needs will be addressed.

4. Environment – how the environment will be organised to demonstrate parent partnership.

5. Inclusion and additional needs – how the parent partnership policy links with the setting's other policies and statutory obligations.

6. Family support and parenting programmes – how these will be promoted and to whom.

7. Liaison with external agencies – how key organisations are facilitated to become active partners.

SECTION 2.1   THE PARENT PARTNERSHIP TOOLKIT FOR EARLY YEARS

Family-friendly version

Parent partnership policy

As parents you are very important in the life of our setting. We want you to feel welcome here so that you and your child enjoy the time you spend with us. As parents you are the most important people in your child's life. We will help you to support your child as they grow and learn by:

- providing you with information about how the setting runs
- sharing information with you about your child's progress
- organising events, activities and information sessions
- asking you what you think about different things happening in the setting.

If you would like to know more, our parent partnership policy is available

from ………………………………………………………………………

We have set out the main parts of our parent partnership policy in our home-setting agreement. Please read this, sign it and give the signed copy to ……………………………………… (setting manager/teacher).

This will help us all to work together to provide the best opportunities for your child.

Figure 2.1d cont

Home–setting agreement

To help you and your child make the most of their time with us,

We will:

- make sure the setting is safe, secure and friendly
- provide well-trained staff and good equipment
- organise interesting activities and experiences to support your child's learning and development
- share information with you
- support your child to behave well
- organise activities to make you feel a part of the life of the setting.

You will:

- keep us up to date with contact numbers
- arrive on time and collect your child on time at the end of a session
- make sure your child is wearing clothes that enable them to join in the day's activities
- let us know if your child is unwell and keep them at home until they are better
- let the staff know of any changes that might affect your child's behaviour during the day
- support your child to behave well
- ask if you want to know anything.

Signed: _____ (Parent)

Signed: _____ (Setting)

SECTION 2.1   THE PARENT PARTNERSHIP TOOLKIT FOR EARLY YEARS

Figure 2.1a

What does our parent partnership policy involve in practice?

Use this audit sheet to find out what procedures need to be put in place to translate policy into practice.

It also provides a useful checklist when monitoring the implementation of the parent partnership policy.

Aspect	Action	Completed	Comments
Organisational information for parents	• Prospectus given/sent to all new parents. • Policy and procedures file on table in reception area. • Notice on parents' noticeboard drawing attention to policy and procedures file. • Newsletter distributed by email or hard copy. • The family forum has a clear remit, meetings are held regularly and action taken on any issues arising.		
Staff protocols	• Staff wear name badges. • Staff photos are up to date. • Information on parent partnership policy in staff handbook.		
Learning and development information for parents	• Information on key experiences is made available to parents. • Photographs and documentation of children's learning is up to date and attractively displayed. • Children's development records are updated regularly and made available to parents on request. • Progress review meetings are held with individual families twice a year. • Families have access to information on children's learning and development and on creating a supportive home learning environment.		

THE PARENT PARTNERSHIP TOOLKIT FOR EARLY YEARS SECTION 2.1

Figure 2.1e cont

Inclusion	• Inclusion/special needs coordinator keeps accurate, up-to-date records and initiates progress reviews on individual children as and when necessary.		
Family support	• Family-support activities run in the setting are well advertised and actively promoted. • Information on other organisations offering family support services is readily available to parents in the reception area. • Parents are signposted to sources of additional support including adult learning opportunities where appropriate/requested.		
Consultation	• Family members are consulted on key issues that affect the setting. • Action is taken on the results of these consultations.		
Active involvement	• Family members are invited/facilitated to participate in the daily life of the setting. • Organising a variety of activities at different times of the day/week means that all parents are actively encouraged to become involved.		

Key points

- It takes time and effort to agree the vision of the setting and its underlying values.
- Agreeing shared values builds the ethos of the setting and creates a shared understanding of how life in the setting will be.
- The process of establishing the vision and values clarifies what the setting is trying to achieve and creates a sense of purpose.
- The vision and values will form the foundation on which parental partnerships can be built.
- Involving parents brings rewards for children, staff and the parents themselves.
- Parents know their individual child well and their views should be sought and listened to.
- Creating a strong relationship with parents is the springboard for all future discussions about a child's progress and development.
- Developing a parent partnership policy provides a framework for auditing existing provision and planning future services.
- The parent partnership policy should be available in a 'parent friendly' form and in a variety of languages if necessary.
- The policy should be checked to ensure that it is compatible with all the other policies of the setting.

Reflective questions

Vision and values

- Do we have a clear, succinct vision of what we are aiming to achieve?
- Have we established a set of shared values to support this vision?
- Who have we involved in agreeing the setting's vision and values?
- When did we last revisit our vision and values?

Involving parents

- Do all staff share an understanding of why it is important to involve parents in their young children's learning and development?
- How do we show that we value parents' contributions and the input they provide?
- How do we help parents to support their child's learning and development at home?
- Do we provide enough emotional and practical support for parents?

Providing information

- Do we know what the language needs of our parents are?
- Do we know how to produce clear, easy-to-read and easily understood information for parents?
- How do we let parents know where to find information that they might find useful?
- How up to date and interesting is the parents' noticeboard?

Parent partnership policy

- Who should we involve in establishing our parent partnership policy?
- Do we know what the statutory requirements underlying the policy are?
- Do our organisation and routines enable us to put the policy into practice?
- Do we have an effective system for monitoring the implementation of our policy?

Home-setting agreement

- Would a home-setting agreement be useful for us?
- Who decides what the agreement should cover?
- How would we use the home-setting agreement once established?
- What will we do if a parent is unwilling to sign the agreement?

Creating a welcoming environment

This section takes a closer look at the different elements of the physical and emotional environment that will influence how comfortable parents feel in a setting. It reviews the important role that the architecture of the building – the layout and organisation of space – plays in supporting or impeding the implementation of the setting's vision and values. The importance of creating a good first impression through paying attention to the physical space and to the welcome that parents experience is also considered. A series of audit sheets is provided to support a review of the physical layout and organisational structures of the setting to ensure that they support effective parent partnership. The content of the section is summarised in a series of key points and there are reflective questions to initiate further discussion and staff training.

An early years setting or children's centre functions as a community, made up of all the children and adults who make use of its services or work there. If the building is to serve its purpose well, the design of the space and how it is used must fully support the setting's pedagogical approach.

For example, it should:

- promote social competence and wellbeing by supporting relationships, respect, responsibility, equality of opportunity and the nurturing of a listening community
- inspire curiosity, creativity and imagination and feelings of self-confidence and self-esteem
- encourage a sense of adventure in a challenging but safe environment.

Environment

The way in which your setting is laid out, how the spaces are arranged and the types of furniture, equipment and resources that are found there will create the foundation on which to build your dialogue with parents about how, collectively, you can support young children's welfare, learning and development.

At a very simple level we can consider the environment in terms of the physical aspects of space – how much room there is, how it is laid out and the way it is accessed. These factors will be largely determined by the size, shape, age and overall use of the building the setting occupies. The physical environment will display key messages about your approach to supporting young children's learning and development, including the importance of listening to young children, the value of play, the need for risk and challenge and the role of parents in supporting their young children's learning at home. Displays and documentation panels capturing young children's learning in action will 'set the scene' and create the backdrop for conversations with parents about the value of partnership between the early years setting and the home (*see Section 2.4: Communicating with parents*).

However, any environment also includes an emotional element determined by how welcome people make us feel in that space. So, creating an environment that parents will feel comfortable in involves getting all elements of the equation correct – the space and the relationships between staff, parents and children. The aim should be to help parents and children feel that the setting is 'their place', somewhere where they can feel welcome and comfortable.

In creating a welcoming environment, time also plays a crucial role. By making sure that interaction with families is given a high priority, practitioners can give a very clear message about how much they value parental involvement. Taking time to create a calm start to the day will be beneficial for everyone – children, parents and practitioners.

In an ideal environment, there will be a synergy between the design and layout of the building and the vision, values and philosophy of the setting. Parents will be able to see and feel, from the moment they approach and enter the building, that this is a space where they are welcome. Achieving this involves being clear about the setting's values, knowing the parents who will be using the setting and paying attention to detail in terms of how the setting presents itself to the families who walk through the door. For examples of how this is handled in the preschools of Reggio Emilia, *see the box on p39*.

Achieving the right balance between maintaining safety and security and creating a welcoming environment is challenging. Children's safety is of paramount importance, but it is worth considering from a parent's perspective how intimidating locked doors and the physical barrier of a high reception desk might be. Key-pad entry systems can also inhibit the free flow of children and staff and make it difficult for everyone to move around the building.

First impressions

The first impression that a family gains of your setting will set the tone for the future relationships that develop between the home and the setting. Poor first impressions are always difficult to overcome and it can take a great deal of time and effort to recover from a poor start. Making a good impression can also be time consuming, but will pay handsome dividends in the long run. As with so many aspects of good management, attention to detail is the key to success.

Take a step back and think about these four aspects of how your setting presents itself to a family arriving there for the first time:

- What sort of a welcome do families experience when they arrive at the setting?
- What sort of information will they take away to remind them about different aspects of the setting and how it functions?
- What impression will they have of the staff who work there and their relationships with children, parents and colleagues?
- What impression will they gain of the space and organisation of the setting and how these are organised to support young children's welfare, learning and development? Think about the entrance area, room bases and outdoor space.

Making parents feel welcome

Every parent wants the best for his or her own child and, by having high aspirations for all children, practitioners can do much to support parents in the childrearing process.

Parent partnerships in the Reggio Approach

The importance of creating the right environment, for adults as well as for children, is very clearly demonstrated in the philosophy and practice of the preschools and infant-toddler centres of Reggio Emilia in northern Italy.

'Our objective, which we will always pursue, is to create an available environment in which children, families and teachers feel at ease.' – Malaguzzi (1998)

Buildings used as early childhood settings in Reggio Emilia range from purpose-built accommodation to converted houses and villas but all are planned to serve clearly identified purposes. The settings are organised so that there is space for children to express themselves, think and reflect, communicate and reinforce their identities. Equally importantly, there are also spaces where parents can engage with their children's learning, hear and be heard, meet with others and participate in the life of the setting. In this respect, early childhood settings in Reggio see themselves very much as an integral part of the local community, playing an important part in the lives of the families that use their services.

To help new parents and children feel comfortable that they understand the layout of the setting, every prospectus contains a floor plan of the building. By sharing this information about where everything is located and giving an idea of what happens in different parts of the building, nobody feels at a disadvantage through not knowing what goes on along the corridor or up the stairs.

Documentation panels showing photographs, transcripts of children's conversations, drawings, paintings and models line the walls of the preschool and infant-toddler centre buildings. These are there to share with parents what goes on in the building and to demonstrate the value that educators place on young children's thinking and learning. Some of the panels relate to projects that may have happened some time ago, but which are still seen as valuable as they help to connect parents to the history of the setting and the experiences that children have had there.

Contributing to the good relationship you build up with parents is the responsibility of all practitioners in your setting. The importance of valuing and respecting parents, from all social, cultural and ethnic backgrounds, must be at the core of your setting's values (*see Section 2.1: Establishing the vision and values*).

The telephone is an essential part of the communication system in any early years setting. For many parents, it will be their first contact with the setting and, once their child attends the setting, it is likely to be used regularly to convey important information. The skills of answering the telephone well may seem very obvious but are well worth nurturing in all members of staff:

- answer the phone as quickly as possible and say who is speaking and the name of the setting so the parent knows who he or she is talking to

- adopt a pleasant and welcoming telephone voice – even if you are feeling flustered and under pressure

- offer information or take a message as appropriate
- always write down messages and make sure they are passed on to the correct person
- follow up on any requests made by phone to make sure something happens.

Failing to pass on messages or follow up on requests could not only affect the welfare of a child in the setting but will also leave parents with the impression that the practitioners are disorganised and disinterested.

A good welcome is important at any time and could involve any number of simple but important acts. This could include:

- making eye contact and displaying open and encouraging body language
- a smile and a welcoming greeting – in the parent's home language if appropriate
- being attentive and noticing when a parent could do with help with opening a door, hanging up a coat or holding a child
- displaying a happy disposition and talking enthusiastically about what is going to happen during the day
- taking time to listen to parents and hear what they have to say
- demonstrating a 'can do' approach to daily challenges and problems.

All these will give powerful messages to parents about their role in the life of the setting. Once families have joined a setting, a good welcome at the beginning of the day will help to ensure that the day gets off to a good start for parent, child and practitioner. Think about the way that fathers are welcomed into the setting. Are they made to feel as welcome as mothers? Will they see images of fathers and children playing together in the entrance area?

In Reggio Emilia, educators pay a great deal of attention to the interactions between people at the beginning of the day, describing the threshold of the setting as 'a hinge between two delicate worlds', the world of the home and the world of the childcare setting.

Information for parents

The many different ways of presenting information to parents are looked at in detail in *Section 2.4: Communicating with parents*. On their initial visit, parents will not want to be overwhelmed with information but will need something to take away with them to remind them about the key aspects of how the setting works. This will include opening times, contact numbers, a brief summary of how the setting is organised and details of any fees payable. Think about including in the information pack a floor plan of the building showing where each of the home bases is located. This will paint a very visual picture of the setting and will convey much more than any amount of written description.

Relationships

Parents visiting a setting for the first time will be very aware of the ways in which staff members interact with one another and with children. Their interest and enthusiasm, the

SECTION 2.2

language they use, the degree of care and concern they show for one another will all be a part of the impression of the setting that parents take away. Parents will be looking and listening for interactions and relationships that reassure them that their child will be happy and well cared for. They will also be picking up key messages about how they will be treated by practitioners and how comfortable they will feel bringing their child to this setting.

Implementing the key person working effectively will play a very significant role in building up a strong and successful partnership with parents (*see Section 2.5: Key person working*). This way of working will need to be carefully explained to parents, and perhaps revisited on several occasions to respond to concerns they may have. The setting's policy on transitions and moving children on from group to group as they get older will also have a bearing on this.

How spaces and organisation support children's welfare, learning and development

The physical layout of the setting will do much to either enhance or hinder the development of good relationships with parents in your setting. General points to consider include:

- whether there are spaces available for parents to meet, make a hot drink and talk to one another
- whether there is space where parents can talk to practitioners in confidence, without being overheard
- where information about the organisation of the setting is kept and how it is presented
- how records of children's learning and development are stored so they are accessible to individual parents but still kept confidential
- the types of images there are around the setting, showing children of all ages and backgrounds actively engaged in learning, indoors and out
- where parents can access information about child development, child health and sources of further advice and support.

Auditing your environment to determine how 'family friendly' it is

The checklists in *figures 2.2a, 2.2b, 2.2c and 2.2d (see p43-46)* have been designed to help you to carry out an audit of how your setting currently presents itself to parents. These should help you to look at the setting the way a parent might do to identify areas you may want to work on to ensure parents gain a very positive impression of your setting and the way in which you want to work in partnership with them.

Using ITERS-R and ECERS-R

Many early years practitioners are using the ITERS-R (Infant-Toddler Environment Rating Scale, Revised Edition) and ECERS-R (Early Childhood Environmental Rating Scale, Revised Edition) as audit tools to look at the suitability of their environments to support young children's welfare, learning and development (*see: www.ecersuk.org/4.html*). These tools give a useful overall picture of a setting by looking in detail at how it is organised and resourced and how it functions, but should only be used by practitioners who have received some initial training in how to use and interpret the scales. Provision for parents is covered in Section 33 of the ITERS document and Section 38 of ECERS.

References

Harms, T, Cryer, D and Clifford, R (2006) *Infant/Toddler Environment Rating Scale (Revised Edition)*, Teachers College Press, New York

Harms, T, Clifford, R and Cryer, D (2005) *Early Childhood Environment Rating Scale (Revised Edition)*, Teachers College Press, New York

Malaguzzi, L (1998) 'History, Ideas and Basic Philosophy', in Edwards, C, Gandini, L, and Forman, G (eds) *The Hundred Languages of Children: The Reggio Emilia Approach – Advanced Reflections (2nd Edition)*, Stamford, CT

Reviewing the entrance space in your setting

Car park	• Is there space for parents to park safely?
	• Are the car-parking rules understood and adhered to by everyone?
	• Can children move safely from parked cars to the entrance of the building?
	• Are the rubbish and nappy-disposal bins stored out of sight?
	• Where do staff go if they wish to smoke?
Outdoor space at the front of the building	• Is the grass cut regularly?
	• Are bushes trimmed and flowerbeds weeded and planted?
	• Does the entrance to the building give the overall impression that it is well cared for?
	• Is there a secure storage area for buggies?
Front entrance	• How easy is it for parents or children with limited mobility to access the building?
	• Is the door-entry system easy to understand?
	• If there is a staffed reception desk in the entrance hall, could you have the entrance door closed but not locked at times when the desk is manned?
	• Review the instructions for gaining access to the building – would parents whose first language is not English be able to understand them easily?
Entrance hall	• How well cared for and tidy does it look?
	• What does it smell like and sound like?
	• Are there interesting things to look at that show what goes on in the setting?
	• Will families from different ethnic backgrounds see things that reflect their own cultural identity?
	• How welcoming are the staff members who first greet visitors to your setting? A smile and a friendly welcome will go a long way towards helping people feel at ease.
	• Is there a place for parents to sit comfortably and have a conversation with the manager or setting leader?
	• Are parents offered a cup of tea?
	• Is there somewhere to hang up a wet coat?
	• Are the toilets signposted and easily accessible?

THE PARENT PARTNERSHIP TOOLKIT FOR EARLY YEARS   SECTION 2.2

Figure 2.2b

Looking at the baby room through a parent's eyes

		Yes	No
1	Is the space tidy and uncluttered?		
2	Is the kitchen area clean?		
3	Are individual children's dietary requirements and any essential medical information displayed where they can be seen easily?		
4	How clear is it that practitioners take adequate precautions to protect babies' health?		
5	Is there space to store coats, shoes and spare clothing?		
6	Is the room clean and well decorated, particularly at skirting-board level, which is what babies will look at most?		
7	Are there comfortable coverings on the floor?		
8	Do we provide space and facilities for breastfeeding mothers?		
9	Is the atmosphere in the room calm and reassuring?		
10	Are artificial and natural light used to change the mood of the environment in keeping with the rhythm of the day?		
11	Are there handrails and pull-up bars to support babies who are beginning to stand up?		
12	Can babies see interesting things, such as mirrors, pictures and photographs, from floor level?		
13	Can parents see photographs displayed around the room showing babies involved in interesting experiences?		
14	How obvious is it that outdoor learning is as important as indoor learning?		
15	Is the baby's key person there to welcome him or her at the start of the day?		
16	Do parents feel comfortable that practitioners in the setting really know their individual child?		
17	Are significant moments, such as a baby's first step, recorded and shared with parents?		
18	Is there time for conversation at the beginning and end of the day?		
19	Do we provide enough feedback at the end of a day about how a baby has been, and what he or she has experienced during the day?		
20	Are we good at managing transition from one room base to another?		

What parents might look for in a preschool room

Relationships	• How happy the children appear to be. • How interested they are in what they are doing. • How the children interact with one another. • How the practitioners speak to the children. • How interested the practitioners appear to be in their work.
Organisation	• How well cared for the room is. • How uncluttered the space is. • Whether there is space for children to move around easily. • What types of activities the children are engaged in. • How easy it is to access the outdoors. • Evidence of children's learning visible around the room.
Resources	• Types of resources that are available and how well cared for they are. • Whether children can access the resources themselves. • How children treat books. • Whether there are books, photographs and displays that reflect their own child's ethnic background. • Whether children can take resources outside.
Mealtimes	• Menus and quality of the meals. • How mealtimes are organised. • Whether staff eat with the children. • How much emphasis is placed on mealtimes as occasions for social interaction and developing physical skills. • Whether children help to serve and clear up at mealtimes.
Children's welfare	• How independent children are when going to the toilet. • Whether they practise good hand hygiene. • What arrangements there are for children to rest during the day. • How well the key person system works. • How information is shared at the beginning and end of the day. • How effectively the setting's transition procedures work.

THE PARENT PARTNERSHIP TOOLKIT FOR EARLY YEARS

SECTION 2.2

Figure 2.2d

Reviewing outdoor spaces

	Always	Usually	Sometimes	Never
Does the outdoor space appear well cared for?				
Is outdoor equipment checked regularly to ensure it is safe?				
Are there areas of shade as well as open spaces?				
Is any litter or rubbish cleared away at the beginning and end of the day?				
Are there interesting resources for children of all ages to use outdoors?				
Are the resources used outside stored safely at the end of each day?				
Can children access the outdoors freely?				
Do babies and toddlers go outside every day?				
Do we have an adequate range of boots and waterproof suits for children to use?				
Do children go outside every day, regardless of the weather?				
Are there opportunities for children to dig and shift sand or soil on a large scale?				
Are children encouraged to learn about and appreciate the natural world?				
Do we provide resources so children can play with water on a large scale?				
Do we use the outdoors to develop children's skills in coping with risk and challenge?				
Are children able to grow things that they can then prepare and eat?				
Are learning opportunities outdoors valued as much as indoor learning?				
Are meals occasionally served outdoors in good weather?				
Do we plans trips and visits to help children learn more about their local community?				
Do we share with parents the importance of outdoor play?				
Do we help parents to understand the importance of children experiencing risk and challenge?				

Key points

- The environment includes not just the physical space but also the emotional environment created by the way that your vision and values are translated into practice.
- The way the environment is laid out can either enhance or inhibit your partnership with parents.
- First impressions are vitally important and lay the foundation for your future relationships with families.
- Regular reviews of the upkeep and state of repair of the building are essential to ensure it supports the messages you want to convey to parents.
- All practitioners in the setting have a part to play in making parents feel comfortable and at ease.
- Parents will want to see images that reflect their own identity and family circumstances.
- A floor plan of the building is a very simple way to convey a great deal of information about how a setting functions.
- Implementing the key person role well will make a huge contribution to making parents feel welcome and valued.
- Look after your outdoor spaces and make them interesting and exciting places to be.
- Try to find space where parents can meet together, talk and relax, making the setting an important part of the local community.

Reflective questions

Managing spaces

- Have we looked objectively at how we use space in the setting?
- Does every space have a purpose and does everyone – parents, staff and children – understand what that purpose is?
- How well do we take responsibility for keeping the setting clean and tidy?
- How can we create a building that parents, children and staff find a pleasure to enter and spend time in?

Making parents feel welcome

- Do we all understand our responsibility to make all parents feel welcome?
- Are we aware of the home languages of the families who use our setting and have we learned how to greet individuals in their own language?
- How good are we at trying to see things from a parent's perspective?
- Do we need a protocol for handling phone calls?

Displaying positive images

- How well do we really know our local community?
- Do we need to improve the range of resources we have so they better reflect the diversity of families using our setting?
- How can we ensure that all the important information about the setting is available in a range of formats and languages?
- Do we display images at the right height for children to see them?

Listening to parents

- How can we make more time to listen to parents?
- How well does our key person system work in practice?
- Do we give parents enough information about transitions from room to room within the setting?
- Do we move children on from room to room too often?

Spaces for parents

- How important is it that we create a space where parents can meet together?
- What should this space look like?
- How would it be used?
- Who should be consulted on how the space is organised and managed?

Listening to parents

This section reviews what is involved in creating a listening culture that demonstrates to parents that their views, of their own child and about the work of the setting, are welcomed and valued. It looks at good practice in listening to specific parental groups – families from ethnic minorities, fathers, teenage parents and parents of children with additional needs. The question, 'Why consult with parents?' is reviewed and there is information on how to manage consultation groups and how to design an effective consultation questionnaire. Examples of questionnaires that would be appropriate for different early years settings are provided, along with sample letters to parents, setting out the framework and purpose of the consultation process. The content of the section is then summarised in several key points and reflective questions that are useful for staff training and professional development.

Caring for and educating young children in an early years setting is a huge responsibility and one that can only be carried out successfully if parents and educators work together in the best interests of the child and their family. Creating an effective partnership with parents is the key to supporting individual children's learning and development. It is dependent on being prepared to listen to and value what parents have to say on a wide range of issues, from those that affect their own child's welfare, learning and development to opinions on wider aspects of the organisation and management of the setting.

Creating a listening culture

From the time that families join your setting, it is important to spend time building up a relationship of trust so that they feel comfortable to share information, knowing that their confidentiality will be respected. Evidence shows that the vast majority of parents try to provide the best for their children, but may face barriers that prevent them from doing this successfully (Whalley et al, 2007; Waylen and Stewart-Brown, 2008). Getting to know a family well will help you to avoid making stereotypical generalisations about how different people live their lives. Meeting with and talking to parents can be a time-consuming process but there is no doubt that it lays the best foundations from which the parent-setting relationship can grow and flourish. It also provides an opportunity to pick up the clues that will help you identify parents who might benefit from additional support to develop their parenting skills (see *Section 2.6: Supporting parent-child relationships*).

It is important to remember that, for many parents, going to a children's centre or early years setting may be the first time they have shared responsibility for their child's welfare with someone outside their immediate family. Introducing parents to the key person who will have particular responsibility for the welfare, learning and development of their child will help to reassure them that their child will be treated as an individual and not an anonymous member of a larger group. Organising home visits provides a very successful way of beginning to build a relationship with a family in an environment in which they feel comfortable (see *Section 2.5: Key person working*).

Showing parents that you are interested in and value their perspective on their child puts organisational demands on the setting and its staff. As a starting point, it is important to create the right emotional and physical environment so that parents feel welcome, comfortable and at ease. There should be space within the setting where parents can talk privately to practitioners, confident that they will not be overheard. This can place heavy demands on many settings where space is at a premium but, with some reordering of priorities and creative 'timetabling' of room use, it should be possible to achieve this *(see Section 2.2: Creating a welcoming environment)*.

Parents need access to a range of written information that they can take away and read at their leisure. This information may cover organisational arrangements, details of how children's welfare, learning and development will be supported and where to access further advice and support. It must be clearly presented, written in an accessible style with no confusing jargon and abbreviations and, if appropriate, translated into several languages *(see Section 2.4: Communicating with parents)*.

Use the *audit sheet in figure 2.3a on p60* to review how well you currently engage with all the different groups of parents who use your setting.

Having time to talk

Perhaps the most important message that you can give to parents, especially in the early stages of building the parent-setting relationship, is that you have time to talk with them, to hear their views, share information and answer their questions. We are all aware of the many demands there are on the time of a busy setting leader or manager. However, prioritising the time spent engaging with parents, rather than seeing it as something to be added on to an already busy day, will bring long-term benefits for children, parents and staff. Establishing the vision and values of your setting and developing your parent partnership policy will provide the framework you need to do this *(see Section 2.1: Establishing the vision and values)*.

Creating a calm and unhurried start to the day will benefit not only the children in your care, but also their parents. Some parents may want to stay and talk, sharing their interest and concerns, while others may rush in and out as quickly as possible. Do not assume that the latter group are not interested in their child; it may be that this is their way of dealing with the separation from their child. Take time to engage with these parents and provide opportunities for them to share their feelings and emotions. While it is well recognised that a parent who leaves a child who has become upset and distressed will welcome a phone call during the day reassuring them that all is well, remember that a parent who leaves a quiet and subdued child may also appreciate this reassurance.

Respecting cultural diversity

The families who use your early years setting will come from a variety of different backgrounds, so it is essential to remember that there will be no 'one-size-fits-all' solution to engaging with and involving parents. At any one time you may have children in your setting from a range of ethnic and cultural backgrounds, living in a variety of different family structures. There may be children with particular physical conditions who have distinct requirements as well as children and families who would benefit from additional social and emotional support. Each of these families is unique and will bring their own interests, understandings and challenges to enhance the life of the setting.

For families whose home language is not English, it is vital that information about the setting is straightforward and easy to interpret (*see Section 2.4: Communicating with parents*). Visual images showing families from a variety of ethnic backgrounds will help parents to feel comfortable, as will the availability of leaflets and notices written in the most common home languages of the families using the setting. If at all possible, the ethnic make-up of the staff of the setting should reflect that of the community it serves. In some situations, it may be possible to call on the support of community champions who will help to bridge the gap between the setting and particular ethnic groups in the community. This is particularly important where local families come from cultures that do not traditionally use childcare and early years services. Community champions can create the all-important first link between the setting and the family, on which practitioners can then build.

Home visits, enabling practitioners to gain an insight into a child's life outside the setting, provide an ideal opportunity to understand how best to make the connection between early years services and the family. Visiting children in their home environment enables the practitioner to build up a more complete picture of family circumstances, language spoken and opportunities available to the child to play indoors and outside. Practitioners can begin to establish relationships, provide information and answer questions in a friendly non-threatening environment where the parent is likely to feel more at ease (see Section 2.5: Key person working and also the box on *reciprocal relationships in the Reggio Approach on p52*).

Resources for work with ethnic minority families

- DCSF (2007) *Early Years and Childcare: LA Developing Practice – Improving Communication and Engaging with Parents*: *www.dcsf.gov.uk/everychildmatters/resources-and-practice/EP00367*

- Fatherhood Institute – downloadable resources and examples of good practice when working with men from African Caribbean and Muslim families: *www.fatherhoodinstitute.org*

- Together for Children, Minority ethnic families case studies: *www.childrens-centres.org/Topics/CaseStudies/MinorityEthnicFamilies.aspx*

- DCSF (2007) *Sure Start and Black and Minority Populations*: *http://bit.ly/SureStartBlackandMinorityPopulations*

- DCSF (2005) *Use of Childcare Among Families from Minority Ethnic Backgrounds*: *www.dcsf.gov.uk/everychildmatters/10454*

- DfES (2006) 'Working with Minority Ethnic Families', Sure Start Children's Centres Practice Guidance, section 16: *www.dcsf.gov.uk/everychildmatters/earlyyears/surestart/surestartchildrenscentres/practiceguidance/practiceguidance/*

> ## Reciprocal relationships between parents, teachers and children
> The Reggio Approach to early childhood care and education places great importance on listening to parents and valuing what they have to say. The reciprocal relationships that exist between parents, teachers and children is a fundamental of the Reggio philosophy and is frequently depicted as a triangle of relationships:
>
>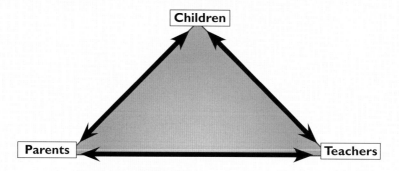
>
> The double headed arrows depict the reciprocal two-way relationships that exist between the groups, each being dependent on and learning from the other.
>
> Educators in Reggio value multiple perspectives, looking at things from several different points of view and valuing everyone's opinion and contribution. They value the opinions and views of individuals of different ages, and from different cultural and ethnic backgrounds and see it as a strength, not a disadvantage, that people hold different opinions about things.
>
> The importance of listening to parents and valuing their views is epitomised in the quality of the documentation that is shared with parents as part of their child's experience in an infant-toddler centre or preschool. Documentation panels on the walls, photographs, visual diaries and beautifully presented narratives of projects help to keep parents fully connected with their child's daily life in the setting. (Thornton and Brunton, 2009)

Listening to fathers

The involvement of fathers in their young children's upbringing from birth onwards has been shown to have a positive effect on both the father and the child. An increasing number of men are becoming involved in young children's early learning and development and it is essential that early years settings embrace this and look carefully at how they ensure equality of opportunity for male parents and carers. To support this work, an increasing range of resources is becoming available through government-funded and charity-sponsored websites, including the Baby Father Alliance, Fatherhood Institute, Think Fathers and Parent Know How.

Consulting with fathers can help practitioners to gain an insight into how their setting is perceived by men, enabling them to implement small changes in environment, organisation or attitudes that can have a big impact. These could include:

- organising the home visit at a time when both parents can be present (see *Section 2.5: Key person working*)
- ensuring the colours and décor of the setting are neutral, rather than predominantly feminine

- including images of men and children playing together as part of the visual display

- moving the children's coat pegs into the setting and away from the door so parents have to come right in to the setting rather than stay on the boundary

- not assuming men are always in a hurry and do not have time to stop and talk about their child

- talking directly to the fathers of the children in your setting rather than addressing them indirectly through their female partners

- organising information or play sessions that focus on fathers' interests (*see Section 3.3: Out and about* and *Section 3.4: Family workshops – exploring together*).

Family Information Direct is a government-funded programme aimed at improving the quality, choice, provision and awareness of parental information and support services. It has a particular focus on meeting the needs of fathers from all backgrounds and includes telephone helplines, digital services, print, video and audio content, and a Family Information Direct Directory. This is an online directory offering parents and those working with them the ability to search for information about childcare and family services, in both their local community and nationally (*www.dcsf.gov.uk/familyinformationdirect*).

Advice on working with fathers, including those from African Caribbean families is also available from the BabyFather Alliance network of Barnardo's (*www.barnardos.org.uk/babyfather*).

The Fatherhood Institute has a wide range of resources designed to support practitioners in engaging more effectively with fathers. These include good practice guides on working with African Caribbean and Muslim fathers and a model consultation format for finding out more about the views of fathers in your setting. The institute is also running a 'Think Fathers' campaign to help setting managers audit how father-friendly their services are. All these resources are downloadable from: *www.fatherhoodinstitute.org*.

Resources for working with fathers

- Father-inclusive services recommended in Every Child Matters: *www.dcsf.gov.uk/ everychildmatters/strategy/parents/pip/PIPrkfatherinclusiveservices/PIPfatherinclusiveservices*

- *Fathers Matter* leaflet from Pre School Learning Alliance: *www.pre-school.org.uk/ documents/238*

- Together for Children, Working with Fathers Case Studies: *www.childrens-centres.org/ Topics/CaseStudies/Fathers.aspx*

- DfES (2006) 'Working with Fathers', Sure Start Children's Centres Practice Guidance, section 14: *www.dcsf.gov.uk/everychildmatters/earlyyears/surestart/ surestartchildrenscentres/practiceguidance/practiceguidance/*

Engaging with teenage parents

Again, it is important to think carefully about the language used and the visual images around the setting to ensure that parents of all ages can feel comfortable in the environment. Young parents have very particular needs, which practitioners will want to address successfully to make sure that the experience they and their children have in the setting is a positive and supportive one. Being organised and coping with regular routines are not skills that come naturally to all young people. Practitioners may find they need to spend time helping younger parents to understand the value of structure in their daily lives, building the confidence of young parents in managing their childcare responsibilities. The early years setting will also be an invaluable source of advice and support, a place to share information about child development and to signpost parents to sources of information on training and career development opportunities.

Resources for working with teenage parents

- DFES (2005): *Reaching Out to Pregnant Teenagers and Teenage Parents: www.education.gov. uk/research/programmeofresearch/projectinformation.cfm?projectid=14536&resultspage=1*
- DFES (2006) 'Working with Teenage Parents', Sure Start Children's Centres Practice Guidance, section 15, see: *www.dcsf.gov.uk/everychildmatters/earlyyears/surestart/ surestartchildrenscentres/practiceguidance/practiceguidance/*
- Together for Children, Young parents case studies: *www.childrens-centres.org/Topics/ CaseStudies/YoungParents.aspx*

Supporting families of children with additional needs

Early years settings have a very important role to play in supporting parents of children with additional needs. All families will want to feel included, accepted and valued by the rest of the early years community and not treated as separate or different. Although the range of needs that different children demonstrate will be diverse, there will be many commonalities in the way in which the setting can engage with parents. Most of the skills needed to establish relationships with families whose children have additional needs are identical to those utilised with all other parents using the setting.

In building up a supportive relationship with parents of children with additional needs practitioners will want to:

- spend time listening to parents in order to understand their hopes and aspirations for their child

- be flexible in organisation and routines to accommodate particular needs

- ensure the family's key person has the skills, knowledge and temperament to support the child and his or her family

- help parents to understand the terminology and processes of the Special Educational Needs Code of Practice (DfES, 2001)

- liaise with other professionals to ensure the setting provides the best opportunities to support the child's welfare, learning and development

- be available to host and attend meetings concerned with supporting the child and his or her family

- support children and families during times of transition

- establish a strong supportive relationship with the family without becoming over-involved on a personal level.

Resources to support families of children with additional needs

- Early support resources – 'Family File', 'Family Pack', 'Background Information' booklets and 'Information for Parents' booklets: *www.dcsf.gov.uk/everychildmatters/ healthandwellbeing/ahdc/earlysupport/resources/esresources*

- Family Information Direct: *www.dcsf.gov.uk/familyinformationdirect*

- DfES/DWP (2005) *Area Special Educational Needs Co-ordinators (SENCOs) – Supporting Early Identification and Intervention for Children with Special Educational Needs*: *www.dcsf. gov.uk/everychildmatters/10168*

- DfES (2006) 'Working with disabled children', Sure Start Children's Centres Practice Guidance: *www.dcsf.gov.uk/everychildmatters/earlyyears/surestart/surestartchildrenscentres/ practiceguidance/practiceguidance/*

- Dukes, C and Smith, M (2007) *Working with Parents of Children with Special Educational Needs*, SAGE, London

---

Consulting with parents

Building a culture of openness and respect in a setting is about more than just responding to the needs and concerns of individual families. It also involves being proactive, consulting with parents and actively engaging them in key issues to do with the life of the setting. The range of issues you choose to consult parents on is very varied, but at different times it could include:

- organisational arrangements to do with the daily running of the setting

- information sharing – what is available and how it is presented

- involvement in specific projects and initiatives

- plans for change or future development.

Devising a consultation timetable setting out different aspects to be consulted on at different times of year will help to embed the 'consultation ethos' in the life of the setting.

Why consult with parents?

Finding the answer to this question is the first step towards designing and implementing an effective consultation strategy that will produce answers that will in turn enhance the life of the setting. Consulting with parents and taking their views into account when planning your provision provides opportunities to:

- improve the organisation and management of the setting by helping to focus on what parents' perceptions are and what is important to them

- minimise misunderstandings and opportunities for dissatisfaction

- add value to the work of the setting by tapping into a broader range of ideas and experiences

- provide a 'gateway' to supplying information to parents about how to support their child's learning and development

- create a platform from which to address child health, welfare and safeguarding issues

- open up a dialogue between the setting and its families about what is 'best' for children.

How to consult

Deciding how best to consult with parents and gain the maximum benefit from the time and effort involved will vary depending on the:

- issue being addressed

- type of information you are trying to gather

- means of communication that the majority of parents feel most comfortable with – written, verbal, IT-based, visual

- timescale of the consultation

- number of individuals with whom you are hoping to consult.

Parent consultation can range from anecdotal evidence gathered in informal conversation with one or more parents to more structured questionnaires designed to gather factual information from as many participants as possible. Each has its place but it is important to vary the ways in which you gather evidence about what parents think to ensure that you are, as far as possible, tapping into the views and opinions of a broad cross section of your parent group.

As with all other aspects of communication with parents, it is essential to make the consultation as inclusive as possible. Written questionnaires are very popular as they enable you to ask a series of structured questions. This provides factual information that can be analysed to help you gauge parental opinion. However, not everyone will be comfortable with the written word. You might consider using a structured questionnaire but talking it through with individual parents face to face or over the telephone. Other parents may prefer to access information electronically and would prefer to complete an online survey. This could be available through your website and certainly provides a very cost-effective way of gathering information. It might also be a good way to reach working parents who do not have a lot of time at the beginning and end of the day.

Discussions in small groups where parents are invited to comment on specific issues can be a relatively non-threatening way of gathering opinions. These can often work well when canvassing opinion on issues that affect a particular group of parents within your setting. For instance, you might want to set up a small group to find out what the setting could do to make fathers feel more welcome and involved. However, it is very important to be aware of

SECTION 2.3 THE PARENT PARTNERSHIP TOOLKIT FOR EARLY YEARS

the dangers of groups such as these appearing to exclude parents who are unavailable at the time the group meets.

Many early years settings have parents' committees or parents' forums, which fulfil a very wide range of functions in supporting the life of the setting. These groups can often be useful sounding boards for trying out ideas and gathering initial opinions but should not be used as the only means of parental consultation. Although they will be proactive and interested in what is happening in the setting, they will not necessarily be representative of the whole parental population, whose views should also be sought.

Organising a consultation group

A little forward planning and organisation can help you to get the most out of everyone's time in a consultation group meeting.

Try to schedule the meeting for a time when the maximum number of people may be able to attend – before the end of a morning or afternoon session is ideal. This has the added advantage of placing a natural limit on the time the group will meet for.

- Invite all parents to attend, giving them as much notice as possible.
- Be clear about the areas you want to consult on and circulate this information in advance so parents have time to think about the issue and how it affects them.
- Organise refreshments; start and end the meeting on time.
- Spend a few minutes at the beginning of the meeting establishing some simple ground rules about respecting and listening to everyone's opinion.
- Try to keep the meeting on track and take notes of the key points being raised. Be aware of other issues that parents might want to talk about, but do not let the meeting go off at a tangent.
- Encourage everyone to speak, perhaps by addressing specific questions to quieter, more reticent parents, and try not to let any one voice dominate the meeting.
- A few key points noted on a flip chart or large sheet of paper will help to reassure parents that they are being listened to and that something will come out of the consultation process.
- If there are important issues raised that are not part of the planned discussion, agree with the parents that these will be 'parked' and addressed on a subsequent occasion. Sometimes it is helpful to write these on a sticky note and stick it on the flip chart so parents can see that the issue is not being ignored.
- Spend five minutes at the end of the meeting summarising what has been discussed so everyone has a clear view of the outcome of the meeting.
- Circulate the information from the meeting as soon as possible to all parents, including any decisions that have been made as a result of the consultation.

57

Using a questionnaire

Although consultation group meetings can be a good way of gauging parents' opinions and identifying issues that may be a cause for concern, they often produce information that is hard to analyse and quantify. Putting together a questionnaire should enable you to ask some more precise questions and tap into a wider cross section of parental opinion.

Types of questionnaire

Questionnaires can be put together in many different ways, depending on the information that you are hoping to gather.

- Structured questionnaires consist of a series of precisely worded questions in a particular order and have the advantage of being relatively easy to analyse.

- Unstructured questionnaires are often used as part of one-to-one consultations, either in person or over the telephone. They are usually made up of a checklist of questions that the person managing the consultation can explore in more depth, depending on the responses they receive. However, the information they provide will be more difficult to analyse because of the more wide-ranging nature of the questions.

- The 'half-way house' is to use a semi-structured questionnaire so you can collect statistical information along with the reasons why people think or do certain things.

Types of questions to ask

A questionnaire will usually consist of questions that fall into three broad categories:

- **Classification questions** – this covers a standard range of information, such as age, gender and number of children. Depending on the topic on which you are consulting, you may want to use a limited number of this type of question.

- **Behaviour** – these questions are to help you gather factual responses about how people behave in different situations. They include questions such as, 'Have you ever…?', 'When did you last…?', 'How often do you...?' Again, these provide numerical information that you can analyse.

- **Attitude** – these are the really interesting questions as they attempt to find out people's perceptions of why they do things. They include questions such as, 'Why do you…?', 'What do you think of...?', 'Would you be interested in…?'

Attitudes are often measured on a sliding scale ranging from strongly agree to strongly disagree or by using emoticons – smiley, neutral or sad faces – to express opinions.

Key steps to producing a good consultation questionnaire

- Be clear about the aim of the consultation to avoid asking irrelevant questions or missing any really important points.

- Think about how the questionnaire will be used. If it is to be completed by a parent on his or her own it needs to be as clear and unambiguous as possible.

- When you are writing the questions, bear in mind the people who will be completing it and the possible answers they might give.

- Make sure questions are grouped together in a logical sequence so particular types of information are dealt with together.

- Make the questionnaire as visually appealing as possible so parents will want to complete it.

- Keep the language and the wording simple and straightforward and do not use any jargon, abbreviations or words that could be misinterpreted.

- If you feel that any of the questions you are asking may be sensitive, think about using response bands (for example, age 20-25, 26-30, 31-35) instead of exact figures. Make sure these bands do not overlap or it will be impossible to complete the questionnaire accurately.

- Decide whether you would like the questionnaire to be anonymous or not. It is probably best to provide an option so parents can make this decision themselves.

It is always a good idea to try reading out loud the first draft of your consultation questionnaire to see if it makes sense. Make any necessary changes and then try it out on someone else. Ask a few parents to complete it to see how easy they find it to use and then make use of their comments to improve the structure and readability of the final version.

To help you in designing your own questionnaires, examples of three questionnaires appropriate to different early years settings are shown in *figures 2.3b on p61, 2.3d on p65 and 2.3f on p70.* These are accompanied by sample letters for parents, describing the focus of the questionnaires and how the information will be used – *figures 2.3c on p64, 2.3e on p69 and 2.3g on p73.*

Feeding back the results of a consultation

Having carried out a consultation exercise and analysed the results, it is important that the findings are fed back to parents as soon as possible. This will help to keep them engaged with the consultation process and make them more likely to participate in the future. The feedback should include the decisions that have been made in response to the consultation. Taking action is the most effective way of showing that parents' views and opinions are valued.

References

DfES (2001) *Special Educational Needs Code of Practice*, see: *www.teachernet.gov.uk/_doc/3724/SENCodeofPractice.pdf*

Thornton, L and Brunton, P (2009) *Understanding the Reggio Approach (2nd Edition)*, Routledge, Abingdon

Waylen, A and Stewart-Brown, S (2008) *Diversity, complexity and change in parenting: Parenting during early and middle childhood and how it changes over time*, Joseph Rowntree Foundation, see: *www.jrf.org.uk/publications/diversity-complexity-and-change-parenting*

Whalley, M and the Pen Green Centre Team (2007) *Involving Parents in their Children's Learning*, SAGE, London

Including all parents

	Yes	No	Action
Parents using the setting will be able to 'recognise themselves' in the visual images they see around them.			
The décor of the setting is neutral and not overtly feminine.			
The books and resources used by the children reflect different cultures, customs and family circumstances.			
We are aware of the different home languages used by our children.			
Our equal opportunities and anti-discriminatory policies are up to date and consistently implemented.			
Staff receive appropriate training as part of their induction and ongoing professional development.			
Staff members are aware of and respect different family structures.			
The verbal and written language we use encompasses both male and female carers.			
Fathers are consulted about how key aspects of the organisation of the setting affect them.			
We actively encourage fathers to become involved in their children's learning and development.			
We provide opportunities for men to act as good role models for their children.			
Groups and activities are organised that interest men and enable them to become involved in the life of the setting.			
We encourage men to work as part of the childcare team and provide them with an appropriate working environment.			
Efforts are made to include all parents in consultation processes.			
We know the support that parents of children with additional needs would welcome and find time to provide it.			
Staff have the training and support they require to identify and support children with additional needs.			
We are aware of the support available to parents from other agencies and can direct them to it.			
The setting recognises and responds to its responsibility to support parents who may need advice and support in fulfilling their roles as parents.			
Parents are consulted about the range of information and support they would find useful.			
Information sessions, drop-in advice sessions and parenting support programmes are organised in response to parental requests/needs.			

SECTION 2.3

Sample questionnaire for a children's centre consulting users on the range of services it provides

Children's centre services

To improve the services we provide for you and your family we would like to ask you a few questions. We will use the answers you give us to plan what happens in the centre during the week.

If you prefer not to provide your name please complete the questionnaire anyway as all the information will be useful.

Please return the completed survey by ……………..………… There is a box in the entrance hall that you can drop it into.

Q1. How many children do you have of the following ages?

Under 1 year _____   1 year old _____   2 years old _____

3 years old _____   4 years old _____   5-8 years old _____

Q2. Do you currently use any of the centre's services?

Yes ☐   No ☐

Q3. If yes, which services do you use? Please tick all the services you use.

Baby club	☐	Breastfeeding support	☐
Toddler time	☐	Stay and play	☐
Story time	☐	Cooking together	☐
Early years provision	☐	Wraparound care	☐

Q4. If no, can you tell us why you do not use these services?

Not at the right time	☐	Too far way	☐
Other childcare responsibilities	☐	Too expensive	☐
Not what I am interested in	☐		

Other reasons – please tell us what:

_____

_____

_____

_____

THE PARENT PARTNERSHIP TOOLKIT FOR EARLY YEARS   SECTION 2.3

Figure 2.3b *cont*

Q5. Would you be interested in using any of these services? Please tick any that you would like to know more about.

Family learning activities	☐	Dads and babies group	☐
Music sessions	☐	Forest school activities	☐
Job hunters' club	☐	Stop smoking	☐

Q6. Can you tell us which groups you enjoy most and why?

Q7. If there are any groups that you have tried and then stopped going to, please tell us what you did not like about them.

Q8. Are there any other groups or services that you would like the centre to set up?

SECTION 2.3 THE PARENT PARTNERSHIP TOOLKIT FOR EARLY YEARS

Q9. Please help us to review how the children's centre works for you by giving us your opinion on these things.

	Strongly agree	Agree	Disagree	Strongly disagree
I enjoy coming to the centre				
I am always made to feel welcome				
I think my child benefits from coming to the centre				
The centre has a good range of groups and activities				
I can usually find the information I need				
The services I pay for are good value for money				

Q10. Please tell us how we could improve the services we offer you.

_____

_____

_____

_____

_____

_____

_____

_____

_____

If you would like to add your name and telephone number, please do. If you prefer not to, that is fine.

Name:

Telephone:

THE PARENT PARTNERSHIP TOOLKIT FOR EARLY YEARS   SECTION 2.3

Sample letter to parents and potential users of children's centre services

Address   **Date**

Dear

Looking at what we do

In the children's centre we try to provide a wide range of services and groups to help you as a family. We have groups for parents of small babies and advice and activity sessions for families with toddlers. We also have a nursery that can provide care and education for children from birth until the time they start school.

We would like to find out how well our services meet your needs as a family. Which things do you think we are doing well and what do we need to improve on?

Please help us by filling in this questionnaire and returning it to us by .... You can drop it in the box in the entrance hall. If you put your name on your survey form we can answer any questions you have. If you prefer not to give your name, please complete the survey anyway as all the information is useful.

When we have looked at what our survey tells us we will put a notice on the parents' noticeboard. This will let you know what we have found out and what we are going to do to improve the services we offer.

Thank you for taking the time to help us improve what we do in the centre.

Yours sincerely,

Name

Position

Sample questionnaire for consulting parents of children attending an early years setting on organisational arrangements

How our early years setting works

In our setting we aim to make sure that your child enjoys the time that they spend with us and that they achieve well. We want to make sure that the setting runs efficiently and meets the needs of you and your family.

We would like you to give us your opinion on different aspects of the organisation and running of our setting. When we have collected all your responses we will look at what they tell us about how we could improve the way the setting runs.

There is a space at the bottom of the form to add your name, but if you prefer not to do this please complete the survey anyway as all the information will be useful.

Please return the completed survey by .... There is a box in the entrance hall that you can drop it into.

Q1. What ages are your children?

Under 1 year _____   1 year old _____   2 years old _____

3 years old _____   4 years old _____

Q2. How many of your children attend the setting?

_____

_____

Q3. Where do you go to find out any information you need about the setting? Please tick all you use.

Prospectus	☐	Procedures and policies file	☐
Parents' noticeboard	☐	Website	☐
Ask key person	☐	Ask manager/setting leader	☐
Ask another parent	☐	Do not have any questions	☐

Other – please specify:

_____

_____

_____

_____

THE PARENT PARTNERSHIP TOOLKIT FOR EARLY YEARS   SECTION 2.3

Figure 2.3d cont

Q4. Please comment on how welcome we make you feel.

	Always	Usually	Sometimes	Never
People greet me by name when I come into the setting				
The entrance area is pleasant, tidy and welcoming				
Staff wear name badges				
People smile at me and know my child's name				
My child is greeted by his or her key person every morning				
I know who to go to if I am unhappy about anything				

Is there anything else we can do to make you feel more welcome?

Q5. Please give us your opinion on the information we provide for you.

	Strongly agree	Agree	Disagree	Strongly disagree
I can find information when I want it				
The information is easy to understand				
The setting provides me with too much information				
I would like more information about how the setting works				
I would like more information about what my child is doing				

SECTION 2.3 THE PARENT PARTNERSHIP TOOLKIT FOR EARLY YEARS

Figure 2.3d cont

Q6. We are interested in your opinion of how our key person system is working.

Do you know who your child's key person is? Yes ☐ No ☐

How well do you feel you understand the role of a key person?

Well ☐ A little ☐ Not at all ☐

Do you think the key person system is helpful:

For you Yes ☐ No ☐

For your child Yes ☐ No ☐

Would you like to know more about the key person system? Yes ☐ No ☐

Q7. We are interested in finding out if our session times work well for you.

Would it be helpful if the setting opened earlier in the morning? Yes ☐ No ☐

What time do you arrive in the morning? _____

What time would you prefer to arrive? _____

What time do you collect your child? _____

What time would you prefer to collect your child? _____

Do you have any other comments about our opening hours?

_____

_____

_____

Q8. How do you feel about the meals we serve?

	Strongly agree	Agree	Disagree	Strongly disagree
The weekly menu is always available on the noticeboard				
My child enjoys the meals she/he has				
I am told if my child does not eat his/her meals				
I think the setting provides a good range of healthy choices				
I feel the meals are good value for money				

67

THE PARENT PARTNERSHIP TOOLKIT FOR EARLY YEARS

SECTION 2.3

Figure 2.3d cont

Please let us have your thoughts on how we could improve our meals:

_____

_____

_____

_____

_____

Q9. Please tell us three things that you think we do well.

1. _____

_____

2. _____

_____

3. _____

_____

Q10. Please let us know three things that we should try and improve.

1. _____

_____

2. _____

_____

3. _____

_____

If you would like to add your name and telephone number, please do. If you prefer not to, that is fine.

Name: _____

Telephone: _____

Sample letter for parents describing the purpose of the questionnaire

Address   **Date**

Dear...

Finding out what works

We are always looking for ways to improve the way our setting runs. Every year we like to ask you some simple questions to find out your opinions about how the setting is organised. We would like as many people as possible to respond so that we can look at ways of changing what we do to suit everyone.

Please complete this short survey and return it to us by...................There is a box in the entrance hall that you can drop it into. You can put your name on the bottom of the survey if you wish. If you do not want to do this, please complete it anyway as all the information is useful to us.

We have asked some questions about things that we feel are important but there is also space at the end for you to comment on any other things that are important to you.

We will look at what the results of the survey tell us and share this with you – in the newsletter and on the noticeboard. We will then make some changes to the way the setting works. If there are things that we cannot change, we will explain why.

Thank you for your help.

Name

Position

THE PARENT PARTNERSHIP TOOLKIT FOR EARLY YEARS   SECTION 2.3

Figure 2.3f

Example of a questionnaire asking parents of Reception class children about their experience of joining a new school

Finding out how you feel

In this survey we would like to find out how well you and your child are settling in to life at .... school.

Please take time to complete it and return it to us by .... There is a box in the entrance area you can put it into or you can give it to one of us when your child arrives in the morning.

Please remember we are always happy to answer any questions you may have. We want you and your child to feel welcome here.

Q1. How many children do you have at the school?

Q2. Which classes are they in?

Q3. Home visits

Did a member of staff visit you in your home before your child started at the school?

Yes ☐   No ☐

If your answer is yes, did you find this helpful?   Yes ☐   No ☐

If your answer is no, would you have liked a visit?   Yes ☐   No ☐

Q4. Key person system

Do you know who your child's key person is?   Yes ☐   No ☐

Do you know how our key person system works?   Yes ☐   No ☐

Q5. Information

How well do you feel you know what is happening in the school?

	Yes	No
I have a prospectus		
I can find what I need to know in the prospectus		
I use the school website for information		
I know where the parents' noticeboard is		
I rely on other parents to tell me what is happening		
I know a little about what happens in the rest of the school		

SECTION 2.3   THE PARENT PARTNERSHIP TOOLKIT FOR EARLY YEARS

Q6. Learning together

We often run family workshops to help you find out more about how young children learn. Which of these might you be interested in?

Learning through play ☐		Exploring numbers ☐
Fun with words ☐		Playing outdoors ☐
Techno tot ☐		Musical magic ☐

Q7. Helping your child at home

We have lots of different things that you can borrow to use with your child at home. Have you borrowed any of these?

Activity packs ☐		Books ☐
Discovery boxes ☐		Storysacks ☐
Number rhyme bags ☐		Good ideas sheets ☐

Q8. What your child is learning at school

Can you tell us how much you know about these things?

	A great deal	A little	Nothing
The Early Years Foundation Stage (EYFS)			
The EYFS profile			
Learning stories			
Phonics			

Q9. Getting involved

We are always happy for parents to be involved in things that are happening in the school. Which of these would you be interested in?

Helping with trips and visits	☐
Helping with a project the children are doing	☐
Coming in to talk to the children about the job I do	☐
Sharing my skills with the children	☐
Helping to organise fundraising and social events	☐

Q10. Room for improvement

Please tell us two things we could do to make your experience of the school better.

1.

2.

If you would like to add your name and telephone number, please do. If you prefer not to, that is fine.

Name:

Tel. no.

SECTION 2.3   THE PARENT PARTNERSHIP TOOLKIT FOR EARLY YEARS

Sample letter for parents of Reception class pupils.

Address   **Date**

Dear Parent

Finding out how you feel

Starting at a new school can be a very exciting time, for children and their parents. We always try to make the new families who join our school feel welcome, so this survey is to help us find out how well we are doing.

Please let us have the answers to these questions by .... There is a box in the entrance area you can drop your completed form into, or you can give it to a member of staff.

Your answers to the questions in this survey are important. They will help us to make sure you have the information you need to help your child make a really good start at .... school. When we have looked at the results of this survey, we will let you know what they say and tell you about any changes we plan to make to the way we do things.

Do not forget that, if there is anything else you want to know, you only have to ask. Your child's teacher is always available at the end of the day to answer any questions.

Thank you for your help.

Name

Position

Key points

- It is vital to spend time building up a relationship of trust so parents feel comfortable to share information, knowing that their confidentiality will be respected.
- It is important to be aware of the different types of family groups using the setting and to plan accordingly.
- Make sure there are visual images around the building that reflect the different families that use the setting.
- Managing the key person system well will give families a direct and dependable link with their child's life in the setting.
- A welcoming physical environment that is not overtly feminine and space to talk in private will help fathers and mothers to feel at ease.
- Parents of children with additional needs may require more flexibility in approach, and support in understanding how assessment procedures work.
- Consulting with parents can take many forms. Consultation groups can be very effective but need to be planned and managed well to be successful.
- If written questionnaires are used to find out what parents think, make sure they are clear and concise and written in language that is easy to understand.
- Provide clear information about why you are carrying out the consultation and make it easy for as many people as possible to express their opinions.
- Do something! If parents find that nothing changes following a consultation they will lose faith in the whole process.

Reflective questions

Making parents feel welcome

- Do we greet parents by name, and in their home language if appropriate, when they arrive?
- Do we know the names of all the children and families and do we take care to pronounce them correctly?
- Do we make fathers feel welcome and at ease in the setting?
- Do all staff always wear their name badges?

Being inclusive

- Are men actively encouraged to become childcare workers and do we have appropriate staff facilities for them?
- Have all staff been trained in equal opportunities and anti-discriminatory practice?
- Do we spend time discussing and reflecting on our attitudes and assumptions about different groups?
- How well do we support families of children with additional needs?

Consulting with parents

- Do we have a shared understanding of why it is important to consult with parents?
- Have we defined the areas we would want to consult on and do we know what the most appropriate consultation methods to use are?
- How will we consult with parents whose first language is not English?
- Have we devised a consultation timetable to spread consultation activity throughout the year and make it part of the culture of the setting?

Creating questionnaires

- Who will design a questionnaire to make sure it is pertinent, unambiguous and easy to understand?
- Are we clear about the questions we want to ask?
- What sort of timescale should we allow and how will we encourage parents to participate?
- Who will analyse the results and how will the findings be fed back to parents?

Managing change

- Have we thought carefully about the changes that might need to happen as a result of the consultation?
- Are we clear about how we will manage these changes?
- Who will decide what these changes will be?
- How will we deal with any issues that arise from anyone dissatisfied with the changes that take place?

THE PARENT PARTNERSHIP TOOLKIT FOR EARLY YEARS   SECTION 2.3

Communicating with parents

This section looks at the range of information that practitioners may want to provide for parents and considers the different ways in which this information could be presented. It highlights the importance of really trying to get to know children and valuing the parents' perspective on and knowledge of their child. The importance of creating a shared view of childhood is highlighted, identifying some of the key messages to share with parents. Ways of sharing information about children's learning and development are considered and there is guidance on how to make letters and documents readable and visually attractive. Techniques for organising meetings where parents feel welcome and comfortable are reviewed as is the key area of supporting staff to develop their verbal and non-verbal communication skills. There are checklists for assessing how well you currently communicate and guidelines for producing easily readable written information. The key points covering the content of the section are summarised and there are reflective questions to prompt personal study and to use for staff training.

Providing parents with the information they need about the many different aspects of a children's centre or early years setting involves a careful balance between making sure they have access to the information they need, and totally overwhelming them. As a starting point, use the *audit checklist in figure 2.4a (see p88)* to help you assess how well you are currently providing information for parents and to plan what to do to improve what you offer.

There is a wide range of different information to be exchanged between the setting and the family in order to ensure good outcomes for children. This can be grouped together under four broad headings:

- For the records – sharing organisational and administrative information.
- Getting to know you – gathering information that helps you to get to know a child as an individual and as a member of his or her family.
- Sharing experiences – providing day-to-day information on a child's experiences in the setting.
- Creating a shared view of childhood – helping parents to understand the setting's overall approach to supporting young children's learning and development.

For the records

Communication is a two-way process. Parents will need to provide the setting with a range of important information about their child and the setting should make sure that parents can access essential information about how the setting is organised.

Basic information you need from parents is:

- up-to-date contact details and emergency contact numbers
- any medical and dietary needs the child may have
- who has permission to collect the child from the setting.

Organisational information to provide for parents is:

- session times and dates
- contact telephone numbers and names
- child safety and security information
- name of the family's key person
- settling in and transition procedures
- how the parent will be contacted and/or kept in touch with what is happening in the setting
- how to contact the setting if they want to know how a child is faring during the course of the day
- fees and charges and how they are structured.

Other information for parents:

The setting's policy documents will cover a wide range of information that parents should have access to. This will include:

- the vision and values of the setting
- how the setting supports equality of opportunity and inclusion
- how health and safety requirements are met
- the procedures for safeguarding and promoting children's welfare
- policies and procedures for fulfilling the learning and development requirements of the EYFS
- how to make a complaint.

As part of your partnership with parents you will also want to share information with them about:

- the day-to-day organisation and running of the setting
- children's learning and development at different ages and stages
- strategies for managing young children's behaviour
- practical ideas to help parents support their child's learning at home
- special events, projects and initiatives that the children are involved in
- tax credits and benefits to help with childcare costs
- sources of help and advice about different aspects of family life and wellbeing.

Getting to know you

Parents are the 'experts' on their own child and have the information that will help the key person to establish a relationship with a child to effectively support his or her learning and development. Listening to how parents describe their child, the words they use, what they say their child is interested in, and what their child enjoys doing, will all help to gain an insight into the character of the child and the relationship between adult and child. Family books (*see Section 3*) provide an ideal way to maintain a highly visible connection between a child's experiences at home and in the setting, highlighting the relationships with the important members of the child's family.

At different times, to support a young child's wellbeing and welfare, you might want parents to share with you:

- a child's sleeping patterns
- the language used for communication in the home
- their views on what their child is interested in and how he or she prefers to learn
- the interesting and exciting things that happen in the child's life that he or she may want to share with the other children and adults
- any changes in family circumstances that may affect a child during their time in your setting.

To create an ongoing dialogue between the setting and the home you will want to share with parents:

- their baby's feeding, sleeping and toileting patterns during the day
- any significant milestones, such as taking a first step or saying a few words
- how happy he or she has been during the day
- what experiences their child has encountered, indoors and out of doors, during the course of the day.

Periodically parents may ask for information on:

- how well their child's learning and development is progressing
- what they can do to support their child at home
- how to manage their child's behaviour constructively
- where they can find help and advice on any aspects of their child's development that are causing them concern.

Consulting with parents (*see Section 2.3: Listening to parents*) to establish what sort of regular feedback they would like about their child's time in the setting will help to keep the exchange of information focused and pertinent. Practitioners will be able to see the importance of collecting and sharing information with parents, and parents will be able to appreciate the value of the information that is being provided for them.

Sharing experiences

Documenting children's learning

Capturing young children's learning and development through taking photographs and recording children's comments and conversations is a very powerful way to share with parents the important experiences that their child is having in the setting on a daily basis. For practitioners, collecting, reviewing and interpreting this information is the ideal way to focus on individual children's ideas and interests in order to plan what to do to extend their learning.

Although the process of documentation focuses on children's learning processes, rather than any product that they might produce, it provides practitioners with a wealth of visual evidence to share with parents. Documentation – photographs, children's words, drawings and models – can be used to help parents to understand the diverse and interesting ways in which young children learn. Documentation can be displayed around the setting to show parents what children are learning when they are involved in activities indoors and out of doors, giving important messages about the value of listening to children and following their ideas.

Sharing documentation with parents at the end of the day when they come to collect their child can:

- help the parent to feel in touch and connected with their child's life in the setting
- create a focus for conversation and discussion with the child later in the day
- suggest ideas and experiences to parents that they may want to follow up on at home.

Documenting young children's learning lies at the heart of the work of the educators in the preschools and infant-toddler centres in Reggio Emilia in northern Italy and is discussed in more detail in Giudici et al (2001) and Thornton and Brunton (2009).

Learning stories

Educators in New Zealand have devised a way of recording young children's learning in narrative form using words and photographs that help to capture not just what a child is physically doing at any particular time, but also the complex interactions and relationships with other people that are a part of the child's learning experience. A learning story will also try to capture the voice of the child and the parent in relation to the learning and development that is happening.

Learning stories attempt to show how 'ready, willing and able' a child is to engage in a learning experience by focusing on his or her interest, involvement and mastery of skills. This gives a more rounded and complete picture of a child's learning and development and provides an ideal starting point for sharing with parents the depth and complexity of young children's learning.

More about the work of Margaret Carr and her team on learning stories can be found in Carr, M (2001).

Documentation panels

By adding some simple information about what children are learning alongside photographs of them engaged in activities, you can help parents to see how children learn through play. This can be a very good way to help parents to see the value of play and to begin to recognise the importance of children having a wide range of different experiences. Key messages, such as the importance of children listening to children, the value of play, and the need for children to experience risk and challenge can all be reinforced in this way.

To have the desired impact, it is important to think about the message you are trying to get across and how you are going to present it. Make sure the photographs you use feature all the children in the setting so parents can see that their individual child's contribution is respected and valued. Provide a commentary for the photographs that highlights what the children are doing and what they are learning. Think carefully about

▶

SECTION 2.4   THE PARENT PARTNERSHIP TOOLKIT FOR EARLY YEARS

the words you use to try to capture some of the excitement, joy and wonder of children's learning.

For example, instead of saying, 'Sam drew a picture of a leaf', you could convey so much more with this commentary:

'Sam rummaged excitedly through the pile of fallen leaves before picking one up to examine more closely. He turned the leaf over in his hands, looking carefully at each side and then gently waved it from side to side to see if it made a sound. He stroked the leaf to see what it felt like and thought carefully before choosing the coloured crayons he used to make his leaf picture.'

Documentation panels can be displayed around the setting to give very striking visual images about the power of children's creative thinking.

Creating a shared view of childhood

Creating a partnership with parents from different backgrounds is essential if children are to thrive in the early years setting. Families will have different views about children and childhood, so it is particularly important to find appropriate ways to share the setting's approach to supporting young children's learning and development. Some of the key messages you will want to share with parents will include the:

- importance of listening to children
- need to give children time and opportunity to become independent
- value of play
- importance of children experiencing risk and challenge.

Listening to children

The image of children as strong, confident and competent will be one that early years practitioners subscribe to, but may not be shared by all the families using the setting. Parents may need support in appreciating the diverse ways in which children explore the world and communicate their ideas and understandings. Sharing information with parents about children's learning and development and acting as good role models for listening to children and following their ideas will help parents to see the benefits of building up this relationship with their child. Practitioners can do this by:

- being interested in what children have to say and giving them time to talk and to listen
- modelling the skills of listening attentively through the use of appropriate body language
- encouraging children to express opinions about what they like and dislike about the layout and routines of the setting
- explaining to parents how planning for children's learning and development is based on children's interests and ideas
- being interested in what happens in children's lives outside the early years setting.

81

Encouraging independence

Learning to become independent and take control of aspects of their own lives is an important life skill for children, which early years practitioners are ideally placed to nurture. For example, for young children to learn how to feed and dress themselves successfully, they need time and lots of practice. In a busy home environment parents may not always be able to provide these opportunities, or may not understand the importance of nurturing these skills. By explaining to parents what children are learning as they master complex processes of this nature, practitioners will be helping them to see the value of giving children time to learn how to do things for themselves.

Practitioners can give important messages to parents about nurturing children's independence by:

- creating a physical environment where children can access resources independently
- demonstrating how to treat equipment with respect
- teaching children the skills they need to get the most out of the resources they are using
- encouraging children to be resilient and solve their own problems
- valuing the learning process not the product
- ensuring children participate in the tidying-away process.

The value of play

For parents from a range of different backgrounds, it may be necessary to explain the value of young children's play to help them to understand what children are learning as they play. Sharing with parents what children are learning from the different experiences they have during a typical day in an early years setting will help parents to understand young children's learning better. This can be done on a daily basis by talking to parents at the beginning and end of the day and sharing photographs and accounts of what their child has been doing. Visual displays and documentation panels around the setting can also be used to show children's learning in action. Organising family workshops to give parents the opportunity to play alongside their children will provide ideal opportunities to share important messages with parents about the importance of play-based learning (see Section 3).

Use the 'Supporting young children's play' factsheet in figure 2.4b (see p89) to share with parents some important messages about how they can support their child's learning and development at home.

Experiencing risk and challenge

Safety is another key area where parents may hold a wide range of different views about what is important for young children. So, helping them to understand the value of young children experiencing risk and challenge is particularly important. Parents will need to be reassured that the children's safety is of paramount importance but that, unless they have opportunities to try out things for themselves and test their own limits, they will not develop the skills they need to keep themselves safe. By helping young children to appreciate what danger is and how to recognise hazards, early years practitioners will be equipping them with essential skills for life. Time spent talking to parents about this approach, helping them to see the benefits of children exploring the world around them, will be time well spent. The occasional minor accident will then become part of a child's overall experience in the setting rather than an issue that has to be dealt with. To support this process, it is essential to ensure that sensible risk assessment procedures are in place and implemented by all staff and that all the necessary procedures are followed to deal with and report minor accidents.

Ways of presenting information

Information for parents can be produced in a variety of formats, depending on the message you are trying to convey and the target audience it is intended for. At different times you may want to:

- talk to individual parents as you show them around the setting
- produce written information in a brochure, booklet or prospectus
- write newsletters with information on current events
- provide information on a website
- use photographs and pictures to create visual displays
- organise meetings on areas of general interest.

Use the *checklist in figure 2.4c (see p90)* to see how you could communicate different types of information to parents.

Show rounds

A show round, or conducted tour of your setting, is the ideal occasion to establish a good relationship with parents on which to build in the future. Giving parents a good welcome has been discussed in *Section 2.2: Creating a welcoming environment.* It is important to remember that, depending on the time of day they arrive, parents may be welcomed into the setting by almost any member of staff, not just the setting manager or leader. The guidelines for welcoming visitors should be known and understood by everyone working in the setting.

Showing parents around the setting should be the responsibility of the manager or a senior member of staff as it requires particular skills and experience. It is an ideal time to impart a range of information about the setting, what it believes in, how it functions and what it is trying to achieve. However, it is also a great opportunity to listen to parents, find out a great deal about their relationship with their child and to tune in to their aspirations and hopes for their child. Paying attention to what parents have to say, verbally and non-verbally, is just as important as talking in this situation. Listening to parents' comments and questions will help to identify important areas where they may benefit from additional support and advice and will give clues as to who is likely to be the most appropriate staff member to act as the key person for that family. For parents who have English as an additional language, it will be important to find the most appropriate language for communication, drawing on external help from bilingual members of the local community if necessary.

Brochure, booklet or prospectus

A prospectus or information booklet is an essential tool for giving parents the basic information about the setting and how it operates. It should spell out the setting's vision and values and contain information about opening times and dates, how the setting is organised, what activities/groups/sessions are available and any fees that are charged. There should be information on staffing, contact numbers and an indication of where to find out more information about the setting, including its policies and procedures. As this is a document that parents will take home with them and refer to from time to time, you may want to include some simple information about how children learn through play and what parents can do to support this at home.

Newsletters

Newsletters can be a valuable tool in keeping parents informed about what is happening on a regular basis. They provide an opportunity to celebrate exciting things that have happened, and to let parents know about things that will be happening in the future. Parents are more likely to read the newsletter if it is written in an interesting 'newsy' style and is attractive to look at. Photographs can add to a newsletter's appeal but may add to the costs and you will require parental permission before you use photographs of the children.

Website

All this information could also appear on your website or could be emailed to parents to save on printing costs and paper. Make sure the design of the website reflects the ethos and values of your setting and try to make it as simple and intuitive as possible to navigate. For some parents, accessing information electronically may suit their lifestyle, but not all parents will have ready access to the internet. Consult with your parents about what they would prefer and act accordingly. The advantage of having information on a website is that it can be updated easily. Make sure you do this regularly, as parents will soon lose interest if the website only has information that is months out of date.

If you have families whose first language is not English you will need to make sure that they can access all the important information about the setting in a way that they can understand, either by translating documents or by producing an audio version that that they can take away and listen to.

Guidelines for producing written information

How easy a piece of writing is to understand will be affected by many different things. These include the style in which it is written, how it is presented visually, how readable it is and how interested the reader is in trying to understand what it has to say. Simplifying documents requires clarity of thought and so can take time. Clear explanations require more consideration as it is often easier to fall back on jargon and statements that can be interpreted in more than one way. This will only confuse the reader and result in the need for even more explanation.

When writing to parents, be aware that you will be addressing both male and female readers. Use inclusive language that avoids giving the impression that the world of young children is a strictly female preserve.

Figures 2.4d and 2.4e (see p91-92) describe the key things to think about when producing written information that is visually attractive and easy to read and understand.

Barriers to communication

We are all aware in our daily lives of how inaccessible some types of information can be. Rather than aiding communication, written information can create a barrier because of:

- The way in which it is presented visually. For example, the difficult-to-decipher information written in small print that is often found in the terms and conditions of contract documents.

- The level at which the information is pitched. Examples include articles or documents that use lots of technical terms, jargon and abbreviations. These assume that the reader has a great deal of background knowledge about the subject being presented.

- The way that language is used. Careless use of grammar and spelling mistakes can make some written information difficult to understand.

- The fact that it is written in a language that the reader is not fully fluent in.

All these are barriers that can be overcome fairly easily by paying a little attention to detail.

Presenting information visually

Displays featuring children's pictures, photographs, comments and conversations are often used to make the setting look interesting and attractive. They can also serve as a way of providing information for parents in a way that is easy to understand. Photographs showing the children in the setting at different times of the day will help parents to connect more with their child's life in the setting, gaining an insight into daily life and routines.

When creating visual displays, try to keep them uncluttered and not too complicated so that someone looking at it can find a visual route through and see the message you are trying to convey. Position them where parents are likely to spend some time and make sure they are in good condition and up to date. Draw parents' attention to the information in the displays and encourage them to look at them to find out more about life in the setting.

You may want to create a PowerPoint presentation or video loop showing photographs of children engaged in activities, with an audio commentary describing what they are doing and what they are learning. You could leave this running in the entrance area and invite parents to spend a short time watching it and finding out more about their child's experiences in the setting. Be careful to include all children so no parent inadvertently feels that their child is not valued.

Organising meetings to share information

Inviting parents to come along to a meeting about a particular subject of interest can be a good way of sharing information and, at the same time, picking up on what an individual parent's interests or concerns might be. The range of topics you may want to cover will come from information gained through your consultation processes (*see Section 2.3: Listening to parents*) and from areas that you, as staff, feel you want to share with parents.

THE PARENT PARTNERSHIP TOOLKIT FOR EARLY YEARS SECTION 2.4

To make it easier for parents to attend, advertise the meeting well in advance, remind people closer to the date – verbally or by text message – and arrange the meeting for a time that is convenient for parents. Deciding what time this is will involve you knowing your individual families so that you understand their working and other commitments. You may want to consider providing childcare if this is feasible; always provide refreshments to make the meeting relaxed and enjoyable.

Think about the needs of particular parent groups and try to organise things that would interest them and encourage them to attend. Helping fathers to feel involved in their young children's learning and development can sometimes be a challenge, so consider organising events that will interest them specifically (see Section 3).

Developing good verbal communication skills

Being a good communicator is essential for all staff in the setting, particularly those with key person responsibilities (see Section 2.5: Key person working).

Some practitioners, particularly younger ones, may not have a great deal of experience in talking to parents and will need advice on how to engage with them, the sort of language to use and the things that it is appropriate to discuss. All practitioners will probably benefit from being reminded from time to time about the importance of confidentiality as the foundation of building up a relationship of trust with parents.

Some parents who come to your setting may feel a little overawed when talking to practitioners, so it is particularly important to build up the skills of being a good listener. To be a good listener you need to hear not just the words that parents are saying but also the message that they are trying to get across. As a good listener, you will be interested in what the parent is telling you and will listen carefully to what he or she is saying, rather than thinking about what you are going to say next. Remember to look at the person speaking and show that you are interested by smiling, nodding and making encouraging noises. Try not to jump to conclusions about what he or she is saying until they have finished speaking. Instead, ask questions and paraphrase what has been said in order to confirm that you have understood. Give parents time to say what they want; try to put yourself in their position and imagine how things look from their perspective. Most of all, treat them with courtesy and respect – the way you would want to be treated yourself.

The non-verbal messages we give – through our body language – are as important as those we convey when speaking. To communicate well, you need to be aware of the unspoken messages you give. When talking to parents:

- Does your posture and stance imply that you are open and interested or do you have your arms crossed in a defensive position?
- Do you look at the person you are speaking to or look past them and talk into open space?

▶

SECTION 2.4   THE PARENT PARTNERSHIP TOOLKIT FOR EARLY YEARS

- What sort of facial expression do you have – friendly and open or bored and uninterested?
- Do you appear calm and unhurried or distracted and keen to get away?

None of us are likely to get this right all the time, but the more aware we are of some of the subtleties of good communication, the more at ease and comfortable we can make families feel.

References

Carr, M (2001) *Assessment in Early Childhood Settings*, SAGE, London

Giudici, C, Rinaldi, C and Krechevsky, M (eds) (2001) *Making Learning Visible: Children as Group and Individual Learners*, Reggio Children

Thornton, L and Brunton, P (2009) *Understanding the Reggio Approach (2nd Edition)*, Routledge

THE PARENT PARTNERSHIP TOOLKIT FOR EARLY YEARS

SECTION 2.4

Figure 2.4a

How well do we keep parents informed?

	Always	Usually	Sometimes	Never
The information on the parents' noticeboard is kept up to date.				
Important information is available in a range of different languages.				
All letters to parents are also posted on the noticeboard.				
Dates for all events, meetings and outings are publicised at least two weeks in advance.				
Meetings are arranged at different times of the day/week.				
Parents are reminded by text message about meetings and events.				
The website is up to date, attractive to look at and easy to use.				
The setting's policies and procedures are available on the website.				
The parents' information area is stocked with leaflets giving sources of help, support and advice.				
Displays around the setting are attractive and reflect activities the children are currently involved in.				
Parents know their key person and understand what the role entails.				
There is time at the end of the session for the key person to share information about a child's day.				
Children's diaries/observation records are up to date and accessible to parents.				
Documentation captures children's learning experiences and this is then shared with parents.				
Staff have been trained to communicate well with parents and receive appropriate mentoring and support.				
Parental comments or complaints are used as a way to improve what we do.				

SECTION 2.4 THE PARENT PARTNERSHIP TOOLKIT FOR EARLY YEARS

Supporting young children's play

These are some of the ways that practitioners in the setting support young children's play.

You may find these ideas useful when playing with your child at home.

- When children are playing we look out for opportunities to introduce new words and ideas, without trying to take over their play.

- We think out loud, asking ourselves questions and posing problems: 'I wonder what would happen if…?', 'How could I…?', 'Is there a way to…?'

- We encourage children to talk about what they are doing, sharing their ideas and thoughts.

- We offer help and support when asked for it, again being careful not to take over an activity a child is involved in. Often this can just mean offering to hold something to assist the child in what he or she is doing.

- We encourage children to be independent by making a wide range of open-ended resources available to them. This means they can choose what to play with and how to combine different things as they explore and investigate.

- We encourage children to play out of doors as well as indoors, even if the weather is wet.

- We try to give children the time they need to become fully absorbed in their play.

- We use everyday opportunities to enable children to begin to see the world from others' viewpoints and to take responsibility for their own actions.

- We encourage children to handle toys and resources carefully and to help to tidy them away when they have finished playing.

- We watch and listen carefully to see what children are interested in and find ways to build on these interests.

Providing information for parents

What parents want to know	Range of information you could provide
How will I know how things work in the setting and who I should talk to if I have any questions?	• Brochure or prospectus • Information sheet on noticeboard • Recent newsletters • Written information on key person working • Information on website • Talk about key person role during introductory visits • Meeting for parents to talk about the theory behind key person working
How will I know if my baby/toddler/preschool child is happy here?	• Verbal feedback from key person • Daily note summarising my baby's day • Photographs displayed around the setting showing children involved in activities • Periodic feedback to parents on children's welfare, learning and development
How can I find out what my child is learning?	• Planning documents displayed in each of the rooms • Displays show children's activities and the areas of learning they are experiencing • Documentation panels and learning stories illustrate children's learning journeys • Information about projects on parents' noticeboard, available on website and in newsletters • Children's learning stories are recorded in their personal diaries • Information about projects and individual children's learning emailed to their parents, with photographs
How can I support my child's learning and development at home?	• Practical ideas leaflets for parents • Lending system for children's books • Resources and ideas packs for parents to use at home • Information leaflets from early years organisations • Learning together sessions and family workshops for parents (see Section 3)
Where can I get help to improve my parenting skills?	• Parents information area stocked with leaflets and contact details of appropriate organisations • Information sessions and support groups • One-to-one advice and help

SECTION 2.4   THE PARENT PARTNERSHIP TOOLKIT FOR EARLY YEARS

Seven suggestions for producing a **visually attractive document**

Creating a visually attractive document involves following some very simple rules:

- Use a font size of at least 12 point, but don't make it too large or the document may look 'childish'.

- Use an easily readable typeface such as **Arial** or **Comic Sans**. The letters are clear and not likely to be confused with one another. Handwriting fonts may look stylish but are not necessarily easy to read.

- Use the normal mixture of upper- and lower-case letters, rather than capitals alone. As we often recognise words by their shape we are more likely to be able to read them easily if they are written largely in lower case.

- Break the text up into short paragraphs so it does not look too daunting.

- Use headings to help to guide the reader through the text.

- Create wide margins at the sides, top and bottom to give lots of white space, which is easier on the eye.

- Be careful when printing on coloured paper as some combinations can be quite difficult to read and impossible to photocopy.

Good visual presentation is no more expensive to achieve than poor presentation and will add value to the range of written information you produce for parents.

THE PARENT PARTNERSHIP TOOLKIT FOR EARLY YEARS   SECTION 2.4

Figure 2.4e

Keeping things simple

Easy-to-read documents convey information in a direct and understandable way so that the reader does not have to wade through lots of irrelevant details to get to the point.

The Campaign for Plain English (*www.plainenglish.co.uk*) has produced guidelines for writing information that is clear and can be understood after it has been read just once. The website has a free guide, *How to write in plain English,* and several downloadable booklets on the use of English grammar and punctuation.

The website also hosts a 'Drivel Defence' tool which you can use to analyse a piece of text you have written to get an idea of how easy it is to understand.

The general rules for writing easy-to-understand information are:

- limit the length of sentences to around 17-20 words
- include one idea per sentence rather than trying to include several ideas and using lots of commas
- use shorter sentences rather than semi-colons in long sentences
- try to keep your writing active and interesting by addressing the reader directly
- use bullet points to convey lists of information
- vary the way that your information is presented – too many bullet points in a document can make it tedious to read.

When preparing any written document, have a typical parent in mind while you are writing. Try to imagine how they will interpret what you are trying to say. If possible, ask someone else to comment on a draft of what you have written.

- Is it understandable? Will it tell them what they need to know?
- Have you used any complicated words or phrases that could be expressed more simply?

To make a more detailed analysis of anything you have written, use the 'SMOG' calculator (SMOG stands for 'simple measure of gobbledygook'), a web-based tool, which you can access on the NIACE website (National Institute of Adult Continuing Education): *www.niace.org.uk/misc/SMOG-calculator/smogcalc.php*

The SMOG calculator will analyse a piece of text, tell you how complex it is and calculate a readability score for the text. The lower this figure is the simpler the text is to understand. You may find it useful to use the SMOG calculator to compare the readability of your policy documents with the 'simplified' versions written for parents. Have you really made it more understandable?

NIACE have also reprinted the readability guide, originally produced by the Basic Skills Agency: *www.niace.org.uk/development-research/readability*. This illustrates the key features of a written document that make it easy to understand.

Key points

- There is a very large amount of information that parents need; vary how you present it and try not to overwhelm them.
- Use a range of different ways to share key messages about children's wellbeing, learning and development.
- Keep written information simple and straightforward and avoid using abbreviations or jargon.
- Think carefully about how to make written material attractive and easy to read.
- Keep your website up to date, easy to navigate and visually appealing.
- Make your key documents available in a range of languages, whether written or as tape recordings.
- Use documentation and learning stories, including photographs and children's comments and conversations, to share what happens in the setting with parents.
- Create a PowerPoint presentation to show parents what their children are learning from day to day.
- Help staff to develop the verbal communication skills to manage the key person role effectively.
- Be aware of the messages that parents pick up from the body language you use.

Reflective questions

Conveying information

- How do we decide what information to provide for parents?
- Do we all understand our key messages and are we consistent in conveying them?
- Are we comfortable to share our knowledge – do we make it easy for parents to find out what they want to know?
- How effectively do we help parents to understand their role in supporting their children's learning and development?

Written information

- Do we take enough care to think about the needs and preferences of the readers?
- Have we checked to see that all our documents are clear and informative?
- How can we make sure our newsletters are interesting and readable?
- How could we improve the way we present written information for parents?

Making use of technology

- Is all the relevant information about the setting available on the website?
- Do we know which parents would prefer to access information by email?
- Have we the time and skills to keep the website updated and informative?
- Would it be an advantage to use text message alerts to remind parents of important events?

Conveying visual messages

- Do we make enough use of documentation and display to give parents important messages about their child's daily experience in the setting?

- Have we the time and skills to make our displays visually attractive and appealing?

- Is it worth investing time in creating a PowerPoint presentation showing photographs of the children engaged in different activities?

- How careful are we to make sure that all parents can find positive images of their own child in the photographs that we display?

Becoming good verbal communicators

- How can we make sure that all staff are aware of the importance of developing good verbal communication skills?

- How aware are we of our body language and the non-verbal messages we give to other people?

- Do we understand what it means to be a good listener?

- Do we always listen to parents as well as we should?

Key person working

In this section we look at the important role played by the key person in consolidating the link between the early years setting and the family. The role of the key person and what it entails is discussed, highlighting the difference between a key worker and a key person. A brief introduction to attachment theory provides the basis on which to build key person working. The practical considerations of organisation and management of key person working are looked at, including resources for auditing and reviewing current systems. The importance of home visits and of managing transitions is discussed and there are checklists and proformas to support these processes. For staff training and professional development purposes, there is a summary of key points at the end of the section and a series of reflective questions for group discussion or personal reflection.

The role of the key person

Managing the organisation and routines of the setting to facilitate effective key person working will make a huge contribution to establishing strong parental partnerships. With the introduction of the EYFS framework, the role of the key person has been strengthened to make it pivotal to the way early years settings establish good working relationships with parents. Previously, many settings organised staffing around a key worker system, but the difference between the two roles is an important and significant one.

Elinor Goldschmied was instrumental in defining and emphasising the importance of the role of the key person in enhancing a child's daily experience in a childcare setting (Goldschmied and Jackson, 2004; Elfer et al, 2003). The change in terminology from 'worker' to 'person' indicates a distinct shift from a functional, job-orientated role involving paperwork and organisation to something that requires the wholesale participation of the individual in order to be successful. A key 'person' will need to create an empathetic and nurturing relationship with a child and his or her family in order to carry out the role successfully.

The key person is the person in the setting who 'looks out for' and pays special attention to a child during his or her time in the setting. This way of working is designed to ensure all children are respected and valued as individuals and to prevent children from becoming anonymous in a group setting. Each key person will have responsibility for a small group of children, getting to know them and their parents and family members well.

To carry out the role successfully the key person will need to:

- spend time getting to know each child's family well, establishing relationships of trust with them

- learn about the interests, behaviours and preferences of each child in his or her key group

- welcome the child and parents into the setting at the beginning of the day

- take time to listen to what parents have to say about their child, using this information to make sure the child has the best possible day in the setting

- reassure parents, share information or highlight sources of help and advice, as appropriate

- as far as possible, attend to the feeding and care routines of the children in the key group

- be available to the children in his or her key group during the day, taking an interest in how each child is feeling and what he or she is doing

- contribute to the observations and documentation of the child's day

- share information – verbal feedback, written observations and photographs – with parents about significant events that have happened in the child's day

- make sure that other practitioners in the setting have the information to feed back to parents if the key person is not present when the child is collected

- encourage parents to become involved with their own child's learning and development at home

- support parents during the transition from one room in the setting to another, or between early years settings.

Attachment theory

The work of John Bowlby, developed by Derek Winnicott (1964) and Mary Ainsworth (Ainsworth et al, 1978), on attachment theory has contributed to our understanding of the importance of the key person approach. Studies on parent-child relationships and the effect on babies and young children of their early environment demonstrate the importance to children of having a secure base from which to experience the world. This secure base will be represented in most instances by the child's primary carer at home, and later shared by the child's key person.

The security a child needs encompasses the physical aspect of this important adult being close at hand and generous with physical contact, hugs and comfort. Importantly, it also includes the emotional elements of feeling safe and secure when supported by an adult who is interested and attentive, quick to smile and encourage, aware of changes in the child's mood and responsive to these changes.

For a variety of reasons, not all children will have had the experience of this secure base from birth onwards. Studies on the interaction between young children and their prime carers have defined four different styles of attachment. The descriptions of these attachment styles are based on how children behave when they are separated for a short period of time from their prime carer.

Styles of attachment

The following information is presented to help practitioners understand the different forms of behaviour they may see being demonstrated by young children. It should not be used to 'label' children, but rather to understand them better and to think about how best to develop the relationship between the key person, the child and the parents when a family joins an early years setting.

Secure attachment

Children who, from birth, have experienced consistent loving relationships with their immediate family and have had their needs met quickly and appropriately will have experienced a foundation of trust on which to build all their future interactions with the world. Such a child can be defined as demonstrating secure attachment.

A child who demonstrates secure attachment will experience feelings of loss and may cry or follow after their carer if the person leaves the room. When the carer returns the child will show joy and relief and may often seek comfort and physical reassurance from a hug or a cuddle. The child will settle down from the experience quickly and go back to being fully absorbed in his or her play.

Evidence shows that babies with a secure attachment grow into confident children who are in tune with their feelings, able to display and handle emotion and handle relationships, are confident about their place in the world and keen to explore everything around them.

Insecure and ambivalent attachment

If a baby's early experiences have been less consistent, where sometimes her cries have been responded to, and sometimes not, she will be uncertain about what sort of response to expect from her primary career. This will cause anxiety and feelings of insecurity. In this case, the child is defined as demonstrating insecure and ambivalent attachment.

If the carer of a child with insecure and ambivalent attachment leaves the room, the child may become very distressed, cry very loudly and be very difficult to settle when the adult returns. He may reject physical contact by pushing away, hitting or kicking and will not find it easy to return to the play he was previously engaged in, constantly checking to see if the adult is still close by.

Children who experience this form of insecure attachment when young may later find it difficult to lose themselves in their play and find it difficult to be independent. They may also start to use their increasing mastery of language to try to exert control in situations where they feel insecure and uncertain.

Insecure and avoidant attachment

Children who have experienced very little emotional support from their primary caregivers when young may display what is known as insecure and avoidant attachment. The caregivers may have expressed very little interest in the child, so there will have been few instances of joyful interaction, non-verbal conversation and shared play.

When a child with this form of insecure attachment is separated from her carer she may not show many outward signs of distress and may carry on playing, albeit not in a fully absorbed way. However, closer examination of the child may reveal an increase in her heart rate. She may follow the movements of her carer carefully with her eyes but is unlikely to initiate physical contact when her carer returns.

Children who develop insecure and avoidant attachment when young grow up finding it difficult to communicate their feelings, find it hard to ask for help in a learning situation and tend to manage their uncertainty and insecurity by distancing themselves from other people.

Insecure and disorganised attachment

This is the least favourable situation for a child, and a family with a child that falls into this category is likely to need a great deal of practical and emotional support from early years practitioners and other professionals. Children are likely to have experienced a disordered and chaotic early life, perhaps with the needs of the parents taking precedence over the needs of the child. There may be safeguarding issues due to children having experienced physical or emotional neglect.

If the child's carer leaves the room, a child demonstrating this form of insecure attachment is likely to react in a disorganised way, demonstrating his or her inability to manage an appropriate emotional response to the situation. Some children may stand still and not move for long periods of time, while others may display rhythmical rocking movements.

Children demonstrating this form of insecure attachment will usually require support from specialist services to help them manage their feelings and emotions, cope with stress and anxiety and learn how to engage in positive relationships with others.

Using attachment theory to underpin key person working

Knowing the basics of attachment theory gives the practitioner a theoretical base on which to build their understanding of the importance of their key person role and how it supports the wellbeing of children and of families. It will help the key person to be aware of the different relationships that exist between parents and their children, and help him or her to provide advice and guidance to parents in a sensitive way to help them in their parenting roles.

Babies and toddlers who come to the early years setting with secure attachment will need consistency in the experiences they have with a new adult who is not their first carer – their key person. While the child is in the early years setting, the key person has the very important role of providing the child with consistent, warm and dependable responses that will reinforce his or her sense of security and wellbeing.

For young children who demonstrate signs of insecure attachment, the key person will be able to provide some of the emotional and physical support that may have been absent from their earlier lives. There will also be opportunities to share information with parents on aspects of child development and on the importance of building strong positive relationships between adults and children.

Defining the key person role

Looking at the different roles and responsibilities of the key person role highlights how integral this role is to the overall organisation of the setting. All practitioners need to fully appreciate the roles and responsibilities of this way of working and understand how it supports the vision and values of the setting. The *key person job description in figure 2.5a (see p103*) highlights the essential requirements of the role. It is designed to be used as a part of the induction procedures for new members of staff. It can also be used as a starting point when reviewing with staff how well current key person procedures work in the setting and prompting a discussion on practical ways to improve policy and practice. The *person specification for a key person in figure 2.5b (see p103)* highlights the key qualities that an individual needs to carry out the role effectively and provides a useful starting point for identifying professional development priorities. *Figure 2.5c (see p104) is a sample key person policy*, which can be used as a template, suitably adapted to take into account the particular needs and requirements of an individual setting.

Sharing information on key person working with parents

As the key person plays such a pivotal role in nurturing the relationship between the early years setting and the individual family, it is vital that parents understand as much as possible about the role and how it will be carried out in the setting. This could include:

- why having a key person is important
- what the role of the key person is
- practical information about how the key person system operates
- where to find out more about key person working
- who to talk to for further information and advice.

You may also find it useful to provide parents with some background information on child development and an introduction to attachment theory.

As this is a lot for anyone to take in, it is useful to have the key facts set out in a letter to parents, which they can take away and refer to at a later date. Use the *letter in figure 2.5d (see p106)* as a template for constructing your own letter to parents, sharing your setting's practical approach to key person working.

Managing key person working

Being a key person places considerable emotional and physical demands on the individual practitioners working in an early years setting (Elfer et al, 2003; Manning-Morton and Thorp, 2003). They will have to balance the needs of a group of children and their families, all of whom will make different demands on and make different contributions to the key person working relationship. To support the practitioner in this important role, it is essential that time is given over to:

- providing training for staff taking on the key person role for the first time
- thinking carefully about how children and parents are allocated to particular key people and being flexible in changing the arrangements if they are not working well
- organising the setting's routines and rotas to ensure staff have time to carry out their role effectively
- making arrangements to allow time for home visits by key persons before a family joins a setting
- managing transition arrangements to minimise the disruption caused by transitions
- having a back-up system in place – for example, buddying or shared key person working – to cope with staff absences through holidays, training or sickness

- reflecting on key person working regularly during staff meetings and training sessions so staff have the opportunity to air concerns and share examples of good practice

- making it clear to practitioners that they are not 'on their own' when working as a key person, but have the support of colleagues and managers in handling situations or issues that concern them.

Use the *audit sheet in figure 2.5e* (*see p107*) to review your systems and structures for key person working.

Taking on the role of a key person is clearly an important and emotionally demanding one. Managing conflicting demands during the course of a day and trying to give each child in a group the attention he or she needs can be exhausting. However, many practitioners have commented on how key person working has improved the quality of their work and their job satisfaction because it has enabled them to see more clearly the significance of the interactions they have with the children in their care and their families.

A shared key person system can go a long way to helping practitioners to cope with the demands of the role. Again, putting thought into how this is organised will pay dividends for all concerned. Matching up two practitioners of different ages and with different skills, qualifications and experience will often provide a good solution.

Home visits

Visiting a family in their own home before a child joins the setting can be a time-consuming process that requires good organisation and commitment in terms of time and money. Home visits are normally carried out by the key person allocated to the family accompanied by another member of staff. Having two people involved in the visit is sensible from a personal security standpoint but also means that one person can focus on talking to the parents and gathering administrative information, leaving the other person free to interact with the child. Find out if it is necessary to have an interpreter present and plan accordingly. Take along some written information about the setting to leave with the parents and some interesting resources for the child to play with. These could be left in the home and returned when the family join the setting. It may be useful to arrange the visit for a time when both parents can be present, to reinforce the message about the importance of fathers being fully involved in the lives of their young children.

Visits should be organised well in advance and their purpose explained fully to the family. Evidence shows that most parents are comfortable with being visited at home and many see it as an important social event. However, home visits should be looked on as a desirable, rather than a compulsory, part of the induction process, leaving families free to decline the offer of a visit. Use the *sample letter in figure 2.5f* (*see p108*) as a template for helping parents to understand what a home visit entails.

For the parents, being visited in their own home by their child's key person:

- provides the opportunity to share information about their child in their own environment where they are likely to feel in control and more comfortable

- is an opportunity to ask questions and gather information about how the setting functions

- enables them to begin to build up a relationship with their key person and begin to feel part of a larger group
- demonstrates to their child the partnership that exists between the home and the setting.

For children, a home visit:

- provides an element of continuity between their life at home and in the setting
- enables them to share aspects of their life at home – showing the practitioner their bedroom for instance – so they are better known and better understood when they are in the setting
- enables them to see the partnership that exists between their family and the people who care for them in the early years setting.

Visiting children in their own home enables the key person to:

- understand more about a child's family circumstances
- see how the child interacts with other family members at home
- hear the language that is spoken at home
- discover more about the child's home-learning environment
- explain settling-in procedures and share information with parents in a non-threatening environment.

Managing transitions

For many parents, bringing their child to an early years setting will be the first time they have shared responsibility for their child's wellbeing and development with someone other than a family member. This is a huge step to take but, when handled well, will reassure parents that rather than losing something they are in fact entering into a partnership with a whole team of experienced, well-trained professionals who will support them in ensuring the very best outcomes for their child.

During their first five years of life, young children go through a series of transitions as they move from home to one or more childcare settings and then on to school. Within a single childcare setting, a child under three will often move room bases frequently as he or she develops from being a non-mobile baby to a mobile baby to a young toddler to an older toddler to a preschool child. The quality of these transitions and how well they are handled will have an impact on children's emotional wellbeing, learning and development (Brooker, 2008).

The first transition children will make will be starting at the setting, either as a baby, a toddler or a preschool child. Well-thought-out and thoroughly implemented settling-in procedures will help to make this a positive experience for both the child and his or her family. Use the *sample 'settling-in' policy document in figure 2.5g (see p109)* as a model for reviewing your existing procedures.

The key person approach has been made statutory within the Early Years Foundation Stage (EYFS) framework to help give children under five a secure base from which to explore the world. If all the physical moves that take place in a setting are accompanied by changes in the family's key person, much of the stability underpinning the key person approach will be lost. Creating an organisational structure whereby the key person progresses through the setting with their key group as they get older may be more complex to manage but does give the continuity needed to benefit everyone.

The secret to successful transition is good preparation. Parents will need to know well in advance when their child is going to move, where they are moving to and who will be responsible for overseeing the move. Children and parents should be given several opportunities to spend time in the new environment, meet new people and find out what goes on there. Try to imagine what the transition looks like from the viewpoint of the child and his or her parent. Use the *information in figure 2.5h (see p110)* to think about how to plan effective transitions to meet the needs of children and parents.

References

Ainsworth, M, Blehar, M, Waters, E and Wall, S (1978) *Patterns of Attachment: A Psychological Study of the Strange Situation*, Lawrence Erlbaum Associates, Hillsdale, NJ

Brooker, L (2008) *Supporting Transitions in the Early Years*, Open University Press, Maidenhead

Elfer, P Goldschmied E and Selleck, D (2003) *Key Persons in the Nursery: Building Relationships for Quality Provision*, David Fulton, London

Goldschmied, E and Jackson, S (2004) *People Under Three: Young Children in Daycare (2nd Edition)*, Routledge, Abingdon

Manning-Morton, J and Thorp, M (2003) *Key Times for Play: The First Three Years*, Open University Press, Maidenhead

Winnicott, D (1964) *The Child, the Family and the Outside World*, Pelican, London

Key person job description

The main responsibilities of the key person are to:

- act as the first point of contact for parents of children in the key group
- participate in a home visit to meet the child in his or her own home
- welcome the child into the setting and manage the settling-in process
- whenever possible, be available to greet the child and parent when they arrive in the setting each day
- provide information for parents on how a child's day has been
- spend time each day with the child, getting to know him or her well and supporting his or her emotional wellbeing
- attend to the physical needs of the children in the key group, using this time to build up the relationship with the child
- be aware of the interests and preoccupations of each of the children in the group and plan experiences for the child based on these interests
- share with other practitioners the observations made of children in the group to support planning and assessment
- gather together appropriate information to pass on when a child moves on to another key person
- support children and parents during the transition process, within the setting or with the move to another setting
- attend training on the key person role and contribute to staff meetings discussing this subject
- share any particular concerns about a child's welfare, learning and development confidentially with the setting manager.

Key person person specification

The important personal attributes of a key person are:

- a broad understanding of the role and a belief that it is important
- the ability to communicate well with a wide cross section of people
- an open and inclusive attitude, valuing difference and individuality
- a calm, confident manner that instils confidence
- a sensitive nature, able to empathise with the worries and concerns of others
- being a good organiser and time manager, able to find the time to talk to parents and build up a relationship with them
- being open to forming relationships with young children
- the ability to be friendly but still professional in approach and comfortable to 'let go' when it is time for a child to move on
- an enthusiasm for professional development and a keenness to find out more about how to carry out the role successfully

Sample key person policy

Date: **Review date:**

Name of person responsible for seeing that this policy is implemented:

Policy

As part of the vision and values of our setting we greatly value the strong positive relationships we build up with the children in our care and their families. Children's emotional wellbeing is an essential foundation for their health, happiness and ability to learn. Every child who attends our setting is assigned a key person to act as the bridge for the child between their home and the setting.

The key person will get to know the child well, become attuned to their likes and dislikes, attitudes and preferences. This relationship will begin at the time the practitioner visits the child at home and continue during the settling-in process as parents and children become accustomed to life in the setting. The key person is there to provide the child with particular support at key times during the child's time in the setting – at the time he or she joins the setting, when the child makes a transition from one home base to another or whenever there has been a significant event in the child's life.

The key person will spend time with the child every day, supporting his or her welfare, learning and emotional and physical development. The key person will be the key point of contact for the parents/carers of the child, able to inform them of what the child has been interested and involved in during the day.

Arrangements for assigning children to a key person will take account of the age of the child, the number of children in each key group and personalities of the individuals concerned.

Ongoing training will be provided for staff to enable them to carry out the key person role, and arrangements will be in place to balance out the number of children assigned to each key person, and to accommodate shift patterns, holiday and sickness absences. Home visits are seen as an essential part of key person working, so time will be allocated to enable this to happen.

The impact of key person working will be a regular topic for discussion at staff meetings and the manager will always be available to discuss any concerns that parents or practitioners have regarding key working.

Procedures

To implement the policy successfully there will be a number of organisational arrangements to be put in place. These will be different in every setting but should include:

- how children will be assigned to a key person
- how shift patterns, absences and holiday periods will be covered — consider implementing a 'shared key person' system
- how parents will be informed about key person working – see figure 2.5d
- arrangements for induction training
- arrangements for ongoing training
- expectations of key person – see figure 2.5a
- how the setting will support practitioners in their key person role.

THE PARENT PARTNERSHIP TOOLKIT FOR EARLY YEARS   SECTION 2.5

Figure 2.5d

Sample letter to parents: key person approach

Dear

Key person working

We know that starting in a new setting is a big step for you and your child. There will be lots of things to find out about, new people to meet and new routines to follow. To help you with all this, we have a system, which we call the 'key person' system.

Before your child starts in the setting, you will be introduced to your child's key person. This is the person who will do their best to make sure your child enjoys the time he or she spends here with us. Your key person will offer to come and visit you at home before your child starts so they can get to know the family. They will be able to tell you all about how things happen in the setting and answer any questions you may have.

Your key person will welcome you to the setting and help you through the settling-in process. While your child is with us, the key person will spend time with him or her every day, getting to know what he or she is interested in. They will also look after your child's physical needs, including changing and feeding. When you come to collect your child at the end of the day, your key person will be able to tell you what your child has been doing during the day. If they cannot be there at the end of the day, they will make sure they pass on all the important information to another member of staff.

If you want to know anything at all about how the setting works, your key person is the one to ask. If they do not know the answer they will know how to find out.

We use the key person system in our setting because it is the best way to give children the security they need to feel happy while they are with us. The key person will form a relationship with your child and look out for his or her interests while he or she is with us. This way of working will support the relationship you already have with your child and respects your role as the person who knows your child best.

If you would like to know anything more about key person working, please ask.

Yours sincerely,

Manager

Name of child:

Name of key person:

106

Managing key person working

		Yes	No
Training	● Do our induction procedures include key person working?		
	● Is key person working included in our programme of ongoing professional development?		
	● Do we have an effective mentoring system for practitioners who are unsure about how to carry out the role?		
	● Is key person working regularly discussed in staff meetings?		
Support	● Is key person working included in practitioners' job descriptions?		
	● Does the manager have the skills and experience to support practitioners in their key person role?		
	● Are difficult issues, particularly around safeguarding of children, dealt with effectively?		
	● Have all practitioners had the opportunity to develop their personal communication skills?		
Organisation	● Is our system for allocating children to key groups working well?		
	● Do practitioners have time to manage their key person responsibilities?		
	● Are suitable arrangements made to allow time for home visits?		
	● Do shift patterns and working arrangements help or hinder our existing way of implementing key person working?		

Figure 2.5.1

Sample letter to parents: home visits

Dear

Home visits

Home visits are an important part of the way we help young children to settle in to our setting. A home visit helps us to get to know you better and gives you the chance to ask us lots of questions about what the setting is like. Here is a short description of what happens during a typical home visit.

What happens during a home visit?

- We will ask you when would be a suitable date and time to come and visit you and your child at home.
- Two members of staff from the setting will come on the visit. One of these will be your child's key person.

We will bring along a welcome pack for you to keep that has some important information about the setting. This will explain about opening times and dates, contact information and any fees or charges. It will also give you more information about the key person system and the settling-in process. While we are with you, we will check that we have all the important information about your contact details and phone numbers.

During the visit, the key person will talk and play with your child, getting to know him or her a little better. We will be interested to know what sorts of things interest your child. You may also like to tell us about sleeping patterns and eating preferences and any other things you feel it is important for us to know.

We will also bring some toys, games or books from the setting for your child. These are for your child to borrow to play with. They can be returned when you next come to the setting.

At the end of the visit we will check that you have all the information you need and that you are happy about what happens next in the settling-in process.

We hope that you will be happy for us to come to visit you at home. We have found that this is a good way of helping children to get off to a good start when they join our setting. If you are not sure whether you would like a home visit, please talk this over with the manager, who will be happy to tell you more about the process.

We are very much looking forward to .... joining our setting and hope you will enjoy being a part of our early years community.

Yours sincerely,

Manager

SECTION 2.5   THE PARENT PARTNERSHIP TOOLKIT FOR EARLY YEARS

Sample settling-in policy

Date: **Review date:**

Name of person responsible for seeing the policy is implemented:

Policy

As part of our vision and values, we want every family to enjoy the time they and their children spend with us in our setting. We recognise that starting in a group setting can be an exciting but unsettling process for both children and parents and we will do everything possible to make the transition from home to setting as easy and enjoyable as possible. Every child is different and each will react in different ways to the experience of being with a group of other children in a new environment. As a staff, we respect these differences and will use our knowledge and experience to help every child and family to settle in comfortably and become a part of the community of adults and children that make up our setting.

To help us do this we have a routine that we follow when new families start in the setting. This starts with a home visit by the designated key person, accompanied by another member of staff. There then follow at least two introductory visits when parents and children spend time in the setting together. This gives parents the opportunity to get to know the staff who will be looking after their child, to see how the daily routines of the setting operate and to understand some of the experiences and activities that a child will be taking part in during the day. This time is an opportunity for parents to ask any questions about how the setting operates, and for us to confirm that we have all the necessary information on a child, including dietary requirements and allergies, as well as up-to-date contact information.

Following these joint visits, most children will be ready to stay in the setting on their own. For the first few sessions, we recommend that children are left only for a short time so they are reassured that parents will come back to collect them. Children frequently become upset and cry at the time parents leave but, with lots of attention from the staff of the setting, they quickly settle and become involved in the activities going on around them. When parents return to collect their child, we encourage them to ask about what he or she has been doing during the day.

Every family will have a key person who acts as the first point of contact between the family and the setting. This will be the person who has specific responsibility for 'looking out' for a child during their time in the setting, ensuring that his or her emotional and physical needs are met, as well as supporting play, learning and development.

The settling-in procedures are covered in more detail below. Parents are encouraged to read these and ask any questions they have about the whole process.

Procedures

List here the procedures for settling in as they apply in your setting. Include details of how parents can contact the setting during the day to check on their child's progress and how staff will feed back information to parents when they come to collect their child – verbally, written record, photographs.

Figure 2.5h

Planning effective transitions

In planning transitions, consider:

1. Where the child is moving to

This could be a new home base in the same setting or a completely new setting. Parents will need to know practical details such as where to drop off and pick up their child and where to hang up coats and bags.

2. Who the child will be moving with

Friendships are as important to young children as they are to us as adults. If children are not able to move with their friends, this will make the transition process more challenging.

Changing key person at the same time as moving to a new environment and becoming part of a new group of children can be difficult. Wherever possible, consider moving a whole group of children along with their key person to provide continuity for all concerned.

3. Who the child's new key person will be

If a new relationship is to be established between the family and a different key person, time should be set aside to establish and nurture this relationship. Information should be passed on from the previous key person to provide an insight into the interests and dispositions of the child.

4. When the move will take place

Give parents plenty of notice and tell them about the procedures you have in place to introduce their child to his or her new environment and peer group. This should include a series of visits at different times of day to experience a range of activities in the new environment. Parents will also want to visit the new environment to meet people and understand its physical layout.

5. What to expect during the period of transition

Different people respond to change in different ways. For some, it is an exciting opportunity to do new things and meet new people, while for others it can be quite intimidating and frightening. If parents have lots of information about the new environment and what happens there, they can talk to their child and help to reassure them.

It is important to reassure parents that even seemingly outgoing children can become quiet and less assured when they initially move to an unfamiliar environment. They may become more dependent for a time before gaining in confidence again and feeling secure enough to explore the world enthusiastically.

Key points

- Effective key person working has been shown to have a very positive effect on the experience that parents and children have of the early years setting.

- The key person 'looks out for' a child while he or she is in the setting, preventing them from becoming an anonymous member of a larger group.

- Understanding attachment theory will help practitioners to appreciate the theory underpinning their key person role.

- Parents will need time and access to information to help them to understand key person working.

- Be prepared to spend time answering parents' questions to explain key person working, revisiting it several times if necessary.

- Practitioners need time to carry out their role, building up a relationship with parents, making home visits and managing transitions.

- Look at transitions within the setting from the parents' and child's viewpoint and find ways to minimise the frequency of change of key person.

- Ensure key person working is included in induction training for new staff.

- Encourage staff members to share with the manager any concerns or issues that arise as part of their key person working.

- Help staff to appreciate the benefits and advantages of key person working.

Reflective questions

Managing key person working

- Do we have a straightforward procedure for allocating children to key groups?

- Could we find a better way to give practitioners the time they need to build up relationships with parents?

- Is it evident that key person working is uppermost in the mind of the person responsible for planning rotas?

- Would 'shared key caring' work well in our setting?

Supporting key person working

- Do younger/less-qualified members of staff have the training they need to take on the key person role?

- Has everyone had access to training on communication skills?

- Does the ethos of the setting encourage practitioners to share concerns and look for solutions?

- Do practitioners feel well supported when difficult situations arise?

Sharing information with parents

- Do practitioners and parents have the same understanding of how information about a child will be shared?
- How well do we ensure every parent is given accurate information about their child when they collect him or her at the end of a session?
- How comfortable do parents feel with sharing information about their child?
- How effectively do we communicate with parents whose home language is not English?

Home visits

- Do we need to improve the uptake of home visits?
- Do all practitioners feel confident in carrying out this role, and do they fully understand its purpose?
- Are there any concerns around personal safety that need to be addressed?
- Have we consulted with parents about their experience of a home visit and asked how it could be improved?

Transitions

- Are all transitions for very young children absolutely necessary or could we find better ways to organise the grouping of children in the setting?
- Do we devote enough time to preparing parents and children for transitions, helping them to understand what to expect?
- When there is a change in key person, is there enough time for the new 'getting-to-know-you' process?
- Could we improve the records passed on during the transition process to make them more useful?

SECTION 2.6

Supporting parent-child relationships

This section looks in more detail at some key information that practitioners can share with parents to support them. It identifies the aspects of child development that many parents would appreciate advice and guidance on and focuses in more detail on helping parents to understand and manage young children's behaviour. The benefits of involving parents in creating the setting's behaviour management policy are discussed, highlighting this as an opportunity to come to a common understanding of what is important for young children. Discussing the setting's approach to safeguarding children can help parents to appreciate the roles and responsibilities that parents and the early years setting share in ensuring children are kept safe from harm. The wide range of programmes to help parents develop their parenting skills is reviewed, accompanied by an information grid identifying the wide range of resources and programmes available. A series of key points summarises the section and there are reflective questions to assist with personal study and staff training initiatives.

Child development

From their training and experience, early years practitioners are in a unique position to offer information, advice and support for parents on many aspects of child development. This can be shared with parents in an informal and supportive way to help them understand and cope with some of the challenges of bringing up young children.

Information can be made available in a variety of ways (*see Section 2.4: Communicating with parents*) including:

- producing in-house information leaflets
- adding links to parent-support organisations on the setting's website
- creating visual displays
- providing leaflets and information from other organisations (*see figure 2.6d: Choosing parent support resources and programmes*)
- arranging workshops with professionals, such as health visitors, dental practitioners, health education coordinators and educational psychologists
- organising events in the setting for parents and children – for example, highlighting healthy eating, being active out of doors, singing and making music together (*see Section 3*)
- creating a parents' lending library of books and DVDs on aspects of child development.

Information on the following aspects of child development is likely to be particularly useful for parents:

Caring for children and meeting children's welfare needs

- Avoiding hazards around the home

113

- The importance of feeling emotionally safe and secure
- Coping with temper tantrums
- Sleeping patterns and managing bedtimes
- Healthy eating for babies, toddlers and preschool children
- Exercise and playing out of doors
- Keeping healthy and free from infection.

Supporting children's intellectual development

- Communicating with babies
- How language develops
- Treasure baskets and heuristic play
- Sharing books with babies and young children
- Schemas and the ways that young children interact with the world
- The value of play and active learning
- Supporting young children to actively explore the world
- Developing problem-solving and thinking skills.

Helping to nurture young children's personal and social skills

- The importance of promoting self-confidence and self-esteem
- Helping your child to become independent
- The value of resilience and learning from experience
- Learning to share and be part of a team
- Forming relationships and building friendships.

Sharing expectations of children's behaviour

One of the most common areas for discussion between parents and practitioners in any setting centres on expectations of how children should behave. Parents and practitioners will want children to be happy in the setting, able to make friends and enjoy their time there. To achieve this aim, it is vital to take time to talk with parents about the setting's expectations of children's behaviour and how children are supported to learn the skills they need, to enjoy being part of a larger group. For a young child, adapting to a group situation and learning how to build friendships with other children are complex skills to master. They will be learning how to share resources and the time and attention of an adult as well as the need to try to appreciate the world from another person's point of view. These skills require a great deal of practice and the support of attentive and empathetic adults.

To function as an orderly community, the setting will have a clear policy on behaviour management that is implemented by all practitioners. Helping parents to understand the thinking behind this policy will enable them to find out why it has been written in the way that it has. The expectations of what constitutes acceptable behaviour in the setting may be

SECTION 2.6   THE PARENT PARTNERSHIP TOOLKIT FOR EARLY YEARS

different from those previously experienced by the child at home. Of course, practitioners are not in a position to dictate how a child behaves at home but they can share with parents the reasoning behind their thinking around young children's behaviour. Parents will be able to see what the expectations of the setting are and there will be opportunities to discuss the importance of children receiving consistent messages about what constitutes acceptable behaviour. The more consistent these messages are, the easier it will be for children to learn how to manage their own behaviour.

Involving parents in agreeing the setting's behaviour management policy

Consulting with parents and involving them in agreeing the setting's behaviour management policy creates the opportunity for some very important and far-reaching discussions about what is important for young children. Experienced practitioners will have much to offer in leading and guiding such a discussion, but will also learn a great deal from the process. When parents have the opportunity to talk about what is important for them in terms of their child's behaviour, it gives practitioners an added insight into children's lives outside the setting.

Engaging a group of parents in a discussion is a chance to share opinions, reflect on other people's attitudes, learn from one another, address challenges and come up with solutions. A behaviour management policy drawn up through a process such as this is likely to be more actively supported and so more effective than something devised by practitioners alone. It will take into account the views and opinions of the parent group and will be 'owned' and championed by them.

A discussion around young children's behaviour can cover a range of important topics including:

- the early years setting as a community of children and adults
- parents' expectations and aspirations for their child
- the vision and values of the early years setting
- valuing and respecting different opinions, cultures and beliefs
- children's rights, duties and responsibilities
- the value of play, first-hand experiences, risk and challenge
- child development and expectations of how children of different ages will behave
- the importance of role models, appropriate language and giving children consistent messages
- strategies for managing difficult behaviour
- the availability of support and advice to develop parenting skills
- roles and responsibilities for safeguarding children.

Figure 2.6a (see p119) is a model behaviour management policy document that can be used as a guide to what your policy should cover.

Figure 2.6b (see p120) is a 'parent-friendly' version of the policy that highlights the key aspects of the policy and where to find out more information.

Safeguarding children

Ensuring children are safe from harm underpins the statutory framework of the Early Years Foundation Stage and will be fundamental to all the policies and procedures that determine how the setting is organised and managed. Early years practitioners have a duty of care for all the children in their setting and a responsibility for safeguarding their welfare. Parents have a similar interest in ensuring the safety and welfare of their individual child, making sure he or she is looked after by responsible, well-qualified adults in a safe and secure environment.

So, practitioners and parents have much to gain from exploring this common interest around keeping children safe from harm. Sharing the setting's safeguarding children policy will be a useful start in this process. *Figure 2.6c (see p121) provides a sample policy document*, outlining what a safeguarding policy should cover. However, to come to some common understanding about what the policy means in practice, it is necessary to share with parents, through a group discussion or workshop session, what the key issues are behind the policy. Although this may seem like a difficult aspect to talk about, by not talking about it, we run the risk of perpetuating attitudes that are not in the best interests of young children. Talking about difficult issues such as this is a very clear indication that, as practitioners, you value a genuine partnership with the parents who use your setting.

Exploring the common interest that we all have in keeping children safe from harm provides an opportunity to:

- listen to parents' concerns about how to keep their children safe
- share a common language when talking about young children
- explain the setting's employment procedures and the checks that are made to ensure only suitable people are employed
- discuss the changes in the attitudes of society towards parental rights, duties and responsibilities – for example, attitudes to smacking
- reflect on cultural differences in bringing up young children
- talk about issues such as internet safety and the use of photographs of children
- look at the barriers that might affect a parent's ability to fulfil their role effectively and identify the services that are available to support parents in their role
- help parents to understand the need for practitioners to ask questions when a child shows unusual changes in behaviour, talks in an inappropriate way or has unexplained injuries
- give parents the knowledge they need to recognise what appropriate early years care and education entails so they can ask questions if they feel an individual practitioner is not fulfilling his or her responsibilities adequately.

The aim of a discussion of this nature is to share information, dispel myths and anxieties and create a real sense of equal partnership in supporting the care and education of young

SECTION 2.6 THE PARENT PARTNERSHIP TOOLKIT FOR EARLY YEARS

children. The better parents and practitioners can understand one another, the better the outcomes will be for children.

Further information and guidance on safeguarding children can be obtained from the following sources:

- DfES (2006) *Safeguarding Children and Safer Recruitment in Education*: *http://bit.ly/ SafeguardingChildren*
- Criminal Records Bureau: *www.crb.homeoffice.gov.uk*
- National Society for the Prevention of Cruelty to Children: *www.nspcc.org.uk*
- Ofsted: *www.ofsted.gov.uk*
- Safe Kids: *www.safekids.co.uk*

Helping parents to develop their parenting skills

As part of their remit to work with families to secure good outcomes for children, many settings have become involved in the delivery of parenting support programmes, either directly or through a partner organisation. Parenting programmes are very diverse in nature and are designed to address a number of different needs. Programmes are delivered in a number of formats, ranging from one or two short sessions to more extensive courses, sometimes leading to qualifications. Practitioners delivering stand-alone parenting programmes will be trained to work to the National Occupational Standards for Work with Parents (*www.parentinguk.org/2/standards/units-and-elements*) to ensure the quality and standards of the programme they are delivering.

The common objective shared by all these courses is to improve the relationship between parents and their children by giving parents the skills and confidence they need to make parenting a more enjoyable and rewarding experience. Parenting programmes aim to develop a parent's understanding of their own and their child's personal, social, emotional, intellectual and physical needs in the context of family life.

The approach to achieving this objective will depend on the identified needs of the target audience. This could encompass:

- helping all parents to understand more about child development and the nature of young children's play
- sharing with parents how to support their child's communication and language skills
- helping parents to manage their child's challenging behaviour
- supporting fathers to become involved with their children's care, learning and development
- working with parents who have themselves had poor experiences of parenting
- increasing the confidence and lifeskills of teenage parents
- engaging with parents from ethnic minority backgrounds to help them connect with the care and education system in the UK
- developing parents' skills to enable them to access work or training

THE PARENT PARTNERSHIP TOOLKIT FOR EARLY YEARS

- addressing the literacy and numeracy skills of parents from a range of backgrounds
- providing information, advice and support for parents of children with additional needs
- supporting parents who themselves have additional needs.

Over the last few years, a great deal of evidence has been gathered on the efficacy of different approaches in supporting parents and developing their skills and confidence. These include a review of international evidence (Moran et al, 2004), the longitudinal evaluation of the Peers Early Education Partnership (PEEP, 2005), the national evaluation of the Sure Start programme (DfES, 2006; DCSF, 2008), and the knowledge review carried out by the Centre for Excellence and Outcomes for Children and Young People's Services (C4EO, 2009). Much of the information on different approaches to parenting support has been gathered together in reports on the Early Learning Partnership Project (ELPP) focusing on work with voluntary sector organisations, and the Parents as Partners in Early Learning (PPEL) project carried out in many local authorities from 2006 to 2008. The DCSF-sponsored Parenting Implementation Project (PIP) also has a wealth of information about good practice in delivering parent support services.

The good practice from these projects has recently been gathered together in a publication from the Family and Parenting Institute, Early Home Learning Matters (*www. earlyhomelearning.org.uk*). This also contains a summary of the training programmes that are available to help practitioners deliver different parenting programmes.

Use the *information grid in figure 2.6d (see p122)* to help you decide which parenting programmes and resources would be most suitable for supporting parents in your setting.

References

C4EO (2009) 'Improving children's attainment through a better quality of family-based support for early learning' see: *www.c4eo.org.uk/themes/earlyyears/familybasedsupport/files/c4eo_family_based_support_progress_map_summary_2.pdf*

DCSF (2008) *Supporting Parents in Promoting Early Learning: The Evaluation of the Early Learning Partnership Project (ELPP)*, see: *http://publications.dcsf.gov.uk/default.aspx?PageFunction=productdetails&PageMode=publications&ProductId=DCSF-RR039&*

DCSF (2008) *The Sure Start Journey: A Summary of Evidence*, see: *http://publications.everychildmatters.gov.uk/eOrderingDownload/Sure_start_journey.pdf*

DfES (2006) *Empowering Parents in Sure Start Local Programmes*, RR NESS/2006/SF/018, see *www.dcsf.gov.uk/research/data/uploadfiles/NESS-2006-FR-018%20-%20Evaluation%20Report.pdf*

Moran, P Ghate, D and van de Merwe, A (2004) *What Works in Parenting Support? A Review of the International Evidence*, see: *www.prb.org.uk/wwiparenting/RR574.pdf*

Parenting Implementation Project, see: *www.dcsf.gov.uk/everychildmatters/strategy/parents/pip/pip/*

Parents as Partners in Early Learning (PPEL) *http://nationalstrategies.standards.dcsf.gov.uk/primary/features/foundation_stage/parents_partners*

PEEP (2005) *Birth to School Study: A Longitudinal Evaluation of the Peers Early Education Partnership (PEEP) 1998-2005*, see: *http://bit.ly/PEEPBirthToSchoolStudy*

Sample behaviour management policy

Date: **Review date:**

Name of person responsible for seeing the policy is implemented:

Policy

Helping children learn how to manage and regulate their own behaviour gives them the foundation on which to build their learning and development. To achieve this, we have simple rules and guidelines to support good behaviour in the setting, which have been drawn up in consultation with parents. Implementing our behaviour policy is dependent on staff acting as good role models at all times and being consistent and fair in their approach to children.

Expectations of behaviour are appropriate to the age and stage of development of the child. Whenever possible, instances of unacceptable behaviour are used as learning opportunities to engage the child, or a group of children, in discussing what has happened, and what should happen to resolve the situation. This gives children the chance to become involved in setting the rules and boundaries for behaviour in the setting.

Children are helped to understand the importance of being kind and helpful, thinking about the effect of their actions on others and keeping themselves and others safe. Opportunities are taken throughout the day to promote children's sense of self-worth through giving attention and praise.

Instructions given to children are simple and clear and explanations are always given of why something should be done. Negative language is avoided as far as possible but, when behaviour is unacceptable, it is always emphasised that it is the behaviour and not the child that is disapproved of.

If any child appears to have a persistent behaviour problem, it will be investigated fully to determine the cause and parents will be invited to collaborate in putting strategies into place to address the problem.

Corporal punishment will not be administered at any time. Children will be removed from the situation that is causing the problem and talked to calmly about their behaviour by a member of staff.

The implementation of the setting's behaviour management policy will be monitored regularly by the manager and any inconsistencies dealt with immediately.

The behaviour management policy will be shared with parents when they join the setting and parents will be involved in the regular review of the policy.

Procedures

To support the policy you should have a list of the behaviour management procedures to be used in your setting. Include details of:

- *how staff should behave*

- *the language they should use with children when discussing their behaviour*

- *any sanctions to be used to deal with unacceptable behaviour.*

Set out the procedures to be used to work in partnership with parents on behaviour management issues and the process by which the implementation of the behaviour management policy will be monitored by the manager. You may also want to include contact details of the local authority behaviour support team and reference to any local guidance.

Sample letter to parents: helping children to behave well

Dear

Helping children to behave well

Being able to make friends and enjoy the time spent in the setting is very important for your child. When he or she joins the setting they will be spending time alongside many different children and adults. To help children learn how to be part of this larger group, we have some simple rules that guide the behaviour of everyone in the setting.

For example, everyone in our setting is expected to be friendly, kind and thoughtful and to look after their own safety and that of other people.

To help children understand what this means we:

- act as good role models
- talk respectfully to children and to one another
- encourage children to behave well and notice when they are doing so
- help children to resolve their own conflicts and disputes
- give children opportunities to talk about feelings and emotions
- show children that they are loved and valued.

Sometimes children behave in ways that can be disruptive and upsetting. This can affect family life at home as well as the child's ability to develop friendships, play and learn in the setting. There may be many reasons behind this disruptive behaviour, but we will always work with you to find effective ways to manage the situation. This could involve providing information and advice about child development and thinking up behaviour management strategies to use at home and in the setting. Occasionally, the solution will be to seek expert advice from other professionals.

If you would like to find out more about different aspects of young children's behaviour please talk to your key person. They will be able to answer your questions, provide you with our advice sheets and leaflets and help you to find the information you need.

Every year we consult parents about our behaviour management policy to make sure it still matches the needs of the children, families and practitioners in our setting. Please share your views as part of this consultation so your opinions can be heard.

Yours sincerely,

Manager

Sample safeguarding children policy

Date: **Review date:**

Name of person responsible for seeing the policy is implemented:

Policy

All practitioners take their responsibility for safeguarding and promoting the welfare of the children in their care very seriously. To support this, the setting has a safeguarding children coordinator who receives up-to-date training in all issues relating to the protection and welfare of children. In addition, all staff are trained in child protection issues, to enable them to respond appropriately to:

- significant changes in children's behaviour
- deterioration in their general wellbeing
- unexplained bruising, marks or signs of possible abuse
- neglect
- any comments children make that give cause for concern.

Guidance and information from the Local Safeguarding Children Board (LSCB) is made available to staff members. This includes advice for staff on how to avoid situations that might make them vulnerable to allegations of abuse.

All incidents or allegations affecting the welfare of children are investigated in a prompt and confidential manner according to LSCB guidelines. Written records are kept of all incidents and allegations and are stored securely in the setting. Information is shared with other agencies and professionals according to the guidelines laid down by the LSCB.

All staff have undergone appropriate criminal records checks and any allegation made against a member of staff will be thoroughly investigated. Allegations of serious harm or abuse will be reported without delay to Ofsted and the LSCB. Full details of the setting's safeguarding children policy and procedures are available in the staff handbook.

The setting's policy on safeguarding children is shared and discussed with parents and time is spent clarifying any issues that arise.

Procedures

List here the procedures to be taken by staff members to report any concerns they have about the welfare of the children in their care. Include the details of the safeguarding children coordinator and where to access information and guidance from the local child protection team.

List the steps that will be taken to investigate an allegation and include incident report forms for recording factual information. Emphasise the confidential nature of the information.

Detail how information on safeguarding children will be shared with parents.

Choosing parent support resources and programmes

Target group/skills need	Programmes and resources
Helping parents to understand more about child development and the nature of young children's play	● *Child Development from Birth to Eight*, Maria Robinson (2008), Open University Press ● *Developing Play for the Under 3s*, Anita Hughes (2006), David Fulton ● Early Home Learning Matters: www.earlyhomelearning.org.uk ● Family and Parenting Institute resources: www.familyandparenting.org/item/publication/42 ● Family Learning Information Pack (FLIP) and First and Foremost series, Pre School Learning Alliance: www.pre-school.org.uk ● Foundation Stage Parents: Partners in Learning http://nationalstrategies.standards.dcsf.gov.uk/node/154690 ● Jump Start and Looking at Learning Together programmes: www.pre-school.org.uk/practitioners/parents/445/looking-at-learning-together ● *Learning Together* leaflets, Early Education: www.early-education.org.uk ● Parents as First Teachers (PAFT): www.parentsasfirstteachers.org.uk ● Parents as Partners in Early Learning, case studies: http://nationalstrategies.standards.dcsf.gov.uk/node/151972 ● *Parents as Partners: Playing and Learning Together* DVD: https://nationalstrategies.standards.dcsf.gov.uk/node/113036 ● Parents, Early Years and Learning (PEAL): www.peal.org.uk ● *Parents, Early Years and Learning: Parents as Partners in the Early Years Foundation Stage, Principles into Practice*, Helen Wheeler and Joyce Connor (2009): www.ncb.org.uk ● Parents Involved in their Children's Learning (PICL): www.pengreen.org ● Peers Early Education Partnership (PEEP): www.peep.org.uk ● *The Wonder Year – First Year Development* and *Shaping the Brain* DVD, Siren Films: www.sirenfilms.co.uk ● *Why Love Matters*, Sue Gerhardt (2004), Routledge

SECTION 2.6   THE PARENT PARTNERSHIP TOOLKIT FOR EARLY YEARS

Target group/skills need	Programmes and resources
Sharing with parents how to support their child's communication and language skills	● Bookstart: www.bookstart.org.uk ● Chatter Matters Family Pack: www.btbetterworld.com/pg/developing_skills/free_resources/Chatter_Matters_Family_Pack/home.ikml ● Early Reading Connects family involvement toolkit: www.nationalliteracytrust.org.uk ● I CAN: www.ican.org.uk
Helping parents to manage their child's challenging behaviour	● *Building Better Behaviour in the Early Years*, Chris Dukes and Maggie Smith (2009), SAGE, London ● *Encouraging Positive Behaviour in the Early Years*, Collette Drifte (2008), SAGE, London ● *Feelings and Behaviour – a Creative Approach*, Anni McTavish (2007), Early Education ● *Managing Difficult Behaviour: Workshops for Parents*, Sonya Hinton (2008), Southgate Publishers ● Parents as First Teachers (PAFT): www.parentsasfirstteachers.org.uk ● Triple P: Positive Parenting Programme: www8.triplep.net
Supporting fathers to become involved with their children's care, learning and development	● Baby Father Alliance network: www.barnardos.org.uk/babyfather ● Father-inclusive services Every Child Matters: www.dcsf.gov.uk/everychildmatters/strategy/parents/pip/PIPrkfatherinclusiveservices/PIPfatherinclusiveservices ● Family Learning Works materials: www.campaign-for-learning.org.uk ● Supporting Young Dads project and Top Dads toolkit: www.continyou.org.uk/what_we_do/parents_and_family_learning/supporting_young_dads ● Family Information Direct: www.dcsf.gov.uk/familyinformationdirect ● Think Fathers campaign: www.fatherhoodinstitute.org ● Working with fathers Sure Start Children's Centres Practice Guidance 2006: www.dcsf.gov.uk/everychildmatters/research/publications/surestartpublications/1854 ● Working with fathers case studies, Together for Children: www.childrens-centres.org/Topics/CaseStudies/Fathers.aspx ● Working with men from African Caribbean and Muslim families: www.fatherhoodinstitute.org

123

THE PARENT PARTNERSHIP TOOLKIT FOR EARLY YEARS

SECTION 2.6

Figure 2.6d cont

Target group/skills need	Programmes and resources
Working with parents who have themselves had poor experiences of parenting	● Early Home Learning Matters: www.earlyhomelearning.org.uk ● Incredible Years: www.incredibleyears.com and www.incredibleyearswales.co.uk ● Parents as First Teachers (PAFT): www.parentsasfirstteachers.org.uk ● Parents Involved in their Children's Learning (PICL): www.pengreen.org.uk ● Peers Early Education Partnership (PEEP): www.peep.org.uk ● Parentline Plus: www.parentlineplus.org.uk ● Parents, Early Years and Learning (PEAL): www.peal.org.uk ● Sure Start Children's Centres Practice Guidance 2006: www.dcsf.gov.uk/everychildmatters/research/publications/ surestartpublications/1854 ● Working with mothers, fathers, carers and families: www.dcsf.gov.uk/everychildmatters/strategy/parents/ workingwithparentscarersandfamilies
Increasing the confidence and life skills of teenage parents	● Busymummy: www.busymummy.co.uk ● *Reaching Out to Pregnant Teenagers and Teenage Parents* (2005): www.dcsf.gov.uk/everychildmatters/healthandwellbeing/ teenagepregnancy/research/strategyresearch/ ● Supporting Young Dads project and Top Dads toolkit: www.continyou.org.uk/what_we_do/parents_and_family_learning/ supporting_young_dads ● Working with teenage parents, Sure Start Children's Centres Practice Guidance 2006: www.dcsf.gov.uk/everychildmatters/research/publications/ surestartpublications/1854 ● Young Parents case studies, Together for Children: www.childrens-centres.org/Topics/CaseStudies/YoungParents.aspx

SECTION 2.6 THE PARENT PARTNERSHIP TOOLKIT FOR EARLY YEARS

Target group/skills need	Programmes and resources
Engaging with parents from ethnic minority backgrounds to help them connect with the care and education system in the UK	● BabyFather Initiative: www.barnardos.org.uk/babyfather ● Working with men from African Caribbean and Muslim families: www.fatherhoodinstitute.org ● *Effective Provision of Pre-School Education (EPPE) Project: Final Report – A Longitudinal Study Funded by the DfES (1997-2004)*, Kathy Sylva et al (2004): www.dcsf.gov.uk/rsgateway/DB/RRP/u013144/index.shtml ● *Early Years and Childcare: LA Developing Practice – Improving Communication and Engaging with Parents* (2007): www.dcsf.gov.uk/everychildmatters/resources-and-practice/ EP00367 ● *Involving Asian Families in Learning*, National College of School Leadership: Leadership library: www.nationalcollege.org.uk/index/leadershiplibrary/leading-early years/working-with-parents-and-carers.htm ● Minority ethnic families case studies, Together for Children: www.childrens-centres.org/Topics/CaseStudies/ MinorityEthnicFamilies.aspx ● Strengthening Families, Strengthening Communities: www.raceequalityfoundation.org.uk/sfsc/index.asp ● *Supporting Children Learning English as an Additional Language* (2007): http://nationalstrategies.standards.dcsf.gov.uk/node/84861 ● *Sure Start and Black and Minority Ethnic Populations* (2007): www.dcsf.gov.uk/everychildmatters/publications/0/1905 ● *Use of Childcare Among Families from Minority Ethnic Backgrounds* (2005): www.dcsf.gov.uk/everychildmatters/10454 ● Working with Minority Ethnic Families, Sure Start Children's Centres Practice Guidance 2006: www.dcsf.gov.uk/everychildmatters/research/publications/ surestartpublications/1854

THE PARENT PARTNERSHIP TOOLKIT FOR EARLY YEARS

SECTION 2.6

Figure 2.6d cont

Target group/skills need	Programmes and resources
Developing parents' skills to enable them to access work or training	• ContinYou: www.continyou.org.uk/what_we_do/parents_and_family_learning • National Family Learning Network: www.campaign-for-learning.org.uk/familylearningnetwork • National Institute of Adult Continuing Education (NIACE): www.niace.org.uk • Parents case studies, Together for Children: www.childrens-centres.org/Topics/CaseStudies/Parents.aspx
Addressing the literacy and numeracy skills of parents from a range of backgrounds	• ContinYou: www.continyou.org.uk/what_we_do/parents_and_family_learning • Family literacy and numeracy resources, NIACE: www.niace.org.uk • Jump Start programme: www.pre-school.org.uk/services/family-learning/jump-start/index.php
Providing information, advice and support for parents of children with additional needs	• Early support resources – 'Family File', 'Family Pack', 'Background Information' booklets and 'Information for Parents' booklets: www.dcsf.gov.uk/everychildmatters/healthandwellbeing/ahdc/ earlysupport/resources/esresources • Family Information Direct: www.dcsf.gov.uk/familyinformationdirect • *Supporting Early Identification and Intervention for Children with Special Educational Needs* (2005): www.dcsf.gov.uk/everychildmatters/10168 • *Working with Parents of Children with Special Educational Needs*, Chris Dukes and Maggie Smith (2007) SAGE, London
Supporting parents who themselves have additional needs	• Home Start: www.home-start.org.uk • Parents as First Teachers (PAFT): www.parentsasfirstteachers.org.uk • Peers Early Education Partnership (PEEP): www.peep.org.uk

Key points

- Practitioners have a wealth of experience about child development that they can share with parents.

- Share information in a variety of ways, thinking carefully about the needs of all parents using the setting.

- The early years setting is the ideal place to provide parents with information about the wide range of services and support organisations available locally and nationally.

- Make good use of the expert advice available from other professionals who provide services for families.

- Most parents will appreciate advice on strategies to manage particular aspects of their young child's behaviour at different ages.

- Involving parents with drawing up the setting's behaviour management policy provides an ideal opportunity to build a mutual understanding of what is important for young children.

- Safeguarding children is a shared responsibility that should be discussed in order to appreciate individual roles and responsibilities.

- A wide range of parenting programmes is available to support parents with particular identified needs.

- Parenting programmes should be delivered by practitioners who are trained and qualified in their delivery.

- Building parents' skills and confidence in fulfilling their role has been shown to have significant positive benefits for both children and parents.

Reflective questions

Child development

- Are we aware of which aspects of child development parents would like to know more about?

- Are there better ways to provide parents with the information they need?

- Would it be useful to provide some information specifically targeted at fathers?

- Could we make better use of our professional links with colleagues in the health service?

Managing behaviour

- As practitioners, do we share a common understanding of what constitutes good behaviour?

- Is our behaviour management policy straightforward, easy to understand and implemented consistently?

- How effective are we at using opportunities to help children to learn how to manage their own behaviour?

- How could we involve parents in reviewing our behaviour management policy?

Safeguarding children

- Are the setting's procedures for carrying out checks on new members of staff up to date and rigorously enforced?
- Are we all comfortable that we fully understand our responsibilities for safeguarding children?
- Are we comfortable to discuss the principles behind our safeguarding policy with parents?
- Do we know who to contact for support and advice regarding the safeguarding of children?

Parenting programmes

- Do we see the promotion of parenting skills as a part of our professional role?
- Are we aware of the full range of parenting support programmes available in our area?
- How effectively do we promote parent support resources as inclusive and helpful for all parents?
- Do we feel comfortable to signpost parents towards programmes and resources that we feel will be useful to them?

Working with other professionals

- Do we invest sufficient time in building up links with other children's services professionals?
- Do we foster a feeling of respect towards our colleagues and actively promote multiagency working?
- Are staff encouraged and facilitated to attend multiagency training events?
- Do we see the early years setting as an opportunity to bring parents and multiagency professionals together?

SECTION 2.7   THE PARENT PARTNERSHIP TOOLKIT FOR EARLY YEARS

Auditing your provision

This section reviews the place of developing parent partnerships in the Early Years Foundation Stage (EYFS) framework and looks at the requirements of the Ofsted self-evaluation form (SEF). It then brings together all the aspects of developing partnerships with parents looked at in Sections 2.1 to 2.6 to create an audit tool for measuring all aspects of your provision to see how effectively it supports partnership with parents. This provides essential information for completing the Ofsted SEF and for planning for improvement.

Early Years Foundation Stage (EYFS) framework

The EYFS framework builds on all the evidence of what constitutes good quality provision for young children as evidenced in the Effective Provision of Pre-School Education (EPPE) and Researching Effective Pedagogy in the Early Years (REPEY) reports (Sylva et al 2004; Siraj-Blatchford et al, 2002).

At a very fundamental level there is a specific legal requirement within the welfare standards ('Safeguarding and promoting children's welfare') of the EYFS to provide parents with information about:

- 'the type of activities provided for the children
- the daily routines of the provision
- the staffing of the provision
- food and drinks provided for the children
- the provider's policies and procedures – for example, admissions policies, equality of opportunity policy, safeguarding children policy
- the complaints procedure (copies to be available on request)
- details for contacting Ofsted and an explanation that parents can make a complaint to Ofsted should they wish
- the procedure to be followed in the event of a parent failing to collect a child at the appointed time
- the procedure to be followed in the event of a child going missing.

In addition, providers must obtain necessary information from parents in advance of a child being admitted to the provision, including:

- emergency contact numbers
- the child's special dietary requirements, preferences or food allergies the child may have
- the child's special health requirements
- information about who has legal contact with the child, and who has parental responsibility for the child.

129

Parents should be allowed access to all written records about their children (except in exceptional cases where data protection laws stipulate it is against the best interests of the child to do so) and, where requested, comments from parents are incorporated into children's records.'

(Source: Statutory Framework for the Early Years Foundation Stage:
http://nationalstrategies.standards.dcsf.gov.uk/earlyyears)

Over and above this, the themes and commitments of the EYFS emphasise the role of parents as partners in commitment 2.2 of the positive relationships theme:

'Parents are children's first and most enduring educators. When parents and practitioners work together in early years settings, the results have a positive impact on children's development and learning.'

It goes on to highlight the importance of:

'Respecting diversity

- All families are important and should be welcomed and valued in all settings.
- Families are all different. Children may live with one or both parents, with other relatives or carers, with same sex parents or in an extended family.
- Families may speak more than one language at home; they may be travellers, refugees or asylum seekers.
- All practitioners will benefit from professional development in diversity, equality and anti-discriminatory practice whatever the ethnic, cultural or social make-up of the setting.

Communication:

- A welcoming atmosphere with approachable staff helps to create effective communication.
- Effective communication means there is a two-way flow of information, knowledge and expertise between parents and practitioners.
- All communication is important, including gesture, signing and body language. Actions can speak louder than words.
- Posters, pictures and other resources on display will show the setting's positive attitudes to disability, and to ethnic, cultural and social diversity. They will help children and families to recognise that they are valued.

Learning together

- Parents and practitioners have a lot to learn from each other. This can help them to support and extend children's learning and development.
- Parents should review their children's progress regularly and contribute to their child's learning and development record.

SECTION 2.7 THE PARENT PARTNERSHIP TOOLKIT FOR EARLY YEARS

- Parents can be helped to understand more about learning and teaching through workshops on important areas such as play, outdoor learning or early reading. Some parents may go on to access further education at their own level.

- In true partnership, parents understand and contribute to the policies in the setting.'

The EYFS statutory requirements and practice guidance make it quite clear that partnership with parents is an underpinning commitment on which the framework is built, not an optional extra. This is reflected in the Ofsted inspection framework and good practice guidance.

Ofsted self-evaluation framework (SEF)

How well practitioners develop partnerships with parents to support young children's welfare, learning and development is a recurring theme within the Ofsted self-evaluation framework. The SEF expects there to be consultation with parents and children to seek their views on the provision and asks for evidence of changes and improvements that have been made as a result of this consultation. The new self-evaluation form published at the end of October 2009 (Ofsted, 2009) requires an evaluation and judgement to be made about 'The effectiveness of the setting's engagement with parents and carers'. This is a new section of the SEF that did not appear in the original version, emphasising the importance placed on effective parent-setting partnerships.

Within the context of evaluating the leadership and management of their early years provision, setting leaders are asked to consider how effectively they:

- provide parents/carers with good quality information about early years provision
- inform parents/carers about their children's achievements and progress
- encourage parents/carers to share what they know about their child, particularly when their child first starts to attend
- encourage parents/carers to be involved in supporting their children's learning and development
- work in partnership with parents to meet every child's individual needs
- liaise with external agencies or services and the parents to ensure a child gets any support they need
- work in partnership with parents and others to safeguard children
- work with parents, carers, other providers, services and employers and take into consideration ethnic background, home language, family background, religion/faith, learning difficulties and/or disabilities and gender to promote children's care and education
- ensure policies and procedures are inclusive, understood by all parents and available in the languages of all the children that attend the setting
- involve parents in the self-evaluation process.

An inspection judgement of 'good' or 'outstanding' will be impossible to achieve without systems and structures being in place to support effective parental partnership.

131

ITERS-R and ECERS-R Scales

An increasing number of settings are making use of the Infant-Toddler and Early Childhood Environment Rating Scales – ITERS-R (Harms et al, 2006) and ECERS-R (Harms et al, 2005) – to help them carry out complete audits of the quality of their provision. Although initially devised for research purposes, these scales, if used properly, can help to gain an overview of the many different aspects that make up the overall quality of any early years setting. Partnership with parents is included as a very small aspect of the overall audit of provision in section 33 of the ITERS and section 38 of the ECERS document.

Auditing your partnership with parents

Figure 2.7a (see p133) is an audit grid that brings together the key issues reviewed in *Sections 2.1 to 2.6*. It will help you to identify those aspects of your partnership with parents that are currently working well and those that require further development. This information can then be used to plan improvements to the way you manage your provision to support better outcomes for children and families.

References

Early Years Foundation Stage framework, see *http://nationalstrategies.standards.dcsf.gov.uk/earlyyears*

Harms, T, Clifford, R and Cryer, D (2005) *Early Childhood Environment Rating Scale (Revised Edition)*, Teachers' College Press, New York

Harms, T, Cryer, D and Clifford, RM (2006) *Infant /Toddler Environment Rating Scale (Revised Edition)*, Teachers' College Press, New York

Ofsted (2009) *Early Years Self-Evaluation Form Amendments*, see: *www.ofsted.gov.uk/Ofsted-home/Forms-and-guidance/Browse-all-by/Other/General/Online-early-years-self-evaluation-form-amendments*

Ofsted Self-Evaluation Framework & Guidance: *https://online.ofsted.gov.uk/onlineofsted/public/launchportal.aspx*

Siraj-Blatchford, I, Sylva, K, Muttock, S, Gilden, R and Bell, D (2002) *Researching Effective Pedagogy in the Early Years (REPEY)*, DfES RR356, see: *www.dcsf.gov.uk/research/data/uploadfiles/RR356.pdf*

Sylva, K, Melhuish, E, Sammons, S, Siraj-Blatchford, I and Taggart, B (2004) *The Effective Provision of Pre-School Education Project: Final Report*, see: *www.dcsf.gov.uk/research/data/uploadfiles/SSU_FR_2004_01.pdf*

Auditing your parent partnerships

Aspect	Key issues to address	Action needed	Date for review
2.1: Establishing the vision and values	• The setting has a clear vision and values that everyone understands. • Parents are actively involved in agreeing the setting's vision and values. • The parent partnership policy is clear, easy to understand and available in several languages. • The induction process for new staff emphasises the importance of parent partnership. • The values of the setting are evident in everyday practice.		
2.2: Creating a welcoming environment	• The physical layout of the environment is reviewed regularly to make it as welcoming as possible. • Visual images around the building are inclusive and reflect the diversity of families using the setting. • The need for safety and security is balanced sensibly with the desire to facilitate access between different parts of the building. • We actively consider how well the building works from a parent's perspective. • Staff understand the role they play in making parents feel welcome in the setting.		
2.3: Listening to parents	• We spend time with each family to build up a relationship of trust and respect. • Time spent talking with parents is seen as a valuable aspect of daily practice. • Staff receive training covering diversity, equality and anti-discriminatory practice. • Parents' views on many different aspects of the setting are sought and acted on. • A variety of forms of consultation are used to include as many different parent groups as possible.		

THE PARENT PARTNERSHIP TOOLKIT FOR EARLY YEARS   SECTION 2.7

Figure 2.7s cont

Aspect	Key issues to address	Action needed	Date for review
2.4: Communicating with parents	● Information is provided in a wide variety of ways ● We are aware of the language preferences of the families we work with ● Written documents are clearly presented and free from jargon ● Visual images are used effectively to convey information about young children's learning and development ● Practitioners receive training to help them develop their verbal and non-verbal communication skills		
2.5: Key person working	● Staff have a clear understanding of the rationale behind, and benefits of, key person working ● We spend time explaining key person working to parents, revisiting this as required ● Practitioners have time to carry out their key person role effectively, including home visits ● The setting is organised to minimise the number of transitions and changes in key person that children have to make ● Staff know who to talk to if they have any concerns about their key person role		
2.6: Supporting parent-child relationships	● We provide accessible information on a range of aspects of child development ● Parents are involved in agreeing the setting's behaviour management policy ● The roles and responsibilities of different parties in safeguarding children are openly discussed with parents and practitioners ● Building parents' skills and effectiveness in their role is seen as an important aspect of the setting's provision ● We are aware of the range of support for parents available in the local area and actively direct parents to this provision		

134

Section 3

Introduction

In all countries of the UK, quality early years provision is underpinned by a commitment to building good relationships with parents and carers. The relationships that exist between parents and practitioners have a major effect on the wellbeing, learning and development of children. Although it is often a challenge for early years settings to find ways of engaging parents, the positive results of successful engagement are well worth the effort.

The resources in this section are designed to support a range of different approaches to engaging with parents and other family members. There are examples of:

- ways to incorporate partnership with parents into the everyday planning and organisation of the setting
- 'one-off' activities to engage with groups of parents, including support materials for running family workshop sessions
- information leaflets for parents about different aspects of children's play and learning, including ideas to use at home.

Structure of Section 3

The ideas and activities are grouped into six sections:

3.1 Creating links with home

3.2 Using collections of everyday things

3.3 Out and about

3.4 Family workshops – exploring together

3.5 Family members as visitors to your setting

3.6 The value of play.

3.1 Creating links with home

This section introduces a range of simple ways to engage with families by building links with home. It includes ideas to use with children of different ages, but many can be adapted to use throughout the 0-5 age range. Each idea is accompanied by a sample letter to parents explaining what you are doing and how they can become involved. These resources provide a quick but effective way of building up the relationship between the setting and the home.

The resources in this section will be particularly useful for:

- empowering practitioners to be actively involved in establishing positive relationships with the children they are directly responsible for
- helping settings to plan a programme of family involvement appropriate for different age groups of children.

3.2 Using collections of everyday things

This section looks at the value of using collections as a focus for supporting parents' understanding of young children's play. It describes the use of collections of natural and reclaimed materials and household objects to share with parents the value of active learning and open-ended exploratory play. The principles behind the use of treasure baskets, heuristic play and Treasureboxes® are described and there are photocopiable parent information sheets for parents (*figures 3.2a, b and c, on p161-165*) to enable parents to use these approaches at home.

Use these resources to help parents:

- understand what children are doing when they are playing
- recognise their individual child's interests and ideas
- see the potential of everyday objects as playthings for children.

3.3 Out and about

The focus of this section is helping parents to make the most of the vast range of opportunities presented by outdoor play. It looks at the reasons why outdoor play is important and then provides three photocopiable eight-page activity booklets to promote outdoor play with different age groups. These contain ideas for parents to use with *babies (figure 3.3a on p169), toddlers (figure 3.3b on p173) and preschool children (figure 3.3c on p177)*.

Use these resources:

- to promote important messages to parents on the theme of healthy living
- as a way of encouraging the active involvement of fathers and other male carers
- to raise the profile of outdoor play among fellow practitioners.

3.4 Family workshops – exploring together

The resources provided in this section can be used to organise and run a family workshop session on the theme of exploration and investigation. The open-ended nature of the activities makes them ideal for use with children of different ages and takes away any fear of failure – for both adults and children. They include a series of workshop activities on the theme of exploring water (*figures 3.4a to 3.4n, on p188-204*), an example of a letter of invitation (*figure 3.4o on p205*) and three ideas and activity sheets for parents to use at home with children of different ages (*figures 3.4p, 3.4q and 3.4r, on p206-208*).

The resources in this section will help you to:

- share with parents the importance of listening to young children and following their ideas
- engage fathers and other male carers in their children's wellbeing, learning and development
- build relationships with family members in a relaxed and enjoyable situation.

SECTION 3 THE PARENT PARTNERSHIP TOOLKIT FOR EARLY YEARS

3.5 Family members as visitors to your setting

This section focuses on the value of inviting family members as visitors into your setting to share their life and work with the children. It helps to address many aspects of young children's personal, social and emotional development and also gives powerful messages to parents about the inclusivity of the setting and the value of diversity. It looks at how to plan for and organise a visit so it is successful for everyone – the children, the visitor and the practitioners (*figures 3.5a and 3.5b, on p215-216*).

Use the resources in this section to:

- build your relationships with the families who use your setting
- nurture an attitude of respect for individuality among parents, children and practitioners
- widen the experience and understanding of parents and children.

3.6 The value of play

This section looks in detail at the important messages practitioners will want to share with parents about young children's play and learning. It discusses the importance of different aspects of play and what young children are learning while they are playing. The five photocopiable leaflets in *figures 3.6a to 3.6e* (*see p225-234*) are designed to help you to share with parents some key information about play and learning across all areas of the early years curriculum. On the back of each of these sheets are ideas for parents to use at home with children of different ages, to complement the work you are doing in the setting.

Use these resources to:

- share with parents what young children are learning through play
- build parents' understanding of the early years curriculum and what experiences their child is having in the setting
- provide ideas for parents to help them support their children's learning at home.

137

THE PARENT PARTNERSHIP TOOLKIT FOR EARLY YEARS   SECTION 3

Creating links with home

> This section introduces a range of simple ways to engage with families by building links with home. It includes ideas to use with children of different ages, but many can be adapted to use throughout the 0-5 age range. Each idea is accompanied by a sample letter to parents explaining what you are doing and how they can become involved. These resources provide a quick but effective way of building up the relationship between the setting and the home.
>
> The resources in this section will be particularly useful for:
> ● empowering practitioners to be actively involved in establishing positive relationships with the children they are directly responsible for
> ● helping settings to plan a programme of family involvement appropriate for different age groups of children.

Introduction

In the UK, there is now an accepted understanding that the home is the most significant environmental factor in enabling children to develop the trust, attitudes and skills that will enable them to learn and develop and to engage positively with the world (Roberts, 2009).

If, as early years practitioners, we accept that a good home environment provides the love, security, support, aspiration, experiences and opportunities that children need in order to flourish, then we must also recognise our responsibility to acknowledge the value of what happens in children's lives at home.

In Reggio Emilia in northern Italy, the educators who work with children in the infant-toddler centres and preschools see parents as active partners in their children's learning and development. Their induction programme is planned to make the family feel at home and a part of the organisation. Opportunities are built into the programme so that educators have the opportunity to talk with the parents, helping them to begin to understand the parents' unique perspective on their own child (Thornton and Brunton, 2009).

The educators in Reggio Emilia place great value on what parents can tell them about their individual children's personalities, preferences, interests and capabilities. They then build on this information to help them to plan for each child's learning and development. In this world-renowned system of early years services, the professionals are humble when they say:

> 'As educators it is our duty to know more about the planet of children. We know too little about how children learn and about how their ideas and opinions are formed.'
>
> (Spaggiari, 2004)

How better to gain the information we need than by learning more about each child's family and listening to what they have to say?

Practitioners often put forward the argument that, for a variety of reasons, parents are unable, or unwilling, to engage in their children's learning and development. As Margy

Whalley, of the Pen Green Centre for the Under Fives and Families, states:

> 'We need to begin with the firm belief that all parents are interested in the development and progress of their own children.'

She emphasises the need to offer a flexible range of options for parents to become involved in their individual child's learning and development (Whalley et al, 2007).

Practical ways of creating links with home

The following resources provide a range of opportunities and ideas to engage parents and families in their children's learning and development. They include suggestions for creating links with home for different age groups of children, but you may find that the ideas can be used throughout your setting if they are modified slightly. The resources are:

- Working with babies – family books and family rolling tins
- Working with toddlers – lending libraries for families and building on children's interests
- Working with 3-5s – Storysacks and Travelling Ted
- Working with 0-5s – Grandparents' Day.

Working with babies

Family books

When very young children start to attend daycare, both the children and their parents are experiencing a vast change in their lives. Suddenly they find themselves in separate worlds during the day when previously they have spent most, if not all, of their time together.

By making family books, you can create a visual link with home and family for babies and toddlers to look at. These books provide a very valuable link with home and their parents' and siblings' lives, and provide the opportunity for families to stay connected during the time the young child is with you. They also give the children's key persons an insight into the families the children come from and help them to have conversations with children that are relevant to them as individuals. The books can be used at different times during the day – to mark the passage of time or to help reassure children if they are unsettled or unhappy. Keep the books where they are easily accessible and where the babies can see them so they can ask to look at the books whenever they want to.

Use either small photograph albums or notebooks to make a collection of photographs of different family members, pets, friends and experiences. Ask working parents to take photographs of themselves at different times of the day – arriving at work, having a break, working – to include in the family books. Either the parents or you, as practitioners, could write short captions to go with the pictures. With babies, begin the family books with pictures of immediate family members. As children become older, you can progressively add more photos, including friends, extended family, pets, events and outings.

Use the *sample letter in figure 3.1a (see p147)* to ask parents to participate.

Family rolling tins

As a variation on the family books theme, you could make some family rolling tins for the babies to play with during the day. You can use these to remind children of their family members, their homes or their favourite toys at home.

Choose a large tin with no sharp edges or a cylindrical container, such as the ones that hold Easter eggs or bottles. Ask parents and carers to send in images of themselves, other family members or of their child's interests and playthings at home.

Glue the photographs to the tin or tube and cover them with clear plastic. Use the family rolling tins to play with the babies. Roll the tins and talk to the babies about the photographs they can see. Ask the babies to point out different family members and things of interest. They will probably be very interested in the family rolling tins of other babies too!

The *letter in figure 3.1b* (see *p148*) explains to parents what family rolling tins are all about.

Working with toddlers

Lending libraries for families

Once babies are mobile, their interests and capacity for enjoying new things and experiences explodes. This can be a very difficult time for parents who are trying to provide enjoyable and challenging experiences for their children, often within a tight budget. One of the ways in which you can both help parents to support their children's learning and development, and influence the quality of the experiences they provide, is to set up a lending library.

You could include a wide range of resources in your lending library, such as:

Books – Include books to introduce families to the value and importance of books in their children's learning.

Include books for babies, such as board and cloth books, books without words, and active books with textures, shapes and flaps.

Books for toddlers and older children will include books with pictures of children doing familiar things, stories about 'hello' and 'goodbye', books with simple themes and clear illustrations. You could also add books of rhymes, stories with predictable patterns or repeating phrases that can be read again and again and simple information books as well as stories.

Make your lending library of books work by:
- storing the books in a separate container
- making sure they are clean and not tatty or too chewed
- removing and replacing damaged books.

You may be able to borrow books from your local library to lend to parents. You could then encourage them to join their local library themselves.

THE PARENT PARTNERSHIP TOOLKIT FOR EARLY YEARS   SECTION 3.1

Toys to develop manipulative skills – Manipulating small objects helps children to develop fine motor control and hand-eye coordination. The resources you will need to provide in your lending library will become more complex as children's skills develop.

They will include:

- toys that babies can squash, stretch and bend
- tray puzzles
- picture puzzles
- floor puzzles
- threading and lacing toys
- hammer and pegs
- shape sorters
- boxes that fit inside one another.

Small world play toys – Including small world play toys in your lending library will help parents provide opportunities for their children to use their imaginations by creating and re-enacting stories, developing language and vocabulary.

You could include:

- wooden cars, trucks and trains
- wooden or good-quality plastic animals and people
- a dolls' house with dolls
- a garage, zoo or farm.

Construction toys – By offering to lend families a range of construction toys, you will facilitate them to provide their children with toys that will enable the children to develop their fine motor skills, experience how different materials behave, and develop spatial awareness and self-confidence as they master new skills.

Resources to use include:

- wooden building blocks
- construction sets
- reclaimed materials, including boxes, tubes, cartons, small empty bottles, tubing, netting
- natural materials, including wood, shells and pebbles
- fabrics for making dens
- Duplo and Lego blocks and shapes.

Use the *sample letter in figure 3.1c (see p149)* to explain how the lending library works and to invite parents to join.

Building on children's interests

As part of their natural stage of development, toddlers often become very interested in particular objects and experiences. Many toddlers show distinct preoccupations with

SECTION 3.1   THE PARENT PARTNERSHIP TOOLKIT FOR EARLY YEARS

repeated actions and ways of doing things. They may be fascinated by transporting things around in bags, boxes or wheeled toys. They may spend long periods of time sorting things, lining them up or putting them in and out of containers. Some children are intrigued by things that go round, by straight lines and boundaries, by stacking, piling up, rolling or even throwing things. This is all part of a toddler's learning and development.

Parents and family members often need support in understanding that, when children are behaving in these ways, they are not being deliberately awkward or badly behaved – they are exploring the world in ways that make sense to them. There is no doubt that this can be very difficult for many families to manage, particularly if their child's preoccupation is not always socially acceptable in the outside world.

Many settings focus a lot of attention on children's interests and schemas – patterns of thought and behaviour (Nutbrown, 2006) and plan much of what they do with the children in their setting accordingly. Parents can often add a great deal of knowledge about their child in terms of what he or she does at home. This information can certainly enrich the experiences that are planned by early years practitioners.

Some settings have gone even further down this route and have provided parents with small Treasurebox® collections to take home and use with their children (*see Section 3.2: Using collections of everyday things*). Parents have been asked to make a record of their children's interests and experiences when playing with the resources. These records have then been used as a basis for planning for the children's learning and development in the setting – a case of true partnership with parents.

You could provide small Treasurebox® collections to lend to parents including:

- a colour collection – coloured tissue papers, cellophane, plastic colour paddles, coloured Perspex shapes, a torch, paint sample cards

- a collection of keys – old keys, new keys, decorative keys, small and large keys, padlocks and their keys, key rings

- a natural collection – pebbles, shells, leaves, twigs, cones and seed pods, dried flowers, skeleton leaves or natural materials from pot pourri.

The *sample letter in figure 3.1d* (*see p150*) explains to parents how they can become involved in using small collections at home.

Working with 3-5s

Storysacks®

Listening to stories helps children to make sense of the world, feeds their imagination and builds their language skills. Sharing books together is a great time for conversations with children and for listening carefully to what they have to say to you. Developing and using a lending library of Storysacks will help you to encourage a love of books shared between children and their parents.

There are two very different ways of setting up a Storysack lending library – the first way is

143

to purchase the ready-made Storysacks® from *www.storysack.com*; the second is to form a group of interested parents to help put together a range of your own Storysacks. You will probably find that you want to use a combination of both ways.

A Storysack is a large drawstring storage bag, which includes a copy of a high-quality children's book for parents to read with their children. The Storysack also includes soft toy characters, props and scenery to encourage role-play. The sack is then completed by the addition of a game, a CD of the story, an activity guide and a guide for parents on how to use the Storysack.

If you use the ready-made Storysacks, your lending library can be up and running in a matter of weeks. If you decide to make your own sacks, you will need to gather together a group of parents, family members and practitioners who will select the books, make the bags and buy or make the characters, props and scenery. You will also need to recruit parents to record the story and to make or buy an appropriate game. A manual to help you make Storysacks and organise parent workshops, along with the activity guides and guides for parents, are also available on the Storysack® website.

Ready-made Storysacks include:

- 'Can't You Sleep Little Bear?' – a perfect bedtime story
- 'Farmer Duck' – an excellent starting point for discussion about teamwork
- 'If Only' – the ideal opportunity to explore self-esteem and outward appearances as well as lifecycles and mini-beasts
- 'Messy Martin' – a story for all messy eaters
- 'Badger's Parting Gifts' – a sensitively told story which provides an excellent introduction to the difficult subject of death and the gifts and memories we leave behind.

Use the *sample letter in figure 3.1e (see p151)* to invite parents to a Storysack workshop session.

Travelling Ted

Sometimes, children are away from your setting for family reasons – perhaps a holiday or a visit to see family members who live abroad. You can introduce Travelling Ted to your setting – a soft toy who can accompany a family while they are away. Travelling Ted can help the child and its family to stay in touch with friends in your setting as well as helping the children who stay behind to gain an understanding of other places from a child's point of view.

Travelling Ted can keep in touch by:

- sending a postcard or letter
- talking on the phone or emailing
- keeping a diary or travel journal
- bringing back souvenirs and photographs to share.

Weekend Ted could be used in exactly the same way as Travelling Ted – helping to make connections between the children's lives with their families and what happens in your setting.

SECTION 3.1   THE PARENT PARTNERSHIP TOOLKIT FOR EARLY YEARS

In *figure 3.1f (see p152), there is an invitation* to take Travelling Ted home and report back on the adventures he has.

Working with 0-5s

Grandparents' Day

Many grandparents make a huge contribution to the lives of their grandchildren, and to their learning and development. More than one-third of the approximately 14 million grandparents in the UK spend the equivalent of three days a week caring for their grandchildren, whether babysitting, providing regular childcare, playing with their grandchildren or learning with them (Al-Azami and Gyllenspetz, 2007).

There are many positive reasons why your setting would want to involve grandparents in the lives of their grandchildren. These include:

- Grandparents will learn more about your setting and be able to support their children more effectively.
- There is an emotional bond between children and their grandparents. Seeing their grandparents actively and positively engaged with your setting will encourage children to become more settled and attached themselves.
- Grandparents' involvement with your setting could help ease the pressure on parents.
- As grandparents find out more about what happens at your setting, parents and grandparents can form an effective partnership to support the child's learning.
- Grandparents may have more time to become involved as volunteers in your setting, offering to share their skills and experiences. They may be able to accompany you on visits, to help out at fundraising events, or to be part of working groups to make and refurbish equipment and resources.

You could decide to hold a regular 'Grandparents' Day', where a range of things could happen. Invite the grandparents of all children well in advance – you may be surprised who turns up.

In addition to showing grandparents around your setting and answering any questions they may have, you could:

- set up activities for grandparents and their grandchildren to do together
- have a shared storytelling session
- organise some outdoor games and races for grandchildren and their grandparents
- find out what grandparents' interests are and ask them to share them with the children
- arrange for children to interview grandparents about their childhood.

Use the *letter in figure 3.1g (see p152)* to invite grandparents to find out more about what goes on in your setting.

References

Al-Azami, S and Gyllenspetz, I (2007) *Grandparents and Grandchildren: Learning with Grandparents*, The Basic Skills Agency

Nutbrown, C (2006) *Threads of Thinking*, SAGE, London

Roberts, K (2009) *Early Home Learning Matters, A Good Practice Guide*, Family and Parenting Institute, London, see: *www.earlyhomelearning.org.uk*

Spaggiari, S (2004) Address at 'Crossing Boundaries' international conference, Reggio Emilia

Thornton, L and Brunton, P (2009) *Understanding the Reggio Approach (Second Edition)*, Routledge

Whalley, M and the Pen Green Centre Team (2007) *Involving Parents in their Children's Learning*, SAGE, London

SECTION 3.1   THE PARENT PARTNERSHIP TOOLKIT FOR EARLY YEARS

Letter to parents: family books

Family books

Dear Parents

In our baby room we have decided to introduce 'family books' to use with your children.

The family books will help your children to make links with their families when they are in our setting.

We will provide a photo album/notebook to hold pictures of your close family. You can help us by sending in photographs of the family members you think your baby will recognise.

We will put the photographs in the album so that we can share the family book with your child at different times of the day. If you have any photos of you taken during the day when you are at work that would be great.

We will also be able to use the family books to reassure your child if she or he is unsettled or unhappy.

When your child is older, we will include photos of other family members and pets. We can include any pictures of special events or trips out.

Could you please let your child's key person have any photographs you want us to use by the end of next week.

With best wishes,

THE PARENT PARTNERSHIP TOOLKIT FOR EARLY YEARS

SECTION 3.1

Figure 3.1b

Letter to parents: family rolling tins

Family rolling tins

Dear Parents

Following the success of the family books we have used in the baby room, we have decided to make some 'family rolling tins' for the children to play with.

Just like the family books, the tins will help your children to make links with their families when they are in our setting. You can help us by sending in photographs of family members, pets or your child's playthings. We also need large round tins (with no sharp edges) or strong cardboard cylinders you no longer need.

We will glue the photographs to the tins and cover them with clear plastic to protect them. We will then use the tins to play with – rolling them and talking to your child about what they can see in the photos.

They will probably want to play with each other's tins too and will get to know the families of the other children in the room.

Could you please let your child's key person have any photographs you want us to use by the end of next week.

You might want to make some picture rolling tins yourself to play with at home. We could supply you with pictures of your child at nursery to put on the tins.

With best wishes,

SECTION 3.1 THE PARENT PARTNERSHIP TOOLKIT FOR EARLY YEARS

Figure 3.1c

Letter to parents: lending library

Join our lending library

Here at [*name of setting*], we have a lending library where parents can borrow books and toys to use with their children at home.

The lending library is open every Friday afternoon from 2 o'clock onwards in the [*area of setting*].

You can borrow one book or toy for each of your children each week.

We make a small charge of [*charge*] to cover the cost of looking after and replacing the books and toys. If this is a problem please talk to [*manager's name*].

We know that accidents can happen but, if you join the lending library, we ask that you encourage your child to look after the books and toys carefully.

Please make sure that you return the things you borrow after a week so that other families can enjoy them. You will be expected to replace any lost items.

We hope you enjoy the books and toys you borrow. Have fun!

The staff at [*name of setting*]

THE PARENT PARTNERSHIP TOOLKIT FOR EARLY YEARS

SECTION 3.1

Figure 3.1d

Letter to parents: Building on children's interests

Building on children's interests

Dear Parents

At [*name of setting*] we plan our activities and experiences for children by building on the things we know interest them.

We are keen to know what interests your child at home, so that we can then build this into our planning.

In [*month*], we are planning to provide experiences connected with colour and we would like you to help us to find out what interests your child on this theme.

We have put together some small collections of things to help you and your child explore colour together. These are for you to take home and use. You might decide to add other things to the colour collection to interest your child.

Please let us know in writing, or by speaking to your child's key person, what your child has been interested in. We can use this information to plan what to do next in our setting.

If you have any questions please speak to [*name*], who will also be able to give you one of our colour collections.

Thank you for your help!

SECTION 3.1 THE PARENT PARTNERSHIP TOOLKIT FOR EARLY YEARS

Letter to parents: Storysacks®

Storysacks

Dear Parents

Here at [*name of setting*], we are hoping to introduce 'Storysacks' as a way for you, as parents, to borrow books and resources to help you share the pleasure of reading with your child.

We are hoping to buy some Storysacks in the next few weeks to begin our collection. After that we will be making some of our own.

Each Storysack will include a good quality book, some soft toy characters, props and scenery, a game, a CD of the story, an activity guide and a guide on how to use the Storysack at home. Everything will come in a strong storage bag.

We hope that you will be able to help us to make the items to go in the Storysacks along with the books. Maybe you are good at sewing or knitting or you would be happy drawing or painting the scenery or recording the story for us.

[*Staff names*] will be holding a Storysack workshop on [*date*] at [*time*], when we will explain how you could help us to make these excellent resources for our families.

If you, or another family member or friend, can come to the workshop, that would be great. If you cannot come but want to help please talk to [*staff names*].

Please let us know if you will be coming to the workshop so that we can make sure we have enough refreshments.

Looking forward to seeing you on [*date*].

[Names]

151

THE PARENT PARTNERSHIP TOOLKIT FOR EARLY YEARS   SECTION 3.1

Figure 3.1f

Letter to parents: Travelling Ted

Wanted – a good home for Ted

At [*name of setting*], we have a bear called Travelling Ted who likes to spend time with children's families – going on holiday, visiting friends and relatives or simply enjoying the weekend! Ted is very well behaved and brings everything he needs with him.

Travelling Ted will let the rest of the children in our setting know what adventures he has. He might send a photograph, write a postcard or letter or send an email. Sometimes he keeps a diary or writes down the story of his adventures for the staff and children to read.

If you would like Travelling Ted to go on a trip with your family or visit you over the weekend, please contact [*name*], who will be pleased to make the necessary arrangements.

Figure 3.1g

Figure 3.1g: Letter to grandparents

Calling all grandparents!

At [*name of setting*], we hear a lot about grandparents from the children in our care. We know how special you are to each other.

To celebrate this, we are holding a 'Grandparents' Day' where we will be able to get to know each other and you will be able to find out what your grandchildren do every day in our setting.

Grandparents' Day will be held on [*day and date*], starting at [*time*], until [*time*]. You can spend as much time with us as you like.

There will be activities to do with your grandchildren, stories to read, music to listen to and games to play.

You are very welcome to stay for lunch at [*time*] or tea at [*time*].

Please let us know if you wish to attend on [*telephone number*] or by emailing [*email address*]. We will need to know if you wish to have lunch or tea.

We are looking forward to meeting you on [*date*].

Best wishes,

(Names)

SECTION 3.2   THE PARENT PARTNERSHIP TOOLKIT FOR EARLY YEARS

Using collections of everyday things
– Treasure baskets, heuristic play and Treasureboxes®

This section looks at the value of using collections as a focus for supporting parents'
understanding of young children's play. It describes the use of collections of natural and
reclaimed materials and household objects to share with parents the value of active learning
and open-ended exploratory play. The principles behind the use of treasure baskets, heuristic
play and Treasureboxes® are described and there are photocopiable parent-information sheets
(*figures 3.2a, b and c, on p161-165*) to enable parents to use these approaches at home.

Use these resources to help parents to:
● understand what children are doing when they are playing
● recognise their individual child's interests and ideas
● see the potential of everyday objects as playthings for children.

Introduction

Collecting things is a natural part of childhood. Most of us can remember collecting leaves,
stones or shells as a small child, moving on to stamps, coins, stickers or erasers as we grew
older. Children, and adults, make collections for all sorts of reasons – to look at, to place and
arrange, to count and sort, to classify, to use imaginatively and to bring back memories of
other times and other places. Making collections of everyday things will be very familiar to
most parents and family members. The children's families will include parents and
grandparents with collections of photographs, commemorative ornaments, spoons from
around the world or sporting memorabilia.

Collections of everyday objects can help children to think creatively and to develop their critical
thinking skills in order to make sense of the world around them. A collection of natural and
everyday objects in a treasure basket offers a baby the opportunity to make choices about
what to select, whether or not to pick up an object at all, when to do so and for how long.
Anita Hughes (2009) explains why it is vital to offer a baby the opportunity to make choices:

> 'Choice implies selection, variety and possibility. Variety implies characteristics and description.
> By being able to select, one is not only embracing variety, but there is also the choice to
> "act" rather than "react" to desires and impulses. The ability to select has become a
> fundamental requirement in this day and age and underpins all decision-making. Being able
> to make decisions in a world of choices is the gateway to being in control of one's life.'

Collections of different objects enable toddlers and young children to engage in heuristic
play when they can discover for themselves what objects will do, where they can be placed
and how they can be used. Toddlers will be fascinated by collections of different objects and
containers – collections for placing and pairing, for piling, posting, rolling and bouncing.

As children progress through the early years, collections can be used to foster the
development of their critical thinking skills. As they get older, their curiosity becomes more

153

focused as they start to look for reasons and explanations for why things happen. Children move from the exploration of a collection of objects to the systematic investigation of a question. They progress from using everyday language to describe objects, events and phenomena to using more precise technical vocabulary to explain events and phenomena. From using simple drawings to communicate their ideas, children move to using more complex forms of representation, such as detailed drawings, diagrams and charts to communicate what they are thinking (Howe and Davis, 2003).

Collections of everyday items can be used to challenge children's thinking. Large collections of toys, shoes, hats or jewellery can be used to engage a group of children, encouraging their curiosity and sparking their creative thinking. Smaller collections of keys, shells, stones, brushes, buttons, rings or nuts and bolts will encourage individuals to become absorbed in what interests them and catches their imagination.

Involving parents

Encouraging families to create and use collections with their children can be used as a focus for involving them in the life of your setting, supporting their children's learning. Invite parents into the setting to see a treasure basket or heuristic play session in action. Use this as an opportunity to talk about the individual ways in which children play with resources and express their interests and preoccupations. Encourage parents to think about how they could provide similar opportunities for their child at home.

Helping to create and maintain the collections of everyday objects will encourage parents and other family members to develop their own skills and knowledge and to benefit from the social interaction they have with other families and staff. For example, asking family members to help you to put together a collection of hats provides an ideal opportunity for staff and families to explore multicultural issues and to gain a shared understanding of different cultures. Being involved in helping to put together collections means that parents and carers will gain an understanding of how and why collections of everyday objects are used with children of different age groups in your setting.

Once you have established the use of collections in your setting, you may wish to encourage parents to do something similar at home. Alternatively, you could set up a lending library of collections so that children and their families can explore, investigate and discover together at home.

Remember that the great benefit of collections of everyday things is that they cost nothing, or very little, to provide. This will be particularly important to many families who are looking for cost-effective ways to support their children's learning and development.

Treasure baskets

Parents of babies, particularly new parents, are often unsure of the ways in which they can best support their child's needs. By providing advice on how to support their child's learning and development from the start, you will be helping parents to lay the foundations for their child's future success.

SECTION 3.2 THE PARENT PARTNERSHIP TOOLKIT FOR EARLY YEARS

Very young babies are dependent on the adults who care for them to provide a wide range of interesting multisensory experiences to support the healthy development of their maturing brains. Treasure baskets are an ideal way to provide these experiences. A treasure basket is a collection of interesting natural and reclaimed resources and household objects put together to give a baby a safe but interesting and intriguing range of objects to explore.

Treasure baskets, as originally conceived by Elinor Goldschmied (Hughes, 2006), are designed to be used by non-mobile babies from the stage they can sit up comfortably until they are old enough to move around. The resources in the treasure basket collection engage very young children's curiosity, prompt them to explore using their sense of touch, taste, sight and hearing and to answer the question, 'What is this object like?'

Making up a treasure basket collection

Ideally the collection should contain 80-100 different objects made from as wide a variety of materials as possible. These should be presented to the baby in a round wicker basket approximately 30cm in diameter and about 12cm high. A basket of these dimensions is large enough to hold the collection but is also very stable and unlikely to be tipped over by a baby exploring its contents.

The treasure basket collection should contain as wide a variety of objects as possible, including things made of wood, cork, fabric, paper, card, metal, leather, rubber, thick glass, along with natural materials such as large pebbles, shells, pine cones, large seed pods and natural sponge. Elinor Goldschmied (1992) was keen to avoid any plastic in her treasure baskets but you may want to consider adding some interestingly textured plastic resources.

Make sure the objects are of a suitable size to be manipulated by small babies. Too large and the babies will become frustrated, too small and the objects may present a choking hazard as the babies explore them with their mouths, lips and tongue. A 'choke tester' is a small plastic device built to mimic the dimensions of a baby's throat. If the object is too large to fit in the choke tester it shouldn't constitute a hazard. Different children will be interested in different objects, so the key to creating a good treasure basket is to include as wide a variety of resources as possible. The types of objects you might include in a treasure basket are shown below

---

Objects to include in a treasure basket

Natural materials

stones	shells	pine cones	driftwood
pieces of bark	twigs	raffia	lemon
pumice stone	gourds	natural sponge	sheepskin
large seed pods	loofah	piece of leather	piece of fur

Household objects

wooden spoons	metal spoons	spatulas	whisk
pastry brush	nailbrush	bunch of keys	length of chain
measuring spoons	bell	bangle	tea strainer
small purse	bean bag	door stop	small metal bowl
shoehorn	hair roller	glass stopper	coaster
nutcracker	garlic press	clothes peg	lemon squeezer

Using a treasure basket

A treasure basket session is a quiet, focused time, organised at the right time of day to ensure that the babies are comfortable, happy and alert. The timing of the session will vary but it is important to be flexible and to timetable the session to suit the moods of the babies and not the routines of the setting. The session will last as long as the babies are interested in exploring the resources – the greater the variety of objects in the basket, the longer the session is likely to last. To get the most out of your treasure basket, plan to have it out every day rather than only once or twice a week.

Treasure baskets can be used with an individual baby or with two to three babies sharing the same treasure basket collection. They should be seated close enough to the basket to be able to reach the contents easily and have clear space around them to discard objects removed from the basket. Make sure the area is free from distractions so that the babies can really concentrate on their explorations.

The adult should sit close by and observe closely, but not interfere. The adult can offer reassurance through gestures and body language, but this is a time to sit back and observe closely rather than trying to direct the activity that is taking place.

By observing closely while a baby is exploring the objects in a treasure basket, the practitioner will be able to learn a great deal about his or her interests, skills and dispositions. Each baby will interact with the objects in the treasure basket in a different way. Some will enjoy rummaging through the basket and investigating a wide range of materials, others will have favourites, which they want to return to every time the treasure basket is out.

You can use these observations to build up a picture of the baby as an individual. Share your observations with the baby's parents and use the knowledge you have gained to plan what to offer the baby next to engage his or her curiosity and extend his or her learning and development.

Invite parents to observe a treasure basket session and use the *'Information for parents' sheet in figure 3.2a (see p161)* to help you to explain the value of using treasure baskets. It will also give them ideas for what to include in a treasure basket collection at home.

Heuristic play

Once babies become mobile they present different challenges for parents and family members as they are constantly on the go, looking for new and exciting things to discover. This is the ideal time for parents to understand the value of heuristic play. The word heuristic derives from the Greek word *eurisko* meaning 'I discover' (Goldschmied and Hughes, 1992). It is used to describe an intuitive way of meeting challenges and solving problems – exactly what young children do when they are engaged in heuristic play.

Toddlers are fascinated by finding out not just what things are but also what they will do. Their natural inclination is to pick things up and explore what they feel like, using their fingers, hands, feet or other parts of their body. They are interested in the texture, shape, colour, weight, flexibility and malleability of different objects. They wave things around to see how they move, drop them to see what they sound like and bang them on a hard surface to see if they change shape or even break. Using their manipulative skills, they push and poke, squeeze and squash, pull and twist the different objects to see what they can do with them. They may be interested in finding out which parts of an object move and which stay still, whether objects will roll or bounce, whether things will stack on top of one another, which things will fit inside other things and how objects can be moved from place to place.

Making up heuristic play collections

Heuristic play is a wonderful opportunity to capitalise on toddlers' curiosity about the objects that make up the world around them. The resources that make up a heuristic play collection will not be the types of objects currently thought of as toys for young children, but they provide equally valuable opportunities for extending children's learning. There is no right and wrong way to play with heuristic play resources, so everyone's ideas are equally valid and worthwhile. The open-ended nature of the resources means that all toddlers can explore and investigate in their own way, applying their own creative ideas and building on their own experiences.

Different children will be interested in doing different things with the resources, so the key to creating a good heuristic play collection is to include as wide a variety of resources as possible. To enable children to get the most out of a heuristic play session, it is important that they can explore their ideas fully, without being interrupted by other children wanting to share the same resources. Children of this age are not old enough to understand the concept of sharing or 'taking turns', so ample quantities of a rich variety of resources should be provided to minimise the potential for conflict.

Your heuristic play collection may include:

- natural materials such as cones, bark, large seeds and seed pods, shells and pebbles
- a range of household objects made of wood, metal, fabric, and rubber – wooden clothes pegs, large corks, lids, lengths of sink plug chain, bunches of keys, lengths of fabric and ribbon, rubber door stop
- a variety of reclaimed materials, either collected yourself or sourced from a creative recycling centre
- rolling things – balls made of different materials, hair rollers, small tubes, cotton reels
- stacking things – sets of coasters, blocks, mug tree with bracelets and wooden rings, set of nesting boxes
- posting things – shoe box with a hole or slot in the lid, coasters, CDs, wooden pegs, large buttons (>50mm diameter)
- carrying things – small baskets, paper carrier bags, ice cube trays.

A variety of containers are an essential part of a heuristic play collection as toddlers will want to explore 'putting things in' and 'taking things out'. These could include:

- tins with smooth rims
- cardboard tubes of different diameters
- nesting baskets
- small bags and purses

- thick-walled glass containers
- wide-necked plastic bottles
- wooden, metal or card boxes
- plastic flower pots

Organising heuristic play sessions

Heuristic play sessions should be timetabled into the daily routine of the setting, ensuring that children have sufficient time to fully satisfy their curiosity about the resources. A typical session might last about an hour, including time for setting up the resources in the room at the beginning of the session and clearing away at the end. Preparation for the session is best done in a room that the children are not occupying.

To avoid confusion, and to focus the toddlers' attention on the heuristic play resources, all furniture should be cleared to the sides of the room to leave the floor space clear. Any storage furniture with open shelving should be covered over or turned around to keep the 'everyday' resources separate from the heuristic play resources.

Set out the different collections of resources in separate, distinct areas of the floor, with plenty of space between them. Arrange the resources so they look interesting and inviting, encouraging children to want to investigate them and see what they will do. When the room is ready, invite the toddlers in and watch carefully to see what they do.

The role of the adult in a heuristic play session is to observe closely, watching how different children interact with the resources. Take note of which things different children are interested in and how they manipulate them. Observe how they set themselves challenges, solve problems, express their creative ideas and engage in critical thinking. Occasionally, a toddler might invite an adult to join in with a particular activity but, largely speaking, the adult should not interfere in the heuristic play session – remember there is no right or wrong way to do things when manipulating open-ended materials.

The last 10 minutes of the session should be used to involve the toddlers in clearing up and storing the resources ready for use the following day. Store the smaller collections of objects that make up the heuristic play collection in drawstring bags so they are easy to access when setting up the next session.

All toddlers will use the resources in a heuristic play collection in their own way. By observing closely which things different children are interested in, how they manipulate the objects and how long they concentrate for, you will be building up your understanding of their individual interests, skills and attitudes. This will provide a wealth of information on which to plan what experiences to offer children next in order to extend and deepen their learning.

Invite parents to observe a heuristic play session and use the *'Information for parents' sheet in figure 3.2b (see p163)* to help them to see the value of open-ended resources and child-initiated play. Sharing your observations with the toddler's parents will give you the opportunity to point out to them what children are learning when they explore and investigate in this way.

SECTION 3.2 THE PARENT PARTNERSHIP TOOLKIT FOR EARLY YEARS

Treasurebox® collections

Treasurebox collections of what may appear to us as adults to be very ordinary objects are an ideal starting point for preschool children's learning and development (Brunton and Thornton, 2006). Children between the ages of three and five are developing their skills of investigation and exploration. They are becoming expert at asking questions and having their own ideas and theories about the world in which they live. Parents can be encouraged to nurture their children's curiosity and enquiry skills by becoming involved in the creation and use of large collections of everyday things, both in your setting and at home. Use the *'Information for parents' leaflet in figure 3.2c (see p165)* to help parents to understand more about making and using Treasureboxes at home.

Making a Treasurebox collection

The starting point for making a Treasurebox might be:

- adult led: starting from a small collection of objects that you have chosen as a focus
- child initiated: arising from the children's interest in a special object or family event.

A typical treasure-box collection would consist of:

- a range of objects connected to the theme of the box
- photographs, postcards or cards related to the Treasurebox collection
- a relevant fiction and non-fiction book
- a suitable box for the collection.

Assembling a Treasurebox can be a valuable experience in which the children, their parents and the other adults in your setting can all become involved. Families, including older and more distant relatives, will often become very engaged in sourcing the resources you need, particularly if there is a personal request from the children. The sorts of places you can encourage parents to look, apart from in their own homes, are:

- charity shops, markets and car boot sales
- craft fairs, souvenir shops or local emporia
- garden centres, builders' merchants
- walks in the local park, country or at the seaside.

Finding the box to put your collection in is a very important part of the whole process of creating your Treasurebox. Parents may have boxes at home that they are willing to donate or they may be happy to visit the setting to help decorate boxes that you provide. When choosing one to house your Treasurebox collection, here are some things you will want to think about:

What does it look like?

- Does it give any clues about the contents?
- How big does it need to be?

159

- How strong is it?
- How easy is it to carry?
- Is it easy to store?
- How long does it need to last?
- Will it clean easily?
- Is it beautiful, exciting, magical?

Using a Treasurebox collection

If you have adopted a topic-based approach to planning, you can introduce a Treasurebox as a focus for learning and teaching. For example, as part of a topic on 'living things' you could use collections such as bird box, window box or egg box. A topic on 'festivals' can be enhanced by Christmas box, light box or letter box collections.

Treasureboxes can also be used to support themes or strands of learning that are of particular interest to children, or that develop specific skills and understanding. Exploring 'pattern' or 'sorting and classifying' can be supported by using a button box. Opportunities for 'designing and making' can be introduced through a hat box, sewing box or music box collection.

Safety first

When you start to build up your Treasurebox® collections, remember to pay careful attention to the health and safety guidelines which apply to your setting.

When selecting items to include in your Treasurebox, you need to apply the same criteria as you would for any other resources used by the children. They should be clean, well maintained and safe for children to handle.

Make sure that children and adults are aware that the resources in the Treasurebox are something special, to be used in a particular way, and not toys for everyday use.

References

Brunton, P and Thornton, L (2006) *The Little Book of Treasureboxes*, Featherstone Education

Goldschmied, E (1992) *Infants at Work. Babies of Six to Nine Months Exploring Everyday Objects*, DVD available from National Children's Bureau Publications, see: *www.ncb.org.uk*

Goldschmied, E and Hughes, A (1992) *Heuristic Play with Objects* DVD available from National Children's Bureau publications. *www.ncb.org.uk*

Howe, A and Davies, D (2003) *Teaching Science, Design and Technology in the Early Years*, David Fulton

Hughes, A (2006) *Developing Play for the Under Threes: the Treasure Basket and Heuristic Play*, David Fulton

Hughes, A (2009) *Problem Solving, Reasoning and Numeracy in the Early Years Foundation Stage*, David Fulton

Information for parents

Treasure baskets at home

In our setting we use treasure baskets with our non-mobile babies. This leaflet gives you some information about what treasure baskets are and why we use them.

Very young babies are dependent on the adults who care for them to provide a wide range of interesting multisensory experiences to support the healthy development of their maturing brains. Treasure baskets are an ideal way to provide these experiences. A treasure basket is a collection of interesting natural and reclaimed resources and household objects put together to give a baby a safe but interesting and intriguing range of objects to explore.

Treasure baskets are designed to be used by non-mobile babies from the stage they can sit up comfortably until they are old enough to move around. The resources in the treasure basket collection engage very young children's curiosity, prompt them to explore using their senses of touch, taste, sight, smell and hearing and to answer the question, 'What is this object like?'

A treasure basket collection contains as wide a variety of objects as possible, including things made of wood, cork, fabric, paper, card, metal, leather, rubber and thick glass, along with natural materials such as large pebbles, shells, pine cones, large seed pods and natural sponge.

If you want to make a treasure basket at home you could include any or all of the things below.

Natural materials

stones	shells	pine cones	driftwood
pieces of bark	twigs	raffia	lemon
pumice stone	gourds	natural sponge	sheepskin
large seed pods	loofah	piece of leather	piece of fur

Household objects

wooden spoons	metal spoons	spatulas	whisk
pastry brush	nailbrush	bunch of keys	length of chain
measuring spoons	bell	bangle	tea strainer
small purse	bean bag	door stop	small metal bowl
shoehorn	hair roller	glass stopper	coaster
nutcracker	garlic press	clothes peg	lemon squeezer

Make sure the objects are of a suitable size to be manipulated by small babies. Too large and the babies will become frustrated, too small and the objects may present a choking hazard as the babies explore them with their mouths, lips and tongues.

(If you want to check the size of the smaller objects in your treasure basket collection, use a 'choke tester', available from Safetots:)

THE PARENT PARTNERSHIP TOOLKIT FOR EARLY YEARS SECTION 3.2

Figure 3.2a *cont*

A treasure basket play session is a quiet, focused time, organised at the right time of day when your baby is comfortable, happy and alert. The session will last as long as your baby is interested in exploring the resources – the greater the variety of objects in the basket, the longer the session is likely to last.

When your baby is playing with a treasure basket, you should sit close by and watch closely, but not interfere.

By watching how your baby is exploring the objects in a treasure basket, you can learn a lot about his or her interests and what he or she can do. Each baby will interact with the objects in the treasure basket in a different way. Some will enjoy rummaging through the basket and investigating a wide range of materials, others will have favourites that they want to return to every time the treasure basket is out.

If you watch carefully, you will be able to see the way your child prefers to learn about the world. This will help you to decide what other sorts of toys your child is likely to be interested in.

SECTION 3.2   THE PARENT PARTNERSHIP TOOLKIT FOR EARLY YEARS

Information for parents

Heuristic play at home

Toddlers are fascinated by finding out not just what things are but also what they will do. Their natural inclination is to pick up things and explore what they feel like, using their fingers, hands, feet or other parts of their body. They are interested in the texture, shape, colour, weight, flexibility and malleability of different objects. They wave things around to see how they move, drop them to see what they sound like and bang them on a hard surface to see if they change shape or even break. Using their manipulative skills, they push and poke, squeeze and squash, pull and twist the different objects to see what they can do with them. They may be interested in finding out which parts of an object move and which stay still, whether objects will roll or bounce, whether things will stack on top of one another, which things will fit inside other things and how objects can be moved from place to place.

In our setting, we use heuristic play as a wonderful opportunity to capitalise on toddlers' curiosity about the objects that make up the world around them. The resources we use in a heuristic play collection are not the types of objects usually thought of as toys for young children, but they provide equally valuable opportunities for extending children's learning.

All toddlers will use the resources in a heuristic play collection in their own unique way. By watching closely which things different children are interested in, how they handle the objects and how long they concentrate for, you will see their individual interests and skills.

We would be very interested in finding out how your child plays with open-ended resources at home. This would help us to plan for his or her learning in our setting. The rest of this leaflet tells you about heuristic play at home.

Heuristic play at home

Heuristic play is all about finding out 'what things will do'. Different children will be interested in doing different things with the resources, so the key to creating a good heuristic play collection is to include as wide a variety of resources as possible.

You could collect these at home for your child to play with:

- natural materials, such as cones, bark, large seeds and seed pods, shells and pebbles
- a range of household objects made of wood, metal, fabric, and rubber – wooden clothes pegs, large corks, lids, lengths of sink plug chain, bunches of keys, lengths of fabric and ribbon, rubber door stop
- a variety of reclaimed materials, either collected yourself or sourced from a creative recycling centre
- rolling things – balls made of different materials, hair rollers, small tubes, cotton reels
- stacking things – sets of coasters, blocks, mug tree with bracelets and wooden rings, set of nesting boxes
- posting things – shoe box with a hole or slot in the lid, coasters, CDs, wooden pegs, large buttons (>50mm diameter)
- carrying things – small baskets, paper carrier bags, ice cube trays.

163

THE PARENT PARTNERSHIP TOOLKIT FOR EARLY YEARS SECTION 3.2

Figure 3.2b *cont*

A variety of containers are an essential part of a heuristic play collection as toddlers will want to explore 'putting things in' and 'taking things out'. These could include:

- tins with smooth rims
- cardboard tubes of different diameters
- thick-walled glass containers
- wide-necked plastic bottles

- nesting baskets
- small bags and purses
- wooden, metal or card boxes
- plastic flower pots

Please let us know how you get on at home.

Information for parents

Making a Treasurebox® at home

Button box

How many of us can look back into the past and recall playing with our mother's, or grandmother's, button box or tin? A simple box of buttons can be explored for hours, providing endless opportunities for learning and development.

Buttons can remind us of clothes that were worn years ago, by ourselves or other members of our families. If you make a Treasurebox of buttons, your child will delight in guessing who the buttons might have belonged to and on which clothes they may have been found.

Buttons can be sorted, counted, paired, matched and used to make patterns. They can be threaded, sewn on to fabric, drawn around and held up to the light – all ways of looking at holes!

Usually a button box contains a collection that is made over a long period of time, with buttons added to it as they become available. It looks like a collection of treasure. When you create your button box collection, you need to think how to give it a sense of history and a 'personality' of its own. An old wooden box, biscuit tin or tea caddy will make your collection feel old. Maybe your child's grandparents can give you an old tin or you could look in charity shops and car boot sales.

You can collect buttons in a variety of ways – 'spare' buttons from clothes you have bought, new buttons from haberdashery shops, old buttons from discarded items of clothing and leftover buttons from dressmaking or knitting.

Your button box collection should include a selection of buttons so that it can be used to support your child's exploration and investigation. Make sure that you include a range of colours, textures, shapes and sizes in your button collection.

You could include:

- **buttons to sort** – by colour, shape, size, material
- **buttons to count or arrange in size order** – sets of buttons, pairs of two different sizes, sizes from tiny to huge
- **textured buttons** – metallic embossed, plastic, wood, silk, satin, ridged, smooth
- **special buttons** – uniform buttons, buttons with motifs, unusual shapes, boot buttons, button eyes from soft toys.

THE PARENT PARTNERSHIP TOOLKIT FOR EARLY YEARS   SECTION 3.2

SECTION 3.3   THE PARENT PARTNERSHIP TOOLKIT FOR EARLY YEARS

Out and about

> The focus of this section is helping parents to make the most of the vast range of opportunities presented by outdoor play. It looks at the reasons why outdoor play is important and then provides three photocopiable eight-page activity booklets to promote outdoor play with different age groups. These contain ideas for parents to use with babies (*figure 3.3a on p169-172*), toddlers (*figure 3.3b on p173-176*) and preschool children (*figure 3.3c on p177-180*).
>
> Use these resources:
> - to promote important messages to parents on the theme of healthy living
> - as a way of encouraging the active involvement of fathers and other male carers
> - to raise the profile of outdoor play among fellow practitioners.

Introduction

Young children benefit in many ways from being out of doors all year round, in all weathers. Too often, children are restricted to playing indoors at home, so it is even more important that they are provided with plenty of opportunities for outdoor play when they are in their early years setting. While many early years settings have long-established systems and routines for ensuring that children have access to the outdoors throughout the year, there are still instances of practitioners who are not willing to take a positive view on children spending time out of doors in all weathers.

The reasons given for not going outside vary from 'It is too cold, wet, windy, slippery for the children' to 'It takes too much time to get ready and parents don't like their children wet, cold or dirty.' More often than not, it is the practitioners rather than the children who do not want to be out in all weathers. Practitioners who have a positive attitude to being out of doors will not only enjoy the experience themselves, but will foster a sense of pleasure in the children as they explore and play together. Providing the right clothing and footwear for children to wear will not only keep children safe and warm but will also allay parents' concerns.

It is also important that early years settings work with parents to help them to understand the value of playing out of doors with their children in terms of their children's learning and development, their wellbeing and their physical and mental health. In addition to explaining to parents the 'whys' and 'hows' of outdoor play in your setting, use the booklets for parents in *figures 3.3a, 3.3b and 3.3c (see p169-180)* to give parents plenty of ideas about what they could do with their children in the great outdoors. Being outdoors with young children is an aspect of play that men may find particularly appealing, providing an effective way to connect with fathers and other male carers (*see Section 2.3: Listening to parents*).

Reasons to be out of doors

- Being out of doors gives babies and young children first-hand experience of the weather, the seasons and the natural world.

167

- The outdoor environment offers children and their families opportunities to do different things and to do familiar things on a larger scale and with less concern about noise levels.
- Playing out of doors gives babies and young children the freedom to explore using all their senses, to use their bodies and to have exuberant fun.
- Being out of doors brings its own challenges and opportunities for risky freedom. Using a torch outside as dusk falls is a safe and exciting way to enjoy the gratuitous fear on which many children, especially boys, thrive.
- Playing outside should not be restricted to warm, dry weather – late autumn, winter and early spring each present unique opportunities for learning.
- Making the most of outdoor spaces, such as gardens or the local park, will give young children the opportunities they need to explore and discover, to express themselves and to relive their experiences through their natural language of movement.

The freedom to play outside using tried and tested activities, such as building a den, climbing a tree, playing hide and seek or chase, enjoying singing and action games or drawing with chalks on a paved area, are all effective in helping children to develop self-confidence and to learn their own physical limits in a safe environment.

The success of children being outdoors in all weathers is very dependent on the attitudes of the adults in the setting. Practitioners who are excited by exploring the world around them and who show enthusiasm for playing and learning outside will be the best role models that young children and their families can have.

Activity booklet
for babies

Outdoor play is very important for children of all ages. In order to be healthy and active, children need exercise and fresh air as well as healthy food and a secure home. Outdoor activities help children to experience the world using all their senses, to use all their muscles, to solve problems and experience risk and challenge in a safe environment.

In this booklet, you will find six different activities for outdoor play with your child, either at home or in another outdoor space, such as a park. The activities provide you with ideas for playing, investigating and exploring. You can talk about living things, watch the weather and the seasons and enjoy building and digging. Remember that playing outdoors means children can run around, use bigger spaces and make more noise and mess than they can indoors.

Activity 6 – **making marks out of doors**

Very young children are beginning to develop the physical skills they will need to express themselves through mark making as they grow older.

Being out of doors gives you the opportunity to offer your baby experiences that will help them to mark make in different ways. You could try:

- bodies – hands, feet and fingers – and paint
- hands and sand
- a stick and mud.

Drawing can be done in lots of different ways with babies:

- some babies are able to manipulate chubby crayons to make marks on sheets of paper
- sticks, including lolly sticks, can be used to draw in sand or mud
- a tray of damp sand can be used with twigs, spoons, brushes or fingers.

Painting with babies can be a very messy activity indeed:

- you can use large sheets of paper out of doors for your baby to paint using his hands, feet, fingers and toes
- you can roll tins, toy cars or balls in runny paint and then on a roll of wallpaper.

Remember that some babies will be able to handle a broad brush and paint. They will be fascinated by the experience of painting with water out of doors. By using water they can 'paint' on a wall, fence or paved area without any permanent damage.

Activity 1 – garden crawl

It is often easier for babies to have the freedom they need to crawl around when they are out of doors. There is more space and less likelihood of knocking into furniture or doors.

You can plan a 'texture crawl' for your baby in the garden or at the local park.

Collect together some small pieces of fabric with different textures and lay them out on the ground. You could use a fleecy throw, some bubble wrap, different textured scarves, carpet squares or corrugated cardboard. Remember that grass is a fascinating surface for babies to crawl over.

Crawl over the different surfaces with your baby. As you crawl talk about what the surfaces feel like. Use words and facial expressions to describe soft and smooth, bumpy and lumpy, rough and tickly.

When your baby tires of the activity, move the different surfaces to another part of your garden or the park. You may be surprised to find that your baby shows fresh interest in the crawling game.

Page 2

ACTIVITY BOOKLET FOR BABIES

Activity 5 – music makers

In the same way that being outside gives you plenty of space for your baby to move around, the outdoors also means that you can often make more noise!

You can sing songs and nursery rhymes and act out action rhymes in your garden, in the park or while you are out for a walk.

Try:

- Rock a bye baby
- Incy wincy spider
- Twinkle, twinkle little star
- Row, row, row your boat.

Use everyday objects to make instruments for your baby to play in the garden or at the park.

Drums can be made from:

- a tin and a wooden spoon
- a pan and a metal spoon.

Shakers can be made from:

- a plastic bottle and rice
- a plastic container and dried peas or beans.

Cymbals can be made from:

- pan lids
- lids from tins or jars (make sure they are clean and not sharp).

A microphone can be made from:

- the empty tube from a paper towel roll – try singing through the tube, making different sounds or repeating the sounds your baby makes.

ACTIVITY BOOKLET FOR BABIES

Page 7

Activity 2 – **natural treasure**

Being out of doors in the garden or the local park is the perfect opportunity to introduce your baby to natural 'treasures'. Different seasons will bring different delights and opportunities to 'ooh' and 'ah' at the wonders of nature.

You will have many opportunities to encourage your baby to use her senses as she explores the outdoor area. You can take a collector's bucket or bag outside with you to collect natural 'treasure' with your baby.

In spring

- Look at the signs of new life. Show your baby buds, new shoots and touch them gently.
- Smell spring flowers and blossom and listen to the birds.
- Collect twigs, stones and different grasses. Ask your baby to pass them to you as you name them.

In summer

- Put a mirror on the ground under a bush or tree. Talk to your baby about what you can see in the mirror – the leaves, branches and the sky.
- Find some dandelion seed heads. Blow the dandelion clocks for your baby to watch, catch and blow herself.
- Collect stones, rocks and shells if you have a trip to the seaside. Place them in lines and watch what your baby does with them.

Activity 4 – **water play**

Water play can be rather messy and the outdoors can be the perfect place to play with water with your baby. You can use a large bowl, a bucket or a paddling pool. You do not need special equipment for water play, just use everyday things that you have around the house.

NOTE! Water play with babies must be closely supervised at all times!

Things to do with water

- Use plastic bowls, bottles and jugs to pour water from one container to another. Let your baby feel the water as you pour it.
- Try squirting water using an empty washing-up liquid bottle. Help your child to squeeze the bottle and watch what happens.
- Play a rain-making game with your baby. Make holes in a plastic bottle and fill it with water. Hold it up in the air and watch the 'rain' fall. Show your baby how to fill the bottle to make rain.
- Dabble your baby's feet in the bowl or bucket of water. Encourage him to kick and splash with his legs and feet.
- When you are playing with water with your baby play silly games with words. Use words that make water sounds such as:

swish   gurgle   squish

splash   splish   splosh

In autumn

- Have fun crawling through a pile of rustling leaves.
- Extend the game by throwing the leaves and trying to catch them.
- Collect leaves, fir cones, conkers and acorns. Help your baby to explore what they feel like in her hand.

In winter

- On a frosty day, go out in the garden to walk and stamp, listening to the crunching noises your feet make on the grass or ground.
- Touch leaves, bushes and fences to feel how cold they are.
- Try to find a frosted spider's web to touch gently.

Activity 3 – garden games

You can play traditional outdoor games with your baby from six months onwards.

Try hide and seek, chase, hide the spoon or ball games. You could also have a baby Olympics, with bouncing, rolling, obstacle races or a wheelbarrow race.

- Find a sheltered spot with a grassy surface in your garden or in the park where your baby can crawl around.
- Have a crawling race across the grass.
- Play hide and seek around a tree, bush or your buggy. See if your baby is able to find you.
- Use a soft ball to play rolling games with your baby. Roll the ball between you and encourage your baby to roll it back.
- You may find that your baby moves on to throwing the ball, enjoying watching you catch it and bring it back.
- Try hiding a shiny spoon or a favourite toy for your baby to find.

Have fun with a baby Olympics

- Sit on the grass and encourage your baby to bounce – either on your knee or standing up, holding your hands.
- Show your baby how to roll if she has not discovered it for herself.
- Have a wheelbarrow race by lifting your baby's legs off the ground and encouraging him to crawl on his hands.
- If you are playing in the garden, you can easily make an obstacle course for your baby to explore. Make a pile of cushions for your baby to climb over or crawl around. Use a large cardboard box as a tunnel to crawl through.

Figure 3.3b Out-and-about activity booklet: toddlers

Activity booklet
for toddlers

Outdoor play is very important for children of all ages. In order to be healthy and active, children need exercise and fresh air as well as healthy food and a secure home. Outdoor activities help children to experience the world using all their senses, to use all their muscles, to solve problems and experience risk and challenge in a safe environment.

In this booklet you will find six different activities for outdoor play with your child, either at home or in another outdoor space, such as a park. The activities provide you with ideas for playing, investigating and exploring. Remember that playing outdoors means children can run around, use bigger spaces and make more noise and mess than they can indoors.

ACTIVITY BOOKLET FOR TODDLERS   Page I

ACTIVITY BOOKLET FOR TODDLERS   Page 8

Activity 1 – digging

Young children like nothing better than to have a place where they can dig, shovel and move earth or sand around to discover what is hiding underneath. Ideally, you could choose a suitable piece of ground in your garden for your child to dig in. Alternatively, you could provide a builders' tray of sand in a smaller space out of doors. Often the local park will have a sand pit especially for young children to play in. Provide your child with a spade, fork, trowel and rake to dig with as well as plastic trays, buckets, bowls, boxes and sieves for filling and emptying.

If you are using a patch of soil in the garden, show your child how to handle any living things she might find. Encourage your child to stop digging as soon as she finds something interesting. This might include a living creature or an interesting stone. It could be other treasure such as a piece of broken china or a coin. Talk to your child about what she has found.

Make sure that your child always washes her hands after digging!

Activity 6—music and movement

In the same way that being outside gives you plenty of space for your toddler to move around, the outdoors also means that you can often make more noise.

You can sing songs and nursery rhymes and act out action rhymes in your garden, in the park or while you are out for a walk.

Try:

- *I'm a little teapot*
- *Five little ducks*
- *Miss Polly had a dolly*
- *The sun has got his hat on*
- *Heads, shoulders, knees and toes*
- *Here we go round the mulberry bush*
- *In and out the dusty bluebells.*

Use everyday objects to make instruments for your toddler to play in the garden or at the park:

- **Drums** can be made from a tin and a wooden spoon or a pan and a metal spoon.

- **Shakers** can be made from a plastic bottle and rice or a plastic container and dried peas or beans.

- **Cymbals** can be made from pan lids or the lids from tins or jars (make sure they are clean and not sharp).

- **A microphone** can be made using the empty tube from a paper towel roll. Try singing or making different sounds through the tube.

Take turns with your toddler playing the instruments and dancing to the music and rhythms that you make.

Activity 2 – a shadow hunt

Toddlers are at a stage in their development where they are becoming very curious about the world around them. They are often fascinated and excited by light and by being in the dark.

When you are outdoors with your child you can have great fun playing with shadows. Although, as adults, we may be very familiar with shadows – big and small – we need to remember that toddlers may be experiencing the wonder of shadows for the first time and will be excited by them.

- Choose a sunny day to explore shadows outside – this could be in the winter as well as in the summer.
- Go on a shadow hunt in your garden, in the street or in the local park.
- Look all around for shadows of different shapes and sizes.
- Look for the biggest and the smallest shadows you can find.
- Talk to your toddler about the shadows you find. Ask him to describe the shadows.

Use the shadow hunt as an opportunity to ask your toddler questions about the shadows you find to encourage him to think carefully.

Try asking:

- 'Where can you see the best shadows?'
- 'Can you catch your shadow?'
- 'Can you stand on your shadow or on my shadow?'
- 'Which of us do you think will have the tallest shadow?'
- 'Do any of the shadows move?'

If it is very hot, remember to protect your child from the sun. Remind your toddler NEVER to look directly at the sun!

ACTIVITY BOOKLET FOR TODDLERS

Activity 5 – catching and throwing

It is very important for their future physical development for toddlers to develop the skills of catching and throwing. This is an activity that needs a large space and is often best done out of doors.

You can play catching and throwing with your toddler at all different times of the year and in many different spaces out of doors – in the garden, at the park or on the beach.

Using a ball you can:

- roll the ball to your toddler and encourage him to roll it back.
- pass a small ball between you and your toddler, gradually increasing the distance you throw the ball.
- Try using balls of different sizes and weights. Use a soft medium-sized ball to begin with and then try an inflatable beach ball, a tennis ball, a solid rubber ball or a table tennis ball. They will all pose very different challenges for your toddler to throw and catch.

You could also practise catching and throwing with:

- a soft toy
- a sock, glove or hat
- pieces of paper or card
- a balloon
- a paper plate
- leaves from the trees in autumn
- a snowball in winter

ACTIVITY BOOKLET FOR TODDLERS

Activity 3 – lifting and shifting

Toddlers often enjoy moving things around. They will spend a lot of time putting different objects into bags or other containers and carrying them from one place to another.

They can have even more fun 'lifting and shifting' out of doors. You can provide opportunities for your child to lift, load and move heavier objects around your garden or patio area. They will gain a lot of experience in problem-solving by moving things around.

You can provide the following things out of doors:

- buckets, bags and baskets
- a child's wheelbarrow or truck
- large stones, pebbles or bricks, small logs, small bags of sand
- plastic bottles and crates.

Talk to your child about the things you have collected together out of doors.

Ask them what they would like to build with the materials. You could suggest making a wall, a path or a den. Many toddlers will simply want to play moving the objects around without making anything in particular, which is fine.

Watch your toddler as she lifts and moves the objects. You will be able to see how she copes with solving problems and how she uses her muscles and the tools you have provided.

As your toddler plays at 'lifting and shifting' you can use new words for her to learn – lift, carry, load, tip, hold, push, pull, heavy, strong, full, empty, build, move, dig.

Activity 4 – outdoors in the wind and rain

Often it is adults, not children, who are keen to stay indoors when it is raining or windy. Being outside on windy or rainy days is the best way for your toddler to learn about the weather.

Choose a windy or rainy day to go out and play with your toddler. Make sure you are wearing appropriate clothes – fleeces or waterproofs and wellies – and try out some of the ideas below.

On windy days:

- Use a plastic carrier bag as a kite. Cut the end of the bag and tie a string to the handles. Run in the wind to fly your kite.
- Make streamers from strips of plastic or ribbons and tie them to a stick or wooden clothes peg. Watch what happens when you run with them in the wind.
- Watch flying seeds – dandelion clocks and 'helicopter' seeds work well.
- Have fun blowing bubbles and watching them float in the wind.
- Make parachutes by cutting squares out of carrier bags, tying strings to the corners and attaching a small toy animal or Lego character to the strings. Throw them in the air or drop them from the top of the climbing frame in the park.

On rainy days

- Play a game of puddle jumping, or simply stamping in puddles to make a splash. Push toy cars through a puddle or ride a bike to see the tracks.
- Give your toddler a sweeping brush to sweep the rain off the patio or path. They can use paint brushes to 'paint' on a wall with the rain water.
- Float boats you have made in puddles in the garden or in the park.

Activity booklet
for 3-5s

Outdoor play is very important for children of all ages. In order to be healthy and active, children need exercise and fresh air as well as healthy food and a secure home. Outdoor activities help children to experience the world using all their senses, to use all their muscles, to play imaginatively, to solve problems and experience risk and challenge in a safe environment.

In this booklet you will find six different activities for outdoor play with your child, either at home or in another outdoor space, such as a park. The activities provide you with ideas for playing, investigating and exploring. You can talk about living things, watch the weather and the seasons and enjoy building and digging. Remember that playing outdoors means children can run around, use bigger spaces and make more noise and mess than they can indoors.

Activity 1 – songs and rhymes

Twenty or thirty years ago, children played many different dancing and singing games in small and large groups, out of doors and on special occasions such as parties. Being out of doors is a great opportunity to play some of the old games that were popular in the past with your child. Invite some of your child's friends along to join in the fun.

Use the space out of doors to have fun with action rhymes with your child.

Show him or her how to sing and move to:

- Ring-a-roses
- Row, row, row your boat
- I'm a little teapot
- Wind the bobbin.

Take a group of children into the garden or to the local park to play some old fashioned circle games such as:

- The grand old Duke of York
- Oranges and lemons
- The big ship sails through the alley O
- In and out the dusty bluebells

Try some other outdoor games from your childhood, such as hopscotch, marbles, jacks (called chucks, fivestones, snobs or dabstones in different parts of the UK), skipping games or conkers.

ACTIVITY BOOKLET FOR 3 TO 5-YEAR-OLDS

Page 2

Activity 6 – investigating snails

Snails provide endless fascination for young children. Snails are easy to catch and are easy for a small child to observe as they move so slowly. You might be able to find snails in your garden, in relatives' gardens or in the local neighbourhood. Different types of snails have interesting and attractive shells. They spiral in different directions, clockwise or anticlockwise, and sometimes have bands or stripes on them.

The best places to look for snails are under stones, in log piles and in heaps of leaves. You may also find them eating the vegetables in your garden. Snails can climb and can be found on walls and fences, particularly if there are plants growing up against them. The best time to find snails is in damp weather or in the early morning after rain or heavy dew.

To help your child begin to understand more about living things try the following:

- Create a snail tank in a plastic fish tank or large plastic sweet jar with a tight lid with holes in it. Put compost on the bottom and add stones and a piece of wood for shelter. Add a dish of water to keep the atmosphere moist and feed the snail lettuce, cabbage, pieces of vegetable and oatmeal. Clean the tank regularly.

- Give your child a magnifier to observe the snails' shells. Look at the shape, pattern of the shells, the eyes on the tentacles and the head and 'foot' of each snail.

- Listen to the snails as they eat cabbage leaves.

- Organise a snail Olympics. Put the snails carefully on the edge of a sheet of black card and see which one wins the race to the other end.

Make sure your child always washes his hands after handling creatures.

ACTIVITY BOOKLET FOR 3 TO 5-YEAR-OLDS

Page 7

Activity 2 – building a den

Den building is an activity that children (and adults!) of all ages enjoy. Dens provide secret places, places to have adventures and special places to be alone or with friends.

You can make all sorts of dens, ranging from ones that can be put up and removed quickly and easily to more permanent huts or tree houses.

Tents can be made using:

- a clothes horse and a blanket
- a rope between two trees or fences with a cover thrown over the rope
- a strong cloth or blanket pinned to a fence and anchored at the bottom a short distance away from the fence
- a real tent pitched on grass or a small pop-up tent.

Screens to play behind can be created by taking two or three strong sticks or broom handles and setting each in a large tin filled with concrete.

Different screens can be made by attaching trellis, garden mesh, fabric or sheets of plastic or cardboard to the sticks.

Boxes are perfect for making dens.

Using a large cardboard box, cut holes in the sides for windows and doors. The den can be painted and curtains made for the windows and doorways.

Alternatively, small boxes, such as shoe boxes, can be used to build the walls of a den.

You can help your child to develop her understanding of numbers and letters by making signs, labels and notices for the den.

ACTIVITY BOOKLET FOR 3 TO 5-YEAR-OLDS   Page 3

Activity 5 – making music

Being out of doors provides all sorts of opportunities to listen to sounds – birds, animals and rustling leaves as well as human voices, traffic, bells and chimes.

Going on a listening walk will help your child to learn to concentrate on what she or he is hearing all around.

Your garden or the local park can be ideal places to music make with your child. You can begin by making music using your bodies – clapping, tapping, using your hands to beat on your legs, arms and bodies. Try playing a body rhythm for your child to copy.

Other ideas for enjoying music making out of doors include those below.

Making instruments using:

- empty tins, bottles, pans, bowls and metal trays for drums
- wooden and metal spoons as beaters
- plastic bottles filled with dried peas, beans, lentils or rice as rattles.

Try tying saucepan lids, kitchen tools and cans to a washing line to see the different sounds that are made when they are struck with a wooden or metal spoon.

Musical mobiles – try:

- hanging old CDs on a string so that they catch the wind and make a noise
- making wind chimes using strings of bottle tops, shells or nuts and bolts.

Dancing and marching

Play music out of doors with your child. Enjoy the freedom of the space to dance and sing. Play marching games along paths and around trees and bushes in the garden or in the park.

Page 6   ACTIVITY BOOKLET FOR 3 TO 5-YEAR-OLDS

Activity 3 – growing things

Watching something grow is always a magical experience for young children.

Being outside enjoying nature, digging in the soil, planting seeds and watching flowers and vegetables grow all provide lasting childhood memories. By growing and harvesting their own fruit and vegetables, children will begin to understand where food comes from and how it is grown.

You do not need a garden to grow your own food. Seeds can be planted in all sorts of containers, which can be kept on a patio or balcony as well as in a warm spot indoors.

Try:

- a hanging basket
- a window box
- a bed made from an old tyre
- an old watering can, bucket or wheelbarrow.

Speedy, and easy, ideas for growing things are:

- Fast-growing salad leaves. These can be grown in any container or in the ground. You can take out the leaves you need and leave the rest to grow again for a second, or even third, harvest.

- Use half an eggshell to make an indoor planter. Paint a face on the shell. Place some fine soil or compost in the shell and sprinkle cress or alfafa seeds inside. In a few days you will be able to watch the 'hair' grow.

- Mustard and cress seeds grow very quickly. Plant them on damp cotton wool or kitchen roll in a plastic tray by sprinkling them on the surface and keeping them moist. You will be able to enjoy egg and cress sandwiches in a few days.

If you have more growing space, radishes, carrots, lettuces and some varieties of peas all grow reasonably quickly.

Activity 4 – numbers and letters all around

Going for a walk in your local neighbourhood will give you the opportunity to talk to your children about the signs, numbers and words that can be found where you live. This will help them to begin to recognise numbers and letters.

When you go for a walk look out for:

- road signs and markings
- street names and door numbers
- parking signs
- signposts
- shop names
- notices and adverts.

Talk to your child about what the signs say and what they mean. You could talk about how the signs help people to:

- find their way around
- know where things are meant to go
- move and play safely
- look after the environment.

Another good way to add fun to your walks with your child is to play 'I-Spy'. You could try different versions of 'I-Spy' when you go the shops or to the park:

- I-Spy numbers on doors
- I-Spy colours
- I-Spy words beginning with...
- I-Spy shop names.

You could give your child a pencil and notebook to 'write down' or draw the numbers, words and signs that they see. They might also enjoy drawing buildings, trees and vehicles that they see on their walks.

SECTION 3.4   THE PARENT PARTNERSHIP TOOLKIT FOR EARLY YEARS

Family workshops – exploring together

The resources provided in this section can be used to organise and run a family workshop session on the theme of exploration and investigation. The open-ended nature of the activities makes them ideal for use with children of different ages and takes away any fear of failure – for both adults and children. They include a series of workshop activities on the theme of exploring water (*figures 3.4a to 3.4n, on p188-204*), an example of a letter of invitation (*figure 3.4o on p205*) and three ideas and activity sheets for parents to use at home with children of different ages (*figures 3.4p, 3.4q, 3.4r, on p206-208*).

The resources in this section will help you to:
- share with parents the importance of listening to young children and following their ideas
- engage fathers and other male carers in their children's wellbeing, learning and development
- build relationships with family members in a relaxed and enjoyable situation.

Introduction

Early years settings and schools are ideally placed to build the confidence of parents and family members through the relationships of trust and mutual respect that develop around the care and education of young children. For many parents, the setting or school will represent their first opportunity for some considerable time to re-engage with a 'learning environment'. This phase of life can act as something of a watershed for parents – a time to consider re-entering the world of work or a stimulus for parents to address their own learning needs to support their child's ongoing development.

Family workshops, with adults and children playing and learning together, are an ideal, non-threatening way to open up the possibilities of parents extending their learning and accessing new skills. Some parents may use this as a gateway to accredited family-learning programmes and then on to focused skills-development programmes. Workshops that focus on science and technology often appeal to male family members who feel comfortable in sharing their expertise with their young children (*see Section 2.3: Listening to parents and Section 2.6: Supporting parent-child relationships*).

Encouraging parents to become involved in their children's learning is an essential part of making sure that young children have the best possible opportunity to enjoy and achieve. Research evidence shows that children do best in all aspects of their lives when parents and family members are actively involved in supporting them (*see Section 1*). Running family workshops as part of your regular programme gives a powerful message to parents about the importance of their involvement in their child's learning.

Exploring Together workshops provide opportunities for parents to be involved in your setting in a meaningful way and demonstrate the value you place on the contribution they make to their child's wellbeing, learning and development (*see Section 2.1: Establishing the*

181

vision and values). These family workshops provide an ideal way to share the philosophy of your setting and to:

- support parents in developing an understanding of the nature of the 'curious child' to ensure that children receive consistent messages about asking questions and having good ideas

- encourage parents to make time for opportunities and experiences that will develop their child's scientific and technological interest at home

- explain that everyday things, found around the house, in the garden and in the local area, can be an endless source of curiosity to young children

- talk about the importance of allowing children to take risks and make mistakes

- show parents the value of open-ended exploration and investigation, encouraging them to value their children's ideas and to follow their interests.

Using the Exploring Together family workshop format

Exploring Together workshops can be used to support the work of early years and childcare, parent support and family learning professionals in many different settings – Sure Start children's centres, day nurseries, schools and parent and toddler groups. They can be delivered in a number of different ways depending on the:

- age of the children

- size of the group

- availability of parents to attend workshop sessions

- timing and structure of existing family workshop programmes.

Exploring Together family workshops provide opportunities for:

- building parents' confidence through activities that are linked to everyday situations, simple ideas and inexpensive resources

- parents to develop positive attitudes towards learning – both for their children and for themselves

- families to make contacts, relationships and friendships

- engaging with male family members through their interest in science and technology (*see Section 2.3: Listening to parents*)

- children to demonstrate their competence and their capacity to manage risky freedom from an early age (*see Section 2.4: Communicating with parents – Creating a shared view of childhood on p81*)

- everyone involved to learn from one another, sharing knowledge, skills and attitudes.

Figures 3.4a to 3.4n (see p188-204) provide examples of the types of activities that might be included in an Exploring Together family workshop. In the example, all the activities are linked to the theme of exploring water. You could use the family workshop format to plan your own activities around a range of different themes, for example, 'what we eat', 'moving things' or 'light and shadow'.

Planning a family workshop

Use this 10-step guide to help you plan the detail of your family workshop sessions.

1. Decide how you intend to incorporate the workshops into the work of your setting. Will they be held during session time or perhaps later in the afternoon or on Saturday mornings?

2. Agree who will be responsible for organising and running the workshops.

3. Identify your target audience – for example, all parents, grandparents or male family members – and decide how best to contact them. This could be:
   - by invitation – invitations from the children themselves work well (*figure 3.4o on p205*)
   - by advert or poster
   - by word of mouth
   - through your regular newsletter
   - by email invitation.

4. Make sure you know how many families are coming by asking the families to book places or respond to the invitation.

5. Choose a suitable venue for the workshops. You will need a space for up to 15 families with tables and chairs that, ideally, are suitable for adults as well as children to use. Some of the workshop activities involve water and making 'interesting' mixtures, so make sure you are prepared for this.

6. Collect together all the resources you need for each activity well in advance. Use the *checklist in figure 3.4a (see p188)* to help you.

7. Allow enough time to set up the workshop activities (45 minutes to an hour) and to clear away afterwards (about half an hour). Make good use of any willing helpers.

8. Make sure you carry out any necessary risk assessments and health and safety checks in line with your normal policies.

9. Decide how the workshops will be staffed and explain in advance to the staff members what they are expected to do.

10. Use the background information in the *section 'Sharing information with parents'* as the basis of a staff-training session before the workshops take place.

Structure of an Exploring Together family workshop

A typical workshop will last between an hour and an hour and a half. Allow a set-up time before the workshop of approximately 45 minutes and about 30 minutes for clearing up afterwards.

Introducing the workshop to the families (15-20 minutes)

Ideally this introductory session should provide the opportunity to talk to family members while the children are being supervised by staff.

Aspects to cover in the introductory session:

- the importance of parents and carers in supporting young children's learning
- children as researchers – encouraging curiosity and creativity
- listening to children and valuing their ideas
- being a good role model
- asking good questions
- the value of recording investigation and exploration.

In addition you will want to talk about:

- parents taking responsibility for their own children at all times
- health and safety considerations – include risky freedom, small objects, hand washing, allergies
- encouraging the parents/carers to allow the children to take the lead as they explore and investigate together
- parents and children exploring as many of the activities as they wish, for as long as they like
- using the question sheets as prompts, or starting points, if they are needed
- reassuring the parents that they can play too, and enjoy themselves.

Exploring and investigating together (45–60 minutes)

- While the workshop is in progress, staff can use the time to support parents and family groups where appropriate.
- Look for opportunities to extend the children's and the adults' experiences and learning.
- Stand back and document what is happening by taking photographs, recording conversations and making notes of encounters and interactions.

Feedback and comments (10-15 minutes)

Adults, children and practitioners together.

- Encourage parents to share their experiences. This might include comments on messy play, risky freedom, the length of time children were able to concentrate and whether they would try these activities at home.
- Provide parents with ideas to use at home – use the information in *figures 3.4p, 3.4q, 3.4r (see p206-208)*.

Sharing information with parents

Exploring Together family workshops are designed to help build up a shared view of childhood (*see Section 2.4, page 84*) and provide opportunities to explore the following key issues with parents and carers:

- children as researchers – encouraging curiosity and creativity
- listening to children and valuing their ideas

SECTION 3.4   THE PARENT PARTNERSHIP TOOLKIT FOR EARLY YEARS

- being a good role model
- asking good questions
- the value of recording exploration and investigation.

You could use the information in the following sections to create a series of information sheets for parents covering different aspects of young children's play, learning and development (see *Section 2.4: Communicating with parents*).

Children as researchers – encouraging curiosity and creativity

Children have their own ideas about how things work and why things happen – they are 'bubbling with ideas'. These ideas or theories are based on all their many different early experiences as babies and young children. Valuing these ideas, encouraging children to share them, and to listen to the ideas put forward by other children, provides the starting point for further investigations, exploration and discovery.

Curiosity is defined as 'an eager desire to know' and is a disposition for learning that should be encouraged in young children. Children can display their curiosity in many different ways, not just through the questions they ask. Curiosity will be conveyed through body language, stance and posture, or through the length of time that a child spends investigating and exploring a particular object or activity, as well as by talking.

In younger children, curiosity tends to be impulsive as they are attracted to new and unusual objects and situations. As they grow older, their curiosity becomes more focused and you will find they pay greater attention to detail and start seeking explanations for the things they see and experience.

When children become involved in investigating and exploring, they often become absorbed and will concentrate for long periods of time. You may find that they will want to revisit a particular activity many times while they extend and consolidate their learning.

In the setting, you can support children's curiosity by being flexible in your approach to the allocation of time, during the course of a day or a week, or perhaps over a longer period to allow children to become involved in the long-term exploration of something that particularly interests them – for example, growing seeds or bird watching.

Children's curiosity can be stimulated by very ordinary and inexpensive things that can be found all around – for example, by discovering which things in the bathroom float and sink or by looking at reflections in a curved spoon.

Providing opportunities for children to express their creativity through science and technology means giving them the opportunities to talk about their ideas, make independent choices and experience the joy of discovering something new for themselves.

Listening to children and valuing their ideas

Children often have very definite ideas and theories about how the world around them works and it is worth investing time to explore their theories and thinking. These make the

185

THE PARENT PARTNERSHIP TOOLKIT FOR EARLY YEARS   SECTION 3.4

ideal starting points for exploration and investigation as they relate directly to the children's interests and first-hand experience of the world. Children's theories will be very creative and may not always be those which are 'accepted' by adults. However, they are valuable because they make sense to the child at the time.

Many adults find science and technology a challenge and lack confidence in their ability to support young children in this area. To help parents to feel more confident you can:

- reinforce the importance of family members as role models, expressing their interest and curiosity in the world around them

- reassure parents that they do not need to know all the answers to children's questions – far better to find out together

- stress the importance of parents listening to their children and respecting their ideas and theories

- explain the importance of giving their children time to talk and listen, to play, to investigate and learn together and, above all, to have fun.

Being a good role model

Acting as a role model for curiosity is the best way to encourage children to be curious themselves. By being curious yourself, by thinking out loud, by saying, 'I wonder why…?' and, 'What would happen if…?' you are conveying important messages that the children will pick up.

By not knowing all the answers but, instead, being an enthusiastic explorer alongside the children, you can play a vital role in building their confidence as independent learners.

Inevitably, there will be occasions when the children need to 'borrow' the skills, knowledge and expertise of an adult. This reminds us of the importance of recognising when and how to share our skills, knowledge and understanding with children in a way that does not inhibit their personal discoveries.

Asking good questions

Asking questions is one of the fundamental ways in which we begin discussions with children and establish the starting point of what they already know. Making sure these are good questions requires thought, organisation, planning and lots of practice.

Open questions invite children to express their thoughts and ideas, build on their previous experience and suggest further investigation and exploration.

Remember to give children time to think and to respond – do not fill the silences with your own questions and comments – and to listen to children's responses before framing the next question.

Ask open questions that encourage children to express an opinion. Remember, you are not looking for the 'right' answer, instead you are establishing what the children already know, what ideas and theories they have. You are setting the scene for investigating their ideas to enable them to find out more.

186

SECTION 3.4 THE PARENT PARTNERSHIP TOOLKIT FOR EARLY YEARS

Using closed questions also has a place – not every question needs to be open ended. In any discussion with a group of children, you might also want to include attention-focusing questions or measuring and counting questions.

Not only is it important that you, as adults, ask good questions, you also need to encourage children to ask questions themselves. You can do this best by providing lots of opportunities for children to ask questions and by showing that you value both their questions and their answers.

The value of recording exploration and investigation

Encouraging the children and parents to make drawings of their investigations or to record the conversations they are having makes an important contribution to the success of the workshop sessions. Provide good quality paper and drawing pencils for both adults and children to use. Inviting adults to write down the conversations they have with their children helps them to focus on what their children are saying and how their ideas develop.

Drawing conveys meaning and can be used as a tool to initiate and communicate ideas. Some individuals who find using words difficult can express their ideas and reveal their thinking through drawing. All children will benefit from the challenge of conveying their thinking through graphic representation – pictures, plans, maps and diagrams. When a child represents her mental images in a drawing she is also representing them to herself, modifying her ideas and developing reasoning skills. Explaining her drawings to an adult provides a further opportunity to revisit, revise and enrich her understanding.

Taking photographs can capture the encounters, events, interactions and stages in an investigation or exploration. Revisiting these at a later date provides parents and children with the opportunity to look back on their earlier experiences and see how the children have made progress over time. Do not forget to share the visual images from the workshop with the wider community.

THE PARENT PARTNERSHIP TOOLKIT FOR EARLY YEARS   SECTION 3.4

Figure 3.4a

Equipment checklist: exploring water

'Exploring water' family workshop

Activities:

1. Floating and sinking   Figures 3.4b, 3.4c, 3.4d

2. Playing with bubbles   Figures 3.4e, 3.4f

3. Drops of colour   Figures 3.4g, 3.4h

4. Making a boat   Figures 3.4i, 3.4j

5. Watching water change   Figures 3.4k, 3.4l

6. Plants need water!   Figures 3.4m, 3.4n

Equipment checklist

Activity	Resources	Comments
Floating and sinking	• Large transparent water container, such as a plastic fish tank • Water tray or several large plastic bowls • Corks • Boat • Lids • Plastic boxes • Sponge • Plasticine • Plastic spoon • Metal spoon • Pebbles • Shells • Wooden bricks • Potato • Apple • Cover for the table top	
Playing with bubbles	• Shallow tray or dish for the bubble mixture • Small plastic bowls for creating 'bubble mountains' • Bubble mixture • Washing-up liquid • Bubble wands • Plastic straws • Pipe cleaners • Plastic-coated garden wire • Balloon whisk • Black and red food colouring • Cover for the table top	

188

SECTION 3.4 — THE PARENT PARTNERSHIP TOOLKIT FOR EARLY YEARS

Figure 3.4: cont

Activity	Resources	Comments
Drops of colour	• Large transparent plastic jars full of water • Plastic pipettes • Food colouring – several colours • Foil • Cotton-wool balls • Make-up remover pads • Water resistant fabric – plastic or rubber coated • Fabric that will absorb water – cotton or woollen • Foil • Dry kitchen paper or coffee filter paper • Damp kitchen paper or coffee filter paper • Cover for the table top	
Making a boat	• Water tray or plastic aquarium or bowl • Foil • Plastic boxes • Lids • Plastic bottle tops • Plasticine • Lolly sticks • Straws • Thick paper • Soap dish • Cardboard • Wood offcuts • String • Elastic bands • Glue • Small world play figures • Photographs and pictures of boats • Cover for the table top	
Watching water change	• Ice cubes in trays or ice-cube bags • Large plastic tray • Balloons • Bowl • Warm water • 'Treasure' – coins, brass paper clips, 'jewels', glitter • Food colouring • Disposable plastic gloves • Hand lens • Access to a freezer	

THE PARENT PARTNERSHIP TOOLKIT FOR EARLY YEARS

Figure 3.4a cont

Activity	Resources	Comments
Plants need water!	• Petri dishes • Clear plastic containers • Blotting paper • Cotton wool • Dry broad bean seeds • Broad beans – soaked in water overnight • Cress seeds • Pictures and photographs of seeds and plants • Magnifier	

Floating and sinking: activity sheet

Exploring water – Floating and sinking

What you need

- A large container of water – ideally a transparent plastic one, such as a plastic fish tank, so you can see through the sides.
- Alternatively you could use a water tray or several large plastic bowls.
- A cover for the table top

- A selection of objects that float or sink, for example:
  - corks
  - lids
  - sponge
  - plasticine
  - metal spoon
  - shells
  - potato
  - boat
  - plastic boxes
  - foil
  - plastic spoon
  - pebbles
  - wooden bricks
  - apple

Ideas and activities to try

- Put the objects one at a time into the water container.
  - Which things sink?
  - Which things float?
  - Record your answers on the floating and sinking chart.
- Can you make any of the floating things sink? How?
- Can you make the sponge float?
- Can you make the sponge sink?
- Try playing with the plasticine.
  - Can you make the plasticine sink?
  - Can you make it float? How?

This activity can become quite exciting!
Protect the table and the floor and have a
mop ready to clear up any water spills.

Floating and sinking: prompt sheet

Put the objects one at a time into the water container

Which things float?

    Record your answers on the floating and sinking chart.

        Can you make any of the floating things sink?

           How?

                Can you make the sponge float?

                    Can you make the sponge sink?

Try playing with the plasticine

Can you make the plasticine sink?

    Can you make it float?

        How?

Floating and sinking: recording sheet

Does it float?

Object	YES	NO
Boat		
Sponge		
Plastic lid		
Cork		
Stone		
Wooden block		
Plastic spoon		
Metal spoon		
Shell		
Apple		
Potato		

Playing with bubbles: activity sheet

Exploring water – **Playing with bubbles**

What you need

- Shallow tray or dish for the bubble mixture
- Small plastic bowls for creating 'bubble mountains'
- Bubble mixture
- Washing-up liquid
- Bubble wands

- Plastic straws
- Pipe cleaners
- Plastic-coated garden wire
- Balloon whisk
- Black and red food colouring
- Cover for the table top

Ideas and activities to try

Investigate the bubble mixture and try blowing some bubbles.
- What do they look like?
- What do they feel like?
- What do they sound like?
- What do they smell like?

How big a bubble can you blow?

Can you use the garden wire to make a square wand?
- Does it make a square bubble?

Can you make coloured bubbles?
- How big a bubble mountain can you make?

Recipe for bubble mixture:

3 parts washing-up liquid

7 parts warm water

1 part glycerine or sugar.

Glycerine helps the bubbles last longer by preventing them from drying out. If you cannot get glycerine, use sugar instead.

This activity can become quite exciting!
Use a protective covering on the table.

SECTION 3.4 THE PARENT PARTNERSHIP TOOLKIT FOR EARLY YEARS

Playing with bubbles: prompt sheet

Playing with bubbles

Investigate the bubble mixture and try blowing some bubbles.

What do they look like?

What do they feel like?

What do they sound like?

What do they smell like?

How big a bubble can you blow?

Can you use the garden wire to make a square wand?

Does it make a square bubble?

Can you make coloured bubbles?

How big a bubble mountain can you make?

195

Figure 3.4g

Drops of colour: activity sheet

Exploring water – *Drops of colour*

What you need

- Large transparent plastic jars full of water
- Plastic pipettes
- Food colouring – several colours
- Foil
- Cotton-wool balls
- Make-up remover pads
- Fabric that is water resistant – plastic or rubber coated

- Fabric that will absorb water – cotton or woollen
- Foil
- Dry kitchen paper or coffee filter paper
- Damp kitchen paper or coffee filter paper
- Cover for the table top

Ideas and activities to try

- Use the plastic pipette to drop some food colouring into the water in the jar.
  - Watch carefully to see what happens.
  - Talk about the patterns the food colouring makes.
  - Can you draw the pattern?
  - Does it look the same from above and from the side?

- Now shake the jar carefully.
  - Add another colour.
  - What happens?

- Drip some water onto the different materials – fabrics, foil, cotton wool, paper.
  - What do you see?
  - Do all the drops look the same?

- Drop some food colouring onto dry kitchen paper.
  - Talk about what you see.
  - What happens if you carefully drip some water onto the drop of colour?

- Drop some food colouring onto wet kitchen paper.
  - What happens?
  - Do all the colours behave the same way?

Use a protective covering on the table and remind parents that food colouring will stain hands and clothing. Hands can be washed, but the colour may be permanent on some clothing fabrics.

SECTION 3.4   THE PARENT PARTNERSHIP TOOLKIT FOR EARLY YEARS

Drops of colour: prompt sheet

Drops of colour

Use the plastic pipette to drop some food colouring into the water in the jar.

- Watch carefully to see what happens.
- Talk about the patterns the food colouring makes.
  - Can you draw the pattern?
  - Does it look the same from above and from the side?

- Now shake the jar carefully.
  - Add another colour.
  - What happens?

Drip some water onto the different materials – fabrics, foil, cotton wool, paper.

  - What do you see?
  - Do all the drops look the same?

- Drop some food colouring onto dry kitchen paper.
  - Talk about what you see.
  - What happens if you carefully drip some water onto the drop of colour?

- Drop some food colouring onto wet kitchen paper.
  - What happens?
  - Do all the colours behave the same way?

Making a boat: activity sheet

Exploring water – Making a boat

What you need

- Water tray or plastic aquarium or bowl
- Small-world play figures
- Photographs and pictures of boats
- Cover for the table top
- A selection of materials including:
  - foil
  - lids
  - plasticine
  - straws
  - soap dish
  - wood offcuts
  - elastic bands
  - plastic boxes
  - plastic bottletops
  - lolly sticks
  - thick paper
  - cardboard
  - string
  - glue

Ideas and activities to try

- Look closely at the pictures of boats.
  - Talk about what you can see.
- Try making your own boat from the materials on the table.
  - What do you need to use?
- Try floating your boat in the water.
  - Does it float well?
  - Is it stable or does it tip over?
  - Will it carry the play people?
  - How many people will it carry?
- Can you make your boat move?
  - How?

Making a boat: prompt sheet

Making a boat

Look closely at the pictures of boats

- Talk about what you can see.

Try making your own boat from the materials on the table.

- What would you need to use?

Try floating your boat in the water.

- Does it float well?
- Is it stable or does it tip over?
- Will it carry the play people?
- How many people will it carry?

Can you make your boat move?

- How?

Figure 3.4k

Watching water change: activity sheet

Exploring water – Watching water change

What you need

- Ice cubes in trays or ice-cube bags
- A large plastic tray
- Balloons
- 'Treasure' such as coins, brass paperclips, 'jewels' or glitter

- Food colouring
- Disposable plastic gloves
- Hand lens
- Bowl of warm water

Ideas and activities to try

- Make some ice cubes before the workshop. Make some clear ice cubes and some coloured ones.
- Investigate the ice cubes in the tray.
  - What do they look like?
  - What do they feel like?
  - What do they smell like?
- Look carefully at the ice cubes using a hand lens. What do you see?
- Watch the ice cubes as they begin to melt.
  - Put some of the clear ice cubes into a bowl of warm water.
  - Watch the ice cubes carefully. What happens to them?
- Now put some of the coloured ice cubes into the warm water. What happens now?
- Make magic ice balloons for the children to take home to freeze or to collect the next day. Fill the balloons with water, put 'treasure' inside and freeze them. Watch what happens when the magic balloons melt!
- Have fun with 'frozen hands' during the workshop or at home. Fill disposable plastic gloves with water and freeze them. When they are frozen peel off the gloves and watch them melt.

SECTION 3.4 THE PARENT PARTNERSHIP TOOLKIT FOR EARLY YEARS

Watching water change: prompt sheet

Watching water change

Investigate the ice cubes in the tray.

- What do they look like?
- What do they feel like?
- What do they smell like?

- Look carefully at the ice cubes using a hand lens. What do you see?
  - Watch the ice cubes as they begin to melt.

Put some clear ice cubes into a bowl of warm water.

- Watch the ice cubes carefully.
  - What happens to them?

- Now put some of the coloured ice cubes into the water. What happens now?

- Make a magic balloon for your child to take home to freeze or to collect tomorrow. Fill a balloon with water, put some pieces of the 'treasure' inside, tie a knot in the end of the balloon and freeze it. When the magic balloon is frozen, remove the balloon and watch what happens when the magic balloon melts. Listen to what your child says about what is happening and what treasure can be found.

- Make a 'frozen hand' at home. Take one of the disposable plastic gloves and fill it with water. Tie a knot in the end of the glove and place it in a freezer. When it freezes remove the glove and watch the frozen hand melt.

201

THE PARENT PARTNERSHIP TOOLKIT FOR EARLY YEARS　　　　　SECTION 3.4

Figure 3.4m

Plants need water!: activity sheet

Exploring water – # Plants need water!

What you need

- Petri dishes
- Clear plastic containers
- Blotting paper
- Cotton wool
- Dry broad bean seeds

- Broad beans – soaked in water overnight
- Cress seeds
- Pictures and photographs of seeds and plants
- Magnifier

Ideas and activities to try

Growing broad beans

Put some dry broad beans in one clear plastic container and the soaked broad beans in another. Look together at the two containers of broad bean seeds.
- What differences do you see?
- Talk about why the beans are different.

Open up a broad bean and look inside.
- How many different parts can you see inside the seed?
- Use the magnifier to help you.
- Can you draw a picture of the inside of the seed?

Choose a broad bean seed to plant.
- Cut some blotting paper to fit around the inside of the plastic container.
- Slide your broad bean seed between the blotting paper and the side of the plastic container.

Talk about why plants need water.
- Pour some water into the container. Watch carefully to see what happens to the blotting paper.
- The seed is now ready to take home.

At home:
- Keep the blotting paper damp.
- Check your seed together every day to see what happens to it.
- Try drawing pictures or taking photographs of your seed as it grows.

Plants need water!: activity sheet

202

Planting cress

Look together at the cress seeds.
- Do you think you could look inside a cress seed?

Help your child to spread some cotton wool over the bottom of a plastic petri dish. Try to make it as flat as possible.

Talk about plants needing water to grow.
- Pour in some water to make the cotton wool damp.

Sprinkle some cress seeds over the cotton wool.
- Try to get the seeds well spread out.

  (The easiest way is to pour some seed into the palm of your child's hand and encourage him/her to pick up a pinch of seeds and sprinkle them over the cotton wool.)

Put the lid on the petri dish to keep the seeds safe on the way home.

At home:

- Take the lid off, put the dish in a warm, light place and keep the cotton wool damp.

- Check the seeds every day with your child, talk about what you can see happening as the seeds start to grow.

- Draw pictures of the cress seeds as they grow.

Plants need water: prompt sheet

Plants need water! – Wet and dry broad beans

- Put some dry broad beans in one clear plastic container and the soaked broad beans in another. Look together at the two containers of broad bean seeds.
  - What is the difference? Talk about why they are different.

- Open up a broad bean and look inside. How many different parts can you see inside the seed?
  - Use the magnifier to help you. Can you draw a picture of the inside of the seed?

- Choose a broad bean seed to plant. Cut some blotting paper to fit around the inside of the plastic container.

- Slide your broad bean seed between the blotting paper and the side of the plastic container. Pour some water into the container.
  - Watch carefully to see what happens to the blotting paper.
  - The seed is now ready to take home.

At home:

- Keep the blotting paper damp.
- Check your seed together every day to see what happens to it.
- Try drawing pictures or taking photographs of your seed as it grows.

Plants need water! – Growing cress

- Look at the cress seeds together.
  - Do you think you could look inside a cress seed?

- Help your child to spread some cotton wool over the bottom of a plastic petri dish. Try to make it as flat as possible.

- Pour in some water to make the cotton wool damp.

- Sprinkle some cress seeds over the cotton wool. Try to get the seeds well spread out.

  (The easiest way is to pour some seeds into the palm of your child's hand and then encourage him/her to pick up a pinch of seeds and sprinkle them over the cotton wool.)

- Put the lid on the petri dish to keep the seeds safe on the way home.

At home:

- Take the lid off. Put the dish in a warm, light place and keep the cotton wool damp.
- Check the seeds every day with your child. Talk about what you can see happening as the seeds start to grow.
- Draw pictures and take photographs of the cress seeds as they grow.

SECTION 3.4

Invitation to parents

Exploring Together family workshop

Exploring water

Please come with me to a special
Exploring Together
afternoon on: [date]

from
[start time]
to
[end time]

There will be lots of interesting things for us to explore and talk about together.

From:

[child's name or picture drawn by them]

Exploring water: ideas for parents – babies

Exploring water
– 10 ideas to use at home with babies

1. Use a sponge so your baby can learn to squash and squeeze in the bath.

2. Use bath time to enjoy splashing – do not fill the bath too full!

3. When you are washing your baby sing *'Heads, shoulders, knees and toes'* as you wash.

4. Put lots of small containers in the bath or in a bowl for your baby to fill up with water.

5. Use kitchen tools with holes in them – funnel, sieve, spoon, whisks – to add fun to bath time.

6. Let your baby smell some different oils or bubble bath before adding them to the water at bath time.

7. Try adding some ice cubes to your baby's bath. Let him feel the coldness of the ice cubes.

8. Blow bubbles for your baby to watch and catch.

9. Sing songs at bath time such as *'Row, row, row your boat'*.

10. Go outside in the rain and let your baby feel the rain as it falls.

Make up songs as you wash your baby's hands after nappy changing, before eating or after playing in sand or soil.

Exploring water: ideas for parents – toddlers

Exploring water
– 10 ideas to use at home with toddlers

1. Have fun floating and sinking different objects at bath time.

2. Use kitchen tools with holes in them – funnel, sieve, spoon, whisks – to add fun to bath time.

3. Sing songs such as 'Five little ducks' when in the bath.

4. Let your toddler smell some different oils or bubble bath before adding them to the water at bath time.

5. When it rains, watch the raindrops as they run down the window pane.

6. After it has rained, go out into the garden or to the park and look carefully at drops of rain on leaves.

7. Wear wellingtons and have fun stamping in puddles or jumping across them. Do it in the rain too!

8. Give your child a child-sized watering can so that she can help water the plants.

9. Use a large bowl, a bucket or paddling pool for water play with jugs, pipes and guttering to encourage your child to learn how to pour.

10. Paint the wall or fence using water and a paintbrush.

Make up songs as you wash your toddler's hands after going to the toilet, before eating or after playing in sand or soil.

THE PARENT PARTNERSHIP TOOLKIT FOR EARLY YEARS   SECTION 3.4

Figure 3.4r

Exploring water: ideas for parents – 3 to 5-year-olds

Exploring water
– 10 ideas to use at home with 3-5s

1. Have fun floating and sinking different objects at bath time, in the kitchen or in the garden.

2. Use kitchen tools with holes in them – funnel, sieve, spoon, whisks – to add fun to bath time. Add different oils or bubble bath to the water to make it different.

3. Make a boat out of a cardboard box and sing songs such as 'Row row row your boat' or 'The big ships sails through the alley-O'.

4. When it rains, watch the raindrops as they run down the window pane. Have a raindrop race.

5. Listen to the different sounds rain makes when it is heavy or light.

6. After it has rained, go out into the garden or to the park and look carefully at drops of rain on leaves. Look around to see which parts of the garden or park are driest and wettest.

7. Wear wellingtons and have fun stamping in puddles or jumping across them. Watch the puddles as they dry. Draw round them with chalk at different times to see what happens.

8. Give your child a child-sized watering can so that she can help water the plants.

9. Make a water play area outside. Use a large bowl, a bucket or paddling pool for water play with jugs, pipes and guttering.

10. Paint the wall or fence using water, a paintbrush or a water spray.

Make up songs as you wash your child's hands after going to the toilet, before eating or after playing in sand or soil.

Family members as visitors to your setting

This section focuses on the value of inviting family members as visitors into your setting to share their life and work with the children. It helps to address many aspects of young children's personal, social and emotional development but also gives powerful messages to parents about the inclusivity of the setting and the value of diversity. It looks at how to plan for and organise a visit so that it is successful for everyone – the children, the visitor and the practitioners (*figures 3.5a and 3.5b, on p215-6*).

Use the resources in this section to:
- build your relationships with the families who use your setting
- nurture an attitude of respect for individuality among parents, children and practitioners
- widen the experience and understanding of parents and children.

Introduction

Young children's personal, social and emotional development is fundamental to their wellbeing and learning. Introducing visitors from a wide range of backgrounds and cultures to your setting can provide the opportunity for children to learn about the wider community in which they live and helps them to develop a respect for, and understanding of, differences (*see the box 'Benefits of inviting a range of visitors to your setting' on p210*).

All settings are different, and the range of cultural and ethnic backgrounds represented by your families will vary. In a multicultural area, it is important to reinforce the positive image that all cultures have of themselves. Inviting in family members from within the local community to talk to the children in your setting is an excellent way to achieve this. In areas of the country where there is little or no cultural mix it is vitally important that young children have the opportunity to meet people from different backgrounds. Learning first hand about life in different parts of the world will bring the experience alive and help children to see similarities and differences between their own lives and those of others.

Inviting a disabled family member into your setting will help children to have an understanding of disabilities and prevent fearful or negative attitudes towards disabled people. The term disability covers a wide range of conditions and you will need to think carefully about who you approach and how you will plan together to make the visit successful for everyone. Within the family circles of the children who attend your setting there may be adults or children who are wheelchair users or who have a hearing or visual impairment. You may want to get in touch with organisations such as the Royal Association for Deaf People (RAD), the Royal National Institute for the Blind (RNIB) or the Guide Dogs for the Blind Association to help you make the most of a visit from a family member with a disability.

There are likely to be several different reactions from parents to the idea of involving family members as visitors in your setting. These will range from enthusiasm and offers to be involved themselves to a degree of apprehension. It is important that you explain to parents how visitors can enrich the experiences provided for children in a safe and secure environment. Use the *sample letter in figure 3.5a (see p215)* to let parents and carers know when you are inviting visitors to meet the children in your setting.

Benefits of inviting a range of visitors to your setting

Introducing a range of visitors to your setting brings benefits for everyone — children, practitioners and the visitors themselves will all gain from a well-planned visit.

Children will:

- have the opportunity to form positive relationships
- learn from adults as guides and role models, developing anti-discriminatory attitudes
- develop an understanding of their own culture and community, fostering a sense of belonging and strong self-image
- begin to develop empathy and sensitivity to the needs of others
- engage in conversation and learn to listen to others
- see things from another point of view.

Visiting family members will:

- have the opportunity to share their knowledge and experience
- promote a positive image of themselves, their community, culture, gender or disability
- increase their understanding of the world of young children
- develop their personal skills — communication, negotiation and problem-solving
- gain personal satisfaction and enjoyment.

Practitioners should:

- act as a positive role model, showing an awareness of the needs of others
- demonstrate respect, politeness, interest, enthusiasm and appreciation
- respond to the children's learning needs and interests
- model effective communication and appropriate language
- take the opportunity to observe children's interactions with other adults
- work with visiting family members to plan experiences that support all areas of learning.

Planning for the involvement of family members

Carefully planned visits by members of the children's families will enrich your planning for personal, social and emotional development (PSED).

- Think about opportunities for including visitors to your setting at the time you are doing your long-term planning.
- At the more detailed planning stage, make sure that you spend time with the children creating the context for the visit and building up their interest and anticipation.

- Help the children get the most out of the opportunity to talk to their visitor, learning to participate in discussions and ask interesting questions.

- After the visitor has been into your setting, think about organising appropriate visits out into the local community to consolidate and extend the children's learning.

See also the box 'Links to early learning and development', below.

Inviting family members from different cultures to come into your setting could be linked to your curriculum planning in one of the following ways:

- **Celebrations**

  Celebrating the festivals of the major religions and cultures provides opportunities throughout the year to extend children's awareness of the wider world. Finding out how weddings, naming ceremonies and New Year are celebrated in different countries will also provide lots of learning opportunities that young children will be able to relate to.

- **Topics**

  A visitor from a different country, culture or ethnic background can bring added interest to a range of topics – for example 'food we eat', 'clothes we wear' or 'our families'– that you may be planning to cover with the children.

  For example, as part of a topic on food, you may spend time over several weeks talking with the children about different types of food, favourite foods, cooking methods and cooking styles. You might then ask your visitor to bring in some examples of the different foods they typically eat, along with examples of cooking and eating utensils. Perhaps you may plan an opportunity to prepare some food together during the visit – remember to talk in advance about the detail of how this will happen, including what types of food it would be appropriate to use, any allergies that children have, and how the resources will be paid for.

Links to early learning and development

Relationships are at the heart of young children's social, emotional and intellectual development. Inviting a range of family members into your setting will broaden the children's experience of people and add another dimension to the topic or theme you are following.

- Inviting parents and carers from the local community to talk to the children about their culture and beliefs will support the early learning goals for a sense of community.

- A visit from older family members who can talk about life in the past and share their skills and experience with the children will underpin the early learning goals for making relationships and for behaviour and self-control.

- Careful and sensitive planning for a visit from a person with a disability will foster the development of children's self-confidence and self-esteem.

▶

> **Welcoming family members into your setting will develop young children's:**
> - self-confidence and self-esteem, helping them to:
>   - respond to significant experiences, showing a range of feelings where appropriate
>   - have a developing awareness of their own needs, views and feelings and be sensitive to the needs, views and feelings of others
>   - have a developing respect for their own cultures and beliefs and those of others.
> - sense of community, helping them to:
>   - understand that people have different needs, views, cultures and beliefs, that need to be treated with respect
>   - understand that they can expect others to treat their needs, views, cultures and beliefs with respect.
>
> **Inviting a disabled family member into your setting will support young children's:**
> - behaviour and self-control, helping them to:
>   - consider the consequences of their words and actions for themselves and others.
> - relationships, helping them to:
>   - form good relationships with adults and peers.
>
> In addition, there will also be opportunities to address aspects of learning in the other areas of the curriculum, including speaking and listening and understanding about communities.

A policy for visiting family members

Inviting family members into your setting can be a very worthwhile and exciting experience. However, remember that successful visits do not happen by chance and need careful planning and preparation. As with all other important aspects of organisation and management, clear guidelines will help to make sure that nothing is overlooked. The following areas should be included in your policy on visitors to your setting:

- A clear statement on the value of including visitors to support personal, social and emotional development and other areas of learning (*see Section 2.1: Establishing the vision and values*).

- How you will inform parents of arrangements for visits – for example, through your information booklet, prospectus, website, newsletters or notices (*see Section 2.4: Communicating with parents*).

- A protocol for inviting visitors, which should include:
  - agreeing which visitors are appropriate
  - establishing who will make the initial contact
  - arranging at least one meeting in advance of the visit.

SECTION 3.5

- Producing guidelines for visitors, which might cover the:
  - purpose of the visit and how it fits with the children's interests
  - appropriate language to use and likely questions the children might ask
  - time and duration of the visit
  - space and equipment needed
  - practitioners' responsibility for health and safety and behaviour management during the visit.

- The responsibilities of the staff for managing any visit:
  - welcoming and thanking the visitor
  - acting as an enthusiastic role model for the children
  - offering refreshments and ensuring the visitor is comfortable
  - taking responsibility for health and safety and behaviour management
  - ensuring the setting's child-protection policy is adhered to at all times
  - follow-up arrangements, including thank-you letters and ways of sharing the valuable outcomes of the visit with parents and the wider community.

Making visitors feel welcome

Good planning and preparation are essential to ensuring that welcoming a visitor to your setting is a successful experience for everyone. When you have the initial meeting with your visitor, use 'A guide for visiting family members' in figure 3.5b (see p216) to help you plan the visit. Remember that you may need to produce the guide in different languages, in Braille or on a tape.

If you intend to invite family members with a disability into your setting, it is important to make sure that their visits are interesting, enjoyable and successful for all concerned:

- It is very important to make your visitor feel genuinely welcome. You will need to make sure that your physical environment is suitable for wheelchairs, is not cluttered and can offer a quiet space for a group of children to meet their visitor.

- Many disabled people experience thoughtless behaviour from adults and you can make a difference by acting as a good role model for the children in your care. When you first meet a disabled family member offer to shake their hand, as you would with any visitor. This simple action of human contact creates a friendly atmosphere for communication. If the disabled visitor is accompanied by a carer, make sure you speak to the disabled person directly and not over their head to their carer.

- You will need to find a comfortable quiet space to talk to your disabled visitor. Wheelchair users are seated at the right height to talk comfortably with young children – make sure that all adults in the room find somewhere to sit at the wheelchair user's eye level.

- A deaf person's speech might sound strange to the children. He or she may speak very softly or loudly or may pronounce some words in an unusual way. Help the children to understand that deaf people cannot hear their own voices and may have learned to speak when they were small without hearing any words at all.

213

- When the children are asking questions they should face the deaf person directly so that lip reading is possible. You will need to make them aware that they do not need to shout. It might be possible to introduce your children to British Sign Language so they can experience the different ways in which deaf people communicate.

- If you invite a blind person with their guide dog to visit your children, the dog will be the focus for lots of interest and excitement. It is important that the children understand that the guide dog has a job to do and must not be distracted from keeping its owner safe.

- Do not forget that a blind person does not have any visual clues to follow such as facial expressions or body language, so it is important that the children take turns to speak and ask questions clearly.

Children will be naturally curious about disabilities and will have different reactions. Remember that young children will stare and make comments. This is an opportunity to talk to the children about the consequences of their actions and words.

Remember to keep parents informed of any visits you have planned for the children and be prepared to deal with any questions they have.

Sources of information

British Sign Language: *www.britishsignlanguage.com*

Guide Dogs for the Blind Association: *www.guidedogs.org.uk*

Royal Association for Deaf People (RAD): *www.royaldeaf.org.uk*

Royal National Institute of Blind People (RNIB): *www.rnib.org*

SECTION 3.5   THE PARENT PARTNERSHIP TOOLKIT FOR EARLY YEARS

Figure 3.5a

Sample letter to parents explaining about visitors to the setting

Inviting visitors to our setting

Dear Parents

The children who attend our setting come from different family backgrounds and have a range of personalities and interests. We encourage them to develop a respect for themselves and for others and to learn how to communicate with adults and other children. Visitors play an important part in this process. They bring many different skills and experiences that they can share with the children.

Inviting visitors into our setting helps children to:

- understand more about the world and their place in it
- learn about the community in which they live
- respect the differences in people they meet
- show interest in other people's points of view
- listen carefully and join in conversations.

When we invite visitors into our setting, they help us to develop the children's interests and the topics they are following.

When we invite anyone in we make sure that:

- they will be a good role model for the children
- we meet them at least once before the visit
- we talk to them about the children's interests
- we explain our policies on child protection, health and safety and behaviour management
- the visitor is aware that the staff of the setting are responsible for the children at all times.

We will always tell you in advance when we are planning to invite a visitor to the setting. You may find that your child talks about the visitor when they are at home with you. We are always happy to share information about what the visitor has talked about and would love to hear what your child has to say at home.

Name   **Position**

If you, or a member of your family, would like to visit the setting to share your experiences and talents with the children please let us know.

215

A guide for visiting family members

Thank you for agreeing to visit our setting to talk to the children. Your visit is part of our programme for supporting children's personal, social and emotional development. This involves encouraging children to be self-confident and feel good about themselves, and to recognise that they are members of a wider community. Meeting new people and hearing about their lives helps children to learn more about the world in which they live and to develop a respect for different cultures and beliefs.

In the section below, we have included some important information to help make sure your visit is enjoyable – for you as well as the children.

Setting contact details:

Date and time of visit:

Size of group: **Ages of children:**

Names of adults who will be supporting the group:

The children will be particularly interested in:

Here are some things to think about when planning your visit:

- As an important visitor to our setting you will be helping our children to learn the skills of being a member of an audience, being polite and listening attentively.

- The adults supporting the group will be responsible for the behaviour of the children and will be there to help you and to make sure your visit is successful and enjoyable.

- Children of this age enjoy having things to look at, such as photographs and pictures, and things to handle. Please make sure that anything you bring in for them to see can be handled safely without the danger of it getting broken.

- Your visit is a wonderful opportunity for children to practise their skills of asking questions and being involved in discussion. You will find that young children need time to think about what they want to say and the questions they want to ask.

- Try to involve all children in the discussions, not just those who find it easy to talk and express opinions. The other adults supporting the group will help with this.

- The children should be able to concentrate for about 30 minutes, including time for them to ask questions and share their experiences.

- Be prepared to make lots of new friends and to be invited back for another visit!

SECTION 3.6   THE PARENT PARTNERSHIP TOOLKIT FOR EARLY YEARS

The value of play

This section looks in detail at the important messages practitioners will want to share with parents about young children's play and learning. It discusses the importance of different aspects of play and what young children are learning while they are playing. The *five photocopiable leaflets in figures 3.6a to 3.6e (see p225-234)* are designed help you to share with parents key information about play and learning across all areas of the early years curriculum. *On the back of each of these sheets are* ideas for parents to use at home with children of different ages to complement the work you are doing in the setting.

Use these resources to:
- share with parents what young children are learning through play
- build parents' understanding of the early years curriculum and what experiences their child is having in the setting
- provide ideas for parents to help them support their children's learning at home.

The serious business of play

Babies and young children are powerful learners from the day they are born, actively striving to make sense of the world around them. As they explore the world they inhabit, they are naturally drawn to learning through playing and being playful.

Throughout the world, play is recognised as being fundamental to children's wellbeing, learning and development; so much so that the right to play is laid down in the United Nations Convention on the Rights of the Child (1989). The commitment to play-based learning is to be found in the early years curriculum guidance of each of the countries of the UK.

The Welsh *Framework for Children's Learning for 3 to7-year-olds in Wales* (2008) states that:

> 'For children, play can be (and often is) a very serious business. It needs concentrated attention. It is about children learning through perseverance, attention to detail, and concentration – characteristics usually associated with work. Play is not only crucial to the way children become self-aware and the way they learn the rules of social behaviour, it is also fundamental to intellectual development.'

Children's play is their work

Play engages children's bodies, minds and emotions. As they play, children are building up the knowledge, skills and attitudes that will make them effective learners. They drive their own learning by the choices they make, by the preoccupations and interests they develop, by the questions they ask and by the ways in which they develop their competencies. Through play, children learn to interact with others, to experience and manage their feelings and to be confident about themselves and their abilities.

Play can help children to build up the attitudes and dispositions they need, both now and in the future. These include:

- finding interests and preoccupations

- making choices and taking decisions
- being willing to explore, experiment and try things out
- raising problems and finding solutions
- making plans and carrying them out
- concentrating, persevering with a task, rising to challenges
- being resilient – finding alternative ways of doing things when things do not work out
- managing their own behaviour and that of others
- playing cooperatively with others, including adults
- understanding the feelings and views of other people.

Play can take many forms in an early years setting. It can range from completely free, unstructured play where children play without adult support, through child-initiated play where the adult's role is to provide an enabling environment and sensitive interaction, to adult-guided, playful experiential activities. Children can benefit from opportunities to experience a balance of each of these types of play and playful activities.

Play at home

Play and playfulness occur across all cultural groups and many families spend a lot of time playing with their children, helping them to learn through:

- playing structured games such as peek-a-boo
- encouraging open-ended play such as water play
- pretending and imagining and acting out different roles
- being playful through humour, jokes, mimicry, riddles and rhymes, singing and clapping games.

Practitioners can help parents to develop their understanding of the importance of play in their child's learning and development by:

- providing them with information on learning through play and its links to future learning
- providing them with ideas to use with their children at home.

The information you might want to share with parents about young children's play is likely to be based on the following themes:

- language for thinking and speaking through imaginative play
- reading and writing through role-play
- maths through games and open-ended play (sand, water, construction)
- science through exploratory play
- play and ICT.

Language for thinking and speaking through imaginative play

As they develop their capacity to play, the ability to pretend has a particular significance for children as learners. When children begin to pretend that one object can represent something else – for example, a building block can be food for a toy dinosaur – they are beginning to understand that things can be symbolic. This, in turn, leads children to think in

SECTION 3.6 THE PARENT PARTNERSHIP TOOLKIT FOR EARLY YEARS

abstract ways that will lead them to use words and images, to express their ideas, to predict and solve problems and to develop as creative and critical thinkers.

Anna Craft has argued that 'possibility thinking' is at the heart of all creativity in young children, whether they are playing alone, in parallel or in collaboration with others. She states that:

> 'Possibilities are generated by children (and adults) in all areas of learning… Possibility thinking is the means by which questions are posed or puzzles surfaced – through multiple ways of generating the question 'what if?'. Fostering children's possibility thinking can be seen as building their resilience and confidence and reinforcing their capabilities as confident explorers, meaning-makers and decision-makers.'
>
> (Craft, 2002; Jeffrey and Craft, 2004).

In order to develop their 'possibility thinking', children need opportunities to play with open-ended resources over long periods of time. By providing a wide range of interesting resources and experiences, practitioners can encourage children to engage in sustained shared thinking as they imagine all sorts of scenarios, encountering and solving problems as they play. Through spending time 'imagining what might be' children will develop the skills of prediction, hypothesising and 'thinking outside the box'.

As they play imaginatively, children will develop a wide range of skills that are important for active learning to take place:

Communication skills of:

- speaking
- listening
- discussing
- recording.

Reasoning and thinking skills including:

- questioning
- speculating
- inferring
- problem-solving
- recognising similarities and differences
- reflecting.

In addition, imaginative play can help develop the social skills of:

- cooperation
- negotiation
- following instructions
- behaving safely
- teamwork and leadership.

Reading and writing through role-play

Role-play is another step in the development of children's imaginative play, when they can become somebody or something else. Role-play provides children with opportunities to 'play out' the events that they experience and observe in their lives. It provides the experience of real-life situations where they can rehearse and develop their skills of language, communication and maths. Role-play can create opportunities for storytelling, reading and writing.

The three most common types of role-play are:

- **Domestic play**, where the home and family are at the centre of the play, with daily routines, such as cooking, mealtimes and housework, taking place.

- **Transactional play**, which involves buying and selling. This may take place in a shop, cafe, garage, travel agent's or garden centre

- **Imaginary-world play**, where the creatures of stories dwell or which takes place in unfamiliar environments, such as on the moon or under the sea.

The props provided for role-play will enhance the quality of the play and can provide excellent opportunities for children to develop their reading and writing skills.

To support the development of reading through role-play you can add:
- notices
- signs
- menus
- recipes
- books/magazines
- brochures
- labels
- prices
- maps/directions.

To support the development of writing through role-play, you can add:
- writing materials
- clipboards
- notebooks
- shopping list
- kitchen noticeboard
- calendars/diaries
- forms to complete.

Maths through games, rhymes and songs

Over time, different terms have been used for children's development in the area of mathematical development, ranging from arithmetic, mathematical development to the current term, 'problem solving, reasoning and numeracy'. Many parents will refer to this area

SECTION 3.6 THE PARENT PARTNERSHIP TOOLKIT FOR EARLY YEARS

of learning as 'maths.' Opportunities for developing mathematical skills occur in all the different play opportunities children experience in an early years setting.

Indoor and outdoor games often require the knowledge, skills and understanding found in this area of learning. For example:

- dominoes and lotto encourage number recognition and counting
- card games such as Snap and Happy Families give practice in matching, sorting and recognising similarities and differences
- board games, including Ludo, and Snakes and Ladders, support counting, number recognition and one-to-one correspondence
- traditional games, such as hopscotch, skipping, hide and seek and 'What time is it, Mr Wolf?', involve number recognition and counting, as well as measuring time
- all types of races involve an understanding of distance, time and 1st, 2nd and 3rd
- team games, such as football and soft cricket, foster an awareness of space and direction as well as encouraging children to play together cooperatively.

Many nursery rhymes and action songs are about numbers and counting. There is a strong connection between the order, timing, beat and rhythm of music and aspects of mathematics, such as counting, sequencing and understanding time and order.

- Many nursery rhymes are counting rhymes – 'One, two, three, four, five, once I caught a fish alive', 'One, two, buckle my shoe'.
- 'Five currant buns in the baker's shop' and '10 green bottles' involve an understanding of taking away and adding.
- Action rhymes, such as 'Two little dickie birds', 'Five little ducks went swimming one day' and 'Five green speckled frogs', involve counting backwards and forwards.
- 'Round and round the garden, like a teddy bear', 'Incy wincy spider' and 'Hickory, dickory, dock' involve the use of positional language, such as round, up and down, as well as numbers.

Most of the nursery rhymes and action songs can be enjoyed by children throughout the early years as they will enjoy repeating well-known words at different ages.

Science through exploratory play

Exploratory play with natural and man-made resources will encourage children to develop their own ideas and interests. When they are exploring the world around them, young children are building up the skills, knowledge and attitudes that will help them to become interested, independent scientific learners. By encouraging children to explore and investigate, and by playing alongside them, you will show them how important you think their ideas and interests are.

When they are engaged in exploratory play:

- **Children explore new things and experiences**
  Children's curiosity about the world leads them to explore using all their senses, to develop their own ideas and begin to make sense of the world.

- **Children talk out loud to themselves**

221

When they talk to themselves, children are clarifying their thoughts and imagining 'what might be'.

- **Children meet physical and mental challenges**
  Working out what to do, trying hard, persevering with problems and finding out for themselves are all opportunities for children to develop a real understanding of the world around them.

- **Children practise doing things**
  Practising skills they have learned helps children to become confident in what they can do and to enjoy their own expertise.

Play and ICT

Young children today live in a technology-rich world. Many parents and family members are extremely ICT literate and will encourage their children to develop their own technological capabilities from a very early age.

However, many parents think that when we are talking about technology, or ICT, we are only talking about computers and not the rich range of technology that is available to children. Others may take a dim view of the use of technology with very young children. Early years practitioners need to engage with parents in order to:

- build up an understanding of each child's home experience of technology by listening to parents' descriptions of how their child uses technology at home

- help parents to support their child's technological development by giving them information about appropriate technological skills, knowledge and understanding

- use technology to involve parents in their children's learning and development through providing family workshops on technology and children's play, using a computer with young children

- keep in touch with the increasing number of families who prefer to use technological means – email, website, e-newsletter – to keep in touch with their child's early years setting.

ICT can be used to enrich all areas of learning in the early years. By using ICT, including electronic programmable toys, digital cameras, computers and other electronic equipment, practitioners can improve the quality of learning and development for all children, perhaps engaging some children who may not be attracted by other provision. Some of the equipment you might want to use to support learning in different areas includes:

- **Personal, social and emotional development** – digital cameras, mobile telephones such as walkie-talkie systems, karaoke machines and microphones will all help children to develop confidence and self-esteem as well as encouraging teamwork and sharing.

- **Communication, language and literacy** – tape recorders, telephones, multi-link headphones, 'talking tins' and 'talking photo albums' are all excellent resources for supporting the development tool of speaking and listening. An interactive whiteboard can be used to develop writing skills on a large scale. Helping children to use a scanner or photocopier will enable them to tell stories, sequence images and create cards, pictures and displays.

SECTION 3.6   THE PARENT PARTNERSHIP TOOLKIT FOR EARLY YEARS

- **Problem solving, reasoning and numeracy** – many digital toys and equipment, such as electronic cash registers, have numbers and function keys that encourage number recognition, counting and problem solving. Remote-controlled cars and simple robots (such as Roamer, Pixie or Beebot) can be used to develop positional and directional language.

- **Knowledge and understanding of the world** – this area of learning specifically includes children's learning and development in ICT. This will range from switching a piece of equipment, such as a cassette recorder or remote-controlled vehicle, on and off, through taking digital photographs and printing them off, to using the internet to print off a photograph or using a scanner, with assistance, to copy a piece of work.

  Some settings have installed sophisticated technological items, such as nest boxes with cameras, digital microscopes or underwater wildlife cameras, to support learning in knowledge and understanding of the world.

- **Physical development** – outdoor play can be enriched by the provision of walkie-talkies, remote-controlled cars or a metal detector. Dance mats and karaoke machines will support physical play – digital heart-rate monitors and stopwatches can be used to show children the effects of their exercising. The manipulation of ICT equipment, such as buttons on an electronic toy or a mouse, will help children to develop their fine motor skills.

- **Creative development** – specialist art programmes are available to use with computers and interactive whiteboards, allowing children to 'paint', 'draw' and mix shades of colours.

  An old-style overhead projector (not the new compact styles, which become too hot) can be used for shadow play, for creating large-scale images on walls and ceilings and for magnifying close observational drawings done by children.

  Electronic instruments, cassette recorders, microphones, dance mats and disco lights will all enrich creative development.

Information for parents

Figures 3.6a to 3.6e (see p225-234) are information sheets and lists of 'bright ideas', which can be given to parents or other family members. They cover:

- language for thinking and speaking through imaginative play (figure 3.6a)
- reading and writing through role-play (figure 3.6b)
- maths through games and open-ended play (sand, water, construction etc) (figure 3.6c)
- science through exploratory play (figure 3.6d)
- play and ICT (figure 3.6e).

You could use the sheets in different contexts, depending on how your setting operates. For example, you could:

- give them to parents as part of an introductory visit
- include them in your prospectus, on your website or in your newsletter
- use them as a basis for a family workshop or parents' evening.

References

Craft, A (2002) *Creativity and Early Years Education*, Continuum, London

Jeffrey, B and Craft, A (2004) 'Teaching creatively and teaching for creativity: distinctions and relationships', *Educational Studies*, vol 30, no 1, pp77-87

Department for Children, Education, Lifelong Learning and Skills, Welsh Assembly Government (2008) *Framework for Children's Learning for 3 to 7 year olds in Wales*

United Nations Convention on the Rights of the Child (1989), Office of the United Nations Commissioner for Human Rights, see: *www.unicef.org/crc*

SECTION 3.6   THE PARENT PARTNERSHIP TOOLKIT FOR EARLY YEARS

Parent leaflet: language for thinking and speaking in imaginative play

Language for thinking and speaking through imaginative play

Imaginative play, and the ability to pretend, is very important for children as learners. When children pretend that one object can represent something else – for example, a building block can be food for a toy dinosaur – they are beginning to understand that things can be symbolic. This then leads them on to think in abstract ways and to use words and images to express their ideas. They begin to use their thinking skills to make predictions and solve problems, developing as creative and critical thinkers.

To develop what has been termed 'possibility thinking', children need opportunities to play with open-ended resources over long periods of time. You can support this by providing your child with lots of interesting resources and experiences. This will encourage your child to develop and share his or her thoughts and ideas when imagining all sorts of scenarios and while encountering and solving problems during play. Through spending time 'imagining what might be', your child will develop the skills that will help him or her to 'think outside the box'.

Through imaginative play, your child will develop a wide range of active learning skills. These will include the communication skills of speaking, listening, discussing and recording.

Imaginative play will also support your child's reasoning and thinking skills, including questioning, speculating, inferring, problem solving, recognising similarities and differences and reflecting.

Finally, imaginative play can help develop the important social skills of cooperation, negotiation, following instructions, behaving safely, and teamwork and leadership.

Practitioners in the setting will be finding many different ways to support young children's imaginative play. You can support this by using the ideas on the back of this leaflet with your child.

Bright ideas to try at home

With babies:

- Place a small box or a pan down on the floor with a toy hidden underneath it. Count 1-2-3 and lift the box or pan to show the toy. Hide the toy again, count 1-2-3 and watch what your baby does. Help her to find the toy.

- Make a recording of the noises your baby makes. Play the sounds to your baby and watch how he responds. Is he excited? Does he talk back to the recording? Try other sounds like sounds from the garden or the street.

With toddlers:

- Collect together some boxes and ask your child to help you make a car, bus or train. Build the vehicle together and use toys as the passengers. Use big boxes to make a vehicle you can get inside.

- Cut some characters out of comics or birthday cards and glue them on to lolly sticks or pieces of strong card to make some stick puppets. Have fun telling stories with the stick puppets. You can also use the stick puppets, or your hand, to make shadow puppets.

With 3-5s:

- Play games with your child where you pretend to be other people or animals. The people or animals could be characters from a favourite book, TV programme or nursery rhyme. Use different voices and expressions and encourage your child to do the same.

- When you are out for a walk, or playing in the garden or the park, try moving in different ways. Say, 'Let's pretend we are soldiers'; 'Let's pretend we are dinosaurs'; 'Let's pretend we are frogs'.

SECTION 3.6   THE PARENT PARTNERSHIP TOOLKIT FOR EARLY YEARS

Parent leaflet: reading and writing through role-play

Reading and writing through role-play

Role-play is another step in the development of children's imaginative play, when they can become somebody or something else.

Role-play provides your child with opportunities to 'play out' the events that he or she has experienced and observed. It provides a child with the experience of real-life situations, where he or she can develop and practise skills in language, communication and maths. Role-play can also provide your child with lots of opportunities for storytelling, reading and writing.

The three most common types of role-play are:

- Domestic play: here the home and family are at the centre of the play, with a focus on daily routines, such as cooking, mealtimes and housework.

- Transactional play: this type of role-play involves buying and selling. The context for this could be a shop, cafe, garage, travel agent's or garden centre.

- Imaginary-world play: this focuses on the places where the creatures of stories live, or perhaps takes place in an unfamiliar environment such as 'on the moon' or 'under the sea'.

To help the development of your child's reading through role-play, there are a number of 'props' you could provide. These include notices, signs, menus, recipes, books and magazines, brochures, labels, price tags, maps and directions.

To encourage writing through role-play you could provide your child with easy access to writing materials, clipboard, notebook, shopping list, kitchen noticeboard, calendars and diaries and blank forms to fill in.

In the setting, practitioners will be providing many different resources to support young children's role-play. You can support this by using the ideas on the back of this leaflet with your child.

227

Bright ideas to try at home

With babies:

- Play a game with different hats or scarves. Put the different hats on your head and sing rhymes to go with them. Let your baby try the different hats, repeating the rhymes as you play.

- When you are feeding your baby, put a favourite toy alongside him in the high chair or next to you on the table. Pretend to feed the toy and make eating noises as the toy enjoys its food. Give your child a bowl and spoon so that he can feed his toys.

With toddlers:

- Give your child bowls, cups and spoons so that he can play at picnics and parties with his toys as the guests. Look through magazines to choose the food the toys will have. Cut pictures of food out of old magazines to use in the party play.

- When you are unpacking your shopping, let your child play 'shops' with the tins and packets before you put them away. Help your child to 'read' the information on the tins and packets that tells her what is inside.

With 3-5s:

- When you are planning a holiday or a trip out for the day, give your child a selection of travel brochures, postcards or timetables to look at. Give them pencils and a notepad so that they can plan the holiday or day out that they would enjoy.

- At the end of the year, give your child old diaries or calendars to play with. Leaflets and forms that are delivered as junk mail make excellent starting points for role-play.

SECTION 3.6 THE PARENT PARTNERSHIP TOOLKIT FOR EARLY YEARS

Figure 3.6c

Parent leaflet: maths through games, rhymes and songs

Maths through games, rhymes and songs

During their play – at home and in the early years setting – young children will have lots of opportunities for developing their mathematical skills. Games that you can play with your child, indoors or out of doors, often require the knowledge, skills and understanding found in the area of learning known in the Early Years Foundation Stage as 'problem solving, reasoning and numeracy', which many of us more commonly refer to as 'maths'.

For example:

- dominoes and lotto encourage number recognition and counting
- card games such as Snap and Happy Families give practice in matching, sorting and recognising similarities and differences
- board games, including Ludo and Snakes and Ladders, support counting, number recognition and one-to-one correspondence
- traditional games, such as hopscotch, skipping, hide and seek and 'What time is it, Mr Wolf?', involve number recognition and counting, as well as measuring time
- all types of races involve an understanding of distance, time and 1st, 2nd and 3rd
- team games, such as football and soft cricket, encourage an awareness of space and direction, as well as encouraging children to play together cooperatively.

Many of the nursery rhymes and action songs you can sing with your child are about numbers and counting. You will find that there is a strong connection between the order, timing, beat and rhythm of music and aspects of mathematics, such as counting, sequencing, and understanding time and order.

- Many nursery rhymes are counting rhymes – 'One, two, three, four, five, once I caught a fish alive', 'One, two, buckle my shoe'.
- 'Five currant buns in the baker's shop' and '10 green bottles' involve an understanding of taking away and adding.
- Action rhymes, such as 'Two little dickie birds', 'Five little ducks went swimming one day' and 'Five green speckled frogs', involve counting backwards and forwards.
- 'Round and round the garden like a teddy bear', 'Incy wincy spider' and 'Hickory, dickory dock' involve the use of positional language, such as round, up and down, as well as numbers.

In the setting, practitioners will be using lots of different opportunities, indoors and out, to support young children's mathematical development. You can support this by using the ideas on the back of this leaflet with your child.

229

Bright ideas to try at home

With babies:

- Choose some action rhymes to sing at nappy changing or bath time – 'Incy wincy spider', 'Round and round the garden, like a teddy bear' and 'Hickory, dickory, dock' work well. Make a splash in the bath at the end of 'Hickory, dickory, dock'.

- Use every opportunity to count fingers, toes and other parts of the body and face. Say '[Name] has one nose, and two eyes, and two ears'.

- Have crawling races with your baby in the garden or at the park.

With toddlers:

- Play 'There were 10 in the bed' with your toddler, rolling over on the floor when you come to the line 'and the little one said "roll over"'.

- Collect together as many toy animals as you can find and act out the song 'The animals went in two by two'. It doesn't matter if you don't have the correct animals in the song.

- Make some props to go with the action rhymes 'Two little dickie birds', 'Five little ducks', 'Five currant buns', 'Five fat sausages sizzling in the pan'. Use two paper birds attached to your fingers, five plastic ducks, cardboard sausages or pictures cut out of magazines and currant buns made out of playdough or real ones!

With 3-5s:

- Play board games, such as Snakes and Ladders, card games such as Snap and Happy Families, picture and number dominoes and lotto, to encourage your child to develop and practise maths skills.

- Think about the games you played as a child – play hopscotch, skipping and ball games, hide and seek, 'What time is it, Mr Wolf?' in your garden or at the park.

- Say more complex rhymes with your child – '10 Green bottles', 'One, two, buckle my shoe' and sing 'The 12 days of Christmas', complete with the actions.

- Try counting to 10 in a different language.

SECTION 3.6   THE PARENT PARTNERSHIP TOOLKIT FOR EARLY YEARS

Parent leaflet: science through exploratory play

Science through exploratory play

Exploratory play with natural and man-made materials will encourage your child to develop his or her own ideas and interests. When they are exploring the world around them, young children are building up the skills and knowledge that will help them to become interested, independent scientific learners.

By encouraging your child to explore and investigate, and by playing alongside them, you will show them how important you think their ideas and interests are.

The following information tells you what children are learning when they are engaged in exploratory play.

- **Children explore new things and experiences**
  Children's curiosity about the world leads them to explore using all their senses, to develop their own ideas and to begin to make sense of the world.

- **Children talk out loud to themselves**
  When they talk to themselves, children are clarifying their thoughts and imagining 'what might be'.

- **Children meet physical and mental challenges**
  Working out what to do, trying hard, persevering with problems, and finding out for themselves are all opportunities for children to develop a real understanding of the world around them.

- **Children practise doing things**
  Practising skills they have learned helps children to become confident in what they can do and to enjoy their own expertise.

In the setting, practitioners will be looking for lots of opportunities to support your child's scientific learning. Why not try some of the ideas on the back of this leaflet at home to help your child learn through exploratory play?

Remember that sharing laughter, fun and enjoyment is the best way to help your child to learn.

231

Bright ideas to try at home

With babies:

- Play games with your baby using rattles. Shake the rattle in front of your baby and watch what he does. Move the rattle to each side and give him time to follow the sound the rattle makes. Make a sound with the rattle behind your baby or somewhere out of sight. Praise him when he works out where the sound is coming from.

- Babies are fascinated by mirrors. Show your baby herself in a mirror. Move her closer to the mirror and away from it. Let your baby hold a suitable hand-held mirror – this is how she will become curious about who she is and what she can do.

With toddlers:

- Have fun playing with a torch. You can use a torch indoors or out of doors when it is getting dark. If you are playing indoors you can make a dark den by placing a thick cloth or blanket over a table – the perfect place to explore light and dark using your torch. Add some shiny things to the den.

- When you go out for a walk, look around for plants, animals, birds and insects. Look for clues that animals have been around, listen to the songs of different birds – talk about what you can see, hear, feel and smell.

With 3-5s:

- When you are cooking or baking, encourage your child to help to make simple things. Talk about what happens when things are mixed, separated, heated or frozen. Help your child to use simple kitchen tools.

- Your child will enjoy using scientific equipment, such as a magnifying glass or a magnet. Have fun in your garden or around the house looking closely at different objects and plants and seeing what the magnet attracts.

SECTION 3.6 THE PARENT PARTNERSHIP TOOLKIT FOR EARLY YEARS

Parent leaflet: play and ICT

Play and ICT

ICT, or information and communication technology, can be used to enrich all areas of learning in the early years. ICT is not just restricted to computers, it also includes a wide range of electronic programmable toys, digital cameras and recording equipment. In early years settings, these resources are used to improve the quality of learning and development for all children, across many different areas of learning.

The following list gives you an idea of how ICT can be used in early years settings to support young children's learning and development in various areas:

- **Personal, social and emotional development** – digital cameras, mobile telephones such as walkie-talkie systems, karaoke machines and microphones will all help children to develop confidence and self-esteem, as well as encouraging teamwork and sharing.

- **Communication, language and literacy** – tape recorders, telephones, multi-link headphones, 'talking tins' and 'talking photo albums' are all excellent resources for supporting the development of speaking and listening. An interactive whiteboard can be used to develop writing skills on a large scale. Helping children to use a scanner or photocopier will enable them to tell stories and to create cards, pictures and displays.

- **Problem solving, reasoning and numeracy** – many digital toys and equipment, such as electronic cash registers, have number and function keys that encourage number recognition, counting and problem solving. Remote-controlled cars and simple robots can be used to develop positional and directional language.

- **Knowledge and understanding of the world** – this area of learning specifically includes children's learning and development in ICT. This will range from switching on and off a piece of equipment, such as a cassette recorder or remote controlled vehicle, taking digital photographs and printing them off, using the internet to print off a photograph or using a scanner, with assistance, to copy a piece of work.

- **Physical development** – outdoor play can be enriched by the provision of walkie-talkies, remote-controlled cars or a metal detector. Dance mats and karaoke machines will support physical play – digital heart-rate monitors and stopwatches can be used to show children the effects of exercising. Manipulating ICT equipment, such as buttons on an electronic toy or a mouse, helps children to develop their fine motor skills.

- **Creative development** – specialist art programmes are available to use with computers and interactive whiteboards, allowing children to 'paint', 'draw' and mix shades of colours. An old-style overhead projector can be used for shadow play, for creating large-scale images on walls and ceilings and for magnifying close observational drawings done by children. Electronic instruments, cassette recorders, microphones, dance mats and disco lights will all enrich creative development.

You can use ICT to support your child's early learning by using some of the ideas on the back of this leaflet.

Bright ideas to try at home

With babies:

- If your child has toys that are battery operated and play tunes, speak or move when different buttons are pressed, spend time showing her how to press the buttons herself so that she can make choices about how she operates the toys.

- Use a CD/DVD player to play music so that you can dance and sing with your baby. Show your baby how you play the music.

With toddlers:

- Some children are fascinated by technology and how things around the house work from a very early age. They can be experts at operating the DVD player or a parent's mobile phone. Use a cardboard box to make a TV or DVD player and give your child an old remote-control handset or mobile phone to play with.

- If you have an inexpensive digital camera, encourage your child to take photos around your house, garden or when you are out for the day. You will get a very good idea of what interests your child and how the world appears from their point of view. Think about buying a child's digital camera for a birthday or Christmas present.

With 3-5s:

- Make a collection of defunct technology equipment for your child to use in his imaginative play. Try collecting a mobile phone, keyboard, computer mouse, telephone, cassette recorder or hairdryer.

- Use walkie-talkies around the house and in the garden to talk to your child about what she, and you, are doing, what you can see and hear.